Kilvert's Diary
and Landscape

John Toman

I go out in the country to *feel* God.
[Frederick Robertson, *Life and Letters of Frederick Robertson*]

The pastoral landscape . . . could be seen as the truest country
of the human heart.
[John Beer, *Wordsworth and the Human Heart*]

Some of the noblest lives are unrecorded upon earth.
They are not thought worthy among men, of being kept in mind.
[*Kilvert's Diary*]

The Lutterworth Press

The Lutterworth Press
P.O. Box 60
Cambridge
CB1 2NT

www.lutterworth.com
publishing@lutterworth.com

ISBN: 978 0 7188 3095 3

British Library Cataloguing in Publication Data
A catalogue record is available from the British Library

Copyright © John Toman, 2009

First published in 2009

Contents

Illustrations

Acknowledgements

Special thanks are due to Dr Philip Dunham (University of Coventry), Dr Martin Crossley Evans (University of Bristol), and Ian Middlebrough (former English Adviser, Oldham), who read and commented on early drafts of the book. I have been greatly stimulated and encouraged over several years by their interest in Kilvert. Dr Marie Mulvey-Roberts (University of the West of England) read a draft of the book and Karoline Leach read parts of it and provided valuable support.

Generous help was also given by the following: Kevin Bacon (History Centre, Libraries and Museums, Brighton), Mike Browning (Bristol and Avon Family History Society), Liz Butler (Quaker Family History Society), Dr C.S.L. Davies, (Archivist, Wadham College, Oxford), Colin Dixon (Archivist, Kilvert Society), Carol Mair Edwards and Dafydd Ifans (National Library of Wales), Rev Peter Gubi (Moravian Church, East Tytherton), the late John Hockin (Dorset), Colin Johnston and Lucy Powell (Bath and North East Somerset Archives), Jennifer Martindale (Dorset County Museum), Ken Osborne (Church Mission Society), Lorraine Parsons (Archivist, Moravian Church Centre, London), Nona Rees (Librarian, St David's Cathedral), Marion Roberts, staff of Bath library, the Bodleian Library, Bristol Library, Bristol University Library, Lambeth Palace Library, the Library of the Society of Friends, and Wiltshire Record Office.

Special mention must be made of Margaret Lockyer, granddaughter of William Powell of Rhosgoch Mill and of Carrie Gore of Whitty's Mill (Clyro). Margaret brought Kilvert's world so much nearer by her graphic accounts of life in the Welsh borderland.

Finally, I wish to express my gratitude to Adrian Brink, who has been a kind, accommodating editor, and to all at Lutterworth Press for their unfailing help and professionalism.

Abbreviations

BCL   Bath Central Library
BRO   Bath Record Office
CMS   Church Missionary Society
DNB   Dictionary of National Biography
ETAMCC East Tytherton Archive Moravian Church Centre
                 (Muswell Hill, London)
NALU   National Agricultural Labourers Union
NEB   New English Bible
NLW   National Library of Wales
OED   Oxford English Dictionary
WRO   Wiltshire Record Office

Note on Sources

The edition used of *Kilvert's Diary* is the three-volume one, edited by William Plomer, published by Jonathan Cape, London (1938-40), reprinted 1971. Details of editions of other *Diary* material are cited in the References and Bibliography.

The Wordsworth edition used throughout is *The Poetical Works of William Wordsworth*, edited by Thomas Hutchinson, London, Oxford University Press, 1905.

The edition used of Wesley's *Journal* is that edited by J. Curnock, London, Culley, 1909-16.

Biblical quotations are from the New English Bible unless otherwise stated.

The literary papers of Kilvert's uncle, Francis, are deposited in Bath Central Library.

Where two dates are given in sources consulted, the first (in brackets) indicates date of original publication, the second is that of the edition used.

Where the word 'evangelical' occurs with a small 'e' it pertains to the Protestant pietism of the Reformation and to its revival by Wesley; 'Evangelical' denotes those of evangelical faith who remained within the Anglican Church, especially in the 1780-1840 period.

Francis Kilvert

Introduction

A landscape in literature is a view, not only of countryside, but of the moral and social attitudes of writer and reader.

[Louis James, in G.E. Mingay (ed.), *The Rural Idyll*]

During the nineteenth century it was taken for granted that real communities could only be found in the English countryside.

[Leonore Davidoff, *Worlds Between: Historical Perspectives on Gender and Class*]

In one sense, the justification for this book is to be found in a remark that Frederick Grice made in 1975 about *Kilvert's Diary*: '[Kilvert's] literary skill ... has still not been properly evaluated'.[1] This remains the situation today. The literary quality of the *Diary* is, as Grice pointed out, 'independent of the interest it may arouse as a sociological or psychological document. It has the self-sufficiency of good art'.[2] Inasmuch as it represents Kilvert's effort to tell the story of his own life, as well as to convey a picture of a society, it falls into the category of 'self-writing' that includes autobiography and biography, a literary field which has experienced a revaluation, particularly in the last thirty years. Nadel, writing in 1984, stated that biographies needed to be treated as 'independent literary texts, judged by the criteria of "style, structure or language" rather than by the usual criterion of "accuracy"' and 'required a critical reading as works of imagination and language if they were to be accepted as works of literature'.[3] My analysis of Kilvert's *Diary* traces the literary and religious influences that caused him to write in the way that he did. These influences not only remain very largely unexplored but certain major ones have not even figured in the conventional account of the *Diary*'s evolution.

Kilvert's reputation as a writer rests chiefly upon his ability to describe people and landscape. It is a basic premise of this book that, for him, the two were intimately connected and hence the concept of landscape used is a unified one — people and the locations in which they live their lives. Schama noted that the word 'landscape' entered the English language at the end of the sixteenth century, signifying 'a unit of human occupation, indeed a jurisdiction, as much as anything that might be a pleasing depiction'. In other words, 'landscape' from its beginning expressed community, a land and its people. Schama also recognised that many cultures have rich nature and landscape myths which overlay particular places so that landscapes are, or can be, cultural products, with 'veins of myth and memory' lying beneath their surfaces.[4] The idea of landscape as a repository of meanings informs Matless's understanding of its power: '. . . the power of landscape resides in its being simultaneously a site of economic, social, political and aesthetic value.' He continued: '. . . the question of what landscape "is" or "means" can always be subsumed in the question of how it works; as a vehicle of social and self identity. . . .' Thus it lies somewhere between nature and culture — a concept involving space, history and memory.[5] In his book, *Landscape and Western Art*, Malcolm Andrews examined our response to landscape as a cultural product, arguing that to appreciate it in this way involved 'learned rather than innate criteria'. It is:

> a concept of a particular entity, "landscape", as distinct from the experience of a random variety of natural phenomena assembled within the view . . . an idea and an experience in which we are creatively involved, whether or not we are practising artists . . . Our sense of our identity and relationship to our environment is implicated in our response to [landscape images]. Landscape in art tells us, or asks us to think about, where we belong. Important issues of identity and orientation are inseparable from the reading of meanings and the eliciting of pleasure from landscape.[6]

Kilvert can be seen to be involved with landscape in exactly this way in his writing, particularly his writing about the landscape of Radnorshire. Its landscape became for him a symbolic form of an ideal world, his relationship with which enlarged his conception of himself. He felt himself to be as deeply involved with it as its traditional inhabitants were. Furthermore, his concept of community depended on seeing people's lives as inextricably bound up with their physical surroundings. The concept of landscape is inevitably bound up with the history of land and of the changes in the way it has been conceived over time. The eighteenth-century view of landscape emphasised the ideal, the general, the timeless, whereas the Romantic approach to it was characterised by actual experience, exact detail, subjective response.[7] The effect of the former was to separate the aesthetic from the practical for, as Williams observed, 'A working country is hardly ever a landscape.'[8] Wordsworth's poems, which were a dominant influence on the Victorians (and on Kilvert), are, however, concerned with particular figures in landscapes (shepherds, cottagers, pedlars, vagrants), with sense impressions of natural objects, with living and working conditions. All the rural writers Kilvert admired and who influenced his writing – Cowper, Burns, Crabbe, Clare, Kingsley, Barnes, Tennyson and Howitt – reflect this new tradition.

Keith stressed that William Howitt was very representative of Victorian attitudes towards the countryside.[9] The view that Kilvert held of it shows clear signs of shaping by Howitt's books.[10] In his *Rural Life of England* (1838), Howitt triumphantly recorded what he saw as the characteristically English 'yearning after the loveliness of nature' that came in with the Romantic poets.[11] He also paid tribute to Bewick's engravings for developing those poets' concern with actual experience of rural life. A 'great increase in country delight' was, he said, owed to his pictures of rural scenery because of their 'sacred fidelity to Nature.' 'See in what a small space he gives you a whole landscape. . . . He is the very Burns of wood-engraving,' by which he meant that his pictures told stories.[12] During the illness of his daughter, Annie, Darwin borrowed from the London Library Howitt's *The Book of the Seasons* and *The Boy's Country Book* to read to her for their account of plant and animal life and of country pursuits.[13] Precise details of natural forms are found in *Kilvert's Diary* but even more characteristic of Howitt's influence is its frequent use of imaginative stories. Thus, the picture that the latter presented of English rural life was intensely patriotic and romantic in tone; it 'purified the spirit and ennobled the heart;' it reflected 'national glory' and, as he walked it, he was aware of a land 'filled . . . with glorious reminiscences.'[14] Of English country houses, he wrote: 'A thousand endearing associations gather about them'[15] and he gave a highly romantic account of Annesley Hall (Notts.), home of Mary Chaworth, 'a spot, where every sod, and stone, and tree . . . is rife with the most strange and touching memories. . . .'[16] Kilvert's tendency to write in this vein is illustrated in subsequent chapters. It may also be assumed that his love of Byron's poem, *The Dream*, which tells the story of Mary Chaworth's doomed affair with the poet, stemmed in part from reading Howitt's account of Annesley.[17] Kilvert's attitude to country houses was, like Howitt's, ambivalent. Both men saw them as institutions of great beauty and power, often overshadowed by the pride and self-indulgence of their owners.

Howitt's vision of landscape was, like Kilvert's, an imaginative one; the sub-title of his *Visits to Remarkable Places* (1842) – 'scenes illustrative of striking passages in history and poetry' – bears this out. The book deals with his walking tours of Durham and Northumberland, chosen for the 'Legend, ballad – song and faithful story' that surround them: 'a twilight of antiquity seems to linger there.'[18] As with Kilvert, Howitt's descriptions of landscape are everywhere informed by his reading. He praised Surtees's history of the county of Durham because its author 'became an antiquary because he was a poet' and poets were the only men who genuinely felt the 'heroic past'.[19] And the outstanding example of such antiquaries was Sir Walter Scott. Kilvert shared this view of Scott, revelling in romantic ruins, tales of noble knights and holy men. Howitt's presentation of Mitford, near Morpeth, which boasted ruins of both a castle and a manor house, typifies his stance: 'To the eye of the poet and the lover of nature, it presents . . . a rich bit of English landscape poetry. . . . To that of the historian and antiquary it offers objects of equal interest.' To the cultivated, imaginative man, the scene 'was rich with all the colours of memory and poetry'.[20] Howitt's love of the stirring exploits of famous families is counter-poised by the deepest respect for ordinary men and women who lived worthy, moral lives or achieved great things from modest beginnings; it is another characteristic that links him to Kilvert and one relished by Victorians in general. Howitt honoured genius that could flower in the humble cottage and cited Chatterton, Burns and Hogg as examples of it.[21]

Archaeology and antiquarianism figured strongly in the life of the Kilvert family in Bath. Kilvert's father recounted how at his grandmother's house he was drawn to Britton's *Beauties of England and Wales*, a book he extracted with difficulty from the lowest drawer of the bookcase (he was only five and the drawer's handle kept coming off). The narrative of his early years reveals other traces of archaeological interest. For example, his grandmother showed him the monuments in Bath Abbey. When he mentioned the church the family attended, he made a point of emphasising its antiquity – 'the old Early English church . . . five or six hundred years old'.[22] His daughter, Emily, acquired her archaeological interest from him and from her uncle Francis, who was 'loved and revered' by all his nieces and nephews.[23] She said that for all the Kilvert children the volumes of *Old England. A Pictorial Museum of Regal, Ecclesiastical, Municipal, Baronial, and Popular Antiquities* were 'a never failing source of pleasure'.[24] A poem written by her uncle Francis, dedicated to 'the father of British Archaeology', is the clue to an influence pushing the Kilvert children towards the buildings, landscapes and annals of the past. Francis's dedication was to John Britton, who was, in terms of archaeology, *the* local hero. Born in 1771, the son of a small farmer and shopkeeper in Kington St Michael, he had a very basic education and went to London where he worked as a cellarman in various pubs. He nevertheless managed to read widely in his limited leisure time. He was asked by a publisher to contribute entries to a topographical work called *The Beauties of Wiltshire*, which appeared in 1801. He was then invited to work on a bigger enterprise, the first number of which came out also in 1801; this was *The Beauties of England and Wales*.

One of the key features of Howitt's books, in terms of their influence on Victorians, was that they stimulated 'popular tourism by foot and rail.'[25] Thus, as a result of improved communications, Victorians became familiar with 'a series of different countrysides with their own physical features, history, customs, dialects, and ways of living.'[26] It was, of course, the spread of railways and increased prosperity that enabled people to visit attractive parts of the country, with the result that 'the Victorian reader became increasingly interested in regional characteristics.'[27] Howitt's own note on the explosion of tourism is ambivalent: 'One of the singular features of English life at the present moment is the swarming of summer

tourists in all interesting quarters.'[28] Wordsworth, too, objected
to the building of a railway line that would bring tourists
into his beloved Lakeland. Kilvert's own hatred of tourists
was extreme.[29] Resentment of forces threatening the beauty
of landscape was but one aspect of the realism informing
Victorian attitudes towards it. Howitt's nostalgia for the past
of song and story he saw reflected in landscape was balanced
by awareness of the poverty, squalor and ignorance of many
peasants' lives. Although 'Victorian novelists of the country
were largely out of touch with the realities of rural life . . . it
is also true that [they] were often aware of what they were
doing when they portrayed idyllic country scenes.'[30] Keith
also denied that Victorian literature as a whole presented 'an
excessively rosy picture' of rural life and that novelists often
set out to show it realistically.[31] In this respect again Kilvert
mirrored a general Victorian tendency, for his diary contains
sentimentalised pictures of the countryside juxtaposed with the
grimmest scenes. The range of 'country house' novels he read
showed the same balance.[32] According to Treble, Victorians
also recognised that cottage life showing happy peasant
children, seen at its best in the paintings of Myles Birket Foster
(1825-99), was 'mythical,' even though it was 'one of the most
powerful images of the Victorian countryside.'[33]

   The image of a rural Arcadia that Victorians treasured while
knowing it to be false was related to the advent of industrialism
and urban living. It was linked also to the concept of domesticity.
Just as the home became increasingly seen, from the 1820s, as
the ideal setting for women, so the village community came to
be seen as the ideal setting for relations in the wider society.
Together, the two themes became 'the very core of the ideal
[which] was home *in* a rural community,' because 'the home,
like the village, was ideally sheltered and separated from the
public life of power.'[34] *Kilvert's Diary* is centrally concerned with
community and in this regard, as in so many others, was affected
by Wordsworth's exalting of the virtues of the country as opposed
to those of the town.[35] Howitt had the same understanding: 'The
state of morals and manners amongst the working population
of our great towns is terrible' and when the country population
came into contact with towns' 'contagion,' it 'suffers in person
and mind.' Thus, 'dwellers of cities . . . long for the quietness
and beauty of the country.'[36] Kilvert was glad he was not a city-
dweller; after a visit to London he wrote: 'I do loathe London.

How delicious to get into the country again.'[37] The change to life in town and work in factories and offices, with the consequent severing of the ties that bound people to each other and to their ancestral village, produced for Victorians 'a nostalgia for a lost world of peace and companionship, of healthy bodies and quiet minds,' according to Houghton. In his view, we should remember this when we read the nature writing of Victorians or look at their landscapes. In his observation that for many Victorians 'the countryside represented the "spiritual values" being destroyed in the unspiritual city,' Houghton came close to Kilvert.[38] We have seen the various ways in which Kilvert's attitudes to the countryside were typically Victorian; the spiritual dimension in his view of landscape is perhaps its most distinctive element. In this, he was like William Howitt. When the latter wanted to explain why the Romantic poets differed from the ancients in their 'more passionate, intense . . . elevated love of Nature,' he found only one cause – Christianity.[39] Kilvert would have agreed.

Kilvert's Diary and Landscape breaks new ground, not only by undertaking the first thorough examination of Kilvert's writing, but also a complete revaluation of the writer himself, which is long overdue. Sixty years ago the Kilvert Society (founded in 1948) set out admirable targets for further research into Kilvert and his *Diary*[40] but little progress has been made towards them, with the result that our picture of the diarist has solidified, even petrified. It is all too common now to find the traditional unexamined responses to him being reiterated. It is generally acknowledged that Kilvert was deeply religious but the nature of his beliefs has not so far been illuminated. Equally well recognised is his love of Nature but that too remains largely unexamined. It is accepted that his literary knowledge, especially of poetry, was the product of his uncle Francis's teaching, yet understanding of that teaching has remained limited because little has been made known of the teacher. There has been a steady tendency to devalue Kilvert's reading — apart from Wordsworth, Tennyson and a few other poets. Thus, we have been told 'he enjoys a great number of ephemeral novels but makes no mention of Jane Austen, Dickens, Thackeray, the Brontës, George Eliot — or even Fielding, Richardson or Smollett'.[41] Another commentator insisted that his choice of books was 'casual and random' and that he read ephemeral literature.[42] Yet another stated that his 'taste in books was . . .

undiscriminating'.[43] Disinclination to examine what Kilvert actually read and to look for patterns in it inevitably led to the conclusion that it was 'casual and random'. Misconceptions about his reading stem partly from failure to give adequate weight to the fact that he was an Evangelical. Evangelicals were extremely punctilious about what they read and 'casual and random' reading was anathema to them. Kilvert had a very good reason for avoiding novels by the major nineteenth-century novelists: they consistently portrayed Evangelicalism (and religion generally) in a poor light. The commentator who designated Kilvert's reading 'casual and random' went so far as to assert that the first instinct of this highly literary man was 'not to reach for a book'. Kilvert of course cared a great deal about what he read and his choices reveal the clearest of patterns, which are themselves a guide to his personality, beliefs, and the way he wrote about landscape.[44]

The undervaluing of Kilvert's literary taste is an aspect of the general disparagement of his intellect. According to Lockwood, he was 'not a profound man' and 'his mind was not academic or critical'.[45] He was of 'third-rate intelligence'[46] and had 'a completely unacademic mind'[47] in the opinion of Le Quesne. A.L. Rowse, though he characterised walking, at which he knew Kilvert excelled, as 'that favourite pursuit of the intellectually-minded, ' felt constrained to add: 'Not that he was an intellectual'.[48] Another commentator keen to impugn Kilvert's intellect is Meic Stephens: 'No intellectual himself, Kilvert is often unacceptably sentimental in the eyes of modern intellectuals'.[49] Sentimentality is a crucial concept with regard to Kilvert and his writing but a good deal of misunderstanding surrounds it in Kilvert studies because of a failure to note the part it played in Victorian sensibility: 'Most Victorians believed that the human community was one of shared moral feelings and that sentimentality was a desirable way of feeling and expressing ourselves morally'.[50] It was in fact a way of defining human nature and one's self. It has been assumed that it was Kilvert's sentimentality that led him to choose 'easy', undemanding fiction, whereas the truth is that he favoured books which gave a prominent place to the ethic of mutual kindness. An important consequence of the steady harping on his sentimentality is that he himself has been sentimentalised, described as a saint, as a man who wouldn't say boo to a goose, who was a bit soft in the head as well as in the heart.

Frederick William Robertson

It has always seemed probable that Kilvert must have had an outstanding example of Christian ministry in his mind that he followed. Several clerical models — e.g. Henry Moule, Charles Kingsley and William Barnes — have suggested themselves, but we have lacked one whose *specific* influence could be convincingly demonstrated. That clergyman was Frederick Robertson. His name occurs only once in the *Diary* in Kilvert's brief note: 'Lent Miss Dew Robertson's Lectures on Corinthians',[51] but behind it lies a major influence on his life, his piety, his ministry, and his writing that has gone unrecognised. Robertson (1816-1853), described in the *DNB* as 'not only a man of genius but a man of unique genius', achieved national fame as preacher, writer and religious thinker so that it was inevitable that Kilvert would have heard of him.[52] Proof that he knew not only Robertson's *Lectures on Corinthians* but also Brooke's *Life and Letters of the Rev Frederick William Robertson* (1865) is to be found in echoes and borrowings from the latter work that surface in the *Diary* and in his poetry, the most important of which is the passage in the poem *Honest Work* where Kilvert talked of recognising 'How hearts are linked to hearts by God, — / And prove themselves the sons to be / Of Heaven-descended Charity'. Brooke quoted a passage from one of Robertson's *unpublished* sermons (thus Kilvert could only have seen it in Brooke's *Life*) in which he said, referring to the origin of friendship: 'Hearts are linked to hearts by God'.[53] The notion of 'hearts' linked to each other by a chain of sympathy was much cherished by Evangelicals.[54] It is important to underline the fact that the publication of Brooke's *Life* in 1865 ('to great acclaim', according to the *DNB*) coincided with Kilvert's arrival in Clyro, Radnorshire, and can be assumed to have played a significant part in shaping both

his conception of Christian ministry and his aspiration to be a
writer.

Robertson was a man who attracted devoted followers and
Kilvert became one of them. Kaplan wrote that Victorians
needed to *love* the writers they admired, not just their books,[55]
and the evidence suggests that Kilvert's love for the Brighton
preacher was intense. This seems to be the explanation for what
he did in the summer of 1869 — he undertook a holiday on the
Continent, as Robertson had done in the summer of 1841 and
also in September 1846, times when he was facing a crisis in his
spiritual life. It is significant that both men's journeys took them
to the Alps, where experiences of particular power, far removed
from those provided by the pastoral landscapes of *Kilvert's
Diary*, could be had: 'a man ought to go [to Switzerland] to feel
intensely at least once in his life,' Robertson advised, and Kilvert
followed his advice. Robertson found the experience of being
alone amid the immensity of the Alps helpful in conquering
his spiritual doubts. One evening, the 'wild, savage scenery'
produced a moment — 'so solemn, so awful, almost holy'
— when 'nature, in all its mystery, is felt'.[56] Kilvert's responses
to landscape are consistently informed by this perception: he
dedicated himself to the search for Nature's *mystery*, to 'holy'
moments which he habitually labelled 'solemn'. Mountains
provided some of his deepest religious experiences too, when
he felt nearer to God, more sure of his faith. One of the best
known in his *Diary* is the view he had of a snow ridge on the
Black Mountains, which prompted the reflection, 'I never
saw anything to equal it I think, even among the high Alps'.[57]
In having Robertson as inspiration and mentor, Kilvert was
modelling himself on a highly exceptional man. He is generally
acknowledged to be a most profound religious thinker and a
brilliant interpreter of spiritual truths. He was also a perceptive
critic: 'His literary criticisms, as displayed in his lectures upon
Tennyson and Wordsworth ... were first-rate....'[58] Kilvert's
love of Wordsworth was doubtless reinforced by the fact that he
knew Robertson was devoted to him.

The accepted view of Kilvert is bedevilled by polarisations
— for example, that his literary taste extended only to 'easy'
writers, a category encompassing (absurdly) Wordsworth and
Tennyson, and couldn't cope with 'hard' ones, such as Dickens
and George Eliot. Linked to this polarisation is another one
— that Kilvert's literary sensibility was entirely separate from

his religion. To him, as to other Victorians, Wordsworth was essentially a religious poet. There has been too much stress on the idea that Wordsworth and Kilvert were involved together in a vague, pantheistic view of Nature that could not be reconciled with orthodox Christianity.[59] Thus, the conventional view of Kilvert's personality commonly pictures a Romantic sensuousness and emotionality in conflict with a strict piety, whereas he steadily endorsed the example of the Christian poet who combined poetry with piety.

Kilvert's uncle Francis wrote a poem, *Je Pense Plus*, in which he outlined the chief traits of his own personality; the similarity between that personality and Kilvert's has often been noted. The *Diary* entry in which he stated 'I hate arguing' has been linked by commentators to the poem's third verse, which reads:

> Though indisposed to speak my mind,
> Little to argument inclined,
> In range of general lore confined,
>   I think the more.

It is true that Kilvert was 'Little to argument inclined' but it seems that this disinclination arose from his awareness that dispute often led nowhere, except to bad feeling among the disputants, which he deplored. It should not be taken to mean that he was a man without ideas or principles. He was in fact showing his Evangelicalism for Henry Venn, mentor of the Clapham Evangelicals, had urged: 'Never on any account, dispute. Debate is the work of the flesh.' Of the personality traits in *Je Pense Plus* belonging to uncle Francis, the one that is never applied to Kilvert is that which represents the poem's theme — 'I think the more'. He was not a profound thinker, as Robertson was, but he *was* a thinker: the books he read, including Brooke's biography of Robertson, which ranges in its 650 pages over a very large number of ideas — literary, philosophical, religious, moral, aesthetic, political — and a very large number of writers, prove this to be true.[60] In the chapters that follow, the range of ideas and writers which informed Kilvert's general moral outlook will become apparent. On occasion, the complexity of his mind and personality has been glimpsed by commentators. It is hoped that this study of Kilvert and landscape, which may be regarded as the second part of a revaluation of the diarist that began with my *Kilvert: The Homeless Heart* (2001), contributes to our appreciation of his complexity.

Chapter 1
To Mind the Living of the Dead

Eighteenth-century sentimentalism is not naïve, simple,
or simple-minded, nor even primarily emotional.
[James Averill, *Wordsworth and
the Poetry of Human Suffering*]

Tears, idle tears, I know not what they mean,
Tears from the depth of some divine despair
Rise in the heart, and gather to the eyes.
[Tennyson, *The Princess*, section IV]

Nature, so far as in her lies, imitates God.
[Tennyson, *On a Mourner*]

None can live and mourn alone,
But some will love them still.
[Kilvert, *Unsuspected Love*]

It seems to me, in reading lives, the question too often
is, whether it be one which in all respects answers
our ideal of life? Whereas the question ought to be,
whether it has strongly exhibited some side or other
of our . . . many-sided life. I am satisfied with One life
— One ideal, and I read all others to understand that,
by illustration or by contrasts of their whole to parts of
it. Now Wordsworth throws some light on its purely
contemplative side.
[Frederick Robertson, *Life and Letters*, Volume II]

———

It is one of the paradoxes of *Kilvert's Diary* that while
generations of commentators have drawn attention to its
remarkable vitality, there is in its pages a steady concern
with death and mourning. William Plomer, the man who
'discovered' the *Diary*, was typical of many in commenting

in his introduction to the first volume on Kilvert's 'ability to seize on essentials and to convey *a sense of life*.'[1] Kilvert had of course a professional involvement with death: his work as a parish priest naturally brought him into close contact with dying people, dead people and the bereaved. He had a profound, sensitive respect for grief. Lily Crichton was the daughter of Kilvert's Clyro friends and she had died as a child. Revisiting Clyro in March 1874, he made a point of seeing her grave:

> I went into the Churchyard and stood by Lily Crichton's grave. It is marked by a beautiful white marble cross upon which is carved the touching emblem of a drooping lily broken from its parent stem. . . .[2]

Kilvert's reference to the 'touching' quality of the lily emblem was not casual or automatic: his capacity to be moved was of considerable importance to him, as was the entire activity of mourning. After visiting a family that had been hit by a series of tragedies, he wrote: ' "It is better to go to the house of mourning than to the house of feasting" '.[3] It seems that he was free from any morbid interest in the dead, a fact that emerges from the entry dealing with the funeral of his relative, Maria Kilvert: 'I had a particular wish to see Miss Kilvert though I usually loathe and abhor the sight of a corpse. . . .'[4]

Nor was there anything morbid about his liking for church-yards. The following entry is typical of many:

> After luncheon I spent a happy half hour in the lovely warm afternoon wandering about Clyro churchyard among the graves. . . . I sat awhile on the old Catholic tomb of the 'Relict of Thomas Bridgwater'. . . . This is my favourite tomb. I love it better than all the tombs in the churchyard with its friendly 'Requiescat in pace', the prayer so full of peace, with its solemn reminder 'Tendimus huc omnes'. . . . There is something much more congenial to my mind in these old Catholic associations than in the bald ugly hideous accompani-ments which too often mark the place of Protestant or rather Puritan burial. The Puritans . . . tried to make the . . . associations of death and burial as gloomy, hideous and repulsive as possible. . . .
>
> A small and irreverent spider came running . . . across

the flat tombstone and scuttling over the sacred words
and memories with most indecent haste and levity.[5]

What stands out here is Kilvert's response to the beauty of
Catholic funerary attitudes, his rejection of gloomy ones, and
his fellow-feeling with the jaunty spider, who refused to take too
seriously the serious business of death. Kilvert refused to take
death too seriously because it was the path to a better life and
he often juxtaposed notions of life and death to accentuate this
understanding. The visit to Clyro churchyard took place amid
the warmth of an afternoon in early spring. It was late spring
when he 'wandered round the church [of Langley Burrell]
among the dewy grass-grown graves and picturesque ivy- and
moss-hung tombstones'.[6] The theme of this passage is also the
need to remember the dead because this churchyard contained,
as he emphasised, the grave of Jane Hatherell, whom he had
tended as she lay dying. Much is made in the entry of the fact
that it was a perfect spring day, which reinforced his belief in
her ultimate immortality. Awareness of failure to remember the
dead tinges the entry recording his visit, this time on a warm
summer afternoon, to the ruined church of Llanlionfel near
Builth Wells. Its 'old tombstones stood knee-deep in the long
coarse grass' and all was desolation and neglect: 'window frames
and seats were gone' although memorial tablets to Marmaduke
Gwynne and his family remained. Its ruined state appealed to
the melancholy streak in him — 'It was a place for owls to dwell
in and satyrs to dance in'[7] — while simultaneously reflecting
the antiquarian influence in his background.

Inevitably the act of remembering the dead was accompanied
by a melancholy feeling but Kilvert knew that he had a peculiar
penchant for melancholy. 'I like wandering about. . . lonely, waste
and ruined places,' he said, they had 'a spirit of quiet and gentle
melancholy'.[8] He also recognised that autumn days brought on
this sad, pensive mood: 'I love to wander on these soft gentle
mournful autumn days. . . .'[9] Another autumn entry combines
the contrast of beauty/life and decay/death with his awareness
of mourning as an ever-present dimension of existence: 'in the
midst of all this beauty and freshness a black shadow stole
over the scene, a hearse with plumes and a mourning coach
rumbled along the road from Chippenham and across the bright
Common.'[10] His sensitivity to the dramatic invasion of the scene
by this memento mori is typical of his melancholy and of the

way in which it is frequently blended into his descriptions of landscape. He turned naturally to funeral images to convey this sombre impression of a winter landscape:

> I walked over to Kington St Michael in a thick blinding snow storm . . . The country was wrapped in one vast winding sheet of snow. . . . Yet before I had reached Kington it had turned into rain. . . . In the fading afternoon light the trees bent and swayed black against the leaden grey sky and the white slopes beyond. It was a strange dreary altered scene. The village was silent. It seemed buried and deserted in the snowy waste. . . .'[11]

A 'strange dreary altered scene' — an outstanding feature of Kilvert's writing is his extreme receptiveness to sudden changes in scenery, producing correspondingly violent shifts of his own mood. His leaving of a friend's home in Shanklin, Isle of Wight, in June 1874 was marked by one of those shifts:

> This morning I left with a sorrowful heart hospitable Newstead and all its dear faces and the beautiful Island. . . . As the Island receded more and more dim across the sea, I became more and more sad. Ten days ago all fresh, strange and unknown. But now, the lessening shores seemed like the face of a dear friend.[12]

The mourning note occurs in relation to other non-human forms:

> Cwmgwanon Wood is being murdered. As I walked along the edge of the beautiful dingle and looked sadly down into the hollow, numbers of my old friends of seven years standing lay below on both banks of the brook prostrate and mutilated, a mournful scene of havoc. . . .[13]

Whenever he had opportunity, he would launch into elegies for the dead, as in the case of Mrs Dewing, whom he had met shortly after her marriage:

> And now she is dead. How well I remember the bride cake and wine on the table and she sitting at the window looking so well, so radiant and happy. . . . So early dead, not 23, and to the poor bereaved husband after the short gleam of happiness all seems like a dream.[14]

In so many *Diary* passages, memories, even happy ones, of the past are suffused by a sense of loss and regret. Various commentators have noted this duality as a characteristic feature of Victorian writing. De Laura, for example, referred to a 'pervasive reminiscental mood', stemming largely from Wordsworth, in which remembering frequently involved the re-experiencing of 'something that has gone', that led to more universal perceptions of 'the still sad music of humanity'.[15] It is an 'elegiac mode', De Laura said, and in early and mid-Victorian literature it centred on memory and its 'melancholy inventory of past experience and loss'. Turner, too, underlined the 'duality in the period's mood: the sense of progress was balanced by a sense of loss',[16] which was caught in Tennyson's lines from *The Princess* that preface this chapter, recording the sudden clouding of a moment of happiness by melancholy. To De Laura, the nineteenth-century tendency to look back amounted to a 'passion for the past', and it often dwelt on ruined monuments of former ages. This, too, is very strong in Kilvert's depiction of landscape, as can be seen in the following examples. The standing stone of Cross Ffordd near Clyro elicited these comments:

> I suppose no one will ever know what the grey silent mysterious witness means, or why it was set there. Perhaps it could tell some strange wild tales and many generations have flowed and ebbed around it.[17]

Visiting Salisbury Plain, he wrote: 'Around us the Plain heaved mournfully with great and solemn barrows, the "grassy barrows of the happier dead" '.[18] Such passages abound in *Kilvert's Diary*. They often dwell on mortality, are Romantic and melancholy in tone, and reveal an abiding interest in archaeological and antiquarian matters, which was a strong current in his background.

All of these elements appear in his haunting description of his visit to Whitehall, which is perhaps the best example of his elegiac mode. The keynote of what is to follow is set by his encountering 'the old deserted kiln house':

> It is a strange country between the kiln and Whitehall. The trees look wild and weird and a yew was stifling an oak. The meadow below Whitehall looked sad and strange and wild, grown with bramble bushes, thorns, fern and gorse. Poor Whitehall, sad, silent and lonely,

Whitehall Farmhouse

with its great black yew in the hedge of the tangled waste grass-grown garden and its cold chimney still ivy-clustered. I walked round and looked in at the broken unframed windows and pushed open a door which swung slowly and wearily together again. . . . Here were held the Quarterly Dances. What fun. What merry makings, the young people coming in couples and parties from the country round to dance in the long room. What laughing, flirting, joking and kissing behind the door or in the dark garden amongst the young folks, while the elders sat round the room with pipe and mug of beer or cider from the 'Black Ox' of Coldbrook hard by. Now how is all changed, song and dance still, mirth fled away. Only the weird sighing through the broken roof and crazy doors, the quick feet, busy hands, saucy eyes, strong limbs all mouldered into dust, the laughing voices silent. There was a deathlike stillness about the place, except that I fancied once I heard a small voice singing and a bee was humming among the ivy green, the only bit of life about the place.[19]

The Romantic quality of the passage resides in a number of things. First it is full of melancholy. The 'great black yew' deepens this melancholy, as does the representation of the farm-house as a human body that is now decayed. The personification of inanimate things is continued in such supernatural details as the yew that was 'stifling an oak' and 'the weird sighing through the broken roof'. There are touches of the picturesque in the wildness of the trees and meadow, while the ivy clustering round the chimney provides the contrast of growth co-existing with decay so beloved of picturesque writers. Central is the dramatic contrast between what Whitehall was — the centre of a rich, happy community — and what it is now. The youth, beauty, vitality that once filled its rooms are replaced now by age, ugliness and death. Kilvert laid heavy emphasis on the difference between time past and time present: 'What fun. What merry makings. . . . What laughing, flirting, joking and kissing . . . Now how all is changed. . . .' 'Song and dance' has given way to 'deathlike stillness', the 'mirth fled away' like the lovers at the end of Keats's *The Eve of St Agnes*. These dramatic contrasts are underpinned by keen observation of telling physical details — the 'tangled waste grass-grown garden', the door swinging 'slowly and wearily', the 'small voice' (real or ghost?) singing, and the bee buzzing among the ivy. Mention of the 'crazy doors' supplies a surreal note. The Gothic element in Kilvert's description is apparent in the way once 'quick feet, busy hands, saucy eyes, strong limbs' are now 'mouldered into dust'. Absolutely nothing of the young people's joy at the Quarterly Dances remains, and the realisation is crushing. Nevertheless, Kilvert was remembering the dead and that is the passage's ultimate significance, apart from the fact that it illustrates the way he presents landscape's decisive role in people's lives, which is what William Plomer meant when he said that Kilvert gave a 'Hardyesque account' of Whitehall.

Though Kilvert did not generally dwell ghoulishly on the details of mortality, in the Whitehall passage there is a hint of a literary tradition that loved the graveyard, a tradition strongly represented in the education — religious, antiquarian, literary — he experienced at the Claverton Lodge home of his uncle Francis in Bath. The Rev Francis Kilvert is known as 'the antiquary' partly to differentiate him from his nephew and partly because he was famous in Bath and beyond for his antiquarian knowledge.[20] Kilvert received the greater part of his school education, both in terms of duration and impact, at Claverton.[21] Uncle Francis's literary remains confirm his 'passion for the past', not only as regards his antiquarian researches but in his considerable classical knowledge and his penchant for eighteenth-century writers.[22] The grounding in eighteenth-century literature which Kilvert received from his uncle is responsible for a highly characteristic aspect of his writing — the pattern of description alternating with reflection commonly found in such writers as Pope, Thomson and Gray. Hagstrum noted that Gray 'places himself in a scene of his own creating, which he then observes and meditates upon'.[23] Eighteenth-century readers would not only demand meditation in a descriptive poem but also human figures capable of arousing their interest and sympathy.[24] James Thomson's *The Seasons* was seen in the eighteenth century as the type of the religious/descriptive poem. Much of what we find in *Kilvert's Diary* is explained by subsequent literary developments. The eighteenth-century's easy assumption that poets would naturally reflect the sense that God was everywhere in Nature did not suit the Evangelical temper of the early nineteenth century, which demanded a more clear and more devotional recognition of personal faith, a strain found in Wordsworth, as subsequent chapters will show. Nevertheless, there was a line of development from *The Seasons* to the poetry of the Romantics because 'Thomson is a precursor, not only of the transcendental claims later made by Wordsworth and Coleridge, but of their poetry of meditative response'.[25] Cowper's *The Task*, part-philosophical satire, part-religious treatise, and part-nature poem, has a place in this line of development, forming a bridge between Thomson's *The Seasons* and Wordsworth's *The Prelude*. Cowper's devotional poetry provided Evangelicals with what they needed and, as later chapters show, Kilvert was familiar with it. Sambrook characterised *The Task* as 'discursive-meditative – descriptive' and noted that it becomes an 'excursion' comparable to Wordsworth's *Excursion*.[26] Typical of its approach is the passage in Book VI in which Cowper stated that a winter walk on a fine day through an avenue of trees, where the only sound, that of a robin 'pleased with his solitude, encourages meditation.' In Nature, 'there lives / A soul in all things, and that soul is God.'[27] Very probably, Kilvert came across in his uncle's study Hervey's *Meditations among the Tombstones* (1745), a work so popular that by 1791 it had gone through 25 editions.[28] Its romantic antiquarianism was likely to have appealed to uncle Francis. Hervey was important, not only for his contribution to the Gothic side of Romanticism, in its

obsession with dead bodies, skulls, ghosts, ruins and tombs, but
also for his contribution to the Nature literature of the period.
Kilvert's Whitehall meditation has all the essential features
of Hervey's: the feel for physical beauty, the emotionality, the
perceptive detail, the melancholy, elegiac quality. In Hervey's, he
suggested that if we could draw back the tomb's covering, 'oh!
how it would . . . grieve us!' Instead of a girl's lovely smile, there
'grins horribly a naked ghastly skull'; the 'lovely lightnings of
her eyes are no more'. The phrase 'mouldered into dust', used
in the Whitehall passage about 'saucy eyes' and 'busy hands',
Hervey applied to the busy hands that built the church that was
the scene of his meditation.[29]

Another central figure in the eighteenth-century graveyard
tradition was Edward Young, whose *Night Thoughts* appeared
in 1742-6. Cornford observed: 'Young's preoccupation with
death undoubtedly gripped the imagination of Europe' and his
poem became 'a seminal work in a secular cult of sepulchral
melancholy'.[30] In a stirring passage in *Night IV*, Young declared
that Nature had the power to transform 'the ghastly Ruins
of the Mould'ring Tomb'. He therefore urged Christians to
'Read Nature; Nature is Friend to Truth; / Nature is Christian,
preaches to Mankind'.[31] Like Hervey, Young believed that the
Christian poet was to seek the sublimity of God in the created
world through the imagination: the stars 'were made to fashion
the Sublime / Of human hearts. . . .' The beauty and grandeur
of Nature then become part of the individual self, which Young
consistently presents as a poetic self.[32] For Young, the ability to
reflect upon Nature came with solitude, as he made clear at
the start of his poem when he invoked 'Silence, and *Darkness*!
solemn Sisters! Twins from ancient *Night* . . .' to come to his aid.
He will have them to thank, even though like all mankind he is
doomed to the grave, for helping him to 'strike Wisdom' from
his soul. Kilvert revealed Young's influence when he wrote in
his poem, *Silence*:

> When vexed by wrangling loud and rude,
>   Or tossed on trouble's sea,
>   Sweet Sister twin of Solitude,
>   Silence, I fly to thee.

With the help of those Sisters, his 'evensong / Shall rise ere
long / To Heaven' from 'among these graves'.

Gray's *Elegy Written in a Country Churchyard* (1751) is often categorised as a 'graveyard' work along with *Night Thoughts* and Hervey's *Meditations* but it lacks their lugubrious tone and invites readers to remember the dead as a means of recognising, not simply their mortality, but their virtues, and it was of central importance to Kilvert for this reason. The sense that it was a sacred text for him is reinforced by his indignant reaction when a member of his Clyro gentry set attributed the verse beginning 'let not ambition mock their useful toil' to Goldsmith instead of Gray: ' I looked round in undisguised amazement but no one seemed to have noticed anything particular.'[33] That the *Elegy* was another work to which considerable attention had been given during the years of uncle Francis's tutelage becomes clear from the echoes of it in Kilvert's *Diary* and in his uncle's literary remains. Kilvert was fond of quoting Gray's line emphasising that no one died and left the world 'Nor cast one longing lingering look behind'.[34] Before examining Kilvert's own elegy in a country churchyard, it is necessary to establish the place of Gray's poem in what Schor has called the 'circulation of texts' that sustained memories of the dead in a 'culture of mourning'.[35] The poem became 'a seminal text', exercising 'a profound influence on the poetry of the next 75 years',[36] helping to make fashionable the 'elegiac' mode, with its emphasis on pathos and sentimentalism. The Enlightenment preoccupation with the idea that the morality of society derived from the character of the emotions and intellect of the people who composed it, owed much to Adam Smith, who saw sympathy for the dead as the basis of social sympathy. He was one of a number of eighteenth-century philosophers who stressed the moral value of sympathy and benevolence.[37] Smith wrote: 'The tribute of our fellow-feeling seems doubly due to [the dead] now, when they are in danger of being forgot by everybody'; by paying 'vain honours' to their memory, we try to keep in mind 'their misfortune'.[38] According to this view, the dead became 'a moral resource', morals became 'the exchange of sympathies' (Schor's phrases), and the truly moral person is one in whom sympathy is a highly developed attribute. Thus,

> Smith's sense of the grave as the source of moral life parallels Gray's enquiry into the nature of virtue within the graveyard framework of the *Elegy*; by mid-[eighteenth] century mourning and morals stood together at the grave.[39]

Gray used his poem to examine the virtues of humble country folk, the 'rude forefathers of the hamlet' who 'sleep / Each in his narrow cell forever laid.'

> Let not Ambition mock their useful toil,
> Their homely joys, and destiny obscure;
> Nor Grandeur hear with a disdainful smile,
> The short and simple annals of the poor.

Although the poet/narrator condemns the vanity of the memorials of the rich and proud, he insists that all people, including the poor, need some memorial, and stand in danger of being forgotten: 'On some fond breast the parting soul relies, / Some pious drops the closing eye requires'. Someone needs to tell their 'artless tale' and that person, by telling it, relates himself to the reader as well as to the dead.[40] Gray goes on to note that the 'thee' who is 'mindful of the unhonoured dead' will himself die and 'Some kindred Spirit' shall enquire what *his* fate was. However, in the epitaph which closes the poem, the narrator is portrayed not as a poet but as a man of God, dealing in sympathies rather than verses.

Kilvert's own elegy embodies a much more Christian view of death than Gray's. It is part of the entry he wrote on Easter Sunday 1876 and begins with a heavy emphasis on church bells 'ringing for the joy of the Resurrection'. After the service he walked among the graves:

> I walked alone round the silent sunny peaceful Church-yard and visited the graves of my sleeping friends Jane Hatherell, Mary Jefferies, Anne Hawkins, John Jefferies, George Bryant, Emily Banks, John Hatherell, Limpedy Buckland the gipsy girl, and many more. There they lay, the squire and the peasant, the landlord and the labourer, young men and maidens, old men and children, the infant of days beside the patriarch of nearly five score years, sister, brother, by the same mother, all in her breast their heads did lay and crumble to their common clay. And over all she lovingly threw her soft mantle of green and gold, the greensward and buttercups, daisies and primroses. There they lay all sleeping well and peacefully after life's fitful fevers and waiting for the Great Spring morning and the General Resurrection of the dead. John Hatherell, the good old

sawyer, now sleeps in the same God's acre to which he
helped to carry the gipsy girl Limpedy Buckland to her
burial more than sixty years ago.[41]

A positive view of death permeates the passage. The sense
of a unified community is strong (he was quoting Psalm 148.12
when he wrote of 'young men and maidens, old men and
children'; echoes of the Psalms often surface in his descriptions
of landscape). The dead are not forgotten by him: in death
they remain his 'sleeping friends'. His sympathy with them
is repeated in the passage by the action of John Hatherell,
'the good old sawyer', who 60 years ago carried the body
of the gipsy girl to her burial.[42] Kilvert said no more than
this of the virtues of the dead but his tribute to Hatherell's
action is a reminder of the mutual acts of kindness on which
community life depends. His depiction of the churchyard as
a place of equality recalls particularly Wordsworth's second
Essay upon Epitaphs.[43] Not only all ages and both sexes lie
together, but also squire and peasant, landlord and labourer,
just as in Gray's poem 'the pomp of power, / And . . . all
that wealth e'er gave, / Awaits alike the inevitable hour', in
the company of the 'rude forefathers'. Nature accepts them
all kindly and caringly — 'And over all she lovingly threw
her soft mantle . . .' — and their sleep is untroubled.[44] The
theological notion of the 'Communion of Saints' seems to
lie behind Kilvert's picture of Christian Community in this
entry. His sleeping dead are not those originally designated
'saints', because they were martyrs or exceptionally holy, but
rather the 'faithful Christians who have died [and] are joined
in communion with Christians on earth.'[45] 'Communion of
Saints' was also extended in later medieval theology to mean
sharers in 'holy things, especially sacraments.'[46] Kilvert was
deriving satisfaction from the sense of continuity involved in
a long span of Christian fellowship when he wrote: 'Stopped
a minute to look at the grey church above the river and to
think of the many generations that have worshipped and lain
down to rest in its God's Acre.'[47] The passage expresses the
attitudes towards time and memory that characterise much
of his writing about landscape.

Cornford, in his book on Young, explained that eighteenth-
century poets frequently accorded to the deaths of friends 'an
essentially public, not private, status'.[48] Kilvert's uncle Francis

had thoroughly assimilated this dimension of eighteenth-century culture and had passed it on to the diarist.[49] Uncle Francis's literary remains are permeated by what Schor has called the 'culture of mourning', in which a whole range of texts kept alive memories of the dead. These texts were not confined to formal elegy but encompassed funeral sermons, obituaries, graveyard meditations, elegiac sonnets, epitaphs, inscriptions and eulogistic memoirs.[50] Uncle Francis had a book devoted entirely to epitaphs, notebooks whose contents were dominated by epitaphs, inscriptions, poetic extracts exemplifying meditations and tributes to good lives, and he published a collection of original Latin inscriptions on famous people.[51] He was also very fond of the poet William Shenstone, who 'excelled as a writer of epitaphs' and who greatly admired Gray's *Elegy*.[52] The importance to Francis of Gray's *Elegy* can be seen from the fact that, like Kilvert, he wrote his own version, *A Churchyard Meditation*, emphasising the 'sacred calm' of the churchyard and the wisdom of musing on mortality. It is evident that he had also absorbed the ideas and sentiments of Wordsworth's first *Essay upon Epitaphs*, in which the poet had written: 'the composition of an epitaph naturally turns . . . upon departed worth. . . .'[53] In his obituary of George Stothert, uncle Francis began by saying, in words highly characteristic of the culture of mourning,

> It is a debt due, both to the memory of *departed worth*, and to the best interests of society, to place on record the character of those, whose extraordinary merits their retiring modesty, or the privacy of their station, or both united, have kept back from public view.[54]

The sentiment here is one of the key ones of Gray's *Elegy* — awareness that humble people, the 'unhonoured dead', had virtues that needed to be made public. Wordsworth expressed the same view: 'the virtues, especially those of humble life, are retired; and many of the highest must be sought for or they will be overlooked.'[55]

It is evident from literary fragments among uncle Francis's papers that Wordsworth was a model for him.[56] For example, he wrote a meditation on the ruins of Tintern Abbey, as the poet had. Of most significance is the fact that he had taken the trouble to copy out lines 37-52 of Wordsworth's *A Poet's Epitaph* that depict the poet:

But who is He, with modest looks,
And clad in homely russet brown?
He murmurs near the running brooks
A music sweeter than their own.

He is retired as noontide dew,
Or fountain in a noon-day grove;
And you must love him, ere to you
He will seem worthy of your love.

The outward shows of sky and earth,
Of hill and valley, he has viewed;
And impulses of deeper birth
Have come to him in solitude.[57]

In common things that round us lie
Some random truths he can impart, —
The harvest of a quiet eye
That broods and sleeps on his own heart.

Earlier in the poem, Wordsworth counselled men in other occupations — lawyers, doctors, philosophers — as to the moral stance they should adopt in life. His advice to the statesman — 'First learn to love one living man; Then mayest thou think upon the dead' — had special importance to uncle Francis, because in the copied lines love is seen as the central virtue. The theme is clear: public morality depended on private, individual sympathy. The source of this sympathy was Nature, as Francis had confirmed by underlining lines 45-8 in which 'impulses of deeper birth' are said to come from viewing the 'outward shows of sky and earth'. To make the connection clearer still, he had written, on the reverse of the copied stanzas from *A Poet's Epitaph*, these lines from Wordsworth's *Prelude* Book III: 'To every natural form, rock, fruit, or flower, . . . I gave a moral life: I saw them feel, / Or linked them to some feeling' (lines 127-30). Confirmation that uncle Francis had an image of the Christian poet (largely in the person of Wordsworth but derived also from Hervey, Young and Gray) as hero,[58] comes in the inscription he wrote in a copy of Sedgwick's *Discourse* that he gave to Frederick Falkner on 16 February 1835.[59] The Falkners were the first of several linked Shropshire families, one of which was the Kilvert family, to come to Bath in the late eighteenth century. The inscription reads:

> To Frederick Falkner the ardent admirer of Nature and
> the humble adorer of Nature's God, this book dictated
> by a kindred spirit and calculated to touch his inward
> sympathies is presented by his affectionate friend F.K.

The inscription's wording and the salient features of
Sedgwick's life are revealing about the beliefs of uncle Francis
and his influence on Kilvert. 'Nature's God' is from Pope's
An Essay on Man, while the phrase 'kindred spirit' is a nod in
the direction of Gray's *Elegy*: it is 'Some kindred spirit' who
is to enquire the fate of the poet. Charles Lyell had published
his *Principles of Geology* (1830-3), which challenged the Bible's
account of the age of the earth, and uncle Francis was passing
on to Frederick a work which accommodated new findings in
geology with traditional religious views. The *DNB* describes
Sedgwick's *Discourse*[60] as an argument 'for the place of geology
within natural theology'. In the much expanded 1850 edition
of it, he pictured Wordsworth, whom he knew, as a religious
teacher helping men find 'a better faith in Nature'.

Uncle Francis, in his inscription to Frederick Falkner, had
highlighted the capacity of Sedgwick's *Discourse* 'to touch his
inward sympathies'. On the page of his notebook that contained
the inscription, uncle Francis had also written his epitaph to
Falkner's son Christopher, who had died in 1846 aged 20: to
the Bath antiquary they belonged to the same emotional/moral
activity and to the same discourse — expanding sympathy,
remembering the dead. These were the consistent themes of
the religious and poetic education that Kilvert experienced
at his uncle's hands. In the latter's obituary of November
1863, two merits are repeatedly emphasised: his impeccable
scholarship (with its steady focus on eighteenth-century poets[61]
and divines) and his sympathetic nature. The sentimentalism
of eighteenth-century poetry is a feature too of the novels of
that period and Kilvert's leaning towards Fielding, Sterne,
Cervantes, Lesage, Maria Edgeworth and Lamb may also be
attributed to his uncle's influence. The key to Kilvert's appetite
for a fiction of moral sentiment lies in his strong interest in
Lesage's *Gil Blas*: 'I picked up a copy of *Gil Blas* which I have
long wanted to possess'.[62] The eponymous hero of the novel
is a basically good-hearted young man who has no hope of
succeeding by honest means in a world which esteems only
rank and money. He struggles to retain his integrity in the

course of adventures in which all classes and aspects of society are satirised.[63] The meanness of the nobility is contrasted with the warm, generous feelings of ordinary folk such as Fabrice: 'My adventures [Fabrice] thought whimsical enough; and testified his sympathy in my present uneasy circumstances'.[64] Characters burst into tears with ease and regularity in Lesage's novel as they do in other novels of sentiment.[65] *Gil Blas*, along with *Roderick Random, Peregrine Pickle, Tom Jones, The Vicar of Wakefield* and *Robinson Crusoe*, made up the 'glorious host' of novels which fed the heart and imagination of Dickens as a boy.[66] Kilvert sought out Sterne's *Tristram Shandy* for this reason.[67] At the heart of the novel is 'The lesson of universal good-will . . . taught . . . by uncle Toby'.[68] Even Evangelicals like uncle Francis and Kilvert, who had been brought up to distrust novels, used Sterne as a model of moral feeling. Mullan explained why: 'novels of sentiment keenly rehearsed the art of comprehending the pathos of narratives; the capacity to respond with tremulous sensibility to a tale of misfortune was represented as a sufficient sign of virtue'.[69] Kilvert enjoyed telling such tales and was delighted when his hearers made a sympathetic response: 'Both my hearers walked entranced as the tales beguiled the way, the beautiful girl beside me . . . wondering, awe-struck or pitiful, according to the progress and passion of the tale, her sensitive features reflecting as a mirror the swiftly changing emotions of her gentle heart.'[70] The eighteenth-century philosopher Hume made sympathy the centre of his *Treatise of Human Nature*: 'No quality of human nature is more remarkable'. It was the means by which people drew together in fellow feeling and was the basis of social morality, Hume argued, because a concern for other individuals was the equivalent of a concern for society.[71]

A very striking fact about the *Memoirs* of Robert Kilvert, the diarist's father, is that over one third of its 65 pages is taken up with deaths, near-deaths, death-bed scenes, funerals, epitaphs and mourning. This preoccupation is partly a matter of his own temperament but must also be a reflection of the influence of his brother Francis (the surrogate father from whom he received a good deal of his pre-university education) and of the discourse of the dead that predominated in the early nineteenth century. Robert's childhood record is filled with stories illustrating the precarious hold he and other children had on life. His youngest brother once told their mother a highly plausible tale of seeing

Robert sink beneath the surface of the canal that ran behind the family home in Widcombe. Later, Robert was surprised to find his mother in tears and himself 'famous' for returning from the dead. Another brother, William, nearly drowned in one of the canal basins when the ice broke and he was only saved after sinking twice. On another occasion, Robert witnessed the near-death by drowning of a boy in the river Avon and his abiding memory of the incident was his own sympathy that took the form of painful identification with the unfortunate victim:

> I have never forgotten the intense yearning pain that struck through me at the sight. In heart and mind I was with him in the water, grasping him and dragging him out. . . .[72]

Closer to home was the death in the canal of a neighbour's boy, another memory that stayed with Robert: 'I can see even now his corded trousers and laced boots saturated with water'.[73] This litany of the dead included family bereavements:

> For the three or four years following 1815, most of my recollections are of a shady and melancholy character. . . . In those years we lost my third brother Thomas, my father, my uncle Kilvert of Worcester, my fifth brother William, and my grandmother.[74]

Throughout Robert's accounts of human tragedies runs a steady emphasis on his own capacity to feel for the suffering victims and for those that mourn, which he obviously regarded as an index of his own moral worth, a means by which his private affections contributed to public morality. This sense is powerfully present in his account of the nation's response to the death of Princess Charlotte in 1817. He felt he had to record his own recollection of this event, thus adding to the vast number of documents published within months of it, constituting, in Schor's words, 'a myriad of dirges, monodies, elegies, and epitaphs', as well as sermons, discourses and memoirs.[75] Princess Charlotte gave birth on 5 November 1817 to a stillborn son (she had married only a year before), who would have been third in line for the crown; she herself died on 6 November. Her pregnancy and her stillborn child were the focal point of the nation's perception and representation of her tragedy. Robert Kilvert made this clear in his reference to her marriage:

> It was believed to be one of real and mutual affection, and promised an unusual amount of happiness. Not the slightest apprehension was entertained of anything being wrong, when in a moment the hopes of the country were dashed to the ground by her giving birth to a dead child and dying herself almost immediately afterwards.[76]

The 'promised . . . happiness' of which Robert wrote was both the prospect of an ideal union of husband and wife and of the male heir; as Schor put it, 'Princess Charlotte's expectations had been those of the kingdom'.[77] This is the keynote of Robert's account: 'There was probably never a more universal or more genuine mourning . . . ,'[78] which reflects the tone of all the documents produced at the time: 'A central theme is the conflation of public and private grief'.[79] The Princess became 'everywoman — everydaughter, everywife, every expectant mother',[80] and thus everyone in the country could not only share the grief of members of her family, but was a better person morally for feeling it so deeply. Schor stressed that most accounts of her funeral 'celebrate the family as a sublime showcase for British morals', a universal coming together in grief in which all differences of religion, class, gender and party were forgotten.[81] Robert Kilvert recalled hearing a sermon commemorating the Princess's death. In spite of perceiving an element of mass hysteria in the occasion, he was keen to emphasise the basic sincerity of the emotion: 'Whatever might have been the mode of expression, the real thing, the deep-seated feeling, was prevalent everywhere'.[82]

By the turn of the nineteenth century, the family had become the channel through which the 'deep-seated feeling' detected by Robert flowed, merging individual and public morals. Women's world was that of home and family and the influence they could exert in the roles of wife and mother was seen to extend far beyond that world, their reward for not seeking wider freedoms.[83] In Evangelical homes like that of the Kilverts, the notion of woman's moral influence was particularly strong. While Kilvert was a pupil at Claverton Lodge, his uncle Francis wrote a poem, *The Loving Heart*, which recommends, as Gray's *Elegy* had, rejection of worldliness ('lust of fame or power . . . ambition's glare . . . Fortune's gifts') in favour of 'That heart [which] with faithful pulse shall heave / Beneath thy nestling head. . . .' Francis ended the poem by urging the reader to recognise that 'affection's unbought throb' was the 'holiest, happiest part' of life.[84] These were understandings born of his marriage in 1822 to Adelaide Sophia de Chièvre, a Moravian count's daughter and a refugee (as a child) from the French revolution. She was brought up in London as a Quaker.[85] The formal education supplied by uncle Francis to pupils at Claverton Lodge was complemented by Sophia's informal kind, the essence of which was contained in her book *Home Discipline*. It would have been natural for her to regard her nephew and the other boarding pupils as extensions, along with the servants, of her family, for whom she had moral responsibility. Moreover, Quakers placed a high value on the home, family life and education. They rejected extreme Evangelical ideas of original sin and the salvation only of a few 'elect' ones among the faithful, placing much more emphasis on the affections as a means of fostering faith. 'The charity which never faileth is a necessary virtue for domestic life', Sophia wrote.[86] Furthermore, 'the mutual duties' of master and servant were best fulfilled where 'the "law of kindness" [was] written in every heart'.[87] In Sophia's ideal family, sympathy and affection were the marks of a wife, whose role was to 'establish . . . the happiness of the house of a beloved husband . . . to consult his private and public well-being . . . to be the depository of his joys and sorrows. . . .'[88] A true lady was not to be recognised by 'Mere elegance of person, of manners. . . .' because these were external things esteemed by worldly people, and 'affect not her heart and understanding'.[89] Sophia paid tribute to Quakers for exemplifying these virtues. Their 'industry and integrity' had often made them rich but they employed their wealth in 'ameliorating the sufferings of mankind' and not in worldly show.

A fundamental principle of her book is the supreme importance of personal example as an influence upon the morality of others. She underlined the 'distressing effects' produced 'both to their children and their various ranks of dependants' when heads of families neglected their responsibilities. She acknowledged that, in those days (the ideas in her book dated, she said, from the early 1820s), 'the feudal tie is indeed dissolved' but 'true and faithful service' could be revived 'when the domestic bond is restored'. 'Living example, giving strength to precept' was the key, and in this regard 'The silent and deep influence of the well-ordered family . . . can scarcely be estimated'.[90] This example had its effects, she argued, on one's children and it 'even transfers itself to our servants' and into 'the neighbourhood'. She conceived this influence primarily as a matter of extending sympathy through charitable acts:

> Neighbour charities are (next to the domestic) our first duty. . . . When the time is once spared for exploring the wants and distresses of those around us, their own pathos will fully recommend them to our sympathy and relief.[91]

The very eighteenth-century emphasis on the sympathetic affections of the 'good heart' responding to the 'pathos' of suffering people is notable here. Sophia was very insistent that 'Christian principle', and not moral sentiment alone, was the only true basis of morality: 'enlightened CHRISTIAN PRINCIPLE was the only foundation on which to build the fabric of our household'.[92] By Christian principle she meant 'the practical sense of right and wrong' derived from the Bible. Some people, she said, felt that their charitable actions were holier if directed at distant sufferers (she clearly had in mind overseas missions to the heathen) but 'there is a self-complacency in following those feelings which is not good for us'. This must have been one of the bones of contention between her family and Kilvert's own, which made much of overseas missions. She was another who argued that circulation of sympathies could be effected within a community not only by the living but by the dead. The example of kindly feelings

> remains long in a neighbourhood, when the heads [of a family] are laid in the grave. . . . The light of its rays is not there extinguished. The rich and poor retain a memorial of it which time is slow to obliterate. Tradition . . . hands down the good and evil deeds which we had power in life to conceal. Happy will it be for us and our survivors, if they were our best deeds. . . .[93]

Thus, 'individual personal obligation', working through the family and neighbourhood, had enormous consequences for the moral fabric of the whole nation: 'I could almost say that a large family is a kingdom within itself. To learn to rule well in a public character, we should look at the first ruling principle in our own family circle'.[94] It was the message of Wordsworth's *A Poet's Epitaph*, which her husband endorsed.

Thus, from his aunt Sophia, from Gray and Wordsworth, from his uncle Francis, and, as was noted in the Introduction, from Howitt, Kilvert learned the importance of hidden lives, of the virtues of the 'unhonoured dead', of the 'short and simple annals of the poor' that were in danger of remaining untold because of their 'destiny obscure'. In Wordsworth's poem *The Excursion*, the Wanderer declares that the Pastor is in a position, because of his close knowledge of the local poor, to 'pronounce authentic epitaphs' upon them as they lay 'Beneath this turf mouldering at our feet', in order that 'we may learn / *To prize the breath we share with human kind; / And look upon the dust of man with awe.*'[95] The given objective has the dual aspect encountered earlier: to mourn the dead while simultaneously to feel sympathy for, to establish fellow-feeling with, the living. The Pastor's initial response is to agree that the living needed to represent to themselves the worth of the lives lived by the dead: 'True indeed it is / That they whom death has hidden from our sight / Are worthiest of the mind's regard'.[96] A memory of these lines informs Kilvert's statement: 'Below Tybella a bird singing *reminded* me of how the words of a good man live after he is silent and out of sight "He being dead yet speaketh".'[97] These last words have become Kilvert's own epitaph and appear on his gravestone in the churchyard of Bredwardine, Herefordshire. His poem, *Honest Work,* is his fullest poetic expression of his understanding that there were hidden lives of beauty and worth, often integral parts of the landscape, that would go down, unrecognised and unrecorded, to the grave:

> Live you, work you, out of ken,
> From the windy praise of men,
> In the humble old abode:
> Every day is hid with God.

His message to them was: 'Think not thou dost work alone; / GOD is ever looking on'. Kilvert also was looking on, and while his poem was one form of recognition of them, he intended his *Diary* to be the much fuller one. From the moment he arrived in Clyro in spring 1865, his love for the community of the Welsh borderland began to grow until in January 1870 he started to record its life, criss-crossing his parish in apparently never-ending solitary walks, very much in the pattern of Wordsworth's Wanderer and Wordsworth himself, and with this spirit and with this objective:

> the lonely roads
> Were open schools in which I daily read
> With most delight the passions of mankind,
> Whether by words, looks, sighs, or tears, revealed;
> There saw into the depths of human souls,
> Souls that appear to have no depth at all
> To careless eyes.[98]

Maria Lake was evidently one whom Kilvert thought worth remembering and he mourned over her ruined cottage: 'her place knows her no more though the wind blown larch still bows over the roof as if mourning for her'.[99] He wrote Emma Halliday's 'authentic epitaph' while she was still alive because he was so impressed by her worth:

> Good Emma Halliday was with old John. Wherever there is sickness or sorrow, or trouble to be taken or help to be given there I am sure to find Emma Halliday. She is beloved by the whole village and no wonder for she is one of the best and kindest neighbours I ever knew. God bless her and reward her.[100]

Behind epitaphs lies a biographical impulse, which is captured effectively in Kenneth Johnston's definition of epitaph — 'the smallest compression of the fullest story'.[101] *Kilvert's Diary* is a compendium of stories of lives, one long narrative made up of scores of short ones. Its author loved stories and collected them as an ethnographer would, favouring especially those told with the authentic flavour supplied by the particular background, experience, personality and style of their tellers. It is the rich flavour of these stories that is responsible for much of the *Diary's* appeal and for the characteristic response it provokes — the desire to fill out the stories of lives of which it is composed.[102] Kilvert was blending epitaphs, biography, history and folklore in order to create a picture of a community he knew was disappearing: his *Diary* is his epitaph for that community. One intriguing aspect of the *Diary* is the readership he imagined for it, since such a large proportion of it is given over to celebrating the lives of cottagers and small farmers,[103] rather than the lives of his own class. Neither the ordinary folk who were his subjects nor gentry would read his account.

He was intent upon recording instances of the 'good heart' — the impulse to act in a kindly and moral way, which is such a

powerful concept in eighteenth-century novels of sentiment.[104]
One explanation of the characteristic melancholy, elegiac mood
of Kilvert's writing is that he felt that the social, moral and
psychological conditions that promoted feelings of sympathy in
a community were under threat. This is why the *Diary* so often
has the feeling of being a lament for the past. The fact that the
Victorian age was the great age of self-writing is one indication of
its fascination with the past. De Laura saw Victorians' emphasis
on personal memory as bound up with their awareness of
being in a period of huge social changes: 'The presentation
of one's own past, as part of the search for new meanings in
a deteriorating cultural situation, is perhaps the most central
binding activity of serious nineteenth century literature'. It
is the 'everywhere evident autobiographical pressure of the
period. . . .'[105] The sentimentalism of eighteenth-century poetry
became assimilated, in Wordsworth's poetry in particular, into a
Romantic search for selfhood, an approach whose egocentricity
Kilvert rejected in favour of one that emphasised the individual's
role in a community. This was a characteristically Evangelical
approach, as well as a Victorian one, as we have seen in Sophia
Kilvert's formulation of the individual's responsibility of
undertaking charitable work in his own neighbourhood.[106] To
those of Evangelical viewpoint, the passage of one's life should
evince spiritual and moral progress, as Sophia made abundantly
clear by the epigraph from Fénelon to her *Home Discipline*: 'Time
is given us that we may take care for eternity, and eternity will
not be too long to regret the loss of our time if we have mis-
spent it'. One corollary of such an awareness is diary-keeping.
The 'minute events and considerations' of daily life may seem
trivial, Sophia wrote, but we should remember that 'trifles make
up the sum and substance of our lives'.[107] As far as is known,
neither Sophia nor her husband kept diaries; Kilvert and his
father did because, presumably, they were more Evangelical.
The Evangelical drive in that direction appears forcefully in this
passage from one of James Hervey's letters to a friend:

> Have you employed your time usefully to yourself or
> to others? . . . Do you keep a diary as you used to do,
> a secret history of your heart and conduct, and take
> notice of the manner in which your time is spent? . . .
> And do you often review these interesting memoirs? . . .
> Keeping a diary is the way to know ourselves. . . .[108]

It was to be expected that Kilvert, raised in the culture of diary-keeping and mourning, should seek out in June 1871 Elizabeth Phelps's *The Gates Ajar* (1868), the ending of which he called 'touching and tearful'. Cast in the form of a journal, the book is all about mourning and concerns Mary Cabot, who grieves for her dead brother (actually her lover) killed in the American Civil War.[109] Her Aunt Winifred gives her much comfort and spiritual instruction,[110] conveyed in long, searching conversations, peppered with references to and quotations from the Evangelical writers — Mary Howitt, Mrs Browning, Cowper, Robert Montgomery, Mrs Hemans, Luther — who figure frequently in the books Kilvert read.[111] Aunt Winifred insists not only that the living cherish the memory of the dead, but that 'our absent dead are very present with us' in the sense that they in death continue to love and remember the living.[112] Among the 'friends' Aunt Winifred looks forward to meeting in heaven is Frederick Robertson, whom she specially valued for his reassuring statement, vis à vis death, 'I am not afraid of the dark'.[113] The writings, preachings and *lives* of devout people form for Aunt Winifred, as for Kilvert, another circle of sympathy, one that sustained their moral and spiritual progress. Robertson had explained in his *Lecture on Wordsworth* that he had 'endeavoured to make Wordsworth's principles the guiding principles of his own inner life'.[114] Several of the *Lecture's* key emphases are found in Kilvert's writing, particularly the idea of experiencing such sympathy with another individual as to achieve almost total identification: to sympathise with another, Robertson wrote, involved 'a power of breathing the same atmosphere'. He himself felt that kind of sympathy for Wordsworth, partly because Wordsworth had such deep sympathy for the unregarded poor, 'the pedlars, broom-gatherers, gipsies and wanderers' of his poems. Wordsworth sympathised with them as 'the stately nobles of nature', seeing in them 'not what they were but what they might be'.[115] We will see, in what follows, the extent to which Kilvert was guided by principles such as these, as well as by writers whom Robertson endorsed.[116]

The self-exploratory element of autobiographies and diaries was one of the purposes behind Kilvert's writing. Chapter two notes his interest in diaries and the fact that a large proportion of the prose works that he read have a diary format. Many *Diary* entries show him explicitly monitoring his spiritual and moral progress as individuals do in those works. There was a natural fit between that purpose and his parish visits: in extending sympathy to parishioners, he was testing his own Christianity, assessing the quality of his own 'heart'. As he recorded his parishioners' struggle with life, he also recorded his engagement with their sufferings, completing the circle of sympathy. Hervey, Young, Gray, Wordsworth and uncle Francis had all recommended finding God in Nature and this too gave a purpose to Kilvert's wanderings. His descriptions of landscape combine the main impulses behind his writing. From childhood, the park of Bowood, home of Lord Lansdowne, had been a landscape of special significance to him. His sister Emily noted that the Kilvert children picnicked there: 'sometimes by special permission of Lord Lansdowne, we went into the lovely grounds of Bowood'.[117] Kilvert valued this aristocratic kindness, though it belonged to the past of 'feudal ties' which his aunt Sophia said had gone forever. In his description, Bowood represents a traditional way of life, which was by the 1870s much threatened, and this goes some way to explain its elegiac tone:

> As the sun shone through the roof of beech boughs overhead the very air seemed gold and scarlet and green and crimson in the deep places of the wood and the red leaves shone brilliant standing out against the splendid blue of the sky. A crowd of wood pigeons rose from the green and misty azure hollows of the plantation and flapped swiftly down the glades, the blue light glancing off their clapping wings. I went by the house down to the lakeside and crossed the water by the hatches above the cascade. From the other side of the water the lake shone as blue as the sky and beyond it rose from the water's edge the grand bank of sloping woods glowing with colours, scarlet, gold, orange and crimson and dark green. Two men were fishing on the further shore of an arm of the lake and across the water came the hoarse belling of a buck while a coot fluttered skimming along the surface of the lake with a loud cry and rippling splash.
>   'The wild buck bells from ferny brake,
>   The coot dives merry on the lake,
>   The saddest heart might pleasure take
>   To see all Nature gay.'
> To eye and ear it was a beautiful picture, the strange hoarse belling of the buck, the fluttering of the coot as

she skimmed the water with her melancholy note, the cry of the swans across the lake, the clicking of the reels as the fishermen wound up or let out their lines, the soft murmur of the woods, the quiet rustle of the red and golden drifts of beech leaves, the rush of the waterfall, the light tread of the dappled herd of deer dark and dim glancing across the green glades from shadow into sunlight and rustling under the beeches, and the merry voices of the Marquis's children at play.

Why do I keep this voluminous journal? I can hardly tell. Partly because life appears to me such a curious and wonderful thing that it almost seems a pity that even such a humble and uneventful life as mine should pass altogether away without some such record as this, and partly too because I think the record may amuse and interest some who come after me.[118]

The quoted stanza provides the main clue to the mood in which the entry was written. In spite of the coot's 'merry' diving, the spirited belling of the buck,[119] and Nature at her most beautiful, Kilvert's heart remained sad. This was partly because he knew the context of the stanza from Scott's long poem, *Marmion*. It occurs in Sir David Lindsay's Tale and describes the fair palace of Linlithgow, which is particularly beautiful in 'jovial June', but 'June is to our sovereign dear / The heaviest month in all the year: / Too well his cause of grief you know, — / June saw his father's overthrow'.[120] The stanza records, therefore, an unhappy event from a feudal world long gone. The entry is of great significance because in it Kilvert linked his epitaph for a whole rural society to his motive for writing his *Diary*: 'Why do I keep this voluminous journal?' The journal was also his own extended epitaph, epitaph to his own humble life. Convinced that landscapes profoundly shaped the lives of the people who inhabited them, he saw landscapes and people's lives as inseparable, and he found a religious purpose in walking through both:

'tis a quiet journey of the heart in pursuit of Nature, and those affections which rise out of her, which make us love one another.[121]

In the landscapes through which Kilvert walked, the dead were united with the living in an unbroken circle of sympathies. His diary tells the stories of their lives and of their landscapes.

Chapter 2
Spirit, Song and Sacrament

Good books are like pious friends conversing with us.
[Ashden Oxenden, *The Pathway of Safety*]

She was one of those who thought still more of the training of the heart than of the mind.
[Grace Aguilar, *Home Influence*]

I hear the wakening birds
At their sweet laud;
So let my rising heart
Sing praise to God

[Kilvert, *Advent*]

———

The introduction outlined some factors in the Kilvert family's life in Bath and in Kilvert's reading which determined his path as a writer and the way he wrote about people and landscape. The present chapter will examine other factors that played a part, one of which is his conception of autobiography itself and his decision to make that form of writing the major literary occupation of his life. It is clear that Kilvert conceived of his *Diary*, in part at least, as autobiography. He was typically Victorian in choosing autobiography which, according to Landow, is

the literary mode so representative of its time.... Victorian autobiographers were writing the stories of their own lives at a particularly interesting moment in the history of human consciousness: romanticism had done much to change the way man thought about and experienced himself, but Freud had not yet appeared on the scene with his radical redefinitions of self, society, and discourse.... Victorian autobiography thus embodies a unique moment in the history of man's conception of himself....[1]

Later chapters will show that Kilvert, like many Victorian autobiographers, looked back to Wordsworth, to his long poems *The Prelude* and *The Excursion*, as one model of writing about the self, the Romantic model of 'solitary self-discovery'.[2]

Kilvert's adoption of autobiography as the dominant form of his writing (he also wrote poems) has its origins in the huge social changes represented by the French Revolution, industrial developments, the growth of cities, tourism, population and communications, the decline of religious belief. Under the impact of these changes, traditional society based on the life of the land with its long-established social hierarchy had begun to give way to an ethos in which economic and class competition became the norm. Bath society at the close of the eighteenth century typified the new spirit. The bankruptcy suffered there by his grandfather at this time continued to haunt Kilvert, as is quite evident from the frequent appearance in the *Diary* of mini-biographies in which individuals and their families suffer dramatic losses of fortune and of status.[3] Out of the social turmoil that gave rise to such social tragedies, emerged the literary form known as autobiography:

> we can observe what appears to be an essential fact about this literary mode: societal disturbances and dislocations, the break-up of a culture, produce that sense of self necessary to write one's own life. When communal bonds dissolve, when a shared sense-of-being fails, the individual finds himself cast adrift and, becoming more self-aware, he may also come to believe that he has something to say that could help others in the same difficulties.[4]

This helps to explain why Kilvert's father felt the urge to write *his* life story, in which, significantly, fear of social change is a dominant theme.[5]

Social change is also the background to Kilvert's autobiography, which can be seen as both a record of that change and a form of resistance to it:[6] 'The mystery as to why [he] suddenly began keeping a diary in January 1870 may be explained, at least partly, by a need he felt to record a traditional society that was changing forever. . . .'[7] In the picture of his ministry that emerges in subsequent chapters, his vision of a community of caring Christian folk has a prominent place; it was his answer to the threat of a society of alienated classes. His declared intention of writing in order to 'amuse and interest' readers represents his more purely literary motive. It has been noted that he was brought up in a family which cherished prints of landscapes; this chapter notes further encouragements he had in the direction of using landscape as a metaphor for the progress of his life. It also examines the contribution which his mother, in particular, made towards his destiny as a writer.

In Kilvert's *Diary*, his mother Thermuthis remains a shadowy figure because, though there are many references to her, few contain information about her personality or beliefs. The impression conveyed of her by her daughter Emily is of a woman forever busy as mother, homemaker, and wife of an Evangelical clergyman, making do on a modest income, although there were always one or two servants. She conducted the children's lessons on Sunday evening and even found time to read to them, though 'she had so much other work to do'.[8] Her mother, Thermuthis Ashe, whose father was both squire and rector of Langley Burrell, near Chippenham, married Walter Coleman of Kington Langley, a neighbouring village, on 15 April 1807. The Colemans had lived there since 1550. Kilvert was generally critical in his *Diary* of the Ashe family. For example, he quoted the memories that Mrs Banks, a Langley Burrell farmer's wife, had of his great-grandmother, Madam Ashe, as she was known, of how she was 'eccentric, self-willed and a little tyrannical'.[9] She took it upon herself to arrange marriages of local people to suit her predilections. She had failed in arranging the marriage of her daughter Thermuthis and it continually rankled. Madam Ashe and her husband had opposed her marriage to Walter Coleman, Kilvert's grandfather, but it went ahead nevertheless, incurring a resentment that lasted for years. Kilvert quoted his great-grandfather's words to Thermuthis on one occasion when she was in tears because the marriage had turned out unhappy: 'My dear, we warned you. You made your bed and now you must lie on it'. Kilvert added that the Ashes had been 'deeply averse' to the marriage.[10]

What he doesn't tell us is why, and we are left to assume it was simply the consequence of Ashe arrogance and resentment that for once their will was opposed. An obvious reason for their disapproval would have been difference in rank between bride and groom. The Ashes were landowning squires with a fine mansion. However, this applied equally to the Colemans.

Old Giles, a Langley Burrell villager, recalled Walter Coleman as 'a very plain man', with no pride about him, in contrast to farmers in 1872, who were very conscious of their status.[11] Squire Coleman would invite Giles, a labourer, to walk with him as he went about his business, something that squire Ashe would never have done. One of Coleman's tenants remembered him as a good landlord.[12] (Kilvert's references to his Coleman grandfather are consistently positive as though compelled to honour him without drawing attention to the fact that he was a Quaker; from various sources Kilvert had compiled a mini-biography, an epitaph, in tribute to the forbear who had nurtured his mother's piety.) In all important respects and by all the measures of the time, Walter Coleman seemed exemplary and it is, therefore, hard to see on what grounds the Ashes rejected him as a son-in-law, nor why he should have provoked such inveterate hatred in them. Since no rational grounds for it are evident, one is pushed into seeking irrational ones and there is only one factor in his background that presents itself as a possible basis for prejudice: he came from a family of Quakers.

For three or four generations before Thermuthis Coleman, Kilvert's mother (named after her mother), was born on 12 May 1808, her family had been Quakers. With the recognition that a religious objection underpinned the Ashe anger, the import of the *Diary* entry for 9 January 1872 suddenly becomes clear. On the occasion referred to in that entry, Madam Ashe said to her daughter, at the end apparently of a fierce argument, ' "God forgive you" '. Kilvert's mother, then fifteen years old, was present at this encounter and asked, ' "Why should God forgive my mother?" "God forgive your mother, God forgive you both," repeated Mrs Ashe', words uttered 'with a vengeance'. The Ashes did not object to Walter Coleman on personal or social grounds; it was pre-eminently sectarian differences that could ignite such fierce hatreds in the early nineteenth century.

The true significance of the picture we have of Walter Coleman emerges when it is examined in terms of the traits Quakers typically possessed and encouraged: the plain man who had no pride and declined to exalt his rank; the good landlord; the 'upright honourable man in all his dealings'. (Kilvert's aunt Sophia had praised Quakers' 'patient industry and acknowledged integrity'.) Walter attended church instead of a Quaker meeting-house, evidence that by his generation the

Quaker element in his background had weakened,[13] reflecting
the decline of Quakerism in Wiltshire, as well as nationally, at
this period.[14] Like all sects, Quakers kept to themselves, watched
over each other's moral progress, founded schools for their
children and traded with each other. They would have been
especially resented by the haughty Ashe family because they
were naturally radical, naturally rebels, naturally democratic.
(They were 'the prime incarnation of the seventeenth-century
spirit of religious and social revolt'.)[15] In addition, they were
typically drawn from yeoman and trading classes and rejected
the aristocratic values[16] represented by the Ashes. The Ashes
were not only leaders of their society but their men were, over
several generations, clergymen for whom Quakers' refusal to
pay tithes and church rates and their disapproval of the Church's
ministers and its sacraments would have been a continual source
of rancour.[17] Kilvert was well aware of the Quaker communities
around Chippenham and gave them favourable mention in his
Diary. Visiting a blind old man in Langley Burrell, he observed
that the man's wife died 'a good Quaker'.[18] It is in entries about
local Quakers that it would have been natural and logical for
him to acknowledge the Quaker element in his mother's story,[19]
but he could hardly feel sympathetic to a sect which regarded
people in his position as, at best, irrelevant.[20] He was more able
to accept another element in his mother's background – her
Moravianism.

Walter Coleman was content that his daughter should
receive her early education in the village school at Langley
Burrell. She attended the school until the end of 1813, then a
significant change occurred: she was enrolled at the Moravian
school at East Tytherton, three miles from her Kington Langley
home. The school was a product of the evangelical revival
that had earlier stimulated Nonconformity in the area;[21] more
particularly, it owed its existence to John Cennick, who had
established the East Tytherton Moravian Church. Born in
Reading of Quaker parents, he was converted as a result of
reading Whitefield's *Journal* in 1738. He went on a preaching
tour of north Wiltshire and visited Kington Langley, as his diary
records: '16 November 1742. We were again sadly misused
at Langley. The rude people . . . cut up the clothes of such
as were at the meeting and threw aquae fortis on them and
pelted them with Cow Dung'.[22] Kilvert knew of the treatment
Cennick received at nearby Lyneham: 'Once when he was

preaching . . . about the Blood of Christ the miserable ignorant people syringed him with blood'.[23] The sympathy and interest shown here permeates the rest of the entry, which concerns a visit Kilvert and his mother were making to the Large family of Currycomb Farm, Tytherton Lucas. 'Miss Large told us a great deal about the Moravians . . . at East Tytherton and . . . also showed us a copy of some verses found in the pocket of John Cennick. . . .'

The Moravians' characteristic form of social organisation was the settlement, consisting of family homes, chapel with minister's house, houses for single male and female brethren, and schools. 'Within this framework the Brethren lived a life of singular regimentation'.[24] They have been described as 'the most distinctive offsprings of the pietistic movement. . . .'[25] The essential basis of the their creed was the supreme importance of the individual and a desire to recapture the spirit and practices of the early Christians. The close fellowship fostered by communal living encouraged mutual spiritual examination, one aim of which was to ascertain how far an individual had progressed in following his Saviour's path. Salvation was to be achieved principally by faith, though a man's good works played a part. Moravians believed in instant conversions. Known above all for simple piety, love of meditation, and 'stillness', it was to be expected that one authority would sum Moravians up thus: 'In general, they have stood for a simple and unworldly form of Christianity'.[26]

One of the things for which they were noted was their zeal for education in order to perpetuate and consolidate their way of life. The East Tytherton community had from its beginning a school for its own children but also established a school for boarders and local day pupils. Kilvert's mother was one of the latter, attending from January 1814, when she was five and a half years old, until summer 1817. In this period, the school would have borne the impress of its founder, Ann Grigg, who died at the end of 1814. She began a boarding school for girls, which opened on 11 June 1794 with eight or nine boarders, reaching fourteen by the end of the year.[27] Aspiring scholars were carefully selected; no girl was admitted without consultation with the community's Elders. Miss Coleman, with her solid Quaker/Anglican background would have been a very acceptable candidate. Day scholars partook of the same educational fare as boarders, though the latter's day began early (six in summer, seven in winter) and was strictly, but not harshly, regimented. The motto attached to the boarders' House Regulations set the tone: 'disorder, discord, idleness, / From every action drive / Irregularity dismiss; / And for sweet Order strive'. The twin virtue of Order was Business, and pupils were urged to remember that early rising and 'dispatch' were 'The life of Business, that half an hour wasted in the morning could not be recovered all day'. The fervency of the school's religiousness is reflected in the following statement: 'that all the scholars under our care may, besides improvement in useful learning, obtain a deep impression in their minds of our Saviour's atonement, and wherever they may live hereafter, adore his doctrine by their walk [sic] and conversation'.[28] Close attention was nevertheless given to the secular aspects of learning because of the Moravian requirement that both men and women were equipped for the mission field.[29]

Nothing is more indicative of the burning Protestant faith shared by mother and son than the way they encouraged each other in the reading that was one of its essential supports. For Evangelicals, faith came from hearing the Gospel but it also 'came and received nurture . . . through reading devotional books about the Bible and the Christian faith. . . .'[30] Birthdays were the occasions on which Kilvert and his mother reminded each other of the need to make spiritual progress by giving each other books to support the journey. Three *Diary* entries recording such gifts from her to him have survived (there were, no doubt, more): Goethe's *Faust* (3 December 1870; since it was bought with money she gave him, it may be supposed that he regarded it — bearing in mind its nature — as her gift), *Lyra Apostolica*, the collection of devout poems chiefly by Newman and John Keble[31] (3 December 1873), and Dorothy Wordsworth's *Journal* (3 December 1874). We know of only one birthday gift from him to her, but it is a significant one – Mary Molesworth's *Stray Leaves from the Tree of Life*[32] (*Diary* entry for 10 May 1870; her birthday was on the 12th). Mary Molesworth (1823-68) was an obscure writer (Kilvert presumably knew of her through Evangelical connections) who had had her first novel published in 1848 when she was only 23. Two more novels followed but *Stray Leaves* (1869) was her only overtly religious work. It consists of eight essays, the first of which considers whether the individual soul faces immediate judgement after death or spends time in some intermediate existence. The book is by no means an easy read and is another indication of the quality of both her piety and her intellect.

Birthdays and New Year provided Kilvert with good opportunities for spiritual stock-taking and his *Diary* affords some examples.[33] 'And here is the end of another year. How much to be thankful for. How much to be mourned over. God pardon the past and give grace for the future. . . .' (31 December 1871). 'May God give me grace that if I should be spared another year I may spend it better than the last' (3 December 1874). A visit to Kington St Michael on 23 February 1875 induced 'musing and praying among the graves of my forefathers' (i.e. the Colemans) and he wrote: 'Am I better or worse, have I gone further forward or backward than I was when I lived here . . . ten years ago?' He enjoyed consulting others over spiritual progress as is clear from his joining the 'Mutual Improvement Society' initiated by his friends, Katharine Heanley and Jessie Russell. In this context, he wrote of Katharine: 'How much nobler and holier her thoughts are than mine, and how much higher she has climbed up the hill than I have done'.[34] It is striking how many of the books he read have as central themes self-improvement and life as a spiritual journey, notions which sit easily with diary-keeping. For example, one prefatory passage (from Wordsworth) to Elizabeth Prentiss's *Stepping Heavenward* (1869), a book that Kilvert liked to pass on to others, talks of 'travelling through the world', while another (from Saint Augustine) urges 'Always walk, always proceed . . . he that standeth still proceedeth not'.[35]

Kilvert was an inveterate walker, partly because he could undertake parish visits in no other way and partly because walking pleased him. However, behind his movement lay also the religious idea of life as a 'walk'. A great deal of importance must attach to the fact that he chose 'We are pilgrims, we are sojourners' for his family crest.[36] Sandwiched between the note recording his choice and his pointed reflections on it, is a paragraph dealing with being sworn in as curate of Langley Burrell, as though the two events were closely connected in his mind. The motto derives from verses 13-16 of Hebrews, chapter 11: 'These all . . . confessed that they were strangers and pilgrims on the earth. For they that say such things declare plainly that they seek a country'. The 'country' is heaven, seen as superior to any earthly home. The idea of life as a spiritual pilgrimage went back to Puritan times, becoming later a commonplace of evangelical thinking and writing.[37] Nevertheless, it had deep meanings for Kilvert (many of his poems have it as a main theme).[38] His diary's prime purpose was to record the development of his own spirit. Of course, it does not read like a spiritual autobiography because so much of it concerns holidays, picnics, excursions, dances, descriptions of pretty girls and of natural scenery. Later chapters will show, however, that he brought a spiritual and moral viewpoint to most of his material. Because the *Diary* is as it is, we have become used to highlighting his playfulness, gentleness, humour, sensuousness and geniality, and insufficiently recognising that he was also a devout, serious and intense man whose main concern was saving souls. Plomer's editing is the reason why the *Diary* reads as it does. In his introduction to volume one, Plomer stated that he cut out 'everything of merely fugitive interest' and retained 'the choicest parts', by which he meant what a twentieth-century reader would find entertaining. In his introduction to volume three, Plomer acknowledged that 'necessary abbreviation . . . prevented a just impression being given of [Kilvert's] constant devotion to parochial duties'. The *Diary's* spiritual dimension was reduced still further by Plomer's tendency 'to cut passages in which Kilvert's passionate devotion to God showed itself at length'.[39] That devotion stemmed largely from his mother's role in his upbringing.

The most impressive evidence of Mrs Kilvert's desire to influence her children's upbringing is her decision to read to them Grace Aguilar's novels, *Home Influence* and *A Mother's Recompense*, 'on weekdays evenings', an experience Emily Kilvert remembered well.[40] There are good grounds for believing that the doctrine of kindness that was such a prominent factor in Kilvert's ministry was communicated memorably to him in his youth, reinforcing a trait he already possessed, via Aguilar's novels. It is easy to see why, with her Quaker and Moravian background, they were chosen by Mrs Kilvert to guide her as a mother. Both Quakerism and Moravianism placed high value on the emotions and played down the intellect. When Methodism and Evangelicalism styled themselves 'religions of the heart', they were acknowledging a debt to the Moravians, for it was a phrase especially favoured by them.[41] Their recognition of the emotional life led them both to reject celibacy and to exalt family life and the home (as did the Quakers).[42] Aguilar's novels endorse these values.

Home Influence, although published in 1847, is set in the period 1820-30, the period of great social changes and unrest which provided the background to Sophia Kilvert's *Home Discipline.* It was also the same kind of book as hers — the *Englishwoman's Magazine* said it contained 'many valuable hints on domestic education'. It is permeated, as Sophia's is, by an eighteenth-century sensibility. Aguilar made a link with the moral sentiments theory of that period by stating that she set out to illustrate the development of individual character through 'the spoken sentiment' (an explanation of the fact that her novel contains much conversation).[43] The characterisation has features found in the novels of Richardson, Smollett and Lesage. *Home Influence* consistently illustrates qualities of heart by focusing chiefly on good and bad examples of child-rearing. The bad examples are usually found in aristocratic families.[44] Aristocrats are shown to be over-attached to rank and indifferent to the needs of others, whereas the truly Christian home developed kindness: 'Kindness begets kindness, and if superiors will but think of and seek the happiness, temporal and eternal, of their inferiors, — will but prove that they are considered children of one common Father. . . .'[45] Basic to this viewpoint is the idea that all men's souls are of equal worth, whatever their social rank may be. And again it is to the Quakers and the Moravians we must turn for the most stirring examples of this idea in practice because both groups suffered persecution for their determination to 'call no man master'. The need for true Christians to meet each other as equals on the level of basic human feelings is emphasised too in *A Mother's Recompense.* 'Sympathy,' we are told, 'is the charm of human life'.[46] Thus, in choosing to read Aguilar's novels to her young children, Mrs Kilvert was declaring her credo as a mother and a Christian.

It is possible to trace Kilvert's propensity for moral reflection, noted earlier, to the religious traditions inherited by his mother and in turn by him. Both Quakers and Moravians were noted for their 'stillness'. With the former, it was represented by the 'inner light', which saw Christ as the spirit of life that touched the soul. Fox wrote of it: '[It] draws off and weans you from all things, that are created and external (which fade and pass away), up to God, the fountain of life and head of all things'.[47] Its tendency was subversive as far as conventional church practices were concerned because it led to the rejection of the sacraments, the ministry, and all set forms of worship.

The 'stillness' of the Moravians has been described thus: 'the restfulness of spirit, the open mind and inward ear, the waiting upon God, which are encouraged by silence'.[48] His mother would have been introduced to meditation at East Tytherton because a habit of reflection was part of the school's daily routine from its beginnings. Ann Grigg, the first headmistress, in a letter to her pupils dated Christmas 1797, told of how, particularly at that time of year, she was led 'into a chain of serious meditation', which she recommended to the young souls in her care. She urged each one of them to ask herself: 'Have I made good use of my time this last half year? . . . Have I improved the talents the Lord hath given me?'[49]

The pattern of 'serious meditation' was also put before Kilvert in the stories of Legh Richmond that we know were part of his life when he was nine years old. Richmond had Bath connections that would have increased his interest for the Kilverts. His father was a doctor there and Richmond married Mary Chambers, who also came from Bath. Ordained in 1797, he became curate that year of the parishes of Brading and Yaverland, Isle of Wight. After reading Wilberforce's *Practical Christianity* – 'a book that has been instrumental in turning many from the error of their ways'[50] – he became an Evangelical. He was a writer of religious tracts, the most famous of which was *The Dairyman's Daughter*, first published in 1811. Visiting Yaverland in 1874, Kilvert recalled 'a beautiful and touching story' he had read 25 years before about the place. The story that he had read was *The Dairyman's Daughter*, in which the practice of 'serious meditation' is recommended several times. It also contains a lengthy passage on the value of memory in relation to meditation: 'In religious meditations the memory becomes a sanctified instrument of spiritual improvement.'[51] Richmond begins the passage by comparing man's mind to a 'moving picture', made up of elements resulting from reflection on immediate events but also of 'fruitful sources of reflection'. In his memoirs, Robert Kilvert has a similar passage that probably had its origin in Richmond's account of memory. Robert expresses man's progress through life in terms of the familiar idea of climbing a hill (his son used the same analogy when comparing his spiritual progress with Katharine Heanley's, as was noted earlier),[52] reaching its top in middle years, and descending it as he approaches old age. Life then becomes a landscape affording views that are both distant and near. To make it quite clear that he saw his reflections in the same kind of religious context as Richmond's, he added, 'Well, let this be as it will, the present story has other stuff in it than "Aids to Reflection" of this sort'.[53] Both Robert and Richmond were demonstrating that they belonged to an ancient and central Christian tradition: 'From Augustine onwards, Christians have been interested in memory ... because memory defines – or helps to define – the self, and thereby constitutes the identity of the believer before God'. It is also 'a faculty through which God can draw the soul of the Christian into closer communion with himself'.[54]

Kilvert was brought up by his mother to see Nature as another means by which an individual drew closer to God. In Aguilar's *Home Influence*, the beauty of natural scenery is shown to have a beneficial effect on Edward (who, in spite of his good qualities, can be haughty and wilful) and Mrs Hamilton explains the reason: 'the presence of a loving God is so impressed on His works. . . . We can so distinctly trace goodness, and love, and power in the gift of such a beautiful world. . . .' Nature, with its pure, fresh associations was, in her view, an antidote to worldliness and prolonged exposure to it gave rise to 'a pure sense of poetry in the Universe and in Man'. The 'poetry' of natural beauty induced feelings of piety. Its other effects, however, were dangerous and could lead to excess of feeling, a species of 'enthusiasm' to be deplored.[55] For the Moravian theologian Spangenberg, created Nature was a central part of his case for the existence of God: 'Whoever surveys and reflects at all upon the earth, with all that is in and upon it . . . cannot but think, who has made and created all these things?'[56]

Seeing God in Nature was also encouraged by Mrs Kilvert's Quakerism, which, because it was a thread that the Kilvert family preferred to hide, requires some unravelling. Its importance lies in the fact that it connects Kilvert's upbringing, his uncle Francis, his literary and religious outlook, and his devotion to Wordsworth, as they affect the way he wrote about landscape. To find where the thread starts, we need to recall that Kilvert's uncle Francis had married a lady reared by Quakers. It is reasonable to assume that a man of such deep piety as uncle Francis would have felt sympathy for the Quaker piety of his wife and evidence tends to confirm this assumption. It seems likely that he studied Quaker thought partly because of a bookplate found among his literary papers showing William Penn, the Quaker leader, among the Red Indians.[57] The plate is from Thomas Clarkson's

Memoirs of the Public and Private Life of William Penn (1813).
Clarkson (1760-1846) and his wife Catherine (1772-1856) were
Grasmere neighbours of Wordsworth – Moorman described
them as the Wordsworths' 'most intimate friends.'[58] Clarkson,
though not himself a Quaker, was intimate with local Quakers
and studied their beliefs. Wordsworth himself had a very close
involvement with Quakerism. The town of Hawkshead, at
whose Grammar School he was a boarder from the age of nine,
was 'an important centre of Quakerism.'[59] He lodged with Ann
Tyson, wife of a joiner, in the nearby hamlet of Colthouse, which
was 'something of a Quaker colony,' and he was taken by her
to its Meeting House.[60] Thus, he was surrounded from an early
age by Quakers and Quaker ideas: 'The influence of Quaker
rhetoric [and] of their dissident ideology . . . will have exercised
a powerful formative influence on Wordsworth.'[61] Similarly,
Kilvert could not fail to have been influenced by Quaker ideology when he boarded at Claverton Lodge, presided over by his
uncle Francis and his aunt Sophia.

Wordsworth's involvement with Quakerism left him with a
permanent sympathy for it, so that he was always aware of
common ground between it and his own poetic outlook. In the
particularly close relationship between his sister Dorothy and
Catherine Clarkson, we find reflections of the Wordsworths'
steady interest in Quakerism. Thus, in a letter of 14 September
1813, Dorothy was urging Catherine to send her a copy of her
husband's *Memoirs of William Penn*: 'We have not received Mr
Clarkson's Book which vexes us much. . . . I long to see it.'[62]
In a joint letter of 1 January 1814 to Catherine Clarkson by
Wordsworth and his sister, the poet was anxious that his long
poem *The Excursion* should sell well: 'I therefore beg that you or
Mr Clarkson will immediately . . . give it what help you can in
the Philanthropist . . . because it circulates a good deal among
Quakers.'[63] To the Quaker William Howitt, *The Excursion* was
'a very bible of Quakerism':

> To show how completely Wordsworth's system [of
> thought] is a system of Poetical Quakerism, I should
> be obliged to take his Excursion, and collate the whole
> with passages from the writing of the early Friends,
> Fox, Penn, Barclay, Pennington, and others. . . . It is
> wholly and fervently permeated by the soul of Quaker
> theology.[64]

The abiding interest of the Wordsworths in Quaker thought is further illustrated by a series of letters written by Dorothy to Catherine Clarkson which shows their eagerness to get their hands on Thomas Clarkson's *A Portraiture of Quakerism*.[65]

Clarkson, who was himself enraptured by the Lake District's beauty, was the first to connect Wordsworth's poetic celebration of it with Quaker thought.[66] In his *Portraiture* he explained that the 'Spirit of God' served man 'as a spiritual teacher or guide' and that the man who was aware of it 'sees the animal, the vegetable, and the planetary world with spiritual eyes. He cannot stir abroad, but he is taught . . . some lesson for his spiritual advantage. . . .' Clarkson quoted Wordsworth's *Expostulation and Reply* to illustrate this process. It underlines that just as the senses are bound to register their impressions of natural objects, so 'there are Powers / Which of themselves our minds impress.' As a result, the mind was fed 'In a wise passiveness,' without the need of books and study. There are good grounds for believing that uncle Francis Kilvert, perhaps following Clarkson, had developed his own understanding of the similarity between Quaker ideas and Wordsworth's poetry and imparted it to his receptive nephew. There is a strong, though unacknowledged, Quaker element in the reverence Kilvert had for Nature as evidence of God's goodness. Chapter one made clear that Wordsworth's poem, *A Poet's Epitaph*, had special appeal for Kilvert's uncle Francis because it encapsulated this idea. His underlining, in his own copy of it, of the stanza which tells how 'the poet has viewed / The outward shows of sky and earth' takes on particular significance when seen through a Quaker perspective: it seems likely that he was connecting its ideas to Quaker ones. Clarkson had written in his *Portraiture* that 'the Spirit of God may teach men by outward objects' which produced, according to Quakers, 'internal monitions' (i.e. spiritual insights). These 'impressions from a higher power' (Clarkson's phrase)[67] correspond to the 'impulses of deeper birth' that 'come [to the poet] in solitude' – the last two lines of Wordsworth's stanza underlined by uncle Francis.

William Howitt pushed the parallel between Wordsworth's and Quaker philosophy further. Howitt's view is important because it is evident that Kilvert was familiar with it. The Kilvert children were brought up with books by the Howitts – William (1792-1879) and his wife, Mary (1799-1888). Emily Kilvert told how she never forgot the picture her mother painted for her in Emily's copy of Mary Howitt's *The Children's Year*.[68] The book records the doings over a year of Mary's two younger children and its preface shows the author's (and Mrs Kilvert's) view of the part Nature played in shaping child consciousness. A home would be happy, we are told, 'if the young are induced to desire those lessons from Nature which Nature is so well able to teach.' An identical emphasis appears in the *Home Discipline* of Kilvert's aunt Sophia: 'God's bounteous goodness, in the natural creation all around us, is . . . our proper theme to our children.' At some point, under these influences and that of his uncle Francis, Kilvert learned with Herbert, the boy in Mary Howitt's story, to appreciate landscape: 'For the first time in his life Herbert saw, this day, the beauty there was in an extensive landscape: he had never thought anything about it before.'[69] The Anglo-Saxon names for the months of the year used by Kilvert in his diary (see chapter eight) were derived from William Howitt's *The Book of the Seasons; or the Calendar of Nature*.[70] Kilvert also showed that he relished the idea that Wordsworth obtained his spiritual insights, not from books, but from Nature itself, when he recounted a story told him by Mary Hutchinson, niece of the poet's wife:

> When William Howitt was at Rydal Mount looking about after Wordsworth's death he fell in with old James the gardener and asked him which was the poet's study. 'This', said James pointing to the arbour and the grass mound from which Rydal Mount takes its name.[71]

Kilvert's exultation in the beauty of landscape, hatred of field sports,[72] and habit of studying and praying outdoors – all bear the impression of Quaker thought, via Wordsworth.

Expressing thanks to God in musical as well as poetical terms for his beautiful world was an important strand of Kilvert's piety. The most influential element as regards devotional music in his family background was his mother. If the Moravian tradition in which she was schooled was known for anything it was music. The Moravian definition of the role of music in worship exerted a critical influence on Protestantism: 'For Protestants, the integration of belief and song had roots in the . . . movement of John Hus . . . who advocated . . . the singing of hymns.'[73] Huss became a Protestant hero in the fourteenth century when he was martyred for his stand against the Church

William Howitt

of Rome. Moravians be-
lieved in hymns and music
as means of expressing
theological truths.[74] Kilvert
believed that all singing
to express happiness and
joy in living was in some
sort an act of worship, as
is indicated by the verse
of his poem, *Advent*, that
prefaces this chapter. It
shows the motivation that,
in a general way, lay be-
hind his aspiration and
his need to write, whether
prose or poetry. His verses
were hymns, which were in turn a form of praise, and that is
the way he regarded the verses of other writers he admired. The
joy and beauty of the song of a skylark he saw as an expression
of praise.[75] In several *Diary* entries, he has hymns rising up
from natural objects: 'The corn seemed to be praising God and
whispering its evening prayer'.[76]

Behind his habit of collecting old hymns from old country-
men, lay a number of motives.[77] He valued old hymns and
songs because they were an intrinsic part of a community
and of the region it inhabited. They were also very often
expressive of the basic feelings of people as Wordsworth
intended the *Lyrical Ballads* to be and the poet had praised
them in his survey of books 'which lay / Their sure foundation
in the heart of man'.[78] Kilvert shared the poet's sentiments, as
he shared his interest in 'the real language of men', which
drew on the ballad tradition.[79] Kilvert's own poems show the
influence of ballads. Recognising that Methodist hymns made
a huge impact on congregations of the poor, Evangelicals
sought to revitalise the church service by making it more
lively and more emotional. They emphasised those parts in
which the liturgy laid down no particular wording and tried
to make it more than an empty form.[80]

William Barnes was a clergyman/poet who, as Kilvert saw
it, praised God in words and music and Kilvert's admiration

for him only slightly exceeded that which he had for Henry
Moule, who introduced him to the famous Dorset poet in
spring 1874. Typically, he registered the day as one which
would live in his memory: 'This will always be a happy and
memorable day in my remembrance'. And as the train took
him towards 'the great idyllic poet of England', the landscape
itself celebrated the significant moment: 'The elms performed
a solemn dance round each of the fine Church Towers of
Somerset . . .' (trees were particularly loved by Barnes, as
Kilvert knew, and when Kilvert used the word 'solemn', it
denoted experiences of spiritual moment). His happiness
was complete when, as a prelude to a poetry reading by
Barnes, the Rev Henry Moule 'repeated to me some beautiful
and touching verses which he had composed. . . . The verses
began "Lord, I love thee".' Moule was not only a poet but a
musician too and 'sang these verses . . . accompanying himself
with a beautiful and appropriate air . . . he had composed
himself'. Barnes, Kilvert noted, 'is very musical himself'.[81] It
is no wonder that with examples like these, Kilvert should
think it a duty that he too should praise God in poetry and
song, especially since uncle Francis had taught him to honour
Christian poets.

Mrs Kilvert is probably the key to understanding the place
that another Christian poet, the Rev John Keble, and devotional poetry celebrating the beauty of Nature, occupied in
Kilvert's background. We have seen that she fostered his interest in Nature by making him a birthday present of Dorothy
Wordsworth's *Journal* (which must have been her *Recollections
of a Tour made in Scotland* — first published 1873; selections
from her journals did not appear until 1897). Another of her
birthday gifts to him was *Lyra Apostolica* (1836), a book of
devotional verse by Froude, Keble, Newman, Isaac Williams
and others. The bulk of the poems (109) were by Newman
but Keble was the other main contributor, with 46 poems (out
of a total of 179). They are grouped under headings — Home,
Remorse, Past and Present, Providences, Solitude, Ancient
Stones — which had considerable significance for Kilvert vis
à vis his stance towards landscape, as later chapters show.
It was clearly the poems' devotional nature that mattered to
Mrs Kilvert, not the fact that their authors were Tractarians.[82]
The collection of poems by Keble called *The Christian Year*
was such a pervasive force in relation to the way Victorians

thought and wrote about Nature that it would have been impossible for a man of Kilvert's generation and interests to avoid it. After its publication in 1827, it was 'unrivalled as a book of devotion in Anglican households'.[83] The poems in Keble's book were linked to the important days of the Church calendar and intended to be used alongside the *Prayer Book*.[84] It is probable that Robert Kilvert made a present of *The Christian Year* to his wife in the early days of their marriage (Cruse noted that it was 'a favourite gift-book').[85] Keble had special significance for Robert. He owed his place at Oriel to his friends' influence with Keble, who was a Fellow there. In addition, Robert had Keble as tutor for two terms, was in his lecture class, and made a hero of him because of what he called his 'simple goodness' and 'unsullied childlike nature'.[86] To Kilvert, Keble's overwhelming significance lay in the fact that he was a Wordsworth disciple, his poetry not only influenced by the Lakeland poet but an influence on the latter's later work.[87]

The popularity of *The Christian Year* helped its author to the post of Professor of Poetry at Oxford in 1831 and he used the lectures on poetry that were a requirement of it to outline his views of the links between poetry and religion. He was keen to endorse Wordsworth's definition of poetry as 'the spontaneous overflow of powerful feelings'.[88] Since the deepest, most powerful feelings were common to both poetry and religion, he saw the former as the 'handmaiden' of the latter. 'Piety and poetry are able [therefore] to help each other'. 'Poetry, which leads men to the secret sources of Nature, supplies a wealth of similes whereby a pious mind may . . . remedy its powerlessness of speech'. Religion then invested such similes 'with so splendid a radiance that they appear to be no longer symbols, but to partake (I might almost say) of the nature of sacraments'.[89] Victorians absorbed these ideas not from Keble's lectures but from *The Christian Year*.[90] The idea of Nature as the means of sacramental grace appears in several of the poems, particularly in the one for Septuagesima Sunday, which is prefixed by the text Romans i.20: 'The invisible things of Him from the creation of the world are clearly seen, being understood by the things that are made'. The poem, which takes as its starting point the idea of the Book of Nature that may be read by those whose senses are spiritually alert, begins:

> There is a book, who runs may read,
>   Which heavenly truth imparts,
> And all the lore its scholars need,
>   Pure eyes and Christian hearts.
>
> The works of God above, below,
>   Within us and around,
> Are pages in that book, to show
>   How God Himself is found.[91]

The penultimate verse explains that it is only man's sin that prevents him from perceiving 'the mystic heaven and earth within'. The fully Christian individual needs the 'pure eyes' and the good heart to 'read [God] everywhere'. In G.B. Tennyson's opinion, this view of Nature was 'a notable strain in the Victorian literary imagination that included a host of other poets, some novelists, and even some naturalists'.[92] Surprisingly, he placed Kilvert in this last category, referring to him not as a diarist, but as a 'clergyman and *naturalist*'. Tennyson found in Kilvert's description of snow on the Black Mountains (see chapter five) 'the echo of the Tractarian response to Nature'.[93]

Keble gave expression to the basic idea of sacrament — of unseen, spiritual things lying behind ordinary material phenomena — in his poem, *Morning*, which became the very popular hymn *New every morning is the love*, one verse of which reads:

> If on our daily course our mind
> Be set to hallow all we find,
> New treasures still, of countless price,
> God will provide for sacrifice.[94]

It is an attitude that underpins Kilvert's writing about landscape, in the *Diary* and explicitly in his poetry. In the quatrain at the end of his poem, *Little Things*, he characteristically summed up his sacramental vision in the idea of the universal hymn of natural forms in which the faithful could discern God:

> Each bird that sings, the rustling trees,
> All simple things and lowly,
> Bring sweet and secret messages
> Where'er the heart is holy.[95]

The poem's penultimate quatrain tells of a 'small and shy' flower 'along the wayside blowing' which to the holy heart 'has a meaning in its eye / And teaches in its growing'. For Kilvert,

Florence Hill (left) and Eleanor Hill

no 'small and shy' human flower surpassed Florence Hill of
Noyadd Farm. The meaning she had for him will be examined
fully later but it is important to show how she figured in his
vision of the landscape around Clyro. In his poem *Hill Flowers*,
she and her sister Eleanor are 'sweet hill flowers' in whose
beauty, humility and piety he found meaning and a moral
lesson:

> Sweet flowers bloom on — in Heaven's sight,
> So lovely for so lowly,
> Still deeply wise to find delight
> In simple lives and holy.

Florence's holy beauty attains sacramental significance in a
Diary passage describing a reunion with her in May 1876:

> It was a glorious sunny evening, but had there been no
> sun the presence and beauty and love of Florence Hill
> would have lighted and glorified the world for me with
> a light that never was on land or sea, a light far more
> tender and beautiful than the shining of the sun on the
> valley and the mountains.[96]

It is important to take note of Kilvert's poems partly because the present chapter seeks to establish the way poetry,
particularly of a devotional kind, easily merged into hymns
for him and for men like Keble,[97] and partly because it is there
that we find him making explicit statements about the purposes

that lay behind his writing. Cowper turned from praising the beauty of God's world in poetry to hymn writing and the result was the *Olney Hymns*; it was a natural development for one who had written (in his poem, *Hope*): 'Nature . . . / Is hand-maid to the purposes of grace.' Kilvert's reverence for George Herbert (he referred to Herbert's parish of Bemerton near Salisbury as having particular 'sanctity')[98] suggests that he too had a high place among Christian poets he valued. Herbert was brought up in a circle of Protestant poets to whom religious rather than secular love was the proper subject of poetry.[99] It is not hard to see the basis of Kilvert's reverence for Herbert because the centre of the latter's piety was a love for the beauty of God's world, which led Blythe to describe his poetry as 'a poetry of total landscape involving all divine and human creativity. . . .'[100] Although Kilvert's poems owe little to Herbert,[101] it is very likely that uncle Francis introduced him to the latter's work, especially *The Country Parson*,[102] in which Herbert expressed the notion of sacrament in terms very like those that Kilvert employed in his poem, *Honest Work*. Herbert stated that 'things of ordinary use are not only to serve in the way of drudgery, but to be washed, and cleansed, and serve for lights even of Heavenly Truths'.[103]

Honest Work was the only one of Kilvert's poems, as far as we know, that he had printed on cards for circulation among his poorer parishioners (he clearly felt its messages were inappropriate for the gentry). Those messages were, therefore, a public declaration of the nature of his ministry. The poem's opening couplet states its main theme: 'Honest work is always holy, / Howsoever hard and lowly'. Underpinning the poem's central theme is the idea of sacrament: he wanted the working population of Clyro to recognise that behind hard and routine jobs lay the opportunity to achieve spiritual insights. 'Toil is sanctified', he told them, 'because we are working at His side' and this meant that in milking cows, ploughing, cleaning houses there were 'meanings sacred, deep'. This was the fundamental lesson 'taught by time' which he wanted them to learn:

> Simple things are most sublime;
> Happiest, wisest, who can see
> In common things what beauties be, —
> The field, the stream, the grass, the flower,
> The changing lights of sun and shower, —
> The glory of a Sacrament.

It is the message of Keble's hymn *New every morning is the love*: 'The trivial round, the common task, / Will furnish all we ought to ask'.[104] In *Honest Work* and other poems Kilvert emphasises that beauty in common things is withheld from all but the 'wisest'. In *The Hill Flowers* it is the 'deeply wise' who find delight in simple and holy lives, while in *Little Things* the messages in bird song are 'secret', accessible to those with holy hearts. Keble's influence may be traced in these references for he did not believe that the 'new treasures' of 'our daily course' could or should be open to all. He was wedded to the Doctrine of Reserve: knowledge of God was to be disclosed only to those who had attained a sufficient level of spiritual development. He stated: 'one most essential feature of all poetry is a due reserve . . . as with sacred things, so here everything must be touched upon with due reserve. . . .'[105] This was partly because the poet 'was betraying the secrets of his heart and the inmost aspirations of his soul', but also because 'nothing is further removed from poetry than the spirit which reduces everything to the mere standard . . . of gain and utility' – the spirit of democracy, 'a system which aims at complete levelling of rank and class'.[106]

Reserve also extended to the 'sacred things' of Nature, as Keble made clear in a number of poems in *The Christian Year*, which is permeated by the idea that a contemplation of natural forms inspired devotion. The poem entitled *The Rosebud*[107] is a complete expression of Reserve:

> When Nature tries her finest touch,
>   Weaving her vernal wreath,
> Mark ye, how close she veils her round
> Not to be trac'd by sight or sound,
>   Nor soil'd by ruder breath?

The poem *Mountain Scenery* contains another expression of Reserve:

> Where is Thy favour'd haunt, eternal Voice,
>   The region of Thy choice,
> Where, undisturb'd by sin and earth, the soul
>   Owns Thy entire control? —
> 'Tis on the mountain's summit dark and high. . . .[108]

The mountain top, free of 'worldly toil', has a purity that is conducive to solitude and meditation:

> Lone Nature feels that she may freely breathe,
> And round us and beneath
> Are heard her sacred tones: the fitful sweep
> Of winds across the steep,
> Through wither'd bents — romantic note and clear,
> Meet for a hermit's ear.[109]

The connections that these lines make with Kilvert's love
of solitude and his respect for hermits are explored in later
chapters. There is, however, one *Diary* passage that is central
to the way he thought about landscape which should be set
alongside Keble's poem:

> It is a fine thing to be out on the hills alone. A man can
> hardly be a beast or a fool alone on a great mountain.
> There is no company like the grand solemn beautiful
> hills. They fascinate and grow upon us and one had a
> feeling and a love for them which one has for nothing
> else. I don't wonder that our Saviour went out into a
> mountain to pray and continued all night in praying to
> God *there*.[110]

Kilvert's emphasis on 'there' finds a corresponding one in
Mountain Scenery. Keble too was convinced that a mountain
top was the place to pray because "Tis there we hear the voice
of God within'.[111] And if the voice is listened to attentively
enough, the hidden secret will be made manifest:

> As this landscape broad — earth, sea, and sky, —
> All centres in thine eye,
> So all God does, if rightly understood,
> Shall work thy final good.

Kilvert had received the same advice from William Howitt
in the context of the 'poetical Quakerism' he recommended.
He had quoted George Fox: 'Come out from all your vain
learning . . . and sit down in the presence of Him, who made all
things, and lives through all things.' Wordsworth and Quakers
were agreed, said Howitt, that 'there is a power seated in the
human soul,' superior to man's reason, which was God's own
voice, heard best outdoors, 'not approachable in temples and
churches, but free as his own winds . . . whispering peace
in the lonely forest . . . adoration on the mountain tops.'[112]
Later chapters will show Kilvert seeking *power* of this kind

in various forms through experience of landscape. That
Robertson viewed landscape in identical fashion is clear from
his statement: 'All this universe is God's blessed sacrament'.[113]
Kilvert also had Robertson to thank for connecting a personal,
spiritual response to a mountain with Keble's poem. At the
end of Brooke's *Life*, a letter is quoted by one of Robertson's
friends which records how, when they were walking together,
a mountain peak showed up in the distance:

> A faint blue mist was slowly rising and had filled the
> hollows. The wind was singing loudly through the
> withered bents of grass. He was silent . . . and then,
> as if to himself, began to repeat Keble's hymn, *Where
> is Thy favoured haunt, Eternal Voice?* When he uttered
> the passage 'Lone Nature feels . . . a hermit's ear', his
> voice seemed to take the tone of the wind, and I cannot
> describe how well the landscape explained the verses,
> and the verses the landscape.[114]

The *Diary* entry on the importance of being solitary on a
mountain was written in response to an invitation Kilvert had
received to join the Woolhope Club, a body of local antiquarians,
in viewing an ancient burial mound recently excavated. The
idea repelled him

> because it was so much grander to visit the old-world
> resting place of the wild warriors alone in the silence
> of the summer afternoon . . . than to be stunned by the
> prattle of the Woolhope Club, or to be disgusted by
> the sight of a herd of Hay holiday-makers and sight-
> seers cutting bad jokes and playing the fool. . . . To have
> found a crowd of persons or a single person near the
> mound or to have had any companion except perhaps
> a child in my visit to the strange old grave would have
> ruined the solemn delight of the hours which will live
> in my memory always.[115]

The feeling here goes beyond mere irritation at having meditative moments spoiled by others; it represents rather, as does
the feeling in entries recording similar occasions during his
Cornish holiday (see next chapter), a belief that the 'solemn
delight' should always be an experience available to a select
few.

Worshipping God through singing was as much a part of

Kilvert's piety as giving thanks for the beauty of the natural world. His readiness to respond to passionate singing was part of his romantic nature and part of his background. That it was hearty congregational singing that brought him closer to God and to people is powerfully conveyed in the *Diary* entry that deals with his visit on Sunday 25 June 1876 to St Paul's Cathedral:

> It was a cloudless glowing evening and from the small upper windows brilliant shafts and rays of sunlight pierced the vast gloom of the Dome like angel visitants. The altar was bright with flowers and each word of the preacher was echoed back from the recesses of the Dome by a voice that seemed like the voice of an unseen spirit solemnly confirming and enforcing the preacher's words. The great congregation took the last hymn up and sang it grandly. It was 'Sweet Saviour bless us ere we go'. The beautiful strains went to and fro like the rolling and surging of the sea and almost brought the tears into one's eyes with an enthusiasm of humanity. There is something deeply touching and wellnigh overpowering in the sight and sound of a vast crowd of people singing. The last sweet notes of the hymn died and the vast concourse of people melted silently away. The evening glow shone upon the high tide in the broad river heaving and lapping against the parapet of the Embankment. There was not a cloud in the sky and the heart of the great city lying in its Sabbath rest was bathed in the vast silent splendid glow.[116]

This passage is a very interesting one for a variety of reasons. Kilvert very infrequently describes an urban landscape but we have one here. The passage is also unique in that it contains a positive view of a large assembly of people; he usually expressed his loathing of crowds, even small ones. Here he makes a point of stressing just how big the crowd in the Cathedral was: it was 'a great congregation', 'a vast crowd of people', 'a vast concourse of people'. It was the huge size of the crowd that gave the singing its sublime quality, which Kilvert expressed in images of rolling and surging water and which almost reduced him to tears. It seems that once again he had echoes in his head of a passage in one of Robertson's letters when he used these images. Robertson had written of 'the sound and healthy [conscience] of humanity, whose tides are distinct and unmistakable in their noble music, like those of nature's ocean in its irresistible swell'.[117] It is another reminder that, for Kilvert, church singing was about *feeling* and about the sense of a group of people being united through it in love. The contrast between this experience and the one he had in another 'great congregation' — the High Church service at St Barnabas Church in Oxford — is very clear. Then he remarked: 'I should think that every eye in that great congregation was quite dry'.[118]

The hymn the congregation in St Paul's was singing was, ironically, by the Tractarian (later a Roman Catholic), Frederick Faber, but its words and sentiments had strong Evangelical appeal. It asked Christ 'Thy Word into our minds instil', it harped on spiritual shortcomings — 'the broken vow, the frequent fall', the blessings it requested were 'joy, sweet fear, and sober liberty, and simple hearts'. And finally, it asked for Christ's grace for loved ones, the poor, the sad, and the sinful. While it asked for the living to be united in one circle of sympathy, Kilvert noticeably enlarged the circle by imagining the voice of the preacher to be a link with the dead. Because the congregation was so large, it was easy for its sense of oneness to expand and to extend in Kilvert's mind into a love for the whole of humanity. There is a close similarity between this moment and those frequently found in evangelical testimony when individuals or congregations experience the Holy Spirit; it seems certain that that is the way Kilvert would have looked at it. He needed the idea of a personal saviour and the devotional singing of the St Paul's congregation to arouse the love of humanity symbolised in the 'vast silent splendid glow' of the sunset.[119]

Chapter 3
The Cornish Dream

In Cornwall, where the wrinkles and angles of the
earth's age are left to show, antiquity plays a giant's part
on every hand.
[Edward Thomas, *The South Country*]

I gave myself up unreservedly to the spirit of the place.
I love to do this always.
[Frederick Robertson, letter of 24 September 1846,
from Cortina in Italy]

The quality of experience in English Romantic poetry is
spiritual as well as natural.
[R.E. Brantley, *Locke, Wesley, and
the Method of English Romanticism*]

———

The introduction to *Kilvert's Cornish Diary* stated that 'he
clearly regarded his stay in Cornwall as something special and
outside the normal run of experience'. The reason given for this
judgment is that 'the motif of the dream runs right through this
notebook and is repeatedly established in the description of his
journey through Devon. . . .' It seems as though Kilvert from
the outset wanted to establish that he approached Cornwall in
a mood of heightened consciousness. Thus beyond Exmouth
with its 'stranded boats' and 'white sails hovering about the
river mouth' lay 'a vision of the dim dreamy blue sea'. From
the train he saw the bay at Dawlish in Devon: 'Boats with red
and white sails skimming across the bay, or lying at anchor
like boats in a dream. . . .'[1] The date was 19 July 1870, and
he was on his way to stay with William and Emma Hockin
at their home of Tullimaar, Perranarworthal, between Truro
and Falmouth. They had become his friends when they rented

Langley Lodge in Langley Burrell, Wiltshire, from March 1867 to around March 1869. It is evident that during that period, Kilvert had become very fond of Emma, which provides part of the explanation for his *Diary* entry on the day he arrived at Tullimaar – 'The fulfilment of the two years' dream'. Dreaming of re-union with her was certainly one element in the magical quality of the Cornish trip but there were others.

The previous chapter has laid emphasis on the role of books in Kilvert's upbringing, on the special importance they had for Evangelicals, helping to supply for them the perspectives through which life and landscape were experienced. *Kilvert's Cornish Diary* is very striking for illustrating the way its overall tone and feeling derives from literary sources. Its editors provided substantial and scholarly notes that demonstrate the complexity of its text, the interconnecting allusions constituting its subtle web. The result is that we have a much clearer understanding of what Kilvert was thinking and feeling as he composed his *Diary* entries than is the case with the three-volume Plomer edition. The other factor that clarifies Kilvert's purposes as a writer in *Kilvert's Cornish Diary* is that the text is unabridged: we have all that he wrote. In order to understand the nature of his individual vision of Cornwall, it is necessary to be clear about its constituent parts, to see which belonged to the general mind-set of people of his class at the time, and which were attributable to his upbringing, education and personality.

One part of that vision was his excitement about revisiting a woman with whom he was more than half in love, excitement considerably intensified by the fact that she was a married woman, the wife of his host, whose house was in Cornwall, which also happened to be the home of King Arthur and of Arthurian romance. Kilvert not only knew the Arthur story but, as *Kilvert's Cornish Diary* continually indicates, went there almost obsessed by it. One of his favourite poets was Tennyson, who had popularised the story in his *Idylls of the King*, the first of which appeared in 1859, the year Kilvert went up to Oxford. The legend that Arthur belonged to Cornwall has been part of Cornish folklore for centuries and is particularly popular with tourists. When Kilvert came to Cornwall that summer of 1870, he was determined to visit the key Arthurian site of Tintagel Castle, home of the Round Table. Kilvert knew the *Idylls* before he went and at Tullimaar embarked on further study of them with Mrs Hockin (William Hockin, her husband, was not included in this study). 'We had been reading and thinking a great deal lately about Guinevere, Arthur and Merlin', Kilvert wrote on the day they visited Tintagel.

The crucial fact about the Arthur story is the illicit love affair between Arthur's queen, Guinevere, and Lancelot, his favourite knight and champion. Two days prior to the Tintagel visit, Kilvert recorded: 'Looking at Mrs H's beautiful copy of the Idylls of the King, Vivien, Elaine and Guinevere, illustrated by Doré'. Vivien, one of the ladies at Arthur's court, is characterised, at the outset of the *Idyll* bearing her name, as 'wily' as she flirts with Merlin in the hope of learning the secret of a magic charm that can provide complete control of another's consciousness. The passage that deals with her attempted seduction of him is highly sensuous. For example, we are told she wore 'a robe / Of samite . . . that more exprest / Than hid her, clung about her lissome limbs. . . .' Merlin initially withstands her charms. She affects tears at this rejection, acting like 'the tenderest-hearted maid / That ever bided tryst at village stile'. She quotes a song sung by Lancelot, the refrain of which is a lover's plea 'trust me not at all or all in all'. The lady replies that they must share any shame that shall overtake them. The poem continues with talk by Vivien of women not trusted, attempted seductions, jealous lovers, adultery, until finally she puts the case of Lancelot's alleged seduction of Guinevere. The poem ends with Merlin's seduction and Vivien triumphant.

The parallels between the content and themes of the *Vivien Idyll* and the relationship linking Kilvert, Emma and William, need no labouring; Kilvert hinted at them in the account he gave of the conversation he and Emma had later that day. He and Emma, with a mood of intimacy already established, went into Truro in the pony carriage. He probably found a greater degree of intimacy in the occasion than she. She shopped while he strolled about the town. During the drive home, there was 'Shakespeare talk, Othello, Merchant of Venice. . . .' Then there follows a quotation of Ophelia's words from *Hamlet* – 'They say the owl was a baker's daughter. . . .' The editors of *Kilvert's Cornish Diary* explain that it refers to a legend in which Christ went into a baker's shop and asked for bread. The baker's daughter rebuked her mother for giving him too much, and was turned into an owl. Noting the sexual implication of Ophelia's explanation of her remark, the editors observe: 'One wonders how far Kilvert and Emma Hockin pursued this discussion. . . .'

Emma Hockin

This refers to the remainder of her speech, in which Ophelia tells of a maiden seduced by her lover.

Understanding the romantic perspective supplied by *The Idylls of the King* helps us understand the nature and intensity of Kilvert's relationship with Emma Hockin. It explains how this central aspect of his Cornish holiday was totally bound up with his love of Tennyson. Kilvert had no doubt used the content and themes of the *Idylls* and his exploration of them with Emma to fuel his passion for her, but it is also important to note the powerful significance they had for Victorians in general as well

as for Kilvert and Emma in particular. When the first four *Idylls*
came out in 1859 they sold 10,000 copies in the first week because
they 'hit the taste of both [Tennyson's] public and his critics . . .',[2]
confirming his reputation as a great poet. Critics were delighted
with their content, the Arthurian legends, though to most of
the public they were unknown. The *Saturday Review* referred to
them as 'a forgotten cycle of fables', which was largely true. It
was Tennyson's aim to relate them to the present. At the time,
their emotional and moral content —adultery and seduction
— was daring and provocative. Tennyson's long poem, *Maud*,
which had appeared in 1855, also dealt with immorality and had
shocked the public more than the *Idylls* did because, in Shaw's
view, the latter showed 'poetic decorum' whereas the former
did not. Moreover, the *Idylls* had a clear moral purpose: the
ideal of moral purity being gradually undermined by adultery
and fornication. Tennyson himself described them as showing
'Sense at war with the Soul'[3] and they appeared at a time when
sexual morality seemed threatened by erotic (mainly French)
novels, free love and prostitution.[4]

Victorians saw in medievalism a link with a more spiritual past
and formulated an idealised version of chivalry to counteract
their age's corruption. Frederick Robertson was one of those
Victorians and Kilvert had read in Brooke's *Life* how Robertson
as a boy 'would become entranced in some tale of chivalry or
imagination. . . . He loved to fancy himself a knight — seeking
adventure, redressing wrongs, laying down his life for maidens
in distress. . . .'[5] Chivalry was a popular code in the public
schools of the 1870s, manifesting itself in knights in armour as
school trophies and in stained-glass windows of school chapels,
in school magazine articles about King Arthur and Tennyson's
Idylls. Perceval, first headmaster of Clifton College in Bristol,
named two of his sons Arthur and Lancelot.[6] Emma Hockin's
emotional involvement with the world of Arthurian legend can
be seen from the fact that her fourth child (baptised by Kilvert)
was christened Lancelot. The legends revived in the *Idylls* were
designed by Tennyson 'to read his contemporaries lessons on
their materialism and sensuality'.[7] He urged two moral lessons:
the code of purity, embodied by Arthur and Galahad, Enid
and Elaine, and the noble faithful passion for a woman. The
contemporary fear of sex was to be replaced by the exaltation
of love. Young men were to consider good women, like their
mothers and sisters, as 'creatures more like angels than human

beings'.[8] A later chapter shows Kilvert identifying himself with Galahad and adhering closely to this ideal of womanhood.

The Cornwall that he journeyed to on 19 July was not just a physical place, though it was exciting enough as that; it was an imaginative one. He was journeying into a dream and Emma was its erotic element. She also partook of its literary/legendary element, which was itself part erotic. On the return journey, with the erotic dream over, the change of viewpoint was agony. 'How different from the journey down. The same objects seen with other eyes and feelings so happily expectant – now how weary and monotonous.' The central idea behind this statement — the experience of seeing the same landscape after an interval of time — is the theme of Wordsworth's *Tintern Abbey*, the profound influence of which on Kilvert is dealt with in a later chapter. However, he found that another poem, Coleridge's *Youth and Age*, formed a more specific parallel to the anguish of his last morning at Tullimaar, when he likened rain water dripping from trees to 'the tears of the morning', a reworking of Coleridge's lines 'Dew-drops are the gems of morning, / But the tears of mournful eve!' *Youth and Age*, like *Tintern Abbey*, is concerned with changes wrought in viewpoint by the passing of time, from the poet's youth to the present — 'the change 'twixt Now and Then'. Youth is personified in the poem so that it becomes almost like a lover known in the past. Kilvert found the poem had special resonance when he too was saying goodbye to a loved one in the morning while being forced to contemplate a 'mournful eve/Where no hope is. . . .' On this occasion, his sympathy was for himself, as he mourned lost love.

An outstanding feature of *Kilvert's Cornish Diary* is the sheer number of literary references, virtually all of them to poets, scattered throughout its pages, indicating the extent to which he felt that experiences of such particular intensity, invested with so much feeling, could only be conveyed through poetic image and vision.[9] It might be expected that the last hours of his stay should be marked by literary allusions: one to Coleridge's poem, one to Hood's *Ode to Melancholy* (dwelling on the hypnotic influence of the moon), one to an unknown poet, and one to Gray's *Elegy*, the theme of which is memory. Kilvert wrote that he cast at the Cornish sea a last 'longing lingering farewell look', a slight paraphrase of Gray's line in which he asked whether there was anyone who ever left the 'warm precincts of the day' without such a backward look as he faced the cold tomb and 'dumb Forgetfulness'. 'Other eyes and feelings' expresses Kilvert's hope of a holiday romance or at least a flirtation with Emma, but it also expresses his awareness of himself as a writer, the awareness that what he experienced was the product of his own shaping imagination and the imagination of others.

Kilvert's lament for the change in his Cornish dream on his return journey centred particularly on his visit to Godrevy, 'the last pleasant excursion'. Emma was with him for much of that day, though they were not alone. The importance of the excursion was made up of other things – the ancient Christian Church of Gwythian, his first sight of a wild seal, the wild sea crashing over Godrevy rocks, Gwythian's 'nice Church and schools', and the picturesque house of its curate. 'I took a strong fancy to this village by the sea', he wrote. Early in the Godrevy entry, he also wrote 'sorrowful dreams', a phrase that must refer to his sadness that his Cornish dream was nearly over. In their note on this entry the editors took the opportunity to show the complexity of Kilvert's original manuscript, with parts written at different times, spaces left for additions, parts pushed in between others, additional proof that the *Diary* is a consciously wrought artefact. He could not compose his life the way he composed his text but was very much aware that its composition was the result of key experiences making a characteristic, individual pattern. Godrevy was such an experience and he knew it: 'the name kept on coming up, Godrevy, Godrevy. With a *mournful* cadence, Godrevy, farewell. Unknown till yesterday. But now how dear, a possession for ever, a memory for ever.'[10] Its landscape had marked him permanently and he was changed as a result.

Memory was of crucial importance to Wordsworth, Kilvert's favourite poet, and Kilvert was thoroughly Wordsworthian in acknowledging its importance for himself. In so many *Diary* entries (and they are often the most significant for understanding his personality and mode of writing) he steadily harps on the way his continuing, developing self was built up from memories. His choice of autobiography, memoirs and diaries as a staple element in his reading is one manifestation of this interest. And, of course, his decision to keep a diary is another. His answer to his own question 'Why do I keep this voluminous journal?' was that he thought it worthwhile to record even his 'humble and uneventful life.'[11] That its events were ordinary was not important; what was important was that they were *his* events and the record was the means of monitoring himself as he developed. It was *his memory* of the park at Bowood near his Hardenhuish home that prompted the reflection about keeping his journal. It, like the memory of Godrevy, was part of his inner landscape of memory. Salvesen uses the phrase 'landscape of memory' as part of the title of his book on Wordsworth,[12] in which, inter alia, he traced a strand of eighteenth-century sensibility that loved to dwell upon the past, accompanied often by a mood of melancholy. Later, it merged into the Romantic movement, when it became particularly linked to personal memory, especially in the poetry of Wordsworth, and Kilvert was a Victorian inheritor of this tradition. One aspect of it was the romantic antiquarianism that suffused his uncle's life and the study at Claverton Lodge in which Kilvert received his early education. It was a dominant element in his vision of Cornish life and landscape in the summer of 1870. The introduction noted that a favourite book of Kilvert's father when he was five years old was Britton's *The Beauties of England and Wales*.[13] Kilvert, too, must have perused the eighteen volumes that made up the *Beauties* series, either at home or at uncle Francis's. Britton was a believer in proper historical research and his books contain several strictures on the excesses of romantic antiquarianism. He declared that 'mankind seem rather to delight in romance than genuine history; and we all know that delusion and mystery are powerful auxiliaries in the machinery of the former'.[14] At another point, he rebuked the observer who indulged in 'the day dreams of antiquarianism'.[15]

It was partly preoccupation with Tintagel Castle as the keystone of the Arthurian legend popularised by Tennyson that drove Kilvert there but he was driven also by the romantic antiquarianism represented so forcefully by the Rev Richard Warner of Bath, indefatigable traveller and writer on things antiquarian. Warner toured Cornwall in 1808[16] and made a point of visiting Tintagel, preparing himself beforehand by reading up on its legends (just as Kilvert's reading of Warner had probably been part of his preparation). Warner too came with a dream of Cornwall in his head, determined as Kilvert was to feed his imagination. He stated that he refused 'to be skeptical as to the existence of his hero' (i.e. King Arthur), 'so as not to miss the magical effect that imagination might throw over such a celebrated scene'. Having toured the site, he concluded: 'Every feature connected with Tintagel Castle is formed to foster flights of fancy'.[17] The contrast between this approach and

Britton's is seen in the latter's brief off-hand comment: 'it has been conjectured that this was once the royal residence of the British King Arthur'.

Kilvert's Cornish itinerary not only replicated closely part of Warner's longer one, but included a similar determination to see Tintagel. In negotiating his itinerary with his hosts, Kilvert made the firm declaration 'I wished to go to Tintagel', and when it was agreed, wrote 'Three cheers'. He approached the site with exactly the same mental attitude as Warner, taking the legend and the poetry as facts and seeking to make its physical features fit them. 'We conjectured as to the place where Merlin found Arthur . . . , a naked child, "Upon the sands of wild Dundagil by the Cornish sea"'.[18] He and the Hockins then set about trying to 'discern a likeness' between the coastal rocks they had before them and those in Doré's picture of the finding of Arthur! It was the most unashamed dream – chasing, as Kilvert made clear when he added, immediately after the passage just quoted – 'the dream came true'. Chasing dreams with his beloved Emma by his side completed his bliss.

The dreams of romantic antiquarians were enhanced and their experiences deepened by awareness of the picturesque in landscape. Travellers of a romantic and imaginative stamp had, from around the middle of the eighteenth century onwards, been seeking out wild countryside which aroused feelings of fear and awe at the powerful, violent and threatening natural forms that composed it. William Gilpin was the leader of this movement and his *Observations, relative chiefly to picturesque beauty made in the year 1772* was a key work in it.[19] He talked of observing landscape according to the 'rules of picturesque beauty'. Kilvert's *Diary* gives ample evidence that he knew these 'rules'. The period in which he was his uncle Francis's pupil at Claverton Lodge seems to be the likeliest time for his introduction to Gilpin and to other guides to the appreciation of landscape. An earlier eighteenth-century school of landscape writers – Pope, Shenstone, Gray, Mason and Richard Graves – were favourites of uncle Francis and consequently were likely to have figured in Kilvert's Claverton Lodge education. Humphreys referred to the 'cheerful and sensible love of Nature' of these writers.[20] Shenstone's small estate of The Leasowes, which sought to create a naturalism that concealed the art behind it, typified their outlook: 'it illuminated . . . a Virgilian rusticity which was near to the heart of the eighteenth century'.[21]

George Henry Jenkins, 'Tintagel', 1875

In this view of landscape, natural beauty was associated with moral virtue and with the idealised pastoral vision of classical poets. Pope was referring to it when he wrote of 'the amiable Simplicity of unadorned Nature, that spreads over the mind a noble Sort of Tranquillity. . . .'[22] Kilvert showed he was drawn to such a picture of rural bliss when he described the landscape of Hardenhuish Park, its 'gentle slopes . . . in their autumn livery' and the garden of a rustic cottage where he 'witnessed a pretty loving meeting between a young mother and a child under the boughs of an apple tree', which reminded him of a 'sweet passage in Virgil so true to nature'.[23] It is a view of landscape which accords well with the impression we have of uncle Francis, rather than the Romantic one which emphasised the elemental power and mystery of Nature. However, it should be noted that Graves (whose work Francis particularly admired), while he approved of The Leasowes, preferred wild scenery, which he thought should be approached in solitude and with reverence.[24]

A large literature of tourist guides to scenery had been accumulating throughout the eighteenth century and it was people like uncle Francis who both wrote them and read them. By the mid-eighteenth century, the tourist around Britain would be likely to pride himself on being primarily an antiquarian.[25] 'It was the Antiquaries . . . who turned their attention to the discovery and preservation of the English past.'[26] Gilpin

typified, as Warner did, the clergyman/antiquarian so common
at the end of the eighteenth century and so much part of the
Kilvert family's life at Widcombe. (Warner was in fact Gilpin's
curate for four years.) The yearning for wild scenery was in
part a reaction against what was seen as the 'taming' of the
countryside by agricultural improvements, enclosure and the
work of landscape artists. Thus, we have Gilpin declaring: 'No
tame country, however beautiful, . . . can distend the mind, like
. . . awful, majestic scenery', and when he talked of the mind
being distended, he meant the 'strong effect on the imagination'
of scenes provoking 'grandeur and horror', and yielding
experience of the 'sublime'.[27] Visiting Tintagel, Warner showed
the teachings of Gilpin, his master. Around the promontory on
which the Castle stood, Warner underlined, lay 'the wildest and
most desolate tract of Cornwall'. The Castle ruins appeared
scattered by Nature's violent 'throes', on every side were 'awful
precipes' and 'horrid rocks'.[28]

In his description of Tintagel, Kilvert does not employ the
conventional adjectives 'awful' and 'horrid' but other characteristic picturesque features are present. One kind of scene
cited by Gilpin as typically picturesque was 'the majesty of
a ruined castle, whose ivied walls, seem a part of the very
rock, on which they stand'.[29] Kilvert enjoyed tracing the same
impression: 'The work of the Castle is so ancient, simple and
primitive, that it looks almost like the natural rock in parts . . .
it is difficult to tell . . . where the rock ends and the masonry
begins'.[30] As was mentioned earlier, the dwelling on the past,
so powerfully provoked by ruin, was often accompanied by
melancholy reflections. Brewer indicates the place this had
in the cult of the picturesque: 'Ancient British ruins not only
provided melancholic reflection on the transitory nature of life,
. . . but conjured up obscure and often frightening images of a
barbaric and brutal past'.[31] Tintagel provoked this reflection
from Kilvert: 'Some distance further on' (i.e. from the Chapel)
'is the graveyard. . . . It is a very solemn place this graveyard
on the cliff, the ancient strange forgotten people, so long, so
quietly asleep in their storm-swept graves'.[32] His Restormel
Castle entry is marked by the same relishing of the sheer
ancientness of ruins: 'The Castle is a strange weird place and
looks as if it belonged to an older world'. As Tintagel had for
Warner, Restormel challenged the imagination of Kilvert and
his friends: '"Ah", said one of our party, "if these walls could

Restormel Castle

but speak and tell their own tale".' These *Diary* entries, dwelling
as they do on graves, ruins and sympathy with the dead, are
very much in the tradition of graveyard meditation outlined in
chapter one. Experiencing the sublime in scenes of wild Nature
was another aspect of eighteenth-century sensibility, whose
'characteristic literary modes, the gothic and the sublime as
well as the sentimental, reflect this reaching after exotic and
extravagant fruit. Instead of an alp or ghoul-haunted castle,
sentimentalism focuses on human suffering, but it differs less
than might be expected from other versions of the era's quest
for emotional energy.'[33] The 'sentimental traveller' of that era
roamed landscapes looking for emotional stimulation.

It is evident that Kilvert was very stimulated by the Logan
Stone near Land's End, which his hosts showed him. Britton,
in his guide to the beauties of England, explained the term
'Logan or Rocking Stone':

> a stone, generally of immense bulk and weight, placed
> on so small a centre, and in so exact an equilibrium,
> that it moves to a certain degree with the application of
> a very small power, as the touch of a hand; but which
> could not be thrown down by any common force.[34]

Kilvert's guide put his shoulder under the Stone and rocked it
and Kilvert followed suit. It was explained to him that 'There
are several Logan Stones of various sizes, half a dozen at

least'.[35] Bearing in mind his great interest in stories of ancient Britons and Druids (see chapter nine), it is odd that he did not give any hint that he was aware from Britton's guidebook that Logan Stones had been linked to these forgotten peoples. The editors of *Kilvert's Cornish Diary* similarly found it odd that, though he referred to another 'peculiar rock, called the "Irish Lady"', he did not tell the legend associated with it, 'which he must have read or been told, and which seems just the sort to appeal to him'.[36] He seemed content to regard Logan Stones as the work solely of Nature. Britton, however, declared that:

> in many instances, the curious eccentricities of nature were improved, and then rendered instruments of super-stition, by the ministers of a long forgotten religion. As there is not the slightest reason for believing that such works were undertaken either by the Romans, Saxons or Danes, they may be securely attributed to the Britons.[37]

He believed that the base of some stones was whittled away, to make them as narrow as possible, 'thereby to produce the effect'. Perhaps Kilvert's respect for Logan Stones was derived from Britton, although he chose not (or forgot) to make explicit what stirred his imagination.[38] Howitt had also mentioned, among walks he recommended, a visit he made to the Logan Rock near Land's End.

Seemingly, Kilvert had no chance to visit the hill of Carn Brea (he made only a brief reference to the 'old ruined castle' on its summit) and therefore missed sites that would have caught his attention.[39] Warner not only mentioned the British fortress there, 'frowning with barrenness, and towering over the adjacent country', but also noted: 'The surface of the hill is covered with circles, cromlechs, and altars . . . within walls that marked the precincts of holy grounds'.[40] Kilvert was drawn to 'holy grounds' of different kinds and was fond of using that phrase to describe landscapes he found significant. Later chapters trace his interest in burial chambers, barrows, cromlechs, stone circles and holy wells, yet during his Cornish holiday he saw nothing of these, even though Cornwall is particularly rich in them. The explanation may be that his hosts had their own agenda of visits, that Kilvert himself had other priorities, and that his time was limited. Or maybe he felt that, as a Christian minister, he should not be seen to be preoccupied with pagan sites.

His sympathetic response to Stonehenge (see chapters eight

and nine) may be explained by the fact that he was accompanied by another clergyman and felt 'supported'.[41] He *was* interested in Cornwall's ancient stones: apart from the Logan Stones and the Irish Lady, he noted, when crossing a moor, 'a gigantic wall in which was a gigantic stile. The wall was very high, and built dry with such enormous stones beautifully and regularly piled upon each other that it looked like an ancient wall made by the old Cornish giants'.[42] He was particularly taken with Cornwall's reputation for giants, something he had derived from Bottrell,[43] whose book begins with stories of them and with the idea that they were the forbears of the Cornish Celts: 'a mighty race of Titans dwelt in our hills, woods, and carns, who were anciently masters of the world and the ancestors of the true Celtic race and . . . who were looked upon as giants'.[44] The 'huge serpentine cliffs and the vast detached rocks' Kilvert saw at Kynance Cove he likened to 'giants guarding the Cove'.[45] Bottrell linked giants to stone burial chambers, of which Cornwall has many. His giant Denbras, sensing his imminent death, requests to be buried within a cromlech (called a 'quoit' in Cornwall).[46] Kilvert's reverence for such ancient stones was part of his sense of kinship with the dead and the ancient past.

The all-important picturesque experience of awe could derive, as was noted earlier, from contemplation of the immensity of time. However, nothing could match the awe provoked by the elemental power of Nature, and *Kilvert's Cornish Diary* is punctuated by passages that reflect it. Almost as important as Tintagel to Kilvert was Land's End. 'The accomplishment of an old *dream*', he wrote as it came into sight (my italics). Ironically, his description of it is short and muted, though he did write of 'rocks . . . very strangely fantastically shaped' which resembled 'baulks of timber . . . leaning against each other'. One of the things travellers in search of the picturesque loved to do was to visit frightening places without being in danger of being killed. Kilvert experienced an agreeable degree of fear by kneeling on a flat rock 'which hangs over a horrible chasm' and which looked through a great cavern behind Land's End. Perhaps the flatness of his response to this site was the result of the tameness of the sea. Gilpin had laid down that the imagination needed 'some *extraordinary* circumstances of beauty or terror' when experiencing romantic scenery, such as that provided by 'the agitation of a storm'.[47] That was what Kilvert missed at Land's End: 'One thing was wanting, a rougher sea', he observed.[48]

Warner was a little disappointed with his visit to Kynance Cove
for the same reason. He found 'a dread solemnity' in its 'horribly
picturesque' rocks but 'we only wanted the terrors of a storm to
afford us a picture of the true sublime'.[49]

One aspect of Godrevy's picturesque charm for Kilvert were
the 'horrible deep chasms' among its rocks and he obtained an
extra frisson of terror and gloom from the grave of a former
curate of Gwythian whose dog had pulled him into one of those
chasms, where he drowned. He also enjoyed Godrevy because
the sea was satisfyingly rough – 'all in a roar and a tumult . . . the
whole bay heaving wild and dark'.[50] Nearby were rocks jutting
out into the sea, 'rearing themselves in wild fantastic masses and
strange awful shapes'. The rest of this impressive description
concentrates on the sheer power of a sea by which 'iron, granite
rocks' are 'split, riven, wrenched, torn asunder'. And, in an
imaginative transformation beloved of the picturesque theorist,
the rocks became an ancient castle, just as at Tintagel the Castle
merged imperceptibly into rocks: 'huge pinnacles and rocks
like castle walls . . . broken, ruined'. Again, the impression left
by such natural violence is terror – the cliffs were 'pierced by
horrible chasm and abyss', with waves always 'threatening'.[51]
Lizard Point impressed him in exactly the same way. 'At the base
of the Point . . . a strange ruin of rocks lies broken in scattered
confusion. . . A little way from the Point rises a low long line of
black broken jagged teeth of cruel rocks. . .'.[52]

The awe and terror inspired by savage natural scenery had a
moral and religious dimension as well as aesthetic educational
ones. When Kilvert toured picturesque sites in Cornwall
and Wales it was still assumed, as it had been from the late
eighteenth century onwards, that knowledge of them was part
of genteel education. However, the religious revival of the
eighteenth century was deeply influenced by the philosopher
Locke, whose *Essay concerning Human Understanding* stated that
God was knowable only through impressions derived from
the senses. Brantley gives an account of how Wesley's writings
passed on Locke's ideas to a wider public and provided the
approach to experience shared by the Romantic poets Blake,
Wordsworth, Coleridge, Shelley and Keats. The supreme
importance of experience, especially of a sensuous kind, in
English Romantic poetry 'derives ultimately from Locke's *Essay
concerning Human Understanding*'.[53] Lamb showed that he had
accurately discerned the link, in terms of attitude to experience,

between Wesley and Wordsworth when he observed in his 1814 review of Wordsworth's long poem, *The Excursion*, that it expressed 'a kind of Natural Methodism'. Throughout his Journal, Wesley shows a love of and a sensitivity to Nature. Gill quotes several passages from autobiographies of Wesley's preachers to show the way their piety was infused with a love of Nature expressed in Romantic terms. Similar evidence in Wesley's writings led Gill to state: 'Wesley's interest in Nature is certainly not less, but if anything more, marked than that of the majority of his contemporaries'.[54] Wesley also encouraged emotion by confirming that it had an important place in religion: 'True religion is love, the love of God and our neighbour'. In his view, a religion of the heart would always produce what he called 'righteousness, peace and joy in the Holy Ghost. These must be *felt*, or they have no being. All therefore who condemn inward feelings . . . , leave no place for joy or peace or love in religion, consequently reduce it to a dry, dead carcase.'[55]

Chief among the qualities of writers like Cowper, Hervey, Goldsmith and Gray, those forerunners of Romanticism, was 'the new prominence of emotion', to use Gill's term. It is notable that all of these, with the exception of Hervey, are referred to by Kilvert. Evidence suggests that Hervey too would have been known to him. It ought to be pointed out too that the common denominator among the poets Kilvert favoured — Wordsworth, Tennyson, Clare, Crabbe, Keble, Barnes, Kingsley, Robert Montgomery, Herbert and Cowper — is that their work combined poetry with piety. A further point, which is of considerable importance, is that two-thirds of these men were clergymen (the exceptions are Wordsworth, Tennyson and Clare; Cowper was not ordained but did some preaching). A blend of poetry and piety was a feature also of novelists he read but it was in poets, especially ones who saw God in Nature, that he found a mirror to his own soul. He saw their poetry as a form of worship, rejoicing in the particularly Quaker emphasis of Howitt: 'The verses of English poets seem to have been composed in the open air.'[56] Their piety included the imagination, passion, sensuousness and sheer joy in the beauty of landscape that Kilvert knew were central elements in his own personality. This is not the kind of piety we normally associate with the Calvinism of Methodism and Evangelicalism but, as Nicholson in his book on Cowper reminds us, it is misguided to associate Evangelicalism with Calvinistic gloom and austerity.

Its 'vigour, sense of adventure, deeply emotional . . . fervour [made it] an essentially romantic movement.'[57]

Coleridge's poem, *Kubla Khan*, stands as the epitome of Romanticism, the supremely sensuous expression of the mysterious, magical powers of Nature and of the imagination. In its representation of the creative powers of the mind, it inhabits the same world as Wesley's 'vital religion', speaking of man's inner life, of the imagination that can see beyond the physical to the transcendent reality beyond, of a moment of 'holy dread' which is simultaneously the joy of attaining Paradise. In images drawn from the landscape of dream (Coleridge called the poem 'a Vision in a Dream') — 'that deep romantic chasm . . . a savage place . . . mighty fountain . . . caves measureless to man . . . caves of ice' — the poet caught the appeal that wild landscape held for imaginative travellers who were drawn to focus on physical objects which gave the impression of immensity and infinity. The objects in Nature that most readily yielded such impressions were its wild and terrifying ones, and experiencing them produced emotions similar to those which an experience of God would produce: 'their immensity evokes the concept of Immensity itself; and their horror and grandeur are *immediate evidence* . . . of the existence and irresistible power of the merciful Creator'.[58] The imagination, seen as the means by which physical sensations produced spiritual effects, then becomes a faculty of special, religious importance. Kilvert had assimilated this view of the imagination chiefly from Wordsworth but also from such Evangelical writers as Grace Aguilar, Cowper, Mrs Hemans, the Howitts and Robert Montgomery. He listed Montgomery with other poets he discussed with his literary-minded farmer friend, Lewis Williams of Clyro.[59] Born in Bath in 1807, Montgomery would have been a local figure of some importance when Kilvert was young, especially to an Evangelical family such as his; Montgomery's long poem, *The Omnipresence of the Deity* (1828), appealed to the mood of the Evangelical society of the time.

It begins with the notion that the imagination has a special role in perceiving the all-pervading spirit of the Infinite. The poem dwells much on the contrast between the insignificance and weakness of man and the vastness and power of natural forms he observed. 'Long may I remain the adoring child / Of Nature's majesty, sublime or wild', Montgomery wrote, confident that all its 'terrors and charms' are in the 'hidden but supreme control of God'. Meditating upon ruins was also productive of a similar contrast because they provided an important moral lesson – the transience of earthly power, the vanity of human aspirations and joys as against the perspective of God's eternity. Montgomery's *Omnipresence* has a lengthy passage on the value of ruins for inspiring awe and moral sympathy.[60] He talked of how 'beneath the wasting wings of Time, / Columns and temples sink in age sublime', of owls' 'dismal dirges' heard at midnight through 'roofless halls'. We have already pointed to the importance memory had for Kilvert, as a means of focusing on experiences deemed crucial in the development of his moral/ spiritual self. Montgomery, too, stressed the power ruins have to cause 'musing Memory to turn aside and to weep', while 'Retrospection draws the moral sigh'.[61] Part of the importance of ruins, castles, churches, churchyards, as well as of disturbing natural scenery, was that they all produce feeling, stimulate 'the feeling heart'.[62] As will be argued later, feeling/sympathy was central to Kilvert's view of the ideal community. He was pleased to get close to humble Cornish people and to record Mrs Hockin's observation that they 'are very kind and neighbourly to each other, especially when they are in trouble'.[63]

In order to indulge both feeling and the imagination and to create conditions conducive to religious reflections, solitude was required. A liking for his own company was a part of Kilvert's character but it was also an element in the eighteenth-century protocol for contemplating ruins and wild scenery.[64] We can see him registering his observance of it in the passage dealing with his visit to Gurnard's Head: 'I sat alone among the wilderness of broken shattered tumbled cliffs. . . . Perfect solitude'.[65] He was afraid that the sombre atmosphere of Restormel Castle would be broken by other tourists; he longed for the 'Reserve' that would protect it. 'Happily we were uninterrupted and the *spell* was unbroken, and the *charm* remains and now will remain'.[66] To have such moments invaded by others was not just a temporary irritation; it meant that a spiritual experience that could have added depth to his moral self was irretrievably lost. 'Spell' and 'charm' have been highlighted here to indicate the extent to which he was conscious of having access to significant experiences, special states of consciousness, that could not be replicated elsewhere. Similar ones were available in the Welsh borderland that he knew so well and it is evident that he came to Cornwall very much aware of the similarities between Welsh and Cornish Celts and between their two cul-

tures. Especially at the beginning of his Cornish journal, there
are numerous references to Wales.

Kilvert had gone to Cornwall knowing that it was a unique
region. He knew Mrs Charles' novel, *The Diary of Mrs Kitty
Trevylyan*, in which the area is portrayed as wild and remote. An
elderly clergyman in the book, used to life in Oxford, describes
Cornwall as 'a region rather on the outskirts of civilisation',
the home of 'native barbarism'.[67] His view was typical of that
current in the mid–eighteenth century, as other commentators
confirm. Hamilton Jenkin stated that for a long time it was
regarded as a place of barbarians and quoted a writer of 1776
who said that 'it presents a wild and strange appearance'.[68]
However, precisely because of its wildness, it became a target
for tourists at this period, as did Wales, Scotland and the
Lakes. Travel books devoted to it appeared in 1749, 1764, 1770,
1771, 1783 and 1789.[69] Lack of good roads and sheer distance
had kept it remote till then. It didn't have the charm of other
remote regions, however. 'Nothing can be more desolate than
the appearance of this province', wrote Southey, in 1802.[70] Even
when Kilvert went there in 1870, it was an area still relatively
unfrequented by tourists according to Pearse, who noted that
the rail link to London came only in 1859 and that Tintagel
was not even mentioned in a North Cornwall guide of 1889.[71]
A significant number of tourists, especially at the turn of the
century, favoured Cornwall because its ancient traditions had
been preserved in towns, villages and people. Tourism of this
kind was therefore a flight from modernity.[72] Kilvert was in
this tradition of travellers. He had found a wildness in Wales
to which he responded passionately and he came seeking it in
Cornwall too. It represented a move beyond the pre-Romantic
view of landscape that emphasised its order and tranquillity.

'So many tourists, in the nineteenth century just as now, came
to Cornwall looking for unspoilt beauty, picturesque scenery
and an old-world way of life; and Kilvert is no exception'.[73] So
wrote the editors of *Kilvert's Cornish Diary*. However, they added
that Kilvert's account of Cornwall is 'highly individual' in that
he described not only the legendary, romantic Cornwall but also
its industrial self. The issue is an important one since it concerns
the extent to which his account presents an imagined place, as
against a real one. The foregoing exploration of *Kilvert's Cornish
Diary* has laid emphasis on his pursuit of a romantic, idealised
Cornwall, a 'dream' location, during those three fevered and

frantic (the pace of sight-seeing was incredible) weeks of summer. However, the *Kilvert's Cornish Diary* editors are right: Kilvert *did* juxtapose the romantic with the industrial in his descriptions. Two questions then emerge: why did he do this and was he 'very unusual' (as the editors claim) in so doing?

By the end of the eighteenth century, a combination of literary fashion and growing urbanisation had created a tension between town and country life and this led to a deploring of industrialisation by writers.[74] Warner, in his journal of his 1808 Cornwall tour, expressed resentment of improvement in public roads because they were 'the means by which luxury spreads her poison from large towns into the quiet retreats of rural simplicity'.[75] Picturesque tourism, of the kind Warner and Kilvert practised, generally ruled out industrial concerns, partly to assert rural harmony in contrast to the perceived ugliness and conflicts of industrial life.[76] However, according to Moir, late eighteenth-century tourists would often combine the viewing of natural scenes with visits to mines and mills to see industrial processes.[77] Sir Colt Hoare, antiquarian of Stourhead, Wiltshire, was only one of a number of travellers in the late eighteenth century who commented on such things (for example, on machines processing velvet and calico in Manchester).[78] Kilvert had the example of Howitt, who, though chiefly intent on noting the conventionally beautiful and picturesque in landscape, made a point of including industrial scenes which stirred his imagination as, for example, the mining country around Houghton-le-Spring and Newcastle-on-Tyne, which he described fully in the chapters on those locations in *Visits to Remarkable Places* (1842). Kilvert, too, could find beauty in the process of steel making, as is evident from the account of his visit to Layard's ship-building yard in Liverpool in June 1872.

It was very interesting to see the forging of the iron when a dozen men opened the furnace door and ran along the grated iron floor holding the long iron bar with pincers and drawing it out of the furnace. . . . The working of the machinery was beautiful, especially the drills which moved up and down . . . boring a hole through a thick plate of cold iron as if it had been a cheese. . . . The lathe too was wonderful, peeling off the outer rusty skin of great iron cylinders and leaving them bright and shining. . . .[79]

When Kilvert described scenes of industry, which he does quite often in his *Cornish Diary*, it is usually to deplore them, their destructiveness and ugliness, as, for example, Hayle: 'ugly town, half seaport, half manufacture . . . a dreary creek by a bridge over which runs a tramway for coal etc'.[80] The spectacle of the 'great mining district' of Dolcooth produced this response: 'The bowels of the earth ripped open, turned inside out in the search for metal ore, the land defiled and cumbered with heaps and wastes of slag and rubbish, and the waters poisoned with tin and copper workings'.[81] There are so many similarities between this description and Warner's, which is given next, that the likelihood that Kilvert was half remembering the older writer's account when composing his own seems very strong. (In the first sentence Warner is referring to Dolcooth; the remainder is from his description of mining around Penrhyn.) '[It is a country] whose very entrails have been torn out by the industry of man. [Mining] penetrates the earth, and covers the neighbouring soil with unproductive rubbish. It proceeds to poison the brooks around with mineral impregnations'.[82] It was Dolcooth, referred to by Warner as 'the largest Copper Mine in Cornwall', that provoked him not only to write a very long description of the largest of five steam engines, but to do so in the style usually reserved for picturesque scenery: 'The unceasing rattle of this gigantic engine, the deep and dark abyss in which it works and the smoke that issued from the horrid mouth of the pit, formed a combination that could not be regarded without terror by those who are unaccustomed to such scenes'.[83] Warner's imagination was sufficiently stirred by this spectacle that he felt compelled to make a picture of it. However, he wasn't concerned only with making pictures. He also provided his readers with 'hard' information of a topographical, antiquarian and archaeological kind. In this respect, Kilvert differs from Warner.[84]

An important aspect of rural identity unspoilt by forces of modernity was folklore. The scientific study of Nature which emerged in the eighteenth century, accompanied by urbanisation and decline in the numbers of people working on the land, was eroding the folklore that for centuries had grown up in connection with the land and reflected man's relationship with it.[85] Popular beliefs about the natural world were rejected as being unscientific and as forms of superstition. Kilvert ensured that he countered this spirit by viewing Cornish life through the medium of Bottrell's *Traditions and Hearthside Stories of West Cornwall*, whenever he was not viewing it through Tennyson's *Idylls* (though they overlapped). In a significant comment, he showed that he conceived of Cornish and Welsh people in much the same way: '. . . reading books and papers especially Bottrell's (the old Celt's) book of Cornish legends. I find many words, ideas and superstitions and customs kindred to those of Wales'.[86] Kilvert was at one with others who travelled in search of traditional ways of life and of the picturesque in believing that through knowledge of folklore one moved closer to the heart of a people. Bottrell's book, which conveniently first appeared the year Kilvert went to Cornwall, offered a traveller a place at the Cornish fire-side. The book's preface underlines the 'closed-in' nature of the region and explains that, 'like all the Celtic race', the Cornish are 'of a loquacious turn and sociable disposition', and consequently passed their evenings telling traditional stories. The book's contents and tone have been well summed up by Hamilton Jenkin: '[full of] humour, and romance, lively dialogue, character portrayal and appreciation of Nature'.[87] Another way to express the essence of the book is to say that it represents *feeling* above all, and this too is an important part of what Kilvert was seeking – spontaneous, unaffected feeling. Those who travelled from the mid-nineteenth century onwards to remote regions of Britain were in search of a simple, natural, traditional way of life that valued feeling, because in the country lived peasants who were strong on feeling, though weak on culture and sophistication.[88]

This was the kind of society that the Wesleys found when they first came to Cornwall in 1743. At first sight, it is one of the oddities of *Kilvert's Cornish Diary* that no mention is made of John Wesley, because Kilvert would have known that Cornwall had a special place in Wesley's heart and that he had a special relationship with its inhabitants. According to Pearce, a native of that county, the feeling was mutual: 'Devotion to the Wesleys and their principles was among the standards by which a Cornishman was measured. They did not think of John as a great historical figure. . . . He was their father; their individual example and guide'.[89] The extent to which Kilvert recognised Wesley as a 'father' is complicated because spiritually he had two fathers — Wesley and William Wilberforce. Because he was devoted to the Church of England and deplored the way Dissent, in his eyes, was forever seeking to subvert it, he would have been chary about acknowledging Wesley as his forbear. This is one reason for his reluctance to mention his name in the account of his Cornish holiday. There would have been some confusion in his mind as well as tacit approval when the curate of Gwythian 'complained a good deal about the people and their ineradicable tendency to dissent'.[90]

Kilvert's visit to the British Church at Gwythian on the memorable last day of his Cornish holiday is a further example of his dilemma vis à vis Wesley's Methodist legacy. Kilvert was greatly indignant to discover, probably from his Hockin hosts, that what he called 'this most interesting relic of the earliest British Christianity . . . has got into the hands of a dissenting farmer who keeps the place for a cattle yard. . .'. The sand hills at Gwythian were always shifting, as Kilvert relates, and covering old buildings, only to reveal them later. In 1827, remains of the ancient chapel of St Gwythian were revealed, not by sand, but by Richard Hockin, the farmer referred to by Kilvert. Hockin was digging a pond, revealed the chapel walls, roofed them across and used the building as a cowshed. He was a Methodist, and, embarrassingly for Kilvert's hosts, was their distant relative. Kilvert's veneration for the site was a mixture of the romantic, the historical and the religious. He saw it as 'the relic of an older world and more primitive ancient simple religion. . . .'[91] — exactly that kind of religion that Wesley and the Moravians sought to regenerate. It was Wesley's aim to revive the discipline and ritual of the Primitive Church and to approach the Bible in the same way as the first Christians did.[92]

Thus, though Kilvert found some release for his resentment of Methodism in blaming a Methodist for disrespect towards the British Church, it was the father of Methodism who had started the religious revival, the basis of which was the tradition that Kilvert held so dear. Moreover, Wesley had shown his respect of the ancient site by visiting it in September 1757.[93] Kilvert must have felt some excitement at visiting the county that had witnessed such an inspiring upsurge of religious faith. If he steadily declined to mention it throughout his Cornish journal, it was not because he was unaware of Wesley's work there. For one of his evening lectures in his Langley Burrell parish, he 'read to the people . . . for a change the account of John Wesley's Cornish preachings and John Nelson's conversion told by himself from *Mrs Kitty Trevelyan's Diary*.'[94] Its author was Mrs Charles (1828-96), daughter of John Rundle, MP for

Tavistock, and it was published in 1864. 'I was like a wandering
bird cast out of the nest, until . . . Wesley came to preach his
first sermon at Moorfields', wrote Mrs Charles of Nelson's
state before he was rescued by Wesley, 'Oh, that was a blessed
morning to my soul!. . .'[95] Autobiographical accounts such as
this by working men, were especially encouraged by Wesley
and by Evangelicals, and were one aspect of the emphasis both
Methodism and Romanticism placed on sincere, powerful
expressions of feeling. Religious accounts usually played up the
pathos, the spiritual struggle, the personal drama involved in
sinners' experiences.

Kilvert knew that in his time the Church signally failed to
influence the masses of the people and he was interested to
know how and why Wesley had been so successful in Cornwall.
In one *Kilvert's Cornish Diary* entry he indicated that he had a
valuable insight into this mystery. On 22 July, he visited the area
around Mullion and wrote this afterwards: 'Drove through the
village to the Old Inn, kept by Mary Munday a genuine Cornish
Celt, . . . impulsive, warm-hearted, excitable, demonstrative,
imaginative, eloquent'. These qualities had immeasurable importance for Kilvert and he believed they were shared by another
Celtic people – the Welsh. Imaginative, warm-hearted, excitable
Kilvert was moved by Celts just as imaginative, warm-hearted,
excitable Wesley had been a century or so earlier. And the Celts
of Cornwall responded to Wesley because they discerned those
qualities in him. He had his strongest response in the western
part of the country which, according to Pearce, was where the
Celtic influence was strongest. Being Celtic for Pearce meant
being 'imaginatively responsive'. 'The Cornish were moved as
they had not been for centuries. Emotion, instinct, disposition
all played a part in the response'.[96] Hamilton Jenkin, in seeking
to explain the response to Wesley among the Cornish, stressed
their innate religious nature, but he too identified that with their
emotional, imaginative quality: 'The Cornish people . . . had
ever been by nature of a fervently religious type, sharing with
their brother Celts of Brittany the need for lively expression of
their intrinsic yearning for worship and devotion'.[97]

It is interesting that the rich folklore and deep vein of
superstition that are features of Celtic peoples and that fascinated
Kilvert should also be an element of some significance in the
interaction between Wesley and Cornish people. He stated in his
Journal that scoffers and sceptics had 'hooted witchcraft out of

the world' and that 'complaisant Christians' had followed their
lead, but, in so doing, they were 'trampling on men far wiser
than themselves'. They were unwise in being so dogmatically
opposed to 'what not only the whole world, heathen and
Christian, believed in past ages, but thousands, learned as well
as unlearned, firmly believe at this day'.[98] Rack noted that more
than 60 supernatural incidents are recorded in Wesley's *Journal*
for 1739-42, 10 per year in the 1750s, and rather fewer later. Wesley
insisted they should appear though friends objected. 'They
were an integral part of what Methodism . . . meant and helped
to explain its peculiar appeal', Rack stated. He also noted that
some commentators have argued that Methodism flourished
in Cornwall because it was an area where superstition, folklore
and magic were particularly strong,[99] but most people of an
evangelical cast of mind believed in supernatural manifestations
as 'the direct action of God'. Kilvert was not only one of those
people but also showed that steady, intense interest in various
aspects of the relations between physical forces and the mind
that identifies him even more closely with the Romantic poets.
A later chapter will explore this interest and its significance with
regard to the way he wrote about landscape and people.

This chapter has indicated both that Kilvert was naturally
drawn to dream-like states of consciousness and that his
approach to expressing the uniqueness of Cornwall and of
his stay with Emma was to represent it as a series of dream-
like experiences. This impression of his Cornish holiday being
'outside the normal run of experience', as the editors of the
Cornish Diary termed it, is increased by the fact that Kilvert
devoted a separate notebook to it and made it (again in the
editors' words) 'self-contained', just as Cornwall itself was.
We have seen how he gave himself up to experiencing, in the
approved 'picturesque' manner, feelings of awe and terror in
places where the impression of the savage aspects of winds,
waves and rocks was overpowering. An important part of his
relationship with Emma was sharing with her the imaginative,
almost mystical, experiences of studying the *Idylls* and viewing
linked Arthurian sites under the influence of Tennyson's descriptions. He also showed his penchant for meditating among
ruins in a spell-like trance, induced partly by imagination, partly
by solitude and partly by the ruins themselves. He was very
aware that his Cornish holiday was a journey into the heart of
imaginative experience because it was a journey into the heart

of a particularly imaginative people who had responded to vital religion like no other people, unless it was the Welsh. And he had prepared for that journey by steeping himself in an idealised, imaginative vision of Cornwall compounded of literary images drawn either from Cornish folklore or from poetry and legend associated with it. The journey recounted throughout the entire *Diary* (not just the Cornish one) is one that he hoped would lead into the depths of his own being, into his own inner landscape, which is how Wordsworth conceived of landscape — landscape seen as the mind of man.

Often for the Romantic poets, the search to discover the self takes the form of a search for a remote, special country such as a fairyland or land of myth, conceived of frequently as having the nature of a dream.[100] The importance of this symbolic world, according to Barth, is that it can be 'the encounter of the poet with his own deepest self, with the world of nature and of men, with the transcendent reality we call God'.[101] And the symbolic or visionary worlds projected by the Romantic poets (Coleridge's *Kubla Khan* is a good example, though Barth was writing of Wordsworth too) are, properly understood, not visions of this or that, but visions of *mystery*, of the *fact* of mystery, lying at the heart of life.[102] For Kilvert, as for the Romantic poets, memory had a crucial role to play in enabling the mind to reflect upon moments when an individual's consciousness was substantially changed, moments when an individual's identity was formed, when insight into the mystery of self was offered.

Chapter 4
The Religion of Gratitude

If we want to see religion in its most simple and pure character, we must look for it among the poor of this world who are rich in faith.
[Rev Legh Richmond, *The Dairyman's Daughter*]

What bonds of Gratitude I feel
No language can declare; . . .
When shall I that blessing prove,
To return thee love for love?
[William Cowper, *Gratitude and Love to God*]

In circumstances the pastor is nearer the peasant.
[Mrs Charles, *Chronicles of the Schönberg-Cotta Family*]

Their emphasis on compassion, or sympathy, . . . in the sense of shared suffering, is an important part of the Romantic legacy.
[Gordon Mansell, referring to the Romantic poets, *English Spirituality from 1700 to the Present Day*]

———

Chapter three showed that Cornwall was for Kilvert both a real and an imagined place compounded of actual experiences but also of memories and perceptions drawn from literature, folklore and superstition. It also showed that the particular character of Cornish people's response to Wesley lay in his appeal to their feelings, to understandings that had not been totally overlaid by Englishness and by modernity, which had been resisted by the region's remoteness and the Celtic traditions of its inhabitants. Kilvert found these cultural qualities in the Welsh borderland and responded passionately to it, because it fed the sensuous and spiritual parts of his nature that came together in the tradition to which both Methodism and Romanticism belonged.

This chapter is the first of several that will explore the influence of Wordsworth on Kilvert. He does not mention Wordsworth's *Lyrical Ballads* but they were central to his vision of landscape. Garber's summing up of the nature of the poems indicates some of their appeal for Kilvert: 'The poems dwell on a combination of sentimental humanitarianism, studies in both normal and abnormal psychology, and the effects of a particular kind of experience of the natural world which ties in very closely with sentimental morality'.[1] The collection, planned with Coleridge and containing poems by him, was published in September 1798 and signalled a revolution in English poetry in terms of subject matter, treatment, themes, language and overall aims. A modern critic has stated that the poems of the *Lyrical Ballads* are 'some of the most significant ever written in English'.[2] The Quaker, William Howitt, wrote of Wordsworth's poems in general, but with particular appropriateness to the *Lyrical Ballads*: 'they are radical, deeply, essentially, entirely radical. . . . [His] heroes are waggoners, pedlars, beggars, hedgers, ditchers, and shepherds.'[3] The stories of the collection, which established a pattern for much of Wordsworth's later work, focus on human suffering and encompass all its main facets: poverty, illness, madness, desertion, death. The purpose of the poems was to describe people's feelings that were common and universal, which was one of the ways in which Wordsworth exploited the notion of simplicity. He elaborated this theme at some length in the *Preface* to the 1801 edition of the poems:

> The principal object . . . in these poems was to choose incidents and situations from common life, and to . . . throw over them a certain colouring of imagination, whereby ordinary things should be presented to the mind in an unusual aspect; and, further, and above all, to make these incidents and situations interesting by tracing in them . . . the primary laws of our nature. . . . Humble and rustic life was generally chosen, because, in that condition, the essential passions of the heart find a better soil in which they can attain their maturity, are less under restraint, and speak a plainer and more emphatic language; because in that condition of life our elementary feelings coexist in a state of greater simplicity; . . . because the manners of rural life

germinate from those elementary feelings and . . . are more easily comprehended.

There was simplicity, too, in Wordsworth's choice of the human fundamentals that provide the poems' subject matter: childhood and old age, pride and greed, poverty and idiocy, love and desertion. Jordan underlined the positive value Wordsworth derived from this kind of simplicity: it enabled him to dwell on 'the real, the durable, the essential'.[4] It will be obvious that this subject matter is, to a large extent, the same as that of many of Kilvert's *Diary* entries, and they share the qualities which, in Jordan's view, characterise the *Lyrical Ballads*: '[The] poems partake at least as much of the head as of the heart, and are touched with common sense, lightened with humour, and warmed by a pervasive joy'.[5] Simplicity of emotion had necessarily to be accompanied by simplicity of language if the poems were to represent faithfully the experience of ordinary country folk.

The crucial thing to emphasise about the emotion encouraged by the religious revival of the eighteenth century is that it was the real emotion of real people. Wordsworth made the clearest connection with this fact in his *Preface* to the *Lyrical Ballads*. He announced that they were to be an experiment in which 'the real language of men in a state of vivid sensation' was to be used. In this, he sought to avoid the artificiality of language and of sentiment of much eighteenth-century poetry. Cowper, too, had rebelled against this artificiality and Wordsworth was consciously following his lead. Cowper, whose ballads are comparable to the *Lyrical Ballads*, also aimed at simplicity of language. His purpose was, he said, 'to make verse speak the language of prose, without being prosaic'.[6] There was clearly something in this approach to poetry that won Kilvert's support because it was the mark of another poet, Robert Burns, whom he greatly admired. In his preface to his *Poems, Chiefly in the Scottish Dialect*, Burns stated that his poems were not the work of someone who 'with all the advantages of learned art' was casting about for 'a rural theme'. Rather he chose to write of 'the sentiments and manners he felt and saw in himself and his rustic compeers around him . . .' and sought to express 'the various feelings, the loves, the griefs, the hopes, the fears, in his own breast'.[7] In paying tribute to Burns, Wordsworth expressed the link that he (and Kilvert) found between the Scottish poet and Cowper: 'the simplicity, the truth and vigour of Burns would have strongly recommended him to Cowper'. Wordsworth went on to acknowledge his obligations to 'these two great authors'.[8]

In the *Lyrical Ballads*, Wordsworth also aimed at reproducing the intense, personal and dramatic feeling, as well as the metrical form, of the traditional ballad; this is one sense of 'lyrical'. He conveyed this by his emphasis on 'vivid sensation' and by his famous definition of poetry in the *Preface* as 'the spontaneous overflow of powerful feelings'. The other sense of 'lyrical' is musical quality: many ballads were meant to be sung. (Kilvert was greatly attracted to ballads, as has been noted.) Wordsworth, however, intended to do more than simply tell dramatic stories. The feeling developed in his poems, he was careful to underline, 'gave importance to the action and situation, and not the action and situation to the feeling'. Thus, the objective was realism, though of a poetic, imaginative, rather than a literal kind. In other words, he aimed to explore the emotional and psychological truth of human situations, not simply to present social and political facts. There had, therefore, to be a reflective quality in the poems, not only the description of someone seeing and feeling, which was typical of much eighteenth-century poetry and fiction, but some critical analysis of it.

The poems' frequent use of superstition and of the super-natural is also a reflection of the simplicity of the uneducated people who are their subjects. The supernatural was sufficiently important to both Wordsworth and Coleridge for it to form a major theme of the *Lyrical Ballads*. Coleridge spoke of the poems being of two kinds: in the first, the incidents were to be 'in part at least' supernatural; in the second kind, 'the characters and incidents were to be such as will be found in every village . . . where there is a meditative mind to seek after them'.[9] Kilvert was at one with Coleridge and Wordsworth in believing that imagination and superstition had the same function, that of giving man some '"imperfect shadowing forth" of what he was incapable of seeing',[10] the means, in other words, of going beyond reason and the visible world. This, in essence, is the basis of religious faith and for Wordsworth it inevitably involved Nature, which formed the link between the seen and the unseen. Country people, who lived close to Nature and whose lives were regulated by it, were as a result highly disposed towards the 'meditative', that is, the religious mind. Kilvert was drawn to such people, as will appear. It was what drew him to Cornish people, whose belief in the supernatural he found reflected in their folklore; it was an integral element of the imaginative dimension shared by all Celts.

Wordsworth does not shun suffering in these poems; on the contrary he seems fascinated by it. (Coleridge noted their 'enthusiastic sorrow'.) When Wordsworth referred to himself as a 'sentimental traveller', he was acknowledging that he owed something to the eighteenth-century literary tradition that included Wesley and Hervey and others who characteristically meditated in graveyards. Universal responsiveness, sympathy as the basis of morality, was the ideal of this movement, as was noted in chapter one. Coleridge recognised its contemporary manifestations in Wilberforce's *Practical Christianity* and in a letter to him in January 1801 he linked that volume to the *Lyrical Ballads*. In the early part of his letter, Coleridge referred to the importance of 'the most sacred affections of the human race' and the need for them 'to lay hold on our sympathies'. 'In your religious treatise,' he told Wilberforce, 'these truths are developed, and applied to the present state of our religion.' He went on to say that, as author of some of the *Lyrical Ballads*, he was convinced that he was 'a fellow-labourer in the same vineyard' as Wilberforce.[11] More than mere sympathy was required in the response Wordsworth aimed at, because if that were enough, sympathy would be no more than sentimentality. Thinking was needed in order to brace the feeling, and just as feeling must not become mere sentimental wallowing, so the moral learning inherent in the situations presented must not consist of moralising. Averill noted Wordsworth's 'meditative pathos', his interest in the 'revolution within the self' caused by contemplating suffering and in the imagination's response to it;[12] there had to be meditation for the moral revolution to take place.

Kilvert's Evangelicalism counselled rigour and discipline of a similar kind. It told him that charity and sympathy mattered but that the important thing about extending them within one's own community was that it provided access to the homes and the hearts of sinners. Thus, though Christianity was, as Wilberforce had said, 'the religion of the Affections [which] God particularly requires', the true Christian was not satisfied with kindly actions; he had to be concerned to 'rectify the motives and to purify the heart'. 'Supreme love and fear of God' had to be the motive behind all actions.[13] Evangelicals were all too conscious that man's sinful nature made him incapable not only of good actions but even of good intentions. It was this kind of awareness that pressured Kilvert into such conscientious, loving care of parishioners, and we find him reflecting on the issues involved in this *Diary* entry: 'The scent of an unseen flower seemed like the sweet and holy influence of a good kind deed which cannot be concealed though the deed itself may be hidden'.[14] The influence of uncle Francis's and aunt Sophia's teaching about people's 'hidden' virtues may be discerned here.

Wordsworth's aims and methods in the *Lyrical Ballads* have been examined in detail in order to show firstly what Kilvert would find attractive in the approach to writing they represented, and secondly to indicate in what ways they were suggestive with regard to his own work. He was a clergyman in a country parish, in close touch every day with the intense, personal feelings of largely uneducated, unsophisticated people. They were, nevertheless, especially in the border country around Clyro, people he admired and for very much the same reasons as Wordsworth admired country people. Wordsworth said he wanted to reflect in his poems their language and their experience because, in their social class and in their narrow, restricted lives, they were 'less under the influence of social vanity', with the result that 'they convey their feelings and notions in simple and unelaborated expressions'.[15] It is not hard to see why the young curate of Clyro, aroused already to a pitch of passionate intensity by the people and landscape of the border, should find in the artistic testament set out in the *Preface* to the *Lyrical Ballads* exactly what he had been looking for as a guide and a justification for his own writing. Given his nature, his background and the particular form of his piety, would he not have recognised in a flash of excitement that the definition of a poet Wordsworth supplied in his *Preface* made it possible to combine the roles of poet and priest to their mutual advantage? The poet, said Wordsworth, was

> a man speaking to men: a man, it is true, endowed with more lively sensibility, more enthusiasm and tenderness, who has a greater knowledge of human nature, a more comprehensive soul than are supposed to be common

among mankind; a man pleased with his own passions
and volitions, and who rejoices more than other men
in the spirit of life that is in him, and . . . has acquired
a greater readiness and power in expressing what he
thinks and feels. . . .

It would not have seemed artificial or inappropriate to Kilvert
to spend as much time as he did, during the long, quiet,
solitary evenings at Ashbrook, his Clyro lodgings, noting with
'enthusiasm and tenderness' the feelings and experiences of
the country people he came to know so well from 1865 and
recording them from 1870, the year he began his *Diary*.

Kilvert found another poet in whom 'enthusiasm and
tenderness' were so perfectly blended that he made a pilgrimage
to meet him in his Dorset home in April 1874. The long *Diary*
entry that he wrote about his visit to William Barnes confirms
that he had made a study of the Dorset man's work. 'I told him
I had for many years known him through his writings. . . .'[16]
It was inevitable that Kilvert would have warmed to one who
had written:

the beautiful in nature is the unmarred result of God's
first creative or forming will. . . . In the forms and
colours of objects in a landscape there is a fitness and
harmony of the good of God's formative will . . . The
aim of high art is the seeking and interpreting the
beautiful in God's works.[17]

The poetry and prose works of Barnes hark back to an
idealised rural society but his vision of the past was in many
ways clear and sophisticated. Forsyth emphasised that he
was no naive countryman, still less 'an untutored yokel',
but was 'an educated and well-informed person with wide
interests'.[18] There is a danger that Kilvert, in his adulation
of Barnes, might similarly be categorised with the former,
whereas he is much more the latter. Nor, insisted Forsyth,
was Barnes merely an amateur poet, a fact well recognised by
his contemporaries.[19]

An Evangelical tone informs Barnes's observation that his
poems would not find favour with those who believed that
'every change from the plough to the desk and from the desk
towards the couch of empty-handed idleness is . . . an onward
step to moral excellence'.[20] His book, *Views of Labour and Gold*

(1859), contains his thoughts on economics and social science and there is evidence that Kilvert was influenced by it. Its theme is that economic structures should be built on Christian kindness. He deplored the enclosure acts in such poems as *The Common A — took in* because they had undermined rural society by depriving cottagers of the bits of land that gave them independence. A happier case is cited in *Views of Labour and Gold* but it is not a representative one:

> We knew an old man who had grown up in a neighbourhood of small holdings and farms, and had begun farming with a calf; he then won a cow, and afterwards a few others, with a little farm, and at last died a land-holder; but no labourer can hope to gain by any work or thrift, capital enough to stock a farm of a thousand a year, and has no incitement to try.[21]

This passage lies behind Kilvert's lament for the loss of a farm that once guaranteed a family a happy and independent life:

> I passed by the ruined sheds which sadly, regretfully, mark the site of the ancient small homestead of Watling Street. The dwelling house has entirely disappeared and the scene of so many joys and sorrows, hopes and fears, is now waste, silent and desolate, and overgrown with nettles and weeds. What a pity that these ancient humble farms should be destroyed and *thrown* into the great farms, thereby taking away all the poor man's prizes and the chance of his rising in the world.[22]

Kilvert found Barnes's word 'thrown' in his poem, *Two Farms in Woone*, so apt to describe the relentless, unfeeling process of aggregation that he employed it in his own account, which contains the beginning of a characteristically Kilvertian elegiac meditation upon ruins and memory in addition to its economic argument. Barnes said that his purpose, in writing of labour and gold, was to show the consequences for labourers' freedom and welfare when the forces of capital created a monopoly and with it wage-slaves. Deprived of land, farmers and labourers faced poverty, dependence and anxiety, which were destructive of the individual home that was the moral basis of the community:

It is to the house that we must look for the growth of many
of the most lovely social Christian graces; the affections
of kindred, a reverence for the kindly feelings, and a
love of home, which, in its full outgrowth, becomes that
bulwark of the safety of a community. . . .[23]

Barnes outlined his methods of writing: that real places
and real people were represented in his poems, that keen
observation and memories were their basis, that every line was
inspired by love and kindly sympathy. 'And this is wholly true,'
Kilvert confirmed, 'All his poems are overflowing with love
and tenderness. . . .' His *Diary* entry about his visit to Barnes
is especially revealing in what it tells us about his problem
in having poets as heroes, when extreme Evangelicalism
counselled him to beware of poetry as a snare and a temptation.
On his return home, he was bubbling with excitement over his
meeting with Barnes and walked up and down the terrace at
Langley Burrell Rectory telling his father about the poet 'and
discussing the advisability of publishing my book of poems. I
wish to do so'. Kilvert's confidence derived partly from Barnes's
example: he was sure that the poetry of the Dorset clergyman
was thoroughly Christian, as was Cennick's, Cowper's, Keble's,
Herbert's and Moule's. It also derived from knowledge that his
own poetry was no less so. His poems, with their sustained
working of Christian themes and devotional tone, give some
indication of how his *Diary* might have read if seen in its entirety.
Given his piety, it is very unlikely that he would have produced
two distinct kinds of writing, one highly religious and the other
secular and recreational.

His son's eagerness to pursue the goal of literary fame fright-
ened Robert Kilvert, whose judgements had been moulded over
the years by reading the *Record*. 'He rather discourages the idea,'
Kilvert noted with some bitterness.[24] The *Record* was the most
extreme of Evangelical newspapers; Kilvert's uncle Francis read
the more balanced and more urbane *Guardian*. Hylson-Smith
referred to the *Record's* 'aggressively Calvinistic editorials . . . Tory
outlook . . . dogmatic uncompromising posture.'[25] Robert Kilvert
had failed to recognise what some evangelicals (Wesley, Cowper
and Newton among them) had recognised: Evangelicalism was
unique in being able to satisfy the temperament of the artist.[26]
The degree of hurt sustained by Kilvert over his father's rejection
of his poetry, and with it his hero, can hardly be over-stated.

When Kilvert was doing his best to represent Barnes as a prophet to his nervous, conservative father, Wordsworth had long been one for him. He could find both enjoyment and the means of reconciling his artistic, imaginative temperament with his religion in a poet who had written: 'The commerce between Man and his Maker cannot be carried on but by a process where much is represented in little, and the Infinite Being accommodates himself to a finite capacity. In all this may be perceived the affinity between religion and poetry.' Christianity, 'the religion of humility', was founded on imagination, 'the proudest faculty of our nature'.[27] That imagination was for him an essential element in religion is made clear in the comment he made about Unitarians: 'Their religion allows no room for imagination and satisfies none of the cravings of the soul'.[28] How Kilvert must have been reassured by such emphases, so redolent of Evangelical theology. What is more, in Wordsworth's statement, 'Poetry is most just to its own divine origin when it administers the comforts and breathes the spirit of religion',[29] he had specific guidance as to the way imaginative writing, far from being at odds with his religious calling, could be easily and profitably blended with it on a day to day basis. It was also, as we have seen, the testament of John Keble. By means of it, Kilvert was able to recognise that recording in his *Diary* his responses to the beauties of Welsh landscape and his encounters with the needs of his flock was an integral dimension of his ministry, as well as a way of sustaining his own piety.

According to Wordsworth, Nature played a part in establishing the affinity between religion and poetry. He is the supreme poet of Nature, and it is in their feeling for natural forms that he and Kilvert meet. Both write most powerfully and most characteristically when representing their spiritual response to Nature. Kilvert was responding to Wordsworth and to Quaker thought when he walked on Langley Common and said his prayers 'in the fresh sweet morning air, and thanked God for having made the world so beautiful'.[30] In *The Prelude* Wordsworth had talked of the importance of the two 'natures' or powers of the mind, 'The one that feels, the other that observes', and, in a highly Methodistical emphasis, of 'the deep enthusiastic joy' that communicated itself to the observer with the open heart from all natural forms.[31] So many of Wordsworth's poems express faith in the regeneration of

man, in man's 'conversion': if man will only trust Nature, he
has the opportunity of being morally and spiritually renewed.
This depends, too, on having an open heart, one capable of
being affected by beauty, suffering, the demonstration of
human courage. It is this facet of Wordsworth that appealed to
the Victorians, particularly Evangelical ones such as Kilvert. It
was, as Hartman observed, 'religion in a new dress, the dress of
feeling. Religion was once more open to all, as in the primitive
Christianity of St Paul.'[32]

To be a poet of Nature on the pattern of Cowper, Barnes
and Wordsworth meant getting close to natural scenery and
to country people. For all of those poets, close observation
was a key element in their work. Barnes told Kilvert that his
poems featured 'scenes and well-remembered events and . . .
faces [that] crowded in on his memory.'[33] The importance of
observation for Wordsworth has been succinctly underlined by
Jones: 'For Wordsworth, Poet meant Observer'.[34] For Coleridge,
Wordsworth's originality lay in his 'meditative observation'.[35]
Wordsworth himself had written: 'The Powers requisite for
the production of poetry are: first, those of Observation and
Description. . . .'[36] Kilvert, with his love of walking, had the
means of observing the landscape of the Clyro hills, a means
that suited both his temperament and his physique (he had
inherited his grandfather's stamina for walking). An earlier
chapter has noted the extent to which the motif of travelling,
of pilgrimage, is commonly found in pietistic writings. The
link between Kilvert's walking and his writing is a particularly
significant one and a later chapter notes that his movement
through landscapes is closely bound up with his exploration
of his own identity. He had been influenced, through the work
of figures like the Rev Warner, by the tradition of walking and
writing that was established towards the end of the eighteenth
century. Jarvis identified a 'crucial transitional period' of the
1780s and 1790s, in which 'the social and ideological meanings
of walking [were] being redefined.' 'Serious' walking was being
undertaken then by middle-class men and some lesser gentry
in what was a new and culturally significant development.
'University scholars and clergymen were prominent among
these early pedestrians, and they wrote and published accounts of their walking tours.[37] The Rev Warner was a leader of
this movement.[38] It had an important socio-economic aspect.
At this time, only poor people walked, so that until middle-

class pedestrianism became popular, walking was 'almost an unmistakable index of poverty.' To do it, therefore, if one could afford not to, was 'deliberate social non-conformism', a kind of social levelling, an identifying of oneself with the poor. Wordsworth engaged in this kind of 'radical' walking when he toured France and Switzerland in the 1790s; it was a stepping outside of the boundaries set by birth and class, an assertion of 'freedom from a culturally defined and circumscribed self'.[39] Such walking had a philosophical aspect too. Several writers of this period spoke of 'an intense . . . inwardness' induced by it (the meditative quality of the *Lyrical Ballads*, noted earlier, is expressive of it).[40] In such philosophical walking, body and mind are inseparably linked, giving rise to 'a hypnotically self-absorbed state,' which promotes 'introspective and . . . creative thought.'[41]

It is relevant here to record Howitt's words about walking as an activity and its implications vis à vis the moral worth of ordinary people. He deplored the 'almost total cessation of walking amongst the wealthy,' noting 'how rarely do you see [them] except in their own luxurious carriages.' And, with his typically Quaker stress on the spiritual benefits of the outdoors, he recommended 'all the wild sounds and aspects of earth and heaven, to be met with only in the free regions of nature.' Those young men he saw 'ranging over moor and mountain . . . in Scotland and Wales, taste more of the life of life in a few summer months than many dwellers in the country ever dream of through their whole existence'. To make the most of country life depended, he said, on 'living more to nature and less to fashion, by using [one's] physical and moral energies.'[42] Understandings like these lay behind Kilvert's zest for walking and he owed them partly to Howitt. They exhibit something of Christianity's ascetic tradition that saw holy men going out into various kinds of wilderness to pray or meditate, punishing the body in order to achieve spiritual insight. We should remember that Kilvert's spiritual guide (apart from St Paul) was a holy man in this mould: Frederick Robertson. Brooke's *Life* of the Brighton preacher emphasises his ascetic, mystical aspects: 'Self-repression, self-sacrifice — these were not mere names to him. . . . No pain, mental or bodily, caused him to omit the smallest portion of his work.'[43] We glimpse this in the pride Kilvert took in his 25-mile walks, his reverence for hermits, his castigation of idleness and luxury, his relishing of extreme weather, and his designation of journeys he made to places he deemed holy as 'pilgrimages'.

Georgia Frank's exploration of the religious sensibility of pilgrims of the fourth century who journeyed to visit living saints throws useful light on what 'pilgrimage' meant to Kilvert. 'The journey,' she observed, 'remains an enduring metaphor for the spiritual life' and 'a physical journey gradually became a spiritual journey.'[44] She laid particular stress on the mode of perception, called by St Jerome 'the eye of faith,' by means of which the physical eye could see beyond physical experiences. Christians of this early period were concerned with the question of 'how the physical senses might recognise, know, and respond to the presence of the sacred' and she quoted Origen: 'in order to know God we need no body at all.'[45] A highly sensuous man himself, Kilvert was continually aware of the way in which the physical could block the path to spirituality. Once, when he was told of immorality in his Langley Burrell parish that he had barely glimpsed, he found consolation in contemplating the spring landscape of leaves 'so brilliant that even their shadows showed a pale faint ghostly green. The shadows looked like the spirits of leaves without the body.'[46] Clearly he wished that human beings too could transcend their corporeal selves. (He believed Robert Burns had achieved that, identifying him in one *Diary* entry – vol. II, 101-2 – with a prophet who 'went out into the wilderness'.)

Wordsworth, too, was as enthusiastic a walker as Kilvert himself and the latter made a point of tracing the poet's journeys in Radnorshire and Herefordshire.[47] Wordsworth was also very fond of using the metaphor of journeying to convey what his poetry was about. In Book VI of *The Prelude* he wrote 'I too have been a wanderer', and the idea that his writings constituted an account of his own development, artistically and spiritually, is caught in the line 'A traveller I am whose tale is only of himself'.[48] These various influences not only fed Kilvert's interest in autobiography but disposed him towards adopting the life-as-a-journey model of it. When he said of the Clyro hills: 'I believe I might wander about these hills all my life and never want a kindly welcome ... the kindness and earnest gratitude one meets with when one calls at the houses is quite touching,'[49] there was a clear suggestion that he saw his life there as involving a journey that provided him, through mutual acts of kindness, with spiritual experiences of inestimable benefit for his own soul, following the example of his aunt Sophia and William Barnes. It is highly characteristic of Kilvert to emphasise kindness as the distinguishing mark of the peasants of the Clyro hills and kindness is the theme of Wordsworth's poem, *Simon Lee*, which had considerable significance for Kilvert and his wanderings.

Simon Lee is one of the peasant heroes of Wordsworth's *Lyrical Ballads* and he lived in 'the sweet shire of Cardigan' where, for 25 years, he had been 'a running huntsman merry', a reference to the mode of hunting in which the gentry followed on horseback the pack of hounds while the huntsman ran to keep up with them. In his prime, Simon was pre-eminent in this gruelling occupation: 'He all the country could outrun, / Could leave both man and horse behind'. So devoted was he to this sport that he neglected to develop any other rural skills, and now old, with his health broken and blind in one eye, he was forced to eke out a subsistence on his little plot of land. Pictured by 'their moss-grown hut of clay' with its 'scrap of land', he and his wife Ruth seem part of the landscape itself, as do many of the characters of the *Lyrical Ballads*. With no children to help him, his wife 'works out of doors with him'. The poem's narrator tells how he found Simon attempting vainly to remove a rotten tree stump from the ground and he offers help to the old man. ' "You're overtasked, good Simon Lee, / Give me your tool", to him I said.' Quickly, the root of the stump is cut and Simon's reaction is described:

> The tears into his eyes were brought,
> And thanks and praises seemed to run
> So fast out of his heart, I thought
> They never would have done.

Simon's gratitude provokes, in turn, the narrator's reaction that forms the poem's concluding lines, which Kilvert quoted:

> I've heard of hearts unkind, kind deeds
> With coldness still returning;
> Alas! the gratitude of man
> Has oftener left me mourning.

The meaning of these ambiguous last lines has been variously interpreted by commentators but it is evident that Kilvert understood them correctly. The correct reading depends on understanding the relationship established in the poem

between narrator and reader. Having outlined Simon's history
and current predicament, the narrator interposes: 'My gentle
reader, I perceive / How patiently you've waited, / And I'm
afraid that you expect / Some tale will be related.' However,
no tale is related beyond the account of the removal of the tree
stump and Simon's excessive thanks for it. In this, Wordsworth
was fulfilling the aim of the poem set out in the 1801 *Preface* to
the *Lyrical Ballads*, which was to place the reader 'in the way
of receiving from ordinary moral sensations another and more
salutary impression than we are accustomed to receive from
them.'[50] By 'moral sensations' he meant sympathy and pity
for suffering individuals. Wordsworth was not going to give
the reader 'a tale' because that would lead him away from the
direct confrontation with the spectacle of suffering old age that
Simon represented.

The ballad tales that Wordsworth wanted to 'improve' generally had sentimental themes and a tendency to be content
with the type of moral cliché that he rejected — about kind
deeds being taken for granted by unkind hearts.[51] He wanted
to go beyond that, to *shock* the reader into *thinking* as well as
feeling. And when he wrote, addressing the reader, 'I hope
you'll *kindly* take it', there was ambiguity in the 'kindly'.
Wordsworth was urging him to adopt a 'kindly', a morally
sympathetic, attitude to Simon. Above all, however, he wanted
the reader to understand that the narrator mourned because
he was angry and hurt that society could exploit a dependant's
best efforts and best years, cast him adrift in old age, and leave
him pathetically reliant on a stranger's help. Wordsworth was
going beyond the mere stimulation of sympathy by pathetic
subjects, which was the tendency of eighteenth-century sentimentalism, to analyse sympathy itself. In Romantic poetry
there is an emphasis on experience and feeling that came
from Locke. Hence the interest in stories of others' lives which
Wordsworth exhibited in the *Lyrical Ballads* and which Kilvert
derived in large measure from Wordsworth.

When Kilvert attended the concert in the school hall at
Llowes (a village near Clyro) on 13 May 1870, he saw one
kind of parallel with Simon Lee's situation and it was this
that pushed him into quoting the ending of the poem. After
the quotation he added 'Dear old Wordsworth', as though
approving of the poet's moral insight.[52] Among the audience
he noted a young girl whom he had met before and, worried

that she had no adult with her, he took her under his wing. In the crowded drawing-room of the Rev Tom Williams' home, to which his friends and the singers returned after the concert, a supper had been laid out and each gentleman escorted a lady to it. The girl had the simplicity and even the pathos of humble people who, Kilvert was determined, should not be forgotten. He escorted her so that 'she might not feel strange or lonely or think herself neglected for people who might be thought by some to be of higher rank or consequence. I believe she saw I was trying to be kind to her . . . and she looked at me so gratefully'. Thus, kindness and gratitude become themes of this part of Kilvert's account. He had already emphasised earlier that she had, in his view, shown kindness by agreeing to sing to replace someone in the concert programme who had dropped out. She '*kindly* assented', he noted, and 'went up on to the platform as *kindly* as the sunshine' (my italics). It is noticeable that when he quoted the poem's last verse, he underlined 'gratitude' in the penultimate line and 'me' in the final one, which indicates his understanding of the ending. When he noted the girl's gratitude, it was not a routine use of the word, as is clear from the word's enormous frequency in the *Diary*. The pattern of kind actions followed by expressions of gratitude is so very common in Kilvert's accounts of his contacts with people that one pays attention to it only when one recognises its importance in Wordsworth's poetry. It is intimately bound up with the poet's feeling for Nature, as he made clear in this extract from one of his letters:

> I never had a higher relish for the beauties of Nature than during this spring. . . . What manifold reason . . . have you and I to be thankful to Providence! Theologians may puzzle their heads about dogmas as they will, the religion of gratitude cannot mislead us. Of that we are sure, and gratitude is the handmaid to hope, and hope the harbinger of faith.[53]

It was Wordsworth's belief in 'the religion of gratitude' that led John Jones to say 'gratitude is at the centre of [Wordsworth's] religious life'.[54] To Wordsworth it was the duty of the man of sympathy and imagination to express his gratitude to God in an acceptable form. It has been suggested earlier that this understanding was in large measure the basis of Kilvert's decision to keep his *Diary*, to write his poetry, and that it derived

from the religious traditions he inherited from his uncle Francis
and his mother.

Abrams noted that Wordsworth's poetic vision 'reflects a
movement in eighteenth-century Pietism and evangelicalism
which emphasised . . . God's "condescension" . . . in revealing
his immense divinity to the limited human mind. . . .'[55] It is
an attitude firmly enshrined in the hymn tradition Kilvert so
much admired. The linked notions of gratitude and kindness
were favourite themes for eighteenth-century evangelical writers whose works Kilvert knew. Watts, for example, included
'gratitude' in his list of spiritual graces. Cowper, too, wrote in
his poem, *Truth* (lines 223-4): 'One act, that from a thankful heart
proceeds, / Excels ten thousand mercenary deeds.' Gratitude to
God for all His gifts is a notion to which Wordsworth's poems
give frequent expression, with humility seen as the attitude
most appropriate as the means of expressing it. Beautiful
country walks he knew from his youth 'cannot be remembered
but with thanks / And gratitude. . . .' Gratitude/ ingratitude is
the theme (with variations) of many of the *Lyrical Ballads*. From
the evidence of Kilvert's poems it is clear that he warmed to
Wordsworth's religion of humility/gratitude (the ethics are
opposite sides of the same coin). And when he quoted the
ending of *Simon Lee* he showed his ability and readiness to
apply its message to situations he encountered as a parish
priest. It is important to stress his 'ability' to apply it because
it throws light on the quality of his literary understanding as
well as on his piety. The ambiguity of the poem's ending has
provided a stiff challenge to twentieth-century critics, yet he
apparently took it in his stride. The complexity and significance of the poem have been stressed by John Danby, who saw
it as an example of Wordsworth's art 'at its subtlest', adding
that the ending, which was the justification of the whole poem,
had 'weight, depth, soberness, measured seriousness and overflowing tenderness.'[56]

Wordsworth, in his Preface to the *Lyrical Ballads*, stated that
one of his aims in the collection was to show that the humblest
of men possessed 'the best qualities'. It was a conviction he
was fond of reiterating, as for example in *The Prelude*: 'There
are among the walks of homely life / . . . men for contemplation
framed. . . .' Wordsworth said he spoke of them 'in gratitude to
God, who . . . knoweth us, loveth us / When we are unregarded
in the world.'[57] Knowing that he himself was 'unregarded in

the world', Kilvert had a fellow-feeling with men like Simon Lee. This was part of his concern for John Morgan of Clyro, the Peninsula War veteran whom he called the 'old soldier'. In his frequent visits to Morgan, Kilvert would sit and listen to his tales of dangers and privations experienced in Spain. He admired Morgan's independence because, like Simon Lee, he lived in his humble cottage with no other help than that of his aged wife. Kilvert offered help to Morgan in his vegetable garden just as the narrator offered it to Simon when he struggled with the tree stump. In one visit (the day before Good Friday), Kilvert's purpose was to administer the Sacrament; afterwards, he felt admiration for the old man's humility and piety, for he was 'very quiet, earnest and *thankful*' (my italics).[58]

Among the Clyro hills Kilvert found many of these 'men for contemplation framed' and paying homage to them, as he did in a host of *Diary* passages, was for him an act of piety. The fact that old Price had been abandoned by his relatives and lived alone in filth and squalor made him a particularly deserving target of Kilvert's kindness. 'The poor old man was lying alone this afternoon parched with thirst,' he wrote. 'I went home and got him some brandy and water. . . . His gratitude for the little attention was very touching.'[59] Kilvert showed kindness to Morgan and Price but he also felt grateful to them for their moral example — their independence, patience and piety in the face of suffering simultaneously inspiring and humbling him, producing a mutuality that he and Wordsworth believed was a much needed dynamic in a community. They helped to keep alive sympathy in others, which was why Wordsworth insisted that such men must not be deemed useless. They represented the principle of kindness begetting kindness of which Aguilar had written. This was the function of the old Cumberland beggar:

> the villagers in him
> Behold a record which together binds
> Past deeds and offices of charity,
> Else unremembered, and so keeps alive
> The kindly mood in hearts which lapse of
>   years. . . .
> Make slow to feel.

The spectacle of his suffering thus kept in the minds of the villagers the needs of others and by reminding them of past charitable actions, he functioned as the community's memory. There was also something to respect, Wordsworth believed, in the sheer age of such persons.

No-one epitomised for Kilvert these qualities of old age more completely than Hannah Whitney of Clyro. She was 90 years old and in spite of her 'withered grey face and white hair', he could still discern the 'ancient beauty' of her 'fine delicate features'. Pious and humble though she was, he in his persevering Evangelical way always had hopes of moving her towards formal acceptance of Christ as her saviour. He recorded in March 1873 (by which time his Clyro curacy was six months in the past) that he administered Holy Communion to her in her home — 'for the first time at the age of fourscore years and ten. I am very happy and thankful about this'.[60] He was grateful that he had been instrumental in her conversion. In turn, she expressed her gratitude for the tea and sugar sent her by Kilvert's mother at his request: 'I keep the sugar to honour the Sabbath morning and evening and God bless the finder.'[61]

Kilvert was particularly impressed by the sheer age of Hannah. She was able to remember from her very early childhood old neighbours, her grandfather's friends, who were born, Kilvert underlined, at the beginning of the eighteenth century, or even at the end of the seventeenth. He was emphasising that the culture she belonged to was an oral one which, in Moffat's words, 'lived in the memories of its people for most of its existence'.[62] From these old folk Hannah had derived some of her superstitious beliefs because at the age of eight, she would sit on a stool 'listening while they told their old world stories of the faries ("the fairies") in whom they fully believed.' Her 'old world stories' fascinated Kilvert too. 'I sat with her an hour . . . listening to her reminiscences . . . of the dear old times, the simple kindly primitive times . . . nearly ninety years ago.'[63] The emphasis on 'simple *kindly* primitive times' reflects the importance both Kilvert and Wordsworth attached to kindness as a response to other human beings. Kilvert also respected the wisdom that went with Hannah's great age: 'I sat . . . listening reverently to the words of wisdom that dropped from her. Hannah is a very wise woman, wise with mother wit matured and broadened by the wisdom of age.' Jones's memorable phrase — 'gatherers up of time'[64] — to describe Wordsworthian solitaries such as Hannah, points towards the wisdom they were seen to possess. In part the wisdom came, as it did for the old Cumberland beggar, simply from enduring so long, but enduring was important, as Kilvert recognised, because with it came calm acceptance: 'She spoke of the blessing of being cheerful and of being able to sit by her own fireside and eat her crust of bread in peace and quietness.'[65]

Hannah Jones, an agricultural labourer's widow, was a mere 65 as compared with Hannah Whitney's 90 years and did not have the latter's charm and wisdom. Nevertheless, she was quite a character, given to smoking a short pipe and to telling stories of fairies. She, too, had spirit and independence that won his admiration. Apart from looking after an 80-year-old lodger, Sarah Probert, she was to be found 'tugging and tearing firewood up the old dingle', to use her own words. When Kilvert read the Bible to Sarah, Hannah overheard but paid little attention, which is perhaps why he targeted pious works on her, a kindness she acknowledged: 'Hannah was very grateful for the little book I brought her *Meditations for Three Weeks*.'[66] One of the *Lyrical Ballads* features an old woman, Goody Blake, who combines several of the characteristics of Hannah Whitney and Hannah Jones and the response that Kilvert made to these old parishioners was exactly the one Wordsworth wished his readers to have towards Goody Blake: the pitiable state which they all shared could not and should not be ignored:

> Old Goody Blake was old and poor;
> Ill fed she was, and thinly clad;
> And any man who passed her door
> Might see how poor a hut she had.[67]

The pattern of kind act reciprocated by gratitude is repeated in one *Diary* entry after another. Mrs Jones of the Harbour farm had come to his attention because of the outstanding kindness she had shown to the daughter of Squire Beavan of Glascwm, who disapproved of her choice of husband, Lieutenant Irwine. On Irwine's death, she was refused a home by her father, who put her on the parish, but Mrs Jones took pity on her and took her in. Davies was a shepherd and lived in Bredwardine, the parish Kilvert took over in November 1877. Davies's son's death was particularly poignant because it occurred just before Christmas 1878 but it gained

immeasurable significance in Kilvert's eyes because Davies
was a shepherd. The important parallel for the diarist was that
Christ was traditionally represented as the Good Shepherd,
an image of loving kindness. Davies, in addition, exemplified
the 'natural piety' valued by Wordsworth and by Kilvert. In
Book VIII of *The Prelude*, entitled 'Love of Nature Leading to
Love of Man', Wordsworth recorded his earliest attachments
to various people and observed that 'shepherds were the
men that pleased me most.' To his youthful understanding,
the shepherd became an almost spiritual creature,[68] more
significant than anything in books, and he now felt privileged
to have had such examples of moral integrity around him as
he grew up. Kilvert emphasised that both the shepherd and
his wife Margaret were stoical and humble in the face of their
loss. As Kilvert knelt with Margaret by the bed of her dead
son, 'she was deeply touched and most humbly *grateful.'*[69]

One could go on citing examples of *Diary* entries that repeat
the pattern of kindness begetting kindness, kind act followed
by gratitude. They occur in all sections of the *Diary* and
provide a consistent theme for Kilvert's work and experience
in all of his parishes. However, they are to be found most
frequently and accompanied by the most explicit emphasis in
sections recording life in the English–Welsh borderland. One
striking illustration of the extent to which he registered all
the kind acts he came across and used them to arrive at some
measure of the moral quality of his communities is the section
in volume three, pp. 260-424. The section begins with an entry
recording the end of his love affair with Ettie Meredith Brown.
He had received a farewell letter from her and though it was
painful for him to read it, he was able to take comfort in her
previous kindness: 'How kind and gentle she has always been
to me'. After staying a few days with his sister at Monnington-
on-Wye, he went again to Clyro where he stayed with friends
(and where the references to kindness multiply noticeably).
He was in a variety of locations after that, but the recording
of kind acts and kind people steadily continues with the result
that in 164 pages (pp. 260-424), there are 31 such references,
or one in every five pages. The sheer number of underlinings
of kindness/gratitude as a moral response is one way of
recognising its importance for Kilvert. It should be pointed
out that he is not simply recording something as trivial as
people saying 'thank you' as a matter of good manners. In

noting expressions of gratitude, he was doing a lot more than counting courtesies. When the words 'gratitude' or 'grateful' or 'kind' or 'kindness' occur, a significant moral/emotional contact is made between people, the basis of which he would have interpreted as Christian.

The contacts usually involve parishioners, mostly those of the humbler classes rather than the gentry.[70] His parish work enabled him to recognise that vulnerable people — the elderly poor, the sick, the bereaved, servants, labourers and children — had feelings and needs. Society not only had a responsibility of recognising their vulnerability but also of recognising their strengths, the example they set in terms of their courage, patience, independence, cheerfulness, wisdom and hard work. In addition, the role they had in stimulating and keeping alive among their neighbours the capacity to feel, to sympathise, to be kind, was of supreme importance. 'Bring with you a heart that watches and receives,' urged Wordsworth, and receiving — the experiencing of others' emotions, others' gratitude in return for acts of kindness — was an *active* virtue.

All of this is epitomised in *Simon Lee*. His rejection after years of devoted service represented, as Wordsworth made clear, a breakdown of relationships.[71] A number of commentators have observed that Wordsworth's poems are centrally concerned with relationship. Writing of *Simon Lee*, Laura Claridge said that it 'insists upon society as the very condition of meaning'.[72] Jordan noted that even more important than the theme of gratitude in the *Lyrical Ballads* were the '"links" that produced it, links of man to nature, man to man. . . .'[73] Wordsworth's poems 'demonstrate the vital quality of relationship, the human interaction and the vital sense of communication between individuals', according to J.R. Watson.[74] They explore both the community of people and the relationship of people to the natural world. Love of natural objects, accompanied by the belief that they are proof of God's benevolence, induced feelings of sympathy towards one's fellow human beings, in Wordsworth's view.[75]

Kilvert highlighted an example of selflessness in the Clyro community in Mrs Jones, when he revisited the village in April 1876: 'The poor old dame was still struggling amidst deafness, blindness, weakness, age, poverty and friendlessness to keep her poor little infant school together.' When Vicar of Bredwardine, he organised an offertory for those who struggled as Mrs Jones

did and in a sermon underscored the interdependence of
community members and the need for all to show sympathy
to those in need: 'I pointed out to the congregation that as
we all had an interest in the Church and its services and a
neighbourly feeling towards the sick and afflicted poor we all
ought to contribute something towards their relief. . . .'[76] As
a good Evangelical, he also knew that 'Good Works were not
meritorious, but evidential',[77] that is, they were confirmation of
one's faith. This is a very obvious emphasis in the *Diary* entry
where he was thanked for his seven and a half years' service in
Clyro by old James Jones (husband of the woman who ran the
infant school): 'The old wizard took my hand lovingly and most
tenderly . . . and gave me his blessing. . . . "You have done great
good in this place," he said.'[78] Jones had pronounced Kilvert's
epitaph and Kilvert was grateful for it. The passage sums up
tellingly the concept of community and relationship that Kilvert
and Wordsworth shared. Its characteristic emphases are there
in an entry that contains further testimony to what Kilvert had
achieved in what he significantly called the 'holy ground' of
the Radnorshire hills.[79] The entry is for 10 August 1872, when
his departure from Clyro was imminent and he was saying his
farewells:

> Dear Sophy Ferris, the warm-hearted Carmarthenshire
> woman at the old Forest farmhouse, overwhelmed me
> with tears in her voice, "You will pray for me?" I will
> indeed. What have I done? What have I done? What am I
> that these people should so care for me? How little have
> I deserved it. Lord requite these people ten thousand
> fold into their bosom the kindness they have showed to
> the stranger.[80]

It was confirmation that the religion of gratitude, of kindly
feeling, worked, and that it worked particularly well in Wales.
He took special pleasure in being able to record the remark Lady
Joscelyn Percy made about the Clyro region: 'Lady Joscelyn
Percy says that in this neighbourhood she never hears people
speaking unkindly of each other.'[81] It was clear to him that the
Cornish and the Welsh, by dint of having the same Celtic origins,
manifested the same characteristics — passion, imagination,
warm-heartedness, responsiveness to natural things, superstition — and these characteristics were the basis of their deep,
innate feel for religion.

Such was Kilvert's affinity with Welshness, he could assert 'Wales, sweet Wales. I believe I must have Welsh blood, I always feel so happy and *natural* and at home amongst the *kindly* Welsh.'[82] The emphasis here on naturalness is notable. The constant theme of his relations with people, especially women, for whom affectation posed the biggest threat, is naturalness, simplicity, genuineness. Kilvert felt at home in Wales because he made the same imaginative response as the Welsh did to people and places. His imagination was similarly stirred by wild scenery, lonely places, strange legends, and ancient traditions, as has been shown in the chapter on his Cornish experiences. That chapter noted the tradition connecting evangelicalism, Romanticism and superstition; the present chapter has explored the *Lyrical Ballads* as a specific example of it. Kilvert recognised that that collection of poems lay within the religious tradition in which he had been raised. Its theme of kindness expressed for him the essence of the Christian faith. Its characters and situations were indistinguishable in all essentials from those that formed the staple of his Clyro ministry and, because they were worthy of meditation, they constituted a model for his own writing, enabling the pious and the imaginative sides of his nature to come together in perfect harmony.[83] The brief stories of simple, good lives that he found in the *Lyrical Ballads* and in his borderland community were an intrinsic part of the larger narrative of his own life contained in his *Diary*.

Chapter 5
Memory

Who knows the individual hour in which
His habits were first sown, even as a seed?
Who that shall point as with a wand and say
"This portion of the river of my mind
Came from yon fountain?"
    [William Wordsworth, *The Prelude*, Book II]

a flood of dear old memories of Clyro Hill. . . . Again
I heard the breeze rustling the dry fern and sighing
mournfully through the gorse clumps . . . and there
before my eyes came a vision of the green mountain-
side, the Radnor Hills.
    [*Kilvert's Diary*, Volume III]

I feel strongly that . . . things can be felt but once; you
cannot recall impressions. You recall only part of them,
softened and altered, bearing the same relation to the
impression itself that the mellowed Italian does to
the original Latin. Pictures, scenery, persons, you can
feel them in this world but once. The first time never
returns. So I write now, that whatever I have to say may
be fresh and living. Memory retains things, but only as
a herbarium holds plants; they become colourless and
withered after a time, retaining only the shape of what
they were, and even that distorted.
    [Frederick Robertson, letter of 27 September 1846]

For Wordsworth, the deepest experience of nature, of
landscape, . . . was a sensuous and spiritual totality,
of past forms remembered, working with present
forms. . . .
    [Christopher Salvesen, *The Landscape of Memory.
A Study of Wordsworth's Poetry*]

The chapter about Kilvert's Cornish holiday showed how his approach to landscape was in part influenced by the idea of the picturesque, the leading exponent of which was Gilpin, who laid down rules by which scenery should be viewed. Aware of the charge of artificiality that could be levelled against it, he attempted a defence. Examining landscape according to rules could, he said, 'seem rather a deviation from *nature* to *art*. Yet, in fact, it is not so: for the rules of picturesque beauty are drawn from nature'.[1] However, by insisting as he did that picturesque beauty resided in the visual qualities of objects themselves and not in an individual's subjective experience of them, artificiality inevitably crept in. The viewer's imagination was, according to him, involved in 'improving' scenes presented by Nature. Thus, when looking at a lake, 'the line of water, which perhaps is straight, the imagination will easily correct' by mentally introducing a promontory or a bay, rearing the 'majesty of a ruined castle' upon a small hill or 'a mouldering abbey' among encircling woods. The objective was the 'composing' of a landscape by 'correcting one part of a nature by another'.[2]

In some of his descriptions of landscape, Kilvert can be seen picture-making in the Gilpin manner. It is most marked in the *Diary* entry (June 1875) concerning his visit to Tintern Abbey, a visit prepared for, as was his visit to Cornwall, by prior reading of guidebooks.[3] In that entry he can be seen first adjusting his own response to the Wye in relation to one encountered elsewhere: 'I have heard great talk of the Wye at Chepstow. . . . I was disappointed at the famous view from the Wynd Cliff'. Gilpin had stated that 'the noble ruin of Tintern Abbey . . . is esteemed . . . the most beautiful and picturesque view on the river'. Kilvert, on the other hand, objected: 'Tintern Abbey at first sight seemed to me to be bare and almost too perfect to be entirely picturesque. One wants a little more ruin and ivy. . . .'[4] His description here is constrained by awareness of what he was *supposed* to see; he knew that ivy was a *sine qua non* of ruins.[5] It was also emphasised in picturesque guides that 'sympathetic' weather was needed to view scenery at its best (noted earlier in relation to rugged Cornish coasts) and accordingly we have Kilvert observing: 'It was a solemn day, very quiet, a perfect day for seeing a ruined Abbey. . . .' In the following description of a sunset he related the experience to picturesque notions of 'sublimity' and 'infinity':

As I came home the western heavens were jewelled
with pure bright sparkling lights of grey silver and pale
gold, and overhead a sublime mackerel sky of white
and blue in its distant fleecy beauty gave me a more
intense and grand sense of infinity and the illimitable
than I ever remember to have had before.[6]

It suited Kilvert's sensibility as a man and as a writer to be free
of the constraints of rules for viewing landscape, as it did for
Wordsworth, who had the greatest impact on the way Kilvert
wrote. Again, one feels that it was from his uncle Francis's
teaching about Wordsworth that Kilvert began to develop his
religious and imaginative vision of landscape. Chapter one
showed that uncle Francis revered the Lakeland poet as a moral
teacher, one who saw natural forms as evidence of a divine
creator, an emphasis reinforced by Quaker influences. One of
the guides to landscape to which he introduced Kilvert was
Wordsworth's *Guide to the Lakes* (as is demonstrated in chapter
nine). In his *Guide* Wordsworth occasionally used picturesque
concepts and terms but did so critically instead of accepting
them as given. His descriptions of scenery relate to what
he actually saw and often provide factual details of natural
processes (fallen rocks, erosion and other geological features),
which show that he was prepared to go beyond the conventions
of the picturesque. (The 1853 edition of the *Guide* incorporated
five letters by Sedgwick on the geology of the Lake District.)
Wordsworth indicated that he differed from picturesque
theorists like Gilpin who were forever 'improving' on scenery:
'let us rather be content with appearances as they are. . . .'[7]
The poet recognised that a concern to observe the conventions
of the picturesque or to compose the most perfect 'picture' of
a scene could come between a viewer and what was actually
there, reducing his personal involvement with it. He praised
the attitude to landscape of his sister Dorothy, emphasising
that her feelings were engaged with what she saw, not simply
her visual sense of 'appropriate' forms: 'Her eye was not the
mistress of her heart; / Far less did rules prescribed by passive
taste, / Or barren intermeddling subtleties, / Perplex her mind.'[8]
The effort to compare 'scene with scene' resulted, he said, in a
focus 'overmuch on superficial things'.[9]

Earlier chapters have underlined the importance for Kilvert
of *feeling*. Chapter one focused particularly on the nostalgia

characterising much Victorian writing, with its strong emphasis on memory, its 'melancholy inventory of past experience and loss' (De Laura's phrase), and Kilvert's description of the landscape of Whitehall was cited to exemplify this 'elegiac mode'. It has been suggested that, among other literary models, the books of William Howitt had a significant role in disposing Kilvert to write about landscape in this way. Some of Kilvert's descriptions of Cornish landscapes illustrate perfectly what Howitt meant when he wrote of Mitford's ruined manor house as 'landscape poetry ... rich with all the colours of memory and poetry.' In Howitt's writing, poet, historian and antiquary come together to provide the *stories* that, for him, were the essence of landscape's meaning. To this end he had meticulously researched his chosen locations, so there is a profusion of detail. Kilvert didn't possess Howitt's knowledge and consequently historical detail is sometimes in short supply, but the poetic feeling is there (as, for example, in his descriptions of Bowood, Yaverland, Draycot House, and various Welsh locations focused on in chapter nine).

We have seen that memory as a means of developing and monitoring one's moral and spiritual self was a key element in the religious tradition which shaped Kilvert. When he was nine he was urged by Legh Richmond to recognise that memory working through meditation was the 'sanctified instrument of spiritual improvement'. Spiritual autobiography played a large part in Kilvert's reading and he read a number of poets — Gray, Cowper, Mrs Hemans, Montgomery, Tennyson, and Barnes — for whom memory was a central theme. His Whitehall meditation on mortality and the vanity of human hopes has a close parallel in Howitt's evocation of the landscape of Annesley, home of Mary Chaworth, whose story, encapsulated in Byron's poem *The Dream*, had taken such a firm hold on Kilvert's imagination that he was always quoting its refrain 'A change came o'er the spirit of the dream' whenever he wanted to mourn over the mutability of human fortunes. Change is the dominant theme in Howitt's account of Mary Chaworth: 'Mary Chaworth was here all life and spirit, full of youth, and beauty, and hope. What a change fell upon her after-life!'[10]

The present chapter seeks to explore the approach to landscape which Kilvert, following Wordsworth, particularly favoured. His approach centred on locations to which an individual became attached by personal feelings so intense that they remained forever alive in his memory. Wordsworth forcefully differentiated this approach from that of the picturesque, rejecting 'pampering myself with meagre novelties / Of colour and proportion', in favour of being responsive to 'the moods / Of time and season, the moral power, / The affections and the spirit of the place. . . .'[11] Before turning to the specific issue of how Wordsworth influenced the way Kilvert wrote about landscape, it is worthwhile to register what Wordsworth meant in general to Victorians of Kilvert's generation.

> The Victorians inherited the cult of noble emotions from the Romantics. . . . Rousseau and Wesley can be thought of as the immediate fountainheads of the two great streams of Victorian morality. It was the earlier Wordsworth . . . who carried this morality alive into the Victorian heart.[12]

The source of this inspiration was the beauty and grandeur of Nature. The supreme importance of feeling in Wordsworth's poetry has been stressed by Prickett:

> We make a mistake to think of his poetry as versified philosophy. . . . It is not merely thought but *feeling*. . . . It is this immense effort to articulate *feeling* that gives Wordsworth his appeal to the Victorians.[13]

Just as the recurrence in the *Diary* of the words 'kind/kindness' and 'grateful/gratitude' signifies the business of relationship that was of profound importance for Kilvert, so the reiteration of 'memory', 'remembering' and 'forgetting', is the mark of another concern that went to his very heart (chapter one noted memory's key role in remembering the dead). It is best to begin here with examples that establish this general concern and to move from them to wider implications. In April 1872 he was facing a crisis: the previous September he had been told by the Rev William Thomas of Llanigon near Clyro to give up his courtship of his daughter Daisy because his prospects were not good enough. Consequently their affair had languished but on 5 April they had met again at a ball and talk with Daisy had turned to the past, to flowers she had given him the previous September which he had 'kept carefully ever since' and to the mountain of Wen Allt where they had picnicked together in August 1869. 'I have one happy sunny memory . . . connected with it and her,' he wrote. After the ball 'all the old feelings of last September have revived again . . . the old wounds are all open'. He 'wandered with slow and melancholy steps' up the hill he and Daisy knew three years before, deriving consolation from 'the Wen Allt always in sight with its crowd of happy memories of long ago'.[14] The phrasing here — 'Wen Allt always in sight' — indicates the way the physical scene linked past and present, his mood then with his mood now.

He eased the pain of his imminent departure from Clyro with a trip to another mountain that had an important place in his memory. It was the May Saturday of Hay Fair and he, determined 'to get out of the sight and sound of it', climbed Penllan where he knew there was a perfect secluded nook where he could read and muse. The mountain containing his nook was associated particularly with the 'mountain beauty', Mary Williams, who lived at the white farmhouse visible from his Clyro lodgings. Penllan's full significance for him is contained in the entry for 24 March 1874 when he was revisiting Clyro. As he looked at the mountain 'a thousand sweet and sad memories came over me and all my heart rose up within me and went out in love towards the beloved place and people among whom I lived so long and so happily.'

What distinguishes the experience contained in the Wen Allt and Penllan entries is the hint that more than mere nostalgia is involved. The Wen Allt passage suggests that the landscape enabled Kilvert to reflect upon changes in himself over time. When he dwelt on the secluded nook of Penllan, he revealed a trait in himself that the mountain accommodated and complemented — the need for solitude. In the second Penllan entry it is clear that the mountain symbolised for him a particularly important phase of his life because, to the region in which it was located, he was indebted for much happiness. Previous chapters have shown that his happiness in the Welsh borderland stemmed from the way it provided him with unique fulfilment both as a parish priest and as a writer. It was a 'beloved place' because it had stimulated significant individual development, enabling him to be himself more fully. His joy in and gratitude for the 'beloved place' (gratitude is again important here) corresponds to the 'affections and spirit of place', which Wordsworth contrasted with the 'meagre novelties' of the picturesque. Wordsworth also spoke of the 'moral power' of particular places, by which he meant the part they played in his own development, especially in relation

to his creative powers as a poet. Vital to those powers was
solitude, a requirement Jones summed up in these terms: 'the
power to write poetry . . . depended for him on the power to
be alone.'[15]

Throughout Wordsworth's poetry there is a huge appetite for,
an obsessive need for, solitude, and the same is true of Kilvert's
diary; his seeking it out on Wen Allt and on Penllan is one sign
of it. The need had always been there for Wordsworth. Writing
of his childhood, he said: 'I was taught to feel, perhaps too
much / The self-sufficing power of Solitude' and 'I would walk
alone under the quiet stars'.[16] As a young man he had 'moods
melancholy, fits of spleen, that loved / A pensive sky, sad days,
and piping winds, / The twilight more than the dawn, autumn
than spring.'[17] Kilvert warmed to a writer with these traits and
revealed identical ones in his own work. 'I love to wander on
these soft gentle mournful autumn days, alone among the quiet
peaceful solitary meadows. . . .'[18] He did go walking in the
company of others but preferred to be solitary: 'I walked alone
along the beautiful road deeply wooded . . .' and 'wishing to
be alone and to escape the intolerable noise and tumult of the
. . . school feast I left Brading . . . and walked home by myself
perfectly happy in the delightful solitude.'[19] Two other *Diary*
passages not only express the same attitudes to landscape that
Wordsworth had but have such similar phrasing to passages
in Wordsworth's poems that it is evident that Kilvert was half-
remembering them. In the first he stressed how much he liked
solitary wanderings: 'I had the satisfaction of managing to
walk from Hay to Clyro without meeting a single person. . . . I
have a peculiar dislike to meeting people, and a peculiar liking
for a deserted road.'[20] For Wordsworth, the 'soul of that great
Power' [i.e. solitude] was epitomised by the hermit, alone in
the 'vast cathedral' of Nature, or by 'a deserted road'.[21] The
second *Diary* entry has no context of experience because
Plomer excised it and focused, understandably enough, on
these striking words: 'I like wandering about these lonely,
waste and ruined places. There dwells among them a spirit of
quiet and gentle melancholy more congenial and akin to my
own spirit than full life and gaiety and noise.'[22]

We have already seen how responsive he was to the 'presences' of 'lonely, waste and ruined places' that he experienced
in Cornwall and to the special modes of consciousness they
evoked. Wordsworth, too, had been marked since boyhood,

he said, by 'Presences of Nature in the sky / And on the
earth! Ye Visions of the hills! / And souls of lonely places!'[23]
The solitary state of shepherds and hermits was important to
Wordsworth because they lived closer to Nature than ordinary
men and therefore were more influenced by it and could be
more sensitive to it. His preoccupation with such figures is
evident from their appearance in several shorter poems and
the long poem *The Excursion*, in which he tells the life story
of the Solitary, a devout man, once a minister, who has lost
his faith, which another character, the Wanderer, attempts
to restore by explaining the source of his own. Wordsworth
intended in his long poem to 'chant in lonely places . . . the
great consummation of man and Nature', a further declaration
of his belief that his creative powers depended on communing
with Nature in solitude. The full significance of this has been
well summed up by Jones:

> Solitude is the preoccupation of his poetry . . . [but] he
> was not concerned primarily with solitude as physical
> isolation . . . its significance lies in his use of it as a token
> of a peculiarly Wordsworthian seriousness, an outward
> state of mind. . . . [It] arises from an attitude towards
> personality; from an eagerness to accept the fact that I
> am myself just because I am not anything else: to be me
> is to be always apart.[24]

It is the thesis of this chapter that Kilvert wandered the Clyro
hills and the Langley Burrell meadows with the meditative
seriousness of the Wanderer, that he too exalted the penchant
for solitude in himself as the result of insight into his own
personality and its needs as both writer and priest.

Wordsworth's communing with Nature, his sensitivity to
the beauty of natural forms — rocks, flowers, sunsets, water,
trees — led him to ask how one thing was different from
another: 'the bodily eye . . . evermore / Was searching out the
lines of difference / As they lie hid in all external forms'.[25] It
is the kind of search that involves identifying what makes
an object what it is, what might be called the 'this-ness' of
it, its essence, its singularity. Many writers and artists have
struggled to reproduce this quality of uniqueness in their
work. Van Gogh, for example, concentrated on drawing
accurately individual elements in a landscape in the belief
that if they were right the rest of the composition would also

be. He gave the example of a willow tree which, he said, had
to be drawn 'as if it were a living thing — and, after all, it
really is.'[26] But he also knew that no willow tree was exactly
like another and the large number of paintings he did of
cypress trees and sunflowers testify to his search for the exact
qualities of *particular* cypresses and *particular* sunflowers.
Kilvert's *Diary* shows him at work in the same search in the
following examples; 'Along the Eastern horizon there was
a clear deep intense glow neither scarlet nor crimson but
a mixture of both. This red glow was very narrow, almost
like a riband and it suddenly shaded off into a deep blue.'[27]
'There was the brown withered heather, the elastic turf, the
long green ride stretching over the hill like a green ribbon
between the dark heather.'[28] 'I came to Hay Bridge where
the long empty sunny white road stretched away straight
over the river to the town. . . .'[29] 'The crescent moon sparkled
through a poplar and between the twin poplar spires hung
the twin stars.'[30] 'The gorse that glowed and flamed fiery gold
down the edge of the hill contrasted sharp and splendid with
the blue world of mountain and valley which it touched.'[31]
On a morning of hoar frost, 'the oaks were still tawny green
and glittering with diamond dews, Hay Church in a tender
haze. . . . A rook shot up out of the valley and towered above
the silver mist. . . .'[32]

Kilvert's *Diary* is full of passages like these and they illustrate
the high level of success he achieved in conveying the actuality,
the 'feel' of scenes, and the consistent effort to be precise, to
capture 'the lines of difference'. It was something he learned
from Frederick Robertson, as well as from Wordsworth.
Brooke tells us that Robertson 'had . . . an exquisite perception
of natural scenery. . . . He had the artist's power of seeing,
italicising, as it were, the essential and characteristic points
of form and colour in the clouds and sky'.[33] Kilvert's over-
use of adjectives (criticised by some) can be seen as part of
the attempt at precision. The examples given above are little
cameos of landscape description. The example below is not
only one of his most sustained and powerful descriptions but
is valuable because it contains an explicit statement of what
natural forms meant to him.

The Black Mountains were invisible, being wrapped in
clouds, and I saw one very white brilliant dazzling cloud

where the mountains ought to have been. This cloud grew more white and dazzling every moment, till a clearer burst of sunlight scattered the mists and revealed the truth. This brilliant white cloud that I had been looking and wondering at was the mountain in snow. The last cloud and mist rolled away over the mountain tops and the mountains stood up in the clear blue heaven, a long rampart line of dazzling glittering snow so as no fuller on earth can white them. I stood rooted to the ground, struck with amazement and overwhelmed at the extraordinary splendour of this marvellous spectacle. I never saw anything to equal it I think, even among the high Alps. One's first involuntary thought in the presence of these magnificent sights is to lift up the heart to God and humbly thank Him for having made the earth so beautiful. An intense glare of primrose light streamed from the west deepening into rose and crimson. There was not a flake of snow anywhere but on the mountains and they stood up, the great white range rising high into the blue sky, while all the rest of the world at their feet lay ruddy rosy brown. The sudden contrast was tremendous, electrifying. I could have cried with the excitement of the overwhelming spectacle. I wanted someone to admire the sight with me. A man came whistling along the road riding upon a cart horse. I would have stopped him and drawn his attention to the mountains but I thought he would probably consider me mad. He did not seem to be the least struck by or to be taking the smallest notice of the great sight. But it seemed to me as if one might never see such a sight again.[34]

Several of the cameos quoted earlier were notable for the feeling they exhibited. This description of snow on the Black Mountains is absolutely charged with feeling. First, there is Kilvert's joy at the sheer beauty of what he sees. Then there is the shock of it that has him 'rooted to the ground', his consciousness suspended, like those in Wordsworth's poem, *Peter Bell:*

> On a fair prospect some have looked
> And felt, as I have heard them say,
> As if the moving time had been
> A thing as steadfast as the scene
> On which they gazed themselves away.[35]

There is also Kilvert's gratitude to God for vouchsafing him
the sight of the snow, which was a revelation of the divine, a
sacramental moment of the kind Keble had written about. And
finally there is excitement at the scene that brings him close to
tears. The passage illustrates perfectly the extent to which he was
not merely a viewer of landscape but was part of it. Salvesen's
comment about Wordsworth that he 'responds to landscape
rather than observes it: he feels it, almost, rather than sees it,'[36]
applies also to Kilvert.

   The carthorse rider is another link to *Peter Bell* because he
is a reminder of Wordsworth's eponymous 'hero' riding his
ass. Peter is a hawker of pottery and a hard, cruel, insensitive
man and, though he travelled through miles of natural
scenery, 'Nature could not touch his heart by lovely forms'.
'A primrose by the river's brim / A yellow primrose was to
him, / And it was nothing more.'[37] Kilvert was afraid that the
man on the cart horse would turn out to be a Peter Bell, to
whom the snow on the Black Mountains would be snow and
'nothing more'. That Kilvert had Wordsworth's lines about
the primrose in his head when he wrote this passage is given
additional credibility by his reference to 'the intense glare of
primrose light' that turned crimson in the sunset, especially as
we know that the flower had very special meaning for him. In
Kilvert's poem, *Primroses*, the flowers symbolise spring, the
renewal of warmth and life, the 'great Resurrection', and the
enduring of faith through the winter of 'cloud and storm'.
Their pale yellow colour is seen in the poem to impart 'a
warmer beauty' to other flowers that are 'too coldly pure' for
men to love. And men needed love if they were to mount to
'Heaven's gate'. It is the theme of *Peter Bell*: he is a solitary
for whom contact with Nature has not been productive of
increased sympathy, but by the end of the poem coldness and
callousness have been replaced by love.

   Wordsworth recorded the way in which his consciousness
from childhood was built up of memories of natural objects
invested with intense feelings:

> To every natural form, rock, fruit, or flower,
> Even the loose stones that cover the highway,
> I gave a moral life: I saw them feel,
> Or linked them to some feeling.

Chapter one noted that Kilvert's uncle Francis highlighted

The Black Mountains

these lines in his notebook; it may be assumed that he
brought them to the attention of his nephew. Natural objects, once 'impressed' on the memory remained there for
Wordsworth as 'presences' — as both ideas and as things,
capable of evoking or reviving emotion. It was this process
that led him to recognise 'In nature and the language of
the sense / The anchor of my purest thoughts, the nurse, /
The guide, the guardian of my heart, and soul / Of all my
moral being'.[38] Its significance was enhanced because it was
the basis of his power to write poetry, which depended on
being able to combine the freshness and intensity of a child's
experience of natural forms with the adult's ability to reflect
upon them and to probe their qualities and connections. He
expressed this last activity as the effort to find 'affinities / In
objects where no brotherhood exists / To passive minds'.[39]
In the poetic memory, sense impressions and the thoughts
aroused by them are merged into a unity so that it becomes
difficult to distinguish one from the other as the natural
forms of landscape enter the mind and take on emotional,
moral and spiritual meanings. Thereby we are given insights
into spiritual reality through simple acts of perception. Out
of these experiences emerged Wordsworth's own identity:

> I had a world about me — 'twas my own;
> I made it, for it only lived to me,
> And to the God who sees into the heart.[40]

It was the unique consciousness composed of such moments that distinguished one person from another: 'Points have we all of us within our souls / Where all stand single . . . / Is not each a memory to himself?'[41] In Wordsworth, Kilvert had a poet for whom memory was the very condition of all his work, for it was he who defined poetry as 'emotion recollected in tranquillity'; his best poems — *Tintern Abbey*, *The Prelude*, the *Immortality Ode* — have as their main theme the link between memories and his own development. It is this which makes him the most representative Romantic poet, since the whole principle of Romantic poetry is 'self-exploration and discovery'.[42]

In his attitude towards memory, as in so many other ways, Robertson was a follower of Wordsworth: 'Certain scenes,' Brooke observed, 'seem to have been engraved upon his memory. . . . Phenomena lay in his brain as pictures upon sensitive paper. . . . His wanderings in the Tyrol and Switzerland were never forgotten'.[43] We have already seen how Kilvert recognised that memories of certain places and moments took on special importance in relation to his search for his essential self, as, for example, his memory of Godrevy. Wen Allt and Penllan too were not just sources of sentimental reflection but were what Wordsworth called 'spots of time', moments of 'renovating virtue, whence . . . our minds are nourished and invisibly repaired',[44] which led to reflection and increased self-knowledge.

One place for which Kilvert had an overwhelming affection was Aberedw and its spectacular rocks, about twenty miles up the Wye from Clyro. In the following passage, dated 12 April 1875, when he was revisiting the area, he indicated his response to the beauty of the landscape:

> As we glided up the valley, sweeping round bend after bend we saw new prospects and beauties still unfolding and opening before us, distant azure mountains, green sunny bursts and dark blue wooded hollows of the nearer hills with gentle dips and dimpling swells on the hillside softly bosoming. Then suddenly came a vivid flash, dazzling with a blaze of diamond sparks thrown off as if by a firework, on the stream suddenly

The Wye Valley at Clyro

caught and tangled amongst broken rocks, swept roaring in a sheet of white foam through the narrowing
channel, or with a stately and gracious bend the river
broadened, peaceful and calm, to a majestic reach, long
and silver shining, veiled here and there by fringing,
overhanging woods and broken by the larch spires
dawning a thickening green. Then Aberedw, the Rocks
of Aberedw. What more need be, can be said?[45]

This description is one of Kilvert's best and most representative,
full of movement and physicality (the precise observation of 'the
stream suddenly caught and tangled amongst broken rocks' as
the intermittent sunlight sparkles on its surface could hardly
be surpassed). The passage builds to his arrival in the town of
Builth and to his declaration that he felt he must have Welsh
blood because he always felt 'so happy and natural' amongst
Welsh people, which was one way in which he expressed his
spiritual affinity with the place. But it is in the entry that he
wrote the following day that the full significance of Aberedw
for him is revealed:

I had not been in Builth since that memorable day to
me, May 29th, 1865, the day never to be forgotten when
I walked alone over the hills from Clyro to Builth and
first saw the Rocks of Aberedw. . . . Then every step
was through an enchanted land. I was discovering a

new country and all the world was before me. How different it is now, just ten years afterwards. But then there was a glamour and enchantment about the first view of the shining slate roofs of Builth and the bridge and the winding reaches of the broad and shining river which even now cling about the place and have never quite been dispelled. A strange fascination, a beautiful enchantment hangs over Builth and the town is magically transfigured still.

Oh, Aberedw, Aberedw. Would God I might dwell and die by thee. Oh, Aberedw, Aberedw. I never pass thy enchanted gorge and look up through the magic gateway of thy Rocks without seeming for a moment to be looking in at the gates of Paradise just left ajar. But there stands the angel with the flaming sword and I may not enter and only look in as I pass by the Gate. Yet memory enters in and brings back the old time in a clear vision and waking dream, and again I descend from the high moor's half encircling sweep and listen to the distant murmur of the river as it foams down the ravine from its home in the Green Cwm and its cradle in the hills. Once more I stand by the riverside and look up at the cliff castle towers and mark the wild roses swinging from the crag and watch the green woods waving and shimmering with a twinkling dazzle as they rustle in the breeze and shining of the summer afternoon, while here and there a grey crag peeps from among the tufted trees. And once again I hear the merry voices and laughter of the children as they clamber down the cliff path among the bushes.[46]

Kilvert had the tendency that most people have to associate places with particular events and people. He had sat in Clifton with his cousin, Adelaide Cholmeley, 'looking down upon the Suspension Bridge talking of Kathleen Mavourneen' (his name for his lover Katharine Heanley). 'I shall never be able to see the Suspension Bridge from the Cliff without thinking of Kathleen. The Bridge, the river at low tide, the steep lofty Cliffs, and the green-fringed dingles and slopes of Nightingale Valley are now inextricably bound up with thoughts of her.'[47] The passage gives a hint, however, of the deeper meanings that landscape held for him because the phrase 'steep lofty Cliffs' is from Wordsworth's *Tintern Abbey*, the poem which contains the most complete and perfect account of the role of memory in relation to landscape. (Tintern Abbey was sanctified for Kilvert by the knowledge – obtained from Brooke's *Life* – that Robertson had visited it by moonlight in summer 1837.) The phrase 'steep and lofty cliffs' occurs in the poet's description of the banks of the Wye at Tintern seen again after an interval of five years.

There had been a gap of time for Kilvert between his first visit to Aberedw and the return one in April 1875 and he too used the latter occasion to dwell upon the effects of landscape on him and the way in which response to it was a means of measuring change within himself. He used the same phraseology that Wordsworth had used to indicate contrast between then and now: 'Once again / Do I behold these steep and lofty cliffs. . . . Once again I see / These hedgerows . . .' wrote Wordsworth, a pattern repeated by Kilvert: 'Once more I stand by the riverside. . . . Once again I hear the merry voices. . . .' He described the state of his consciousness on 29 May 1865 (shortly after his arrival in Clyro), 'the day never to be forgotten' when 'every step was through an enchanted land'. Noticeably, images of a magical state of consciousness multiply: 'I was discovering a new country . . . there was glamour and excitement about the first view . . . a strange fascination, a beautiful enchantment . . . enchanted gorge . . . magic gateway. . . .' What he was seeking to convey here is the Romantic conception of creativity, of the imagination as the vital part of the individual self. Aberedw had released his creativity and he knew it. His mind had entered into a special relationship with the Welsh borderland in exactly the same way as Wordsworth said his had with Grasmere and the Lakes in *The Prelude*. For both men, the coming together of mind and landscape had marked the beginning of a journey into themselves, into their own individuality. To writers in the Romantic tradition all creativity is an aspect of the self and the key to creativity lies in the relationship between the self and the larger world outside it. Experience is the means of achieving full individuality, full identity.[48]

Clyro and its region had been the means of extending Kilvert's mind and soul as he himself acknowledged when he had been away from it for only six weeks: 'I have a sort of lingering longing for the old country and its beauty and romance'.[49] The magical

beauty of Aberedw was the symbol of the 'old country'. His
reference to its 'romance' is further confirmation that he saw it
as the source of his creativity, the 'enchanted land' of Romantic
poetry. That his mind was thoroughly permeated during the
writing of the second Aberedw passage by recollections of
particular Romantic poems is clear from what has already been
said of its links to Wordsworth's *Tintern Abbey*. The prevailing
tone of melancholy comes chiefly, however, from Keats's *Ode
to a Nightingale*, in which, as he listened to the bird's song, he
wished he could die and escape from the world of human
suffering to become identified totally with its ecstatic music.
Kilvert sought the same dissolution, paradoxically losing his
identity to achieve a finer one: 'Would God I might dwell and
die by thee', meaning by Aberedw's 'enchanted gorge'. In the
penultimate stanza of his *Ode*, Keats had expressed his sense
of the enchanted land of the poetic imagination, symbolised
by the perfection of the nightingale's singing. Its voice 'hath /
Charm'd magic casements, opening on the foam / Of perilous
seas, in faery lands forlorn'. However, the final stanza brings
in a note of sadness: 'Forlorn! the very word is like a bell / To
toll me back from thee to my sole self'. The poet then loses
his oneness with the nightingale in an ideal, timeless universe
and the memory of its 'plaintive anthem' fades and he asks
sadly 'Was it a vision, or a waking dream? / Fled is that music:
— do I wake or sleep?' Kilvert's memory is, however, capable
of bringing back 'the old time' in 'a clear vision and waking
dream', though the sadness persists because he has lost the
self that he once had. He could no longer enter the 'magic
gateway' of Aberedw's Rocks, his way barred by 'the angel
with the flaming sword', an allusion to Genesis 3.24, which
tells of the driving of Adam and Eve from Eden by 'cherubim
and a flaming sword', after the eating of the forbidden fruit.
George Fox had alluded to this Biblical passage in his *Journal*
(volume I) with the same emphases and the same reverential,
ecstatic feeling as in Kilvert's *Diary* entry:

> Now was I come up in spirit through the flaming sword,
> into the paradise of God. All things were new. . . . I knew
> nothing but pureness, innocency and righteousness . . .
> so that I was come up to the state of Adam, which he
> was in before he fell.

Another part of the *Diary* passage's melancholy stems from

Tintern Abbey. Kilvert was as thankful as Wordsworth was in that poem for what memories of 'beauteous forms' had meant in the years between first seeing them and now. For Wordsworth, revisiting them was nevertheless tinged with 'a sad perplexity' associated with painful events in the interim. However, just as the moment of sadness and of loss for the poet is quickly banished, powerless to deprive the Wye of its capacity to soothe and energise, so for Kilvert the 'shining river' still had 'an enchantment . . . never quite . . . dispelled'. There is a further layer of associations drawn from Romantic poetry in the Aberedw passage that should be noted. In Kilvert's reference to 'a vision and waking dream' there are echoes of 'a Vision in a dream', the words Coleridge used to describe *Kubla Khan,* and Kilvert's 'enchanted gorge' is a reminder of the 'romantic chasm' in Coleridge's poem. We recall too the young man at the end of that poem who, like Kilvert and Adam, had fed on 'the milk of Paradise'. In *Kubla Khan,* as in Kilvert's Aberedw, a river appears as the symbol of poetic energy, which yields deeper insight into the self. Coleridge's wild 'sacred river', flowing in 'caves measureless to man', corresponds to the Wye, which 'foams down the ravine from its home in the Green Cwm', giving way at last, as the river of *Kubla Khan* does, to a mood of calm, 'when the evening shadows lie long and still across the broad reaches of the river' (surely one of Kilvert's loveliest phrases). The Wye may seem too sedate a river to stand beside Coleridge's but it is worth noting that in his poem, *The Rocks of Aberedw,* Kilvert wrote of hearing 'the flashing river rave / Through the Rocks of Aberedw', which shows that he thought of it in terms of power and energy. This is true also of the first Aberedw passage quoted above where the river is 'roaring' through a 'narrowing channel'.

Kilvert's preoccupation with memories of his earliest experiences is most visible in that portion of the *Diary* which covers the period 1872-6 when Clyro was behind him and he was again serving as his father's curate in Langley Burrell. It might be expected that living in the region where he had grown up, his attention would centre on people and places that were significant then but it could well be the case that, removed from the 'enchanted land' of Clyro and with a consequent diminution of his creative powers, he filled the void as far as his thinking, feeling and writing were concerned, with looking back. In the many entries which nostalgically trace his beginnings, he was perhaps looking for sparks that might re-ignite the imaginative intensity symbolised by Aberedw. His visit to the village of Lanhill, where he had lived briefly, took place in fact in his Christmas holiday 1872 before he left Clyro but it typifies the pattern characterising later entries. 'After dinner I went to see old Jacob Smith. . . . We talked over the old times and the old people and we had many ancient memories in common.'[50] Something of the fascination that time had for him is seen in the fact that the 'ancient memories' could not have been more than seven to eight years old. Another re-visit to Lanhill in 1875 is much more revealing of the mood of intensity that frequently surrounded moments of return to his personal past.

> As I came down from the hill into the valley across the golden meadows and along the flower-scented hedges a great wave of emotion and happiness stirred and rose up within me. I know not why I was so happy, nor what I was expecting, but I was in a delirium of joy, it was one of the supreme few moments of existence, a deep delicious draught from the strong sweet cup of life. It came unsought, unbidden, at the meadow stile, it was one of the flowers of happiness scattered for us and found unexpectedly by the wayside of life. It came silently, suddenly, and it went as it came, but it left a long lingering glow and glory behind as it faded slowly like a gorgeous sunset, and I shall ever remember the place and the time in which such great happiness fell upon me.[51]

The passage is as puzzling to the reader as the experience was to Kilvert since the exact source of the 'delirium of joy' is not made clear. It would have helped to have had the whole of the original entry — Plomer cut it, adding 'The walk is described at length'. It is possible that a particular aspect of the landscape he saw stimulated his joy but this seems unlikely because some reference to it would have occurred in the part of the entry that has survived. Furthermore, he makes it clear that his feeling could not be explained in that way. The explanation seems to lie in the experiences Wordsworth said he first had as a boy of ten when he 'held unconscious intercourse with beauty / Old as creation, drinking in a pure organic pleasure',

a spontaneous response not linked to any external object. It
was rather a response of the senses simply to beauty:

> Those hallowed and pure motions of the sense;
> . . . that calm delight . . .
> Which . . . surely must belong
> To those first-born affinities that fit
> Our new existence to existing things,
> And in our dawn of being, constitute
> The bond of union between life and joy.[52]

The 'first-born affinities' are the child's unselfconscious reactions to external Nature that are unaccompanied by reflection.
Two other aspects of the Lanhill entry require comment.
The first is Kilvert's effort to convey his joy by comparing
it to a 'gorgeous sunset'. He was particularly receptive, as
Wordsworth was, to sky scenes — sunsets, cloud patterns and
movements, sunrises, moon and stars.[53] The second notable
aspect is the insistence (found in the Cornish Godrevy entry
and in entries considered later) that the special moment would
never be forgotten.

The entry's concern with continuity of experience is to be
found in a whole sequence of entries that will eventually lead
us to his almost obsessive attempt to pin down the mystery of
his own self, how it began, in what experiences and memories
it could most clearly be seen to reside. He used to trace out:

> the ancient footpaths and mossy overgrown stiles
> between farm and hamlet, village and town, musing
> of the many feet that have trodden these ancient and
> now well nigh deserted and almost forgotten ways and
> walking in the footsteps of the generations that have
> gone before. . . .[54]

Such footpaths represented some of man's oldest marks upon
the landscape and Kilvert's awareness of the fact is tinged
with reverence, so that his entry becomes a mini-meditation in
which remembering the dead by walking in their ways played
a part.

The very strong emphasis here and in the Lanhill entries on
preserving the continuity of experience, its connectedness, is
also found in another which tells of his visit to the old Manor
House, home of the Colemans, his mother's family, though
it was let then by his uncle Walter to a tenant. In two visits

on succeeding days, Kilvert kept returning to the idea of
generations of pretty girls (for him they *had* to be pretty ones)
sitting at the house's mullioned windows. What is striking
about the entries is that he imagined the girls' spirits 'looking
out at us their descendants', as though the continuity was
unbroken,[55] very much with the emphasis on remembering the
dead by maintaining sympathetic contact with them that was
examined in chapter one. To encounter breaks in the line of
experience linking him to his past produced feelings of misery
and even terror. Revisiting Oxford in May 1874:

> All was as usual, the copper beech still spread a purple
> gloom in the corner . . . , the fabric of the college was
> unchanged. . . . But all else was altered, a change had
> come over the spirit of the dream.

(This last phrase had a particular importance for him as a later
chapter will show.)

> The familiar friendly faces had all vanished. . . . One or
> two of the College servants remembered my face still,
> almost all had forgotten my name. . . . I felt like a spirit
> revisiting the scenes of its earthly existence and finding
> itself strange, unfamiliar, unwanted.[56]

Here he has become one of the disembodied dead, a lonely,
wandering spirit haunting the landscape it once knew and
seeking sympathy, but shut out from others' remembrance. His
sense of self here was so undermined that he felt negated, without
identity.[57] There was a slight anxiety when he accompanied his
mother in October 1872 to Allington, from where his birthplace
of Hardenhuish was visible, because he missed seeing people
he had known as a child and there were 'new strange faces at
all the old familiar cottage doors'. However, the unchanged
landscape was reassuring — 'the dear old Rectory, the white
house on the hill among the elms where we were all born.'[58]

In Kilvert's time, for most ordinary folk, the place where
one was born and died was usually the same, a circumstance
that gave extra emotional force to meditations in churchyards.
Behind headstones' bare summary of a person's life lay a long
unbroken chain of days all lived in the same location. It was
a notion which Kilvert, and others who loved 'musing' among
gravestones, found satisfying because it not only reinforced
the sense of community but it also meant that 'home' was

a repository of an even richer store of memories. On Easter Sunday 1876 when Kilvert wrote his 'elegy' in Langley Burrell churchyard, he was drawing on an eighteenth-century tradition in which, to use Salvesen's words, 'time is felt to be a condition of one's whole existence'.[59] Gray's *Elegy Written in a Country Churchyard* was central to this tradition and Legh Richmond's *Annals of the Poor* derived from it (he owed his themes and his title to it). When Kilvert wrote in his elegy 'There they lay, squire and peasant, landlord and labourer . . . crumbling to their common clay', he was paraphrasing Legh Richmond's words in *The Dairyman's Daughter*: 'There the once famed ancestors of the rich, and the less known forefathers of the poor, lay mingling their dust together',[60] just as Richmond was paraphrasing Gray's *Elegy*. The idea that rich and poor would find the same quietus in death was a main theme of Gray's poem. He also insisted that it was wrong of the rich and proud 'to impute to [the poor] the fault / If Mem'ry o'er their Tomb no Trophies raised', and he paid tribute to the 'useful toil . . . homely joys . . . the short and simple annals of the poor'.[61] It was in order to compensate the poor for their lack of memorials that Gray wrote his *Elegy*, Richmond his *Annals of the Poor*, Wordsworth his *Lyrical Ballads*, Kilvert his *Diary* and his poem *Honest Work*.

Kilvert made sure that he remembered children, another vulnerable group, in 'the secret drawer' in his desk where he kept 'the lock of our dear Emmeline's hair, with my other such memorials'. The hair was used both to commemorate a child who meant a great deal to him (she was the daughter of his close friend, David Vaughan, Vicar of Newchurch) and to measure the passage of time: 'It seems but yesterday since I saw the beautiful golden-haired child for the first time'.[62] Remembering loved ones, especially dead ones, was a duty which he did his best to observe faithfully; forgetting them produced sharp grief and guilt. 'Today I found in a book a red silk handkerchief worked with the words "Forget me not", and I am sorry to say that I have entirely forgotten who gave it to me. One of my many lovers no doubt.'[63] 'Lovers' in this context meant child sweethearts, of which he had many. The anguish he felt over forgetting a 'lover' was much greater in the entry for 4 September 1874. That night as he sat reading at home in Langley Burrell, from his book fell a bookmark, backed with a purple ribbon on which a book shape was worked with 'the short sweet simple prayer "Forget me not". It was a gift from a child sweetheart. But from which? I

gazed at the words conscience-stricken, "Forget me not". And
I had forgotten. "Forget me not. Forget me not" besought an
imploring voice. There was a sweet and gentle reproach in
its tone'. And then he imagined the child, 'with fair head and
pure eyes' dutifully stitching the marker as 'a labour of love',
finishing it and saying 'I will send it tomorrow and he will
not forget'. Kilvert commented finally 'Oh the fickleness and
forgetfulness of men and the faithfulness of women'. The length
of the entry (it becomes a meditation) and its poignancy indicate
how important the business of forgetting was for him: it was to
break the circle of sympathies. It is there in entries dealing with
reunions with the child lovers Lizzie Harris and Selina Williams
in April 1876. After kissing Lizzie's 'pale sweet lovely face once
more' — his link with the past — comes his anxious questioning
'do you remember me? Do you love me?' The link with Selina's
and his past is his memory of the 'grand romp I had with her
once . . . when she was a little child' and he expressed the hope
'perhaps she thought of it too'.[64]

Just as being forgotten was a disturbing sign that one was
loved no longer, so being remembered was confirmation that
one was the object of enduring love. An element in his grief for
lovers who had been forgotten was concern that he too would
be forgotten by those who claimed to love him. This is very
evident in the entry for 4 October 1873 when he was visiting his
Langley Burrell parishioner Joseph Hatherell and was driven to
recall Jane Hatherell, who died in childhood:

> I seemed to be sitting once more by the bedside of the
> suffering girl . . . and now she sleeps beneath the elm in
> Langley churchyard. . . . I felt an inexpressible longing
> to see her again and speak to her. . . . She loved me I
> believe as few have ever loved. Perhaps she loves me
> now. I hope she does. I think she does. I think she still
> remembers the old days.

He needed to believe that she could retain, even after death, a
memory of him and could vouch for his love and kindness in the
court of eternity. His own memory could furnish proof that he
had not missed out on the best experience that life on earth could
offer: 'Well. I have lived and I have been loved, and no one can
take this from me.'[65] The capacity to give and receive love was
obviously the very core of the moral sentiments. However, the
fear was never far away that he would be forgotten by both his

child lovers and his adult ones, which was tantamount to never having been loved by them at all. As the train took him away from Cornwall and Emma Hockin, his agony was epitomised in his prayer 'Forget me not, oh, forget me not'.[66] It was to show that he remembered his lover, Ettie Meredith Brown, that he visited her house in Nonsuch at a time when his love affair with her had fallen apart. He had the consolation of knowing that the landscape near her home would always be there and that his memory of it would forever be entwined with his lost love. When their separation was finally made irrevocable, he wrote 'But oh, I hope she will not quite forget me'.[67]

During his last two years he experienced a series of small mysterious illnesses, probably indicative of depression resulting from the failure of several relationships. In March 1878, he had an illness that could be clearly defined — congestion of the lungs — and it gave him anxiety that his own death was imminent. On 6 March, in spite of feeling better, he wrote: 'How calm, bright, peaceful and homelike is the dear old home. How long will it last? How long will it be "home"? So going forward.'[68] The implication of the last sentence is obscure but it seems to express his awareness of life as a journey with the accompanying idea on this occasion that the progress of his developing self could be suddenly and fatally interrupted. 'Home' was of course the way he and other Evangelicals envisaged the landscape of eternity, the home that was superior to any earthly one, to which all who were 'strangers and pilgrims' on earth aspired. Although he was much attached to the home of Langley Burrell that he referred to when death threatened, the earthly home that mattered most was the one where he was born and it is the subject of the most astonishing *Diary* entries celebrating the power of memory in establishing his sense of identity. First, we have the place evoked by a memory characteristically couched in clear and strong sense impressions:

> As I went across the fields . . . and looked back up at the dear old white house upon the hill, backed by the dark mass of the trees . . . and overtowered by the cupola of the bright green ivied church, and saw the brown and grey farm buildings . . . at the foot of the hill, my heart rose up and went out towards my old house, and the tears came into my eyes as a thousand sweet and happy memories swept across my soul.[69]

It is the kind of remembering that occurs again and again in Wordsworth — specific natural objects associated with deeply personal emotions. In *The Prelude* he wrote of 'scenes so bright / . . . Habitually dear, and all their forms / And changeful colours by invisible links / Were fastened to the affections.'[70]

In the next three entries in which Kilvert extolled the meaning of the landscape of home for him, memory can be seen working in the same strongly sensuous way, chiefly through the visual sense. He was conducting a baptism at Hardenhuish Church one hot June afternoon and

> A hundred sweet memories stirred within me at the old familiar place and scene. There towered the elms as of old round my birthplace and the church of my baptism. There lay the wide fair plain smiling in the summer afternoon sunshine, as I used to see it from the nursery window. . . . Below me at the foot of the hill rose the brown rough tiled roofs of the old grey farmhouse. . . .[71]

The intense feeling inherent in these memories indicates that they represented for him the 'first-born affinities' of which Wordsworth had written. It is evident that in passages like these something more than sentimental recollection of the past is involved. Kilvert seems to be fascinated by the relationship between memory and landscape, and to be questioning the nature of the act of perception in which he is involved. The repetition of 'there' and 'there' and the insistent focusing on physical details remembered from the past emphasises not only the unchanging quality of the landscape, but also evokes a mystical feeling for the relation between time passing and his individual awareness of it. He underlined the time that had gone by with a reference to 'my own Christening . . . more than five-and-thirty years ago'. The signs of the external world remain unchanged exactly as he remembered them, the elms towering 'as of old', the 'wide fair plain . . . as I used to see it' but they are inside him at the same time as memories that now have powerful emotional and moral and spiritual associations.

A number of Wordsworth critics have sought to explain this phenomenon of the merging of the objective and the subjective, the outer landscape and the inner landscape of the mind. Jones wrote of Wordsworth in *Tintern Abbey* addressing the question of the spiritual presence of natural forms enduring through physical absence, of his surveying the landscape of the Wye, comparing it with memories of the same landscape experienced five years earlier, and becoming aware of a third landscape, that of inner consciousness, which provides insight into 'the life of things', i.e. their inner reality.[72] Salvesen referred to the 'sense of fusion' in *Tintern Abbey*, 'a state of uncertainty between inner and outer worlds' so that when Wordsworth looked at the cliffs of the Wye ('Once again / Do I behold these cliffs . . .'), he described them 'in what is an act of memory as much as an act of observation'. The cliffs, having impressed themselves on his mind, in the past, in memory, as well as at that moment, led him to transfer that impression and the thoughts evoked by it, to the whole scene. Thought and image are as one.[73] The essence of the process is contained in this account of the way Wordsworth's Wanderer looked at landscape:

> his spirit drank
> The spectacle: sensation, soul, and form,
> All melted into him; they swallowed up
> His animal being; in them did he live,
> And by them did he live; they were his life.[74]

Abrams was seeking to convey the sense of passages like these in Wordsworth when he wrote: 'Natural objects enter, flow, are received and sink down into the mind, while the mind dwells in, feeds on, drinks, holds intercourse with, and weaves, intertwines, fastens and binds itself to external objects, until the two integrate as one.'[75] This, wrote Abrams, is the 'marriage between mind and Nature', an emphasis found in Hartman, who said that what interested Wordsworth was the reality of the relation between Nature and the mind, a reality whose essence depended on recognising that the past is not simply a body of experience but also the spirit which permeates it.[76]

A further aspect of what memory and landscape meant for Kilvert is illustrated by reference to Cowper, known as the 'laureate' of Evangelicalism.[77] He knew Cowper's long poem, *The Task*, which describes how 'village bells / . . . With easy force opens all the cells / Where memory slept', enabling him 'in a few short moments [to] retrace / The windings of my way through many years'.[78] In addition to the idea of identity composed of memories, Cowper puts forward the notion of memory as a form of emotional/spiritual ownership in phrasing very similar to that used by Kilvert when describing

Hardenhuish. Writing of a lover of Nature's natural forms, Cowper asked:

> Are they not his by a peculiar right.
> And by an emphasis of interest his,
> Whose eye they filled with tears of holy joy,
> Whose heart with praise, and whose exalted mind
> With worthy thought. . . ?[79]

When Kilvert wanted to assert how much and in what way the landscape of his home had become part of his consciousness, he wrote:

> Sweet Harden Ewyas. My Harden Ewyas. Mine and mine
> by a higher right than the bare possession of houses and
> fields, mine by the ownership of the spirit, mine by an
> inalienable right, my birthplace. Sweet Harden Ewyas,
> on the lone hillside my heart rose up and stretched out
> her hands to thee with a cry of unspeakable love. My
> old home, mine own dear home.[80]

There is also an unmistakable echo here of that central Victorian statement on memory, Tennyson's *In Memoriam*, perhaps Kilvert's favourite poem (he called it his 'beloved *In Memoriam*'). Tennyson referred in section 128 to his dead friend Arthur Hallam as his 'dear heavenly friend that canst not die, / Mine, mine, for ever, ever mine', and attributed to his death his own ability to believe that there was a heaven beyond earth, 'a dream of good' that enhanced his view of mortal life. It is reasonable to suppose that what *In Memoriam* had to say about memory and the search for identity Kilvert found acceptable. The panic that he experienced at the idea of loss of identity, of ceasing to have any significance as an individual, is mirrored in Tennyson's poem. Just as Kilvert feared that being forgotten by a loved one made one nothing, so for Tennyson, Hallam's death resulted not only in the loss of his sense of himself, but of any faith in a meaningful universe: 'Behold, we know not anything', he wrote, and found that faith in God was impossible when it was clear that Nature is 'So careless of the single life.' He was left in the situation of the helpless infant: 'but what am I? / An infant crying in the night'.[81]

The last Hardenhuish entry to be examined includes the orthodox strains of piety which characterise the Cowper passage, plus all the other themes to be found in the *Diary*

passages focused on earlier. Again a visit to Lanhill and meetings with old cottagers from there and Hardenhuish had set
Kilvert's mind on the past: 'How pleasant and familiar all
the old Lanhill faces did look!' Hardenhuish House was the
former home of the Clutterbuck family, friends and patrons of
the Kilverts since their Widcombe days, and the inhabitant of
its lodge told Kilvert of the regret locally that the Clutterbucks'
tenure of the estate was broken: 'All the cry seems to be for the
old family, the beloved and honoured family, . . . to come back
to their own again.' At dusk, Kilvert left the lodge 'and went
up the familiar hill past the farm at its foot and the Church
and the Rectory, my own sweet birth-place on its brow. . . .'
And suddenly he was struck by the numbing feeling that his
continuity in the village was broken as was the Clutterbucks'
and the moment was recorded in the words he used on his
return to Wadham College, where the memory of him had
also faded: 'I felt like a spirit revisiting and wandering about
the old haunts and scenes of its mortal existence. . . . Harden
Ewyas, strangers dwell in thy houses and walk in thy gardens
and the old familiar faces have passed away.'[82] Tennyson had
written, in *In Memoriam*, of his pain when the rectory he had
known since childhood was taken over by another family:

> We leave the well-beloved place
>   Where first we gazed upon the sky;
>   The roofs that heard our earliest cry
> Will shelter one of stranger race.
>
>   And year by year the landscape grows
> Familiar to the stranger's child. . . .
>   And year by year our memory fades
> From all the circle of the hills.[83]

In Tennyson's account of the moment, he too has a spirit
wandering the place it has loved in its mortal life.

Kilvert found consolation for being dispossessed of the
physical home in the continuity that resided in memories of
landscape forms — 'the lights at the Folly' shining cheerfully
across Hardenhuish Park, 'the rooks and jackdaws [that] rustled
and flapped . . . in the tops of trees'. Although strangers now
lived in the home where he was born, he was able to assert
the 'ownership of the spirit' which, in the Cowperesque entry,
transcended all other forms of ownership: the knowledge that

the place had entered into him and become part of his identity — 'but still I am there and thou art mine'. However, from
what follows it is clear that he was also struggling once again
to express his awareness of the strange fusion of mind and
landscape:

> The house remains the white house on the hill where I
> was born, there is the ivied Church across the lane to
> which I was first carried to be baptized, there are the
> meadows and gardens where I first played and gathered
> flowers. Each field and hill and bank has its own bright
> memories and its own sweet story.

He was seeing familiar features of the scene as external things but
the emotion-laden memories that he was recalling at the same
time were so strong that the two kinds of knowing became one.
The result is that the natural forms took on dream-like qualities,
standing out with a strange intensity[84] while he gazed at them
as though in a hypnotic trance or a waking dream: 'The house
remains the white house on the hill . . . there is the ivied Church
. . . there are the meadows and gardens. . . .' In the following
entry, he showed a conscious awareness of the way in which
his perception imparted to the objects in the scene a glowing
quality often encountered in dreams:

> How quiet and sunny and lovely the village was this
> evening as I went to the Vicarage to dinner. There was
> not a person in the roads or moving anywhere. The
> only living creature I saw was a dog. An intense feeling
> and perception of the extraordinary beauty of the place
> grew upon me in the silence as I passed through the
> still sunny churchyard and saw the mountains through
> the trees rising over the school, and looked back at the
> church and the churchyard through the green arches of
> the wych elms. Then the glowing roses of the Vicarage
> lawn and the blue mountains beyond broken by the
> dark Castle Clump.[85]

That Kilvert was doing more in the last Hardenhuish entry
than indulge in a typically sentimental Victorian celebration
of 'home' is evident from the fact that though there is strong
feeling in the writing, it does not centre on recollection of
people and events. In fact, the absence of reference to parents or
siblings is remarkable; only his nurse is mentioned. The focus

is rather on the landscape's physical features and his actual experiencing of memories of them. Throughout his *Diary*, he steadily declined to give any details of his childhood days at Hardenhuish (it seems very unlikely that Plomer would have cut them), even though he had several entries in which such recollections would have been natural. It is one more of the Kilvert stories that somehow could not be told.

He did have a characteristically Evangelical conception of 'home' — the place of sacred domestic affections and of piety — but none of that appears in this or any of the other Hardenhuish entries. The focus is exclusively on landscape and on the agency of memory in relation to it. The words Salvesen used to describe what landscape meant to Wordsworth are appropriate to sum up what is happening in this *Diary* passage and others considered in this chapter: 'Nature is an idea, continuously embodied and recalled both in his native landscape and in his own continuing and feeling self — a state of perfection'.[86] One of Kilvert's other main guides to the operation of memory — Legh Richmond — had emphasised its tendency to form idealised pictures of past scenes:

> Memory retraces past events, and restores an ideal reality to scenes which are gone by for ever. They live again in revived imagery, and we seem to hear and see with renewed emotions what we heard and saw at a former period.[87]

The emotional tone of Kilvert's recollections is consistently positive: 'dear old Hardenhuish ... sweet story ... sweet memories ... mine own dear home ... a thousand sweet and happy memories. . . .' The emphasis is on one single fact — that Hardenhuish was the place of his birth, as though he was concerned with the problem facing all autobiographers of finding his beginning, of 're-experiencing it and re-presenting it'.[88] Religious overtones are present towards the end of this last celebration of Hardenhuish but here again the emphasis is on the importance of remembering, or rather on not forgetting, which recalls Kilvert's fear of suffering oblivion:

> God be very gracious and merciful and lift up the light of His countenance upon thee my sweet birthplace and the dear house of my childhood. I have ever loved thee and ever shall until my heart die. If I forget thee let

my right hand forget her cunning. Yea, let my tongue
cleave unto the roof of my mouth if I prefer not Harden
Ewyas in my mirth.

Kilvert was paraphrasing two sources here. The first sentence
(up to 'upon thee') is from Numbers 6.24 and is part of the
blessing that God instructed Moses to give to the Israelites.
What follows is from Psalm 137, which begins 'By the waters of
Babylon we sat down and wept when we remembered thee, O
Sion', referring to the Israelites' wanderings and their difficulty
in retaining a memory of their home in a strange land.

Kilvert could see a link between himself and the Israelites,
partly because he was 'a pilgrim and a stranger' in search of
a home but, importantly, also because he knew that, having
entered into a special relationship with the landscape of the
Wye, he would be seriously diminished when he was separated
from it. The enchanted dream landscape of Aberedw was the
source of his moral sympathy, of his creativity, the means to
his self-fulfilment, and he so mourned its loss when he had to
leave it that he pictured himself as an exile:

> Exiled, in distant lands I seem
> Happy once more to walk in dream
> Through sweeping cloud and sunny gleam,
> By moor and vale and lake and stream,
> To the Rocks of Aber Edw. . . .
>
> Oh! may once more these pilgrim feet
> Tread those dear hills, these eyes still greet
> Love-yearning those twin valleys sweet,
> Within whose breast the waters meet
> By the Rocks of Aber Edw.[89]

Kilvert's 'love-yearning' stemmed from his awareness that
the borderland and its people had provided him with a home
which enabled him to grow as both writer and priest, and his
poem is a declaration that he would never forget the debt he
owed to its shaping power.

Memory was of huge importance to him because both
Evangelicalism and Romanticism assured him that it was the
key to his personal past and future development. Memories
were things to be treasured, reflected on and explored; they
were not only an accumulation of past experiences but were
themselves experiences, a way of feeling and responding to

life, and of being linked to others in love and sympathy. Kilvert saw a continuity between physical/emotional experiences and the mark they left on memory. Landscapes were a significant part of his past, distilled in memory. The anxiety he showed over breaks in continuity of memory may have been in part a consequence of the Evangelical desire to account for every day. It was also connected to his belief in love as the pre-eminent Christian virtue so that forgetting, or being forgotten by, a loved one was seen as a fall from grace. He had learnt from Wordsworth to see God in Nature, especially in the wilder landscapes of Radnorshire. Cut off from his best source of creative power, the focus of his writing shifted (when he was living once more in Wiltshire) to his childhood. This too was an area of experience in which Wordsworth's influence was particularly strong and it forms the subject of a later chapter. In the series of *Diary* entries dealing with his birthplace, Kilvert explored his earliest memories in an effort to discover the roots of his identity, showing the same curiosity that Wordsworth had shown in the process by which landscapes become part of individual consciousness.

Chapter 6
The Very Culture of the Feelings[1]

He that saith he abideth in Him ought himself so to
walk, even as He walked.

[I St John]

As we journey on our pilgrimage
Through this vast wilderness of mortal life
We cross the path of many travellers,
And stand a single moment face to face.
[Francis Kilvert, *The Pilgrimage*]

Poetry is passion: it is the history or science of feelings.
[William Wordsworth, *Preface* to the *Lyrical Ballads*;
note on *The Thorn*]

Romanticism is spilt religion.
[T.E. Hulme, *Speculations*.
Essays on Humanism and the Philosophy of Art]

Landscape inspires devotion.
[Legh Richmond, *The Young Cottager*]

────────

Extending sympathy to others was one strand of Kilvert's poem,
The Pilgrimage, which he believed had close correspondence
with his mother's view of life because he wrote it especially
for her birthday on 12 May 1870, devoting a good deal of time
and effort to it to ensure it was right.[2] The following passage
expresses the main theme of the poem:

We have come
Out of the spaces of Eternity,
The immeasurable vast, to meet each other,
Brought thither by the Hand and Thought of God,

> Who loves, thinks, cares for each, and painfully
> Plans every little incident of life
> For our advantage.

The purpose of these divinely arranged meetings was that of 'bringing comfort and sweet sympathy / To those that mourn', the opportunity 'to bind up broken hearts', a reference to Cowper's ideal clergyman in *The Task* (Book I, 372), who 'binds the broken heart'. Kilvert's lines obviously have particular relevance to the minister's role — extension of sympathy to bereaved parishioners — but, as this chapter shows, Kilvert was also thinking of a general circulation of sympathies, of meeting others in the spirit of shared humanity that so moved him in St Paul's as the great congregation sang their hearts out. Other lines from *The Pilgrimage* show what he had in mind: 'for if / Two souls have touched, though 'twere but for a moment — / It is the will of God. . . .' This transitory touching of souls was important, but more lasting relationships were intended when he wrote, quoting Robertson, of 'how hearts are linked to hearts by God'.

The basic scenario of *The Pilgrimage* is life envisaged as a series of encounters in which a person could show himself a true Christian by loving his neighbour as himself. Central to it is the life-as-a-journey image but the journey is essentially one that leads into the community, for it is there, in relationship with other people, that the individual's moral worth will be tested. Further consideration is given in this chapter to *Kilvert's Diary* as a record of physical and spiritual travelling, particularly among the people of his Welsh borderland parish of Clyro. This aspect of the *Diary* has been opened up in a fruitful way by Dunham in an essay that examined the relationship between landscape and identity.[3] He noted the way in which 'walking through the Clyro landscape and writing about his experiences in journal form, Kilvert effected an unfolding and interweaving of different narratives of self and landscape. . . .' The emphasis here on *walking* is notable because it links with aspects of his background that highlighted walking. The sense of 'walk' as Christian pilgrimage was a commonplace of the religious tradition in which he was raised but no doubt had particular meaning to him. He himself adopted as his family motto the notion of pilgrimage, with all its overtones of challenge and discipline. Walking was also something he took pride in, partly because his coach-builder grandfather excelled in it and partly because his guides to landscape as a source of spiritual enrichment – Cowper, Legh Richmond, Warner, Robertson, Howitt and Wordsworth – had insisted that the only way to experience it was on foot.

In a highly perceptive insight, Dunham observed that 'a strong relationship existed between Kilvert's movement and his writing . . . the importance of this relationship cannot be overstated.' This enquiry into Kilvert and landscape has so far laid emphasis, inter alia, on his awareness of landscape as a significant factor in the development of his identity. This is also Dunham's understanding vis à vis the diarist: Kilvert set out to create in his writing 'a desired self-identity' through his experience of landscape. 'In this sense, the diary emerges as a structured narrative of self and landscape,' one that enabled him both to be true to landscape writers he admired and to the religious goal of self-improvement. (His experiencing of the mutuality of kind acts, cited earlier, exemplified how this self-improvement could proceed.) Both objectives were subsumed in what Dunham referred to as 'a unifying purpose to [Kilvert's] movement and his writing: namely, to experience and record particular moments of encounter with the Clyro countryside.' The focus of the *Diary* is 'the careful delineation of *moments* of encounter with landscapes and figures.' Dunham underlined 'moments' because he wanted to show that Kilvert's encounters were transient, fluid, unexpected, so that 'he was continually engaged in the struggle to produce them. . . . It is this that makes him such an effective writer of landscape and identity.' Dunham stressed that this was a characteristically Romantic stance towards experience and writing.

In this chapter, *Diary* passages are examined in which Kilvert can be seen placing himself in relation to other people and, in the process, effecting exploration both of his own identity and of theirs. To Langan, the process is central to Romanticism and is exemplified most characteristically by Wordsworth, who indicated that his aim in the *Lyrical Ballads* was to delineate 'The dignity of individual man', not an 'abstraction' or a 'shadow' of man, but the reality itself, by taking to the public road.[4] Walking the public road put the poet on the same level as the vagrants he met and the poetry describing the meetings produced, in Langan's words, a 'figurative identity,' an analogical relationship between himself and them.

'What matters,' Langan stressed, 'is the fact of travelling,' in other words, it is on the basis of 'actual mobility' that the figurative identity and the social/political equality is achieved (this is the 'radical' walking that was referred to in chapter four). Wordsworth's 'Romantic vagrancy' involves a certain idealisation of the vagrant, conveying an internal condition as much as an external object.[5] The individuals who figure in the *Diary* passages examined later in this chapter were not all vagrants but their experiences, impoverishment, and solitariness make them very much the same kind of people as Wordsworth's vagrants.

As a recorder of encounters with landscape and people, Kilvert was in the position of an ethnographer, an outsider who had moved into a community, which he was seeking to study from the inside. He sometimes noted that he was a 'stranger' because he came from Wiltshire and was English. Under the patronage of his Clyro vicar, he gained temporary admission to the highest social circle of the district, but his poverty meant he was essentially an outsider. He won the friendship of cottagers and farmers through dutiful parish visiting but his background, education and position in the Church excluded him from their community. Dunham also noted that Kilvert's unmarried state — his lack of family and home – compounded his 'social marginalisation and "betweenness."' Not only that, but his Clyro was 'part of a quintessentially borderland landscape, one which straddled the physical, cultural and political boundaries of England and Wales.'[6] Kilvert's borderland self, blurring the boundary between Self and Other, has much in common with the Romantic poets for whom the key to creativity lay in the relationship between the self and the larger world beyond it.

His exploration of this relationship led him to record mini-biographies of (often) suffering individuals encountered in his travels. They are not only numerous but exhibit a fascination with the circumstances of their lives and an effort to shape their stories in significant ways. His life-stories had a moral purpose akin to that which guided Wordsworth in his *Lyrical Ballads*, of which he wrote:

> each of them has a worthy *purpose*. Not that I always be-
> gan to write with a distinct purpose formally conceived,
> but habits of meditation have, I trust, so prompted and

regulated my feelings, that my descriptions of such objects as strongly excite those feelings, will be found to carry along with them a *purpose*.[7]

In his poem, *The Excursion*, Wordsworth gives a loving portrait of the Wanderer, based on a devout clergyman of Lakeland whom Wordsworth admired. We are told that the Wanderer studied the people he met among the hills, much as Kilvert did in Clyro. He studied

Their passions and their feelings; chiefly those
Essential and eternal in the heart,
That, 'mid the simpler forms of rural life,
Exist more simple in their elements,
And speak a plainer language.[8]

As this 'Enthusiast' travelled around, he was 'alive / To all that was enjoyed wher'er he went, / And all that was endured.' As a result, he was well versed in 'the history of many families' and because he was 'in himself happy, and quiet in his cheerfulness', he could 'afford to suffer / With those whom he saw suffer'. 'Indulgent listener was he to the tongue / Of garrulous age' and thus, 'in our best experience, he was rich'.[9] There could hardly be a more complete description than this of Kilvert's progress among the farms and cottages of Radnorshire and Wiltshire.

The Wanderer may have been one source of inspiration for Kilvert; Frederick Robertson, in whom many of the Wanderer's chief qualities were replicated, was bound to have been another. The latter's deep affinity with natural things was the mark too of Robertson who, according to his biographer, found that his personality blossomed not only when he was in congenial company, but also under 'the aspect of outward nature, which was society to him'.[10] He also had enormous sympathy for others. Even among his parishioners in Cheltenham, where he was generally ill at ease, he was too open and trusting and suffered as a result, as he explained in a letter he wrote from Heidelberg on 11 November 1846:

I have at last decided upon my course with respect to Christchurch. You were perfectly right, I was most unwise to bare my feelings even to the extent I did. A man who 'wears his heart upon his sleeve' must not be surprised if he finds it a temptation 'for daws to peck

at'... Yet, yet, say what I will — when any one soothes
me with the semblance of sympathy — I cannot for the
life of me help baring my whole bosom in gratitude
and trust.[11]

His sympathy grew, according to Brooke, out of his own
intense sensitivity, a fact that Robertson himself acknowledged:
'My misfortune or happiness . . . is power of sympathy'. In
Robertson's adverse experiences in his ministries, Kilvert had
the example of a priest who became convinced that 'he is
not fit for work among the upper classes' (Brooke's words).[12]
The example was an important one for Kilvert and he must
have pondered it when he encountered similar problems. His
intensity, extreme sensitiveness and impulsive nature — all
qualities he shared with Robertson — rendered him vulnerable
to shallow, insensitive people in exactly the way Robertson
was.

One of the closest parallels between the two men is their
tendency to target their ministry towards the lower-class
members of their parishes and to experience a tension between their work with them and their relationship with
gentry parishioners. Robertson tried to clarify his thinking on
fundamental issues and among those that he said he felt 'certain
of' was that 'Moral goodness and moral beauty are realities,
lying . . . beneath all forms of religious expressions. . . . In the
thickest darkness, I tried to keep my eye on nobleness and
goodness'.[13] He believed that among simple country people
moral goodness was to be found in greater abundance and
lying more open than among the sophisticated. It is clear from
the following passage that he was powerfully influenced in
this direction by the propositions in Wordsworth's *Preface* to
the *Lyrical Ballads*:

I spent some hours in the village of Lindfield, where I
strongly felt the beauty and power of English country
scenery and life to calm, if not to purify, the hearts of those
whose lives are habitually subjected to such influences.
Not that human nature is better there, but life is more
natural, and real nature I hold to be the great law of our
life, both physical and religious. Physical does, in fact,
by derivation, mean natural —physics being the study
of nature. I am sure that religion is the recall to real
instead of perverted nature, just as the medicinal art is

the recall of the body to natural health. There are false
systems in both, as well as true, being marked in each
case by the artificial and unnatural mode of dealing
with the diseased part.[14]

The essence of this passage — the contrast between naturalness
and artificiality — is contained in this entry from *Kilvert's Diary*:
'What an elegant ease and simplicity there is about French
manners and ways of domestic country life, and how favourably
it contrasts with our social life, cumbrous, stiff, vulgarly
extravagant, artificial, unnatural.'[15] In restating Robertson's basic
thesis, Kilvert made use of almost identical phrasing. 'Ways
of domestic country life' corresponds to Robertson's 'English
country scenery and life', and 'our social life . . . artificial,
unnatural' to Robertson's 'artificial and unnatural mode. . . .'
For both men, the artificiality came down finally to worldliness
— a concern for wealth, rank, luxurious living, accompanied
often by an over-elaboration of manners that discouraged easy,
natural expressions of feeling. For both men, worldliness was
'perverted nature' and the enemy of true religion, which was
the expression of uncorrupted natural impulses. According to
Brooke, 'the qualifications Robertson lays down as necessary
for comprehending the poetry of Wordsworth were his own
qualifications — "unworldliness".'[16]

Robertson was both too intelligent and too honest to
persuade himself that uneducated country people were
abounding in moral and aesthetic perceptions, and criticised
Keble for implying they were. The actual circumstances of
country living for the poor did not produce 'any real elevation
of character'. 'It is little more than an animal existence, and
all those notions of peasant purity and pastoral innocence
are miserably false and sentimental. . . . It is education which
draws out the beauty of . . . things'.[17] This understanding
did not, however, prevent him from appreciating the virtues
of the rural poor: 'How precious in the sight of God those
qualities are which we think of almost meanly — plodding
habits, meekness of heart, sense of dependence. . . .'[18] And
with such people, he was patient and understanding and 'did
not despise the dullest intellect'.[19] This thesis of the moral
superiority of humble rural life is implicit in much of Howitt's
writing but Kilvert had come across an explicit statement of
it in the chapter on 'Cottage Life' in *The Rural Life of England*.

There Howitt had castigated the 'corruptions of pride and luxury, false taste, frivolous pursuits' of country house society and their tendency to 'weaken domestic attachments'. Like Robertson, he nevertheless recognised that 'poverty and ignorance' laid grave restrictions on the outlook of cottagers. 'Yet the simplicity of cottage life, . . . the strong sympathies awakened by its trials and sufferings, tend to condense the affections, and to strike deep the roots of happiness in the sacred soil of consanguinity.'[20]

The quality of sympathy epitomised by the Wanderer in his dealings with country people has been recognised over the years as the outstanding one in Wordsworth's poetry. John Simon, medical tutor at King's College, London, indicated in a letter of 1841 to Wordsworth that he valued his poems' capacity of bringing consolation in the face of suffering. Simon said that from them he had derived the benefits of 'humbler reliance on the Divine rule — fuller love of Man — deeper and holier sympathies with Nature — in trial and suffering the stay and comfort of religious wisdom.'[21] J.R. Watson described the problem of finding appropriate consolation in the face of terrible suffering as 'one of the central mysteries of Wordsworth's poetry'.[22] Much has been written about it but only one aspect will be focused on here: the relationship between suffering people and the landscape in which they live. At one level, the beauty of landscape and its accessibility to all is a compensation for the suffering of the poor, a point Kilvert underlined in *The Rocks of Aberedw*: 'The sweet wind freshens o'er the moor, / God's breath alike for rich and poor.' He showed, in his *Honest Work* poem, that he shared Wordsworth's belief that people's character and morality were formed by their intense attachment to their land and by the experiences their work provided. It will be recalled that this idea was put forward in the *Preface* to the *Lyrical Ballads* as one of their principal aims: 'Humble and rustic life was generally chosen because in that condition, the essential passions of the heart find a better soil. . . .' It is a dubious proposition and one that can never be proved, but Wordsworth believed it and he himself always needed to live near great permanent objects, objects that shared the nature of infinity and stirred the deepest feelings of his heart.

An important aspect of the concept of 'heart' is spontaneity and sincerity of feeling. Romanticism was concerned with the personal testing of experience (often extremes of experience) as a means of establishing a sound morality. This effort was distorted by the Victorians so that sincerity became the test of poetic worth and the germ of this distortion was Wordsworth's emphasis, in the *Preface* to the *Lyrical Ballads*, on poetry as the 'overflow' of powerful feelings. This idea became merged with the older, mainly religious connotations of 'sincerity', that is, passionate expression of religious faith, so that a 'sincere' poet was one who expressed Christian ideals.[23] This explains why Wordsworth was taken up so eagerly by Evangelicals and others in the 1830s and 1840s.

Kilvert's response to *The Dairyman's Daughter* supplies not only important clues to some of the things he valued in writing, but also helps us to understand the spirit in which he recorded the lives of his parishioners. He called Legh Richmond's story 'beautiful and touching', a phrase that shows one of his key literary criteria: the power of a book to convey and to arouse emotion.[24] He also valued Legh Richmond's story because it was *true*. Richmond was very keen to emphasise that the heroine, Elizabeth Wallbridge, was a real person and that her story of a sinner's conversion was based 'on real life and circumstances'. This emphasis was also Richmond's way of excusing the fact that his tract reads very much like fiction because, in spite of their hostility to novels, Evangelical writers were forced to acknowledge, in their periodicals and tracts, their readers' craving for wonder and excitement. Thus, 'long before fiction was admitted to their pages, "true fact" material offered a substitute of a sort'.[25] Because his formative literary experience included the stories of Richmond and Aguilar, Kilvert was quite comfortable blending fictional with religious elements in the *Diary* entries featuring worthy lives that are focused on in the latter part of this chapter. It was important too for him that Elizabeth and her story were permanently linked to a landscape, a fact he underlined when he referred to the old manor house of Yaverland, where she was in service, as 'a romance and a paradise to my imagination' and to his visit there after the long interval of 'a quarter of a century' as 'Yaverland at last. The dream has come true.'[26] The phrasing here is very revealing. *The Dairyman's Daughter* satisfied, as he said, his 'soul' chiefly for its religious meaning, but her story (it is significantly a spiritual biography) of triumph over sin and suffering also had a romantic aspect that had retained its grip on his imagination for 25 years. It stood, therefore, for the power of memory — 'the sanctified instrument of spiritual improvement'.

Richmond himself was influenced by the Romantic poets and was distinctly Wordsworthian in the way he used landscape in his writing. He visited the Lakes in 1818 and Scotland in 1820, writing letters home from these tours which conveyed 'a vivid appreciation of the beauties and grandeur of natural scenery and evince . . . that pervading spirit of Christianity which in his case was blended with the common occurrences of life.'[27] Elizabeth Wallbridge's story is also one of self-sacrifice in that she first met Richmond when he officiated at the funeral of her sister, who died of T.B. As a result Elizabeth had to leave her job at the manor and return home to help her frail parents on their little dairy farm, where she contracted T.B. and died a pious death. All of this was part of the 'romance' that her story presented to the Evangelical mind.[28]

Kilvert's Diary is full of stories illustrating the bond between morality and landscape and his love of them connects him to Mrs Gaskell, Howitt and to William Barnes. In her biography of Mrs Gaskell, Jenny Uglow noted how 'she loved rich, wide-ranging talk', how stories 'were intrinsic to her cast of mind'.[29] Kilvert had the same cast of mind, perhaps inherited from his great grandmother, Elizabeth Caink, and had an eager appetite for stories from the people he knew. He also loved his parishioners' stories partly because they enabled him to draw closer to them and partly because he was fascinated by what they revealed of the rich and strange life of the Radnorshire hills, the sufferings and the piety of small farmers and cottagers. He had also relished the experiences of Dorset cottagers distilled in Barnes's poems. His *Poems of Rural Life in the Dorset Dialect* claimed (in his 'dissertation' that accompanied them) to be written out of rural experience and permeated by the 'sound Christian principles, kindness and harmless cheerfulness' characteristic of Dorset families. Barnes aimed to show 'the better feelings and more harmless joys of the small farm house and happy cottage'.[30]

Legh Richmond used Elizabeth Wallbridge and other characters in *Annals of the Poor* to extol the wholesome morality of cottages whose inhabitants are 'precious in God's sight — they ought to be so in ours'.[31] As Elizabeth tells Richmond, very near her death, of her faith in Christ, he looks round the cottage interior and comments: 'Surely this is none other than the house of God'.[32] Wordsworth's Wanderer expresses the same sentiment: 'How feelingly religion may be learned / In smoky cabins'.[33] The *Diary* entry for 24 March 1876 encapsulates all the virtues of the cottage home and is one of Kilvert's most complete statements on the morality of humble rural life and is a reminder of his own yeoman roots.[34] The family life described exhibits the key Kilvertian values: kindness, benevolence, courtesy, humility, piety, hospitality, love of children, endurance, hard work, independence and self-sacrifice:

> The family at the little farm of Gastons seems to me a very happy family. I think they have the true secret of happiness. When I entered they were all sitting at tea, round the table. There was the patriarchal grandfather, Robert Crook, with his white smock-frock, rosy face, and the sweet kindly benevolent look in his eyes. The kindly people asked me to join them at their humble meal and I did not want a second invitation. The old man took up the sheet of music and looked at it. He is a musician and used to play the flute at Tytherton Church. Presently the old man rose with a courteous apology and went out to attend to the business of the little farm. "Daddy! Daddy" cried the children as their father passed the window and the strong comely pleasant-faced carpenter Palmer came in from his day's work, greeted me kindly, and sat down by the fire while his wife prepared his tea. I think he is a God-fearing man, and a fond husband and father. He told me how for ten years he had walked to and from Chippenham in the early morning and late night in wild weather, often in times of flood and in such darkness that he had sometimes to go down on his knees with his little lantern to see if he was in the path, but how he had always been cheered and brightened and helped by the thought of the beacon light of home and the wife and children and the love that awaited him there.

The passage exemplifies perfectly how, in the cases of Robert Crook and the 'comely . . . carpenter', Palmer, 'a character of purity and strength was built up' (to use Robertson's words) out of the experiences of country life.

The Evangelical focus on the individual's struggle with hardship, illness, suffering, spiritual temptations and doubts, and the use of such struggle for the purposes of meditation and extension of sympathy is one key to understanding Kilvert's mode of writing about his parishioners. The other key is the way in which this concern coincides with a very similar Romantic concern — the exploration of the individual self, often through extremes of experience. Patricia Ball demonstrated that 'the taproot of Romantic art . . . reaches down to . . . the sensation of an individual life' and is concerned with the complexity of the experiencing self.[35] This helps to explain the interest that all the Romantic poets had in unusual or heightened forms of consciousness. In the *Lyrical Ballads*, the use of different voices, different points of view, and the shifting role of the narrator, push the reader into a critical examination of experience.[36]

It was these features that led Garber to designate Wordsworth's poetry, especially the *Lyrical Ballads*, as 'poetry of encounter'. In those poems, the poet was concerned with a kind of 'knowing', called by Garber 'object consciousness'. This knowing, because it entailed the intensification and extension of awareness, was a process of encounter:

> In it the self comes to meet something outside (some aspect of a person or an object — some thing); it is an event in which the self may break through to a fleeting, incomplete, but definite understanding of something about the world of the other, an understanding which can result in a permanent increase of self and its knowledge.[37]

Kilvert had learnt from Robertson that there were some experiences of Nature (he cited the Alps particularly – see Introduction), the sheer intensity of which revealed the mystery of Nature itself. We have also seen that Kilvert was concerned in his writing to capture what Wordsworth called the 'lines of difference' between objects, those features in which resided their uniqueness or singularity. Garber used Wordsworth's *The Solitary Reaper* to illustrate this concern. In the poem, the poet struggles to come to terms with the meaning of his encounter with the figure of the girl, whose singularity is repeatedly underlined:

> Behold her, single in the field,
> Yon Solitary Highland Lass!
> Reaping and singing by herself; . . .
> Alone she cuts and binds the grain,
> And sings a melancholy strain.

The series of words, 'single, Solitary, by herself, Alone', presents the girl as object, separate from all similar objects, each word forcing her with increasing intensity towards the centre of the observer's vision. She becomes, as object, 'not so much more purely itself . . . as a pure distillation of what has meaning for the observer', so that he becomes more aware of what he himself is thinking and feeling, of what is personal and unique about himself.[38]

While an important element of the encounter is this movement inward towards the self, the encounter depends just as much on things happening outside the self. There are aspects of the girl's singing — it is like birdsong and is in an unknown language — which place her in a separate realm of being, making the problem of knowing her all the more acute:

> A voice so thrilling ne'er was heard
> In spring-time from the Cuckoo-bird,
> Breaking the silence of the seas
> Among the farthest Hebrides.

The poet is fascinated, enchanted by her singing and desperately wants to understand it in order to understand who and what she is: 'Will no one tell me what she sings?' Even though the communion between him and the girl is imperfect and transient, there is an intensity to it that he feels to be significant. The intensity is conveyed partly by the girl's singing, which continues to haunt him:

> Whate'er the theme, the Maiden sang
> As if her song could have no ending;
> I listened, motionless and still;
> And, as I mounted up the hill,
> The music in my heart I bore,
> Long after it was heard no more.

The Wordsworthian encounter brings observer and object into a transient situation of wholeness, 'creating a continuity between them which may leave pain or joy for a memory, but creating it nonetheless'.[39] Where this experience meets the experience of encountering individuals struggling with intense suffering is in the moment of *shared feeling* between observer and object. Hartman, in his comments on *The Solitary Reaper*, drew attention to the issue of feeling and to the manner in which small incidents and insignificant moods are so frequently invested in Wordsworth's poems with dispro-portionately strong feeling. It is a characteristic feature of *Kilvert's Diary* and provides much of the basis for the charge of sentimentality levelled at it. Hartman emphasised, however, that the point about *The Solitary Reaper* is not that the poet does not, or cannot, explain why the figure of the girl moves him so much, but that he *is* moved. He allows the emotion 'to invade and renew his mind'.[40]

There is much common ground between Wordsworth in this mode and the solitary Clyro wanderer pictured by Dunham at the start of this chapter, seeking different encounters, which he could capture in all their intensity and singularity in his writing. In those encounters, Dunham argued, Kilvert was able to 'let himself go, to indulge the moment of experience and to struggle to be worthy of it through the medium of writing.'[41] To Wordsworth and to Kilvert, worthwhile forms of knowledge were those that led to expansion of the self, increase in awareness and sympathy. It was encounters with particular places and people which, Kilvert said, made Clyro and its environs 'holy ground'. His choice of a family motto which cast him in the role of pilgrim and stranger has a bearing on these issues because both aspects signified for him the kind of seriousness which was the goal of all Evangelicals, and seriousness was the mark too of the Wordsworthian poet. It went with the solitude that was the key to being able to write poetry. Furthermore, Wordsworth's observer is consistently a stranger, 'an outsider alone and with difficulty becoming aware that he is separate', whose apartness can be overcome, though never completely.[42] He can recognise elements in the experience of encounter that may allow some sort of relationship, at the level at least of shared humanity.

Seriousness, singularity, intensity — these three words are central to the encounters that feature so prominently in *Kilvert's Diary* and Wordsworth's poetry. It is noticeable that, in the lines from Kilvert's *The Pilgrimage* which are one of the epigraphs to this chapter, he wrote of travellers standing a '*single* moment face

to face', and, in *Diary* passage after *Diary* passage, stressed that
natural objects were 'solitary'. Plomer picked up the significance
of singularity and intensity when he highlighted Humphry
House's observation that Kilvert's great virtue is the power of
conveying 'the physical quality of everything he describes'.[43]
Kilvert demonstrates, in other words, the importance of close
observation that he had learned from the Lakeland poet. Garber
pointed out that Wordsworth attacked Gray's use of language
because it did not provide 'precise, accurate information about
objects': by contrast, Wordsworth sought 'immediacy of understanding'. For him, 'singularity means . . . a concentration
of intensity'. He 'dwells on single objects alone in their kind,
things more often than people but people too, because he could
get closer to understanding when there were no distractions
of duplication'. The closer the observation, the less the chance
of 'dispersal of intensity' which characterised poor writing.
'There are various kinds of Wordsworthian seeing, but the kind
associated with the objects in encounter requires all that can be
drawn up of concentrated, intensified force. . . .'[44] Wordsworth
spelt out plainly the workings of singularity in this passage
from *The Prelude*:

> As the black storm upon the mountain-top
> Sets off the sunbeam in the valley, so
> That huge fermenting mass of human-kind
> Serves as a solemn background, or relief,
> To single forms or objects, whence they draw,
> For feeling and contemplative regard,
> More than inherent liveliness and power.[45]

It is evident that one aspect of what Wordsworth was describing here is simply the notion of contrast — that between the
'black storm upon the mountain-top' and the 'sunbeam in the
valley', the 'single form' seen against 'background'.[46] However,
there is also, and importantly,[47] the particularly Wordsworthian
concept of 'power'. Single objects could 'draw' power that
exceeded their 'inherent liveliness' (vitality) and 'power'. This
additional power concerned the single objects' impact on the
observer, his 'feeling' about them, his 'contemplative regard' for
them, concerned, in other words, his imaginative comprehen-
sion of them.

Kilvert made explicit recognition of this power of intensity,
of singularity, in the passage examined towards the end

of chapter five, where he wrote of the 'intense feeling and perception' he had of the 'glowing roses of the Vicarage lawn and the blue mountains beyond. . . .'. The frequency with which single objects are made to stand out in his description of landscape leaves no doubt that he was making his own attempt to realise the power of intensity that could accompany them. Often they show, as Wordsworth's example does, the effect of sudden bursts of light, as in these examples: 'Brilliant sun, black cloud and slight shower. The column of a rainbow sprung out of Herefordshire from among the blue hills'; 'A gleam of sunshine shot across the green sea . . .'; 'The mountain was veiled in a tender gauze of green mist and a sudden burst lit the country with a strange violent glare'; 'A beautiful gleam of sunshine lit the rainy mountains into tender showery lights of blue and green'; 'The dingle was gloomy and one yellow tree burnt above the Burnt House like a flame'; 'As I went across the fields the white monks' house shone ghostly down in its lonely hollow in the dusk'; 'Then there was a gleam of silver over the dark heather stems and Llanbychllyn Pool lay in its hollow like a silver shield'.[48] Sometimes a figure in a landscape is strikingly presented: 'A solitary fern cutter was at work on the Vicar's Hill mowing the fern with a sharp harsh ripping sound. . . .'[49]

Singularity is also used to highlight shapes, as in these passages: 'Solitary barrows rose here and there upon the heaving down'; 'the great tower of Colerne Church standing lofty and solitary upon its ridge against the sky'; 'O'er lone Tynessa's cabin roof / The wind-blown larch was bending'; 'the strange grey dark old house lying in the wet hollow among the springs, with its great dismal solitary yew. . . .'[50] In several of these examples it can be recognised that the relatively bleak landscapes which Kilvert saw around Clyro and Wordsworth saw in the Lakes were particularly suited to the technique of singularity. 'Bleakness,' observed Garber 'may come to be seen primarily, and positively, as a way of being without interference. . . . A single object in a bare landscape offered a means of capturing and, for a meaningful duration, holding onto an awareness of the meaning of the presentness of an object that few other kinds of situation could approach in intensity, directness, and purity'.[51]

'The disembodied voice is for Wordsworth the final point to which an object can be purified and still retain a tie to the

sensuous reality of things'.[52] It was an interest that reflected
the general Romantic concern with the meaning of immediate
physical experiences,[53] but the Romantics were always wanting to know what lay beyond the sensuous moment. The
number of times that the disembodied voice (usually of a
bird, of course, as in Wordsworth) occurs in *Kilvert's Diary* is
striking.[54] Sometimes he is interested simply in the meanings
attached in folklore to birds' songs. When he noted 'a storm
cock . . . singing in the top of a tree', it intrigued him that 'the
bird was not wrong in its presage' because he was suddenly
overtaken by a snow storm. Similarly, one July evening at dusk
he heard from some woods 'the strange continuous chirring of
the wheel of "the old woman spinning" as in Wales they call
the nightjar. . . .' Usually, disembodied voices of birds carried
religious overtones, which birds in general had for him. For
example, he recorded his enjoyment of a 'holy autumn day'
when 'a tender haze brooded melting over the beautiful
landscape', adding that it was only the 'clear sweet solitary
notes of a robin singing from the copper beech' that broke the
silence.[55]

Kilvert was brought up to follow Wordsworth by looking
for 'impulses of deeper birth' beyond 'the outward shows
of sky and earth', to view the universe as 'God's blessed
sacrament', as Robertson and Keble did, and to recognise
the 'truths' which the poet could impart through 'common
things'. In this enquiry into the way Kilvert wrote, these twin
strands of Romanticism and evangelicalism have been seen to
be continually reinforcing each other in their stance towards
Nature. Both strands combine in Kilvert's poem, *Little Things*,
the theme of which is contained in the line (repeated in each
verse) 'It seemed a little thing. . . .' It represents another instance
of Kilvert's exploration of Wordsworthian ideas, in this case
the idea of singularity. Aspects both of human interaction and
of interaction between observer and natural objects are treated
in the poem and both are summed up in these lines:

> Oh, little things! *if such there are*,
> How vast a power a given
> To you to keep our spirits far —
> Or draw them nearer Heaven.

The words 'if such there are' have been italicised because it
is clear that Kilvert dismissed the idea that 'little things' had

no serious import. The examples the poem gives of them in human relations — the meaningful glance, the telling of a tale 'best left unspoken', the 'whispered hint', the 'hasty word' — are familiar and ordinary enough. Their importance lay, as he emphasised, in their impact on relationships, their capacity to alienate, 'to keep our spirits far', or to *draw* them nearer Heaven'. Wordsworth used 'draw' in the *Prelude* passage, quoted earlier, in which he spoke of the capacity of single things to 'draw' or hold, for the responsive, contemplative person, power beyond that which normally inhered in them. This is the 'vast power' to which Kilvert referred in the lines above. Again, the matter of responsiveness, of feeling, is paramount as he recognised when he reiterated

> How small a thing has power to bless
> With tender influence moving,
> To give an hour's pure happiness
> To simple souls and loving!

The poem closes with the examples of the 'small and shy' flower that nevertheless has 'meaning in its eye / And teaches in its growing', and of other 'simple things', such as singing birds and 'rustling trees', that held 'secret messages.' The triteness of some of the poem's ideas and its conventional piety can disguise what is really going on in it, but the close parallel between its ending and the ending of Wordsworth's *Immortality Ode* confirms the nature of the exploration Kilvert was making. Wordsworth's poem ends:

> Thanks to the human heart by which we live,
> Thanks to its tenderness, its joys, and fears,
> To me the meanest flower that blows can give
> Thoughts that do often lie too deep for tears.

The *Immortality Ode* is about recovering wholeness, relationship, with the natural forms that surround us, recovering the power of imaginative seeing and knowing, 'the hour of splendour in the grass, of glory in the flower'. *Little Things* is Kilvert's expression of the notions of relationship and imaginative modes of knowing that underpin the Wordsworthian encounter. The influence of sentimentalism and of evangelicalism are evident in the emphasis on 'loving' souls being moved by 'tender influence', i.e. the pathos of situations. 'Tender' occurs frequently in Kilvert's descriptions of natural objects

quoted earlier in this chapter. (He also used it in relation to
Florence Hill's 'presence' — see chapter two.) It was important
for observers to approach the mystery of single things with
reverence because the kind of knowing that was involved was
'a special kind of love',[56] one that had obvious affinities with
the idea of sacrament.

This focus on Kilvert's experiments with the Wordsworthian
encounter has largely emphasised the singularity of *things*;
more needs to be said about the singularity of *people*. In
chapter five we saw his concern with the way memories of
landscapes became incorporated into a person's identity,
shaping it one way or another. We also saw that memories
of his Hardenhuish childhood held a deep fascination for
him, his insistent questioning of particular *forms* of those
landscapes — the 'white house on the hill', the elms, the
'ivied church' —because he knew that his knowledge of them
was unique, marked by their intensity and by his increased
awareness of the act of perception involved in them. It is
appropriate to see them in the context of the Wordsworthian
encounter, since the perception involved is directed inwards
towards the observer's consciousness, producing in him 'a
consciousness of consciousness'.[57] It is also helpful to see
Kilvert's near obsession with objects connected to people, the
'memorials' he kept in his 'secret drawer', as further evidence
of a concern with the *singularity* of things. His urgent need to
remember individuals and to be remembered by them was
tied up with the objects he associated with them. In his 'secret
drawer' he could continue to 'encounter' those individuals,
could continue to 'know' their singularity, the sense in which
they were uniquely themselves and no-one else, through the
singularity of the objects. The objects therefore held intensity,
power, for him and in cases especially where he had (horrors!)
forgotten who gave them to him, he would gaze intently at
them, willing them to give back the knowledge they withheld.
It is worth recalling that Robertson was concerned with the
kind of knowing, of 'sympathy', that produced the total
identification of one individual with another (see chapter
one).

In the *Prelude* passage in which Wordsworth referred to the
'power' of 'single forms and objects', he went on to speak of the
mystery of identity that intrigued him when he was living in
London:

> How oft, amid those overflowing streets,
> Have I gone forward with the crowd, and said
> Unto myself, "The face of every one
> That passes by me is a mystery!"

The facets of this kind of singularity are 'privateness and separateness, uniqueness and unusualness', to use Garber's words,[58] and knowledge of it is difficult to come by except by some form of imaginative vision (Wordsworth referred to the means of such knowing as 'incommunicable powers'). To Garber, the powers come with the state of being single oneself:

> The powers seem tied in with the state of singularity itself, so that something that is alone can, at least potentially, have an immensely potent capacity to reveal the might of hidden forces connected with the insights afforded by imaginative vision.[59]

These ideas offer some explanation for a remarkable *Diary* passage in which Kilvert is unmistakably grappling with the mystery of 'knowing' another human being. The two Miss Halls were staying at the Venables' Vicarage and he was given the job, as he put it, of 'explaining the country to the young ladies'. When he referred to the Miss Halls again it was with sadness and frustration because he had mistaken the time when they were to leave Clyro and had missed them.[60] 'Provoking, vexing,' he wrote, 'I would have given a sovereign to see them and speak to them once more'. The absence of the Miss Halls, indeed their literal *non-presence*, was intensely painful to him, as he repeatedly underlined. He saw Mrs Venables and her baby in the drawing-room, 'but in spite of them how cold blank dull and empty the room looked'. Already there is a sense of utter desolation which hardly seems to be explained by the simple fact that he had missed seeing two girls who attracted him. The desolation grows as the passage proceeds. But first he focused on a number of single objects which held his sense of the girls' earlier 'presentness'. '*There* was the table at which they used to sit writing letters'. 'There' has been highlighted to show the statement's similarity to the Hardenhuish childhood passages of chapter five, in which 'there' is repeated as Kilvert focused on the singularity of the objects that held his sense of his past. He had been drawn especially to Kathleen Hall and his sense of her was bound up with his memory of her 'making up the primroses into bunches for the primrose crosses'. And he recalled a number of other 'little things' — Church on Good Friday, the drive to Boughrood, 'the place where she sat by the Maiden's Stile'.

The words he used to sum up the experiences — 'Well. Such is life, comings and goings and meetings and partings' — repeat the themes of *Little Things*, *The Pilgrimage* and *Honest Work*, the three poems which most explicitly addressed the mystery of the singularity of objects and people, of how people come 'out of the spaces of Eternity . . . to meet each other', of how 'hearts are linked to hearts', and of the 'beauties of common things'. He missed seeing the Miss Halls because they were 'nice sweet girls, so natural and genuine' and he had cherished the hope of romance with one of them. 'I thought I was not going to care for any one again. I wonder if there is any receipt for hardening the heart and making it less impressible.' For Kilvert to entertain the idea of 'hardening the heart' was little short of blasphemy. He was a man raised in a 'religion of the heart', in the belief that the essence of Christianity was Love, that sympathy, responsiveness, feeling were the highest virtues; to will on himself indifference and callousness was to will moral and spiritual death. However, his reaction to the loss of the hope of romance was so extreme that it is clear that the experience had a more profound meaning for him. The irritation of the early part of the entry gives way to total demoralisation: 'I went sadly back to my room . . . feeling as if all was dull and blank and as if some light and interest had suddenly gone out of life'. This is a man experiencing a profound sense of aloneness, a sense that all possibility of relationship has been lost.[61]

The prospect of an individual cut off from all forms of relationship seems to be the source of the unease Kilvert felt when visiting the Solitary of Llanbedr. One of the ways in which Kilvert modelled himself on Wordsworth (and on Robertson) was in his embracing of solitariness, which amounted to a determination, especially where landscape was concerned, to be alone. It was not merely a trait of character that he happened to share with the Lakeland poet, but grew out of understanding of his own personality and of the claims made for the value of solitariness by the latter as the source of his creative powers: the power to write poetry depended for Wordsworth on the power to be alone, as Jones observed. In the special state of consciousness solitude induced was to be found intensification of experience and insight, which made possible the deepest apprehension of landscape. Thus, the Wordsworthian solitaries appear as intrinsic parts of landscape (Wesling referred to them as 'fragments of landscape').[62] This is the basis of Kilvert's respect for the Solitary of Llanbedr. He was fascinated by the impulses that had driven the 'Revd John Price, Master of Arts of Cambridge University and Vicar of Llanbedr' to isolate himself in a filthy hut on a remote hillside. Kilvert generally warmed to solitaries but the particular form of solitariness represented by Price went beyond even his understanding. His sense of the incongruity of his situation is there in his recital of Price's qualifications and title and in his description of the squalor in which he lived.

Throughout the entry concerning his visit to Price's hut works the sense of a man making an effort to understand another human being. The incongruity he perceived in Price's lifestyle is balanced by his evident respect, amounting to reverence, for the discipline, asceticism, seriousness, purity of his singularity. He called him an 'anchorite' and said that in an earlier age he would have been 'canonised as a Saint'. And once again, the note repeatedly struck is pathos. We are told that Price had 'a mild thoughtful melancholy blue eye', that he looked 'dilapidated and forlorn', that he spoke 'plaintively' of coming to live there, that it was 'touching' to hear him speak 'mournfully' of his failing health and his loneliness was 'touching'. Most importantly, Price won Kilvert's admiration because he was moved by landscape: 'The Solitary was infinitely pleased to learn that the grey rocks which looked at us across a cwm from the opposite hill side had been observed and admired by other people than himself'.[63] That was an important relationship, but Kilvert was not happy about the total nature of Price's isolation; community was also important to Kilvert. He knew that Wordsworth's solitaries discovered relationship with their communities and with Nature. 'Solitude is fine when relationship is possible, but the possibility of relationship . . . had first of all to be established. Solitude without relationship is isolation and radical loneliness'.[64] In the emphases that close Kilvert's account there is the suggestion that Price had lost his way: 'There was a *resigned* look in his quiet *melancholy* blue eyes. The last I saw of him was that he was leaning on the gate looking after us. Then I saw him no more'. And it is significant that he *did* see Price no more. In all his revisitings of Clyro, there is no mention of seeking him out.[65]

The world of human relations in the *Lyrical Ballads* is frequently disrupted because of injustice, greed, or failure to respond to the needs of others. This is a noticeable feature of the *Diary* passages examined next, some of which are juxtaposed with particular *Lyrical Ballads* in order to show their similarity of content, theme and treatment. In the *Diary* passages, Kilvert can be seen following the literary credo Wordsworth set out in his *Preface* to the *Lyrical Ballads*: 'The principal object . . . was to choose incidents and situations from common life and . . . to throw over them a certain colouring of imagination, whereby ordinary things should be presented to the mind in an unusual aspect'. The story told to Kilvert about the tragic suicide of William Jones is the first of a number of 'encounters' which exemplify the singularity of human beings, the effort to 'know' them, and the impact upon the observer's self-knowledge. The *Lyrical Ballad* with which the case of Jones has most affinity is *The Old Cumberland Beggar*, in which the Beggar, 'a solitary Man', stands in danger of being deemed useless and sent to a workhouse by administrators who were too ready 'to rid the world of nuisances'.

Kilvert's interest in Jones's story was twofold. Firstly, he was disposed to draw out the moral implications: the pride and courage which made the old man resist becoming a dependant of the parish. In that respect he shared Wordsworth's interest in similar *Lyrical Ballad* stories, which Averill described as 'experiments in pathos . . . analogous to contemporary experiments in natural philosophy'. The poet was engaged in 'questions about human beings as poetic objects, about readers who enjoy tales of suffering, and about poetry that exploits pathos as a source of energy'.[66] Kilvert's horrified fascination with Jones's state of mind led him to present the unfortunate man as a poetic object, which was Kilvert's second interest.

> I could not get out of my head a horrible story Wall was telling me this evening of a suicide committed by an old man named William Jones in the old barn, now pulled down, which stood close by Chapel Dingle cottage. The old man used to work for Dyke at Llwyn Gwillim, but becoming helpless and infirm he was put upon the parish. It is supposed that this preyed upon

his mind. He was a very good faithful servant and a man of a sturdy independent character who could not bear the idea of not being able any longer to maintain himself and hated to be supported by the parish. 'I used to bake his bit of meat for him that was allowed him by the Board', said Mr Wall, 'for Rachel Williams with whom he was lodging at the Chapel Dingle was out at work every day. My baking day was mostly Friday. On Friday he had been up with his meat and I did not notice anything more than usual about him. At noon on Saturday Rachel's step-children missed him. They had seen him go towards the barn some hours before. They went and looked through a lancet hole of the old building and saw the old man lying on the floor, and they came back saying that old William Jones was lying in the barn dead. The master and I went down to the barn. Inside the barn there was a door leading into a beast house. The old man could not shut the barn door from the inside, so he had gone into the beast house and had shut himself in. Then he had leaned his stick up in a corner quite tidy. He had then taken out a razor, unsheathed it, putting the sheath back into his pocket. He was lying on the floor on his face when we saw him. The master turned him over. Heaven send I never see such a sight again. His head was nearly cut off, both arteries were cut through, the tongue was unrooted and, (perhaps in his agony), he had put his hand into the wound and torn his "keck" and everything out.[67]

From Kilvert's account emerges a total image of the man's appalling death, grounded in graphic concrete details. The narrative produces a focus which steadily brings the observer closer and closer to the object. The 'lancet-hole' through which the children and the reader view Jones's body becomes a lens that compels us to look. The sense of a camera moving closer and closer is reinforced by the way Jones went first into the barn, then into the beast house that lay within it, and then into a corner, where he 'leaned his stick . . . quite tidy'. That stick is now a compelling object, loaded with meaning, intensifying our impression of the kind of man Jones was. His tidiness extended even to putting the sheath of the razor back in his pocket. Then comes the moment of terrifying close-up as the body is

turned over. The imaginative mode of seeing objects, which
is the essence of the Wordsworthian encounter, is apparent
in the way physical details now become images representing
psychological reality — the mind of Jones, the agony of Jones.
At that moment the reader contemplates, not just the man's
face, but the singularity of his case, the intensification that
is the outstanding feature of the single object: 'Whatever a
single object may be, it is not diffuse but, quite the opposite,
packed and concentrated in intensity. It is not merely alone
... but also single, the unique example and representation of
its kind'. All that is significant about the object that is Jones
is concentrated in the 'pure example that the observer has in
front of him'.[68] In the final part of the image, the observer is
forced to contemplate suffering of such intensity that a man,
already in agony, could somehow find the will to put an end
to it by tearing 'everything out'. The story that Kilvert heard
from Mr Wall must have been horrible enough but in writing
it down he produced a masterly piece of narrative that marks
him out as an imaginative artist of high quality.

Behind the next brief entry may be discerned the shadow of
another tale of suffering:

> The sick woman at Cross Foot, Mary Price, cowering
> before a roaring fire. She said, 'Six weeks ago I was in
> bed at night and suddenly a young one came on my left
> arm, like a little angel. It was not one of my own. It was
> dressed in white clothes long and it had a cap like the
> dear little children when they are put into their coffins'.
> She told the story in such a strange weird way that I felt
> uncomfortable. It was not a dream, she said, she was
> broad awake.[69]

A number of things stand out from this passage. Kilvert points
up, as he did in the case of the suicide, his awareness of the
events narrated as a 'story', that is, a shaped, imaginative
artefact and not simply a collection of social facts, and of
himself as listener. He is showing awareness of the distinctive
literary dimension that belongs to a significant number of the
Lyrical Ballads — both that a detached viewpoint was required
of the reader and that the response of the reader/observer/
narrator is a crucial part of the poems' experience. Kilvert's
stance towards the 'stories' of Mary Price and of Jones is like
that of the wedding guest in Coleridge's *Rime of the Ancient*

Mariner (one of the *Lyrical Ballads*) — he 'cannot choose but hear'. The other thing worth pointing out in Mary Price's story is that it concerns 'a waking dream', which was a state of consciousness that intrigued Romantic poets. There is no doubt that it also intrigued Kilvert, as chapter eight shows. He was very fond of *I wandered lonely as a cloud* and probably knew the note added to it by Wordsworth in 1815, explaining that it resembled an 'ocular spectrum', that is, the kind of images that passed through the mind when half-awake. Kilvert continually recalled the poem whenever spring brought daffodils.[70]

'It was a fine clear starry night and the young moon was shining brightly.' This is the ballad-like opening to another *Diary* entry which, in all essentials, has the quality of the *Lyrical Ballads* or one of the poems, such as *Maternal Grief, The Affliction of Margaret,* or *The Sailor's Mother,* that Wordsworth grouped under the heading of 'Poems of the Affections'.[71] The entry is based on the account given to Kilvert by 18-year-old Henry Estcourt Ferris, whom he met one night on the moonlit road through Langley Burrell. His account, which Kilvert pointedly called 'a simple touching tale', deals in the 'elementary feelings' Wordsworth deemed worthy of portrayal. There is young love, desertion of a mother and a newborn baby, death-bed declarations, poverty, homelessness, and hard-heartedness balanced by love and charity. In his retelling, Kilvert made a point of highlighting *feeling*. The youth was tramping the district looking for work; he was very 'downcast and out of spirits' when the diarist met him. 'But have you no father or mother?' Kilvert asked. 'The simple question touched a heart still tender and bruised with great sorrow and opened the floodgates of his soul. The lad suddenly burst into tears.' Ferris's mother had died that very day and he would have attended her funeral but he had no black suit and couldn't afford to buy one. 'She was the best friend I had in the world and the only one,' he continued. The emphases here belong more to Legh Richmond and the world of Evangelical tracts than to Wordsworth; their common denominator is feeling, pathos.

In the youth's story Kilvert found material worthy of moral reflection, placing more of an emphasis on sin than is found in Wordsworth. Ferris's father, a labourer, had deserted his wife six months before he was born, which elicited this observation from Kilvert: 'Alas, the old, old story. Trust misplaced, promises broken, sin and sorrow, and the sins of the parents visited

upon the children.'[72] Kilvert walked with Ferris the two miles
from Langley Burrell to Sutton Benger in order to try to cheer
him up. 'The poor fellow was very humble and grateful,'
Kilvert stressed (the word 'gratefully' occurs two lines later).
With a handshake and a 'kindly "Goodbye"' he took his leave
'for ever probably in this world, of the motherless boy'. The
entry's closing words recall the lines from Kilvert's poem, *The
Pilgrimage*, about individuals being brought 'to meet each
other . . . by the Hand of God . . . for our advantage'. He felt
gratitude for the opportunity Ferris had given him (with God's
help) to play the Good Samaritan and to show, as the *Lyrical
Ballads* set out to show, awareness of the needs of others.

The essence of Ferris's story was the bond between parent
and child; if that could be the paradigm of all relationships
then human society would be an earthly paradise. Kilvert's
efforts with parishioners and with people like Ferris, whom
he met in encounters which he firmly believed were not
products of chance, were all directed to this end. Idiots and
mad people formed a sizeable element in nineteenth-century
rural communities and they were a challenging part of
Kilvert's responsibility. The 30 references to them in the index
of the *Diary* are confirmation of this but are also a reflection
of his personal concern. A number of entries centre on the
painful issue for relatives as to whether the afflicted family
member should be confined in an asylum.

Kilvert showed a steady interest in the love mothers showed
for their children, particularly in adverse circumstances as in
this entry for 13 July 1870:

> The maternal instinct and love must be happily very
> strong to enable them to go on loving their children in
> spite of all they have to endure. Perhaps that is the very
> reason and they love their children all the more for the
> trouble they give them. But that wailing and crying of
> a sick child must be terribly wearing. The patience of
> women. It is extraordinary. And happily, for it is all
> wanted.[73]

Kilvert's interest in the maternal instinct has a close parallel
in that shown by Wordsworth in his poem *The Idiot Boy*.
He described the intention behind the poem as 'to trace
the maternal passion through many of its more subtle
windings'.[74] Some indication of what these 'windings' were

can be gathered from the letter he wrote to John Wilson, who had doubts about the poem's tastefulness:

> I have, indeed, often looked upon the conduct of fathers and mothers of the lower classes of society towards Idiots as the great triumph of the human heart. It is there we see the strength, disinterestedness, and grandeur of love.

Wordsworth saw the potentiality of an idiot as a poetic object, which 'calls out so many excellent virtuous sentiments' and which discouraged all feelings of 'disgust and aversion'.[75] *The Idiot Boy* is a comic tale that tells how the idiot Johnny was sent out one night on a pony by his mother, Betty Fry, to fetch the doctor to Susan Gale, a neighbour who was ill. Betty wants her son to have the experiences and opportunities of a normal boy, such as running an errand, but, as time goes by and he does not return, she is overwhelmed with anxiety and guilt at the risks she has forced him to run. Her fears are contrasted with his carefree enjoyment of the moonlit landscape through which he rides. He is as unaware of his mother's anxiety as he is incapable of explaining where he has been for so many hours; he is only able at the end of the story to recall, with evident pleasure, the hooting of owls and 'the sun that did shine so cold'. His strange apprehension of landscape and his capacity to arouse such feelings of love in others are the basis of Wordsworth's reverence for Johnny. Jacobus referred to Johnny's idiocy as 'a significant state of imagination' and to the fact that 'a mysterious inner life sets him apart'.[76] To Watson, the poem has a moral insight which 'directs the reader to see madness as potentially more valuable than sanity' and to recognise the imaginative qualities of madness.[77] (There is an implication in the poem that Johnny is responsible for Susan Gale's recovery from illness since she grows so anxious about him that 'as her mind grew worse and worse, / Her body — it grew better' and is 'as if by magic cured'.) Johnny, locked into his permanent childhood, is for Pirie a child 'who may be able to see more than any other character in the poem', by which he means that he can see a unity and harmony in the world denied to adults.[78]

It is noticeable that Kilvert made a point of acknowledging idiots' imaginative capabilities wherever he could. Out among the hills behind Clyro, he was moved by 'a sweet voice singing'

near 'an ugly abject-looking farmhouse'. (It is another instance
of the 'disembodied voice'.) At first, he couldn't locate the singer
then he saw 'a crazy girl with a coarse ugly face under an old
bonnet in the field . . . singing to herself something like a hymn
tune in a rich mellow voice. . . .'[79] He knew of another idiot girl
in Kington St Michael, Wiltshire, whose mother, 'though sorely
tried' by her, was pleased to recognise that she was 'very fond of
music and caught up tunes with an exceedingly quick ear'.[80] The
closest parallel in the *Diary* to Wordsworth's *Idiot Boy*, because
it illustrates a mother's patience and tenderness towards an
idiot child as well as her faith in its capabilities, is the case of
Prissy Price and her step-daughter of Bredwardine.[81] Prissy
was another old woman like Hannah Whitney whom Kilvert
admired for her endurance and wisdom; she was 77 years old
and her step-daughter was 55. Asked on one visit to read and
pray, he was moved by her piety as she knelt painfully on the
cottage floor, saying to the idiot 'kneel down my dear', and by
the idiot's humility as she 'knelt down in front of the fire with her
head almost in the ashes'. The affectionate relationship between
the two was further illustrated by Prissy's story of the help the
idiot managed to provide when her stepmother suffered a burst
blood vessel.

> "The blood spouted up," said Prissy. "Yes!" thundered
> the idiot. "She held my head," explained Prissy. "Yes!"
> roared the idiot. "There was no one here but her," said
> Prissy. "No!" shouted the idiot. . . . "She had to run out
> into the deep snow," said the step-mother. The idiot
> step-daughter measured the depth of the snow upon
> her thigh.[82]

Like Betty Fry, Prissy can communicate with her idiot child in
only a very limited way yet she talked to her and loved her as
though she were a normal child and showed the same anxiety
over her as she faced taxing circumstances.

Emma Griffiths was a normal child but her life on the land
had brought her terrible suffering. She lived in Chapel Dingle
in the hamlet of Bettws, which was part of Clyro parish. Kilvert
went to see her on Good Friday 1872 to let her know that she
was remembered. 'There was a smile in her sweet sky-blue
eyes . . .but her voice and manner were very sad and quiet.' The
sadness he attributed partly to the fact that she was suffering
from face-ache but he knew it had a deeper cause. She was

married, but her child kept her at home.[83] 'She was scarcely ever able to leave home and went nowhere and heard nothing,' wrote Kilvert, paraphrasing what he was told but adding, in Emma's own idiosyncratic words: 'I have not been in sight of places'. A farm servant since she was 10 and married at 19, she had been shut out from any wider experience. When she was 11 she was attacked by a bull. Kilvert then allowed Emma to tell the rest of her story.

> I saw the bull coming after me. . . . I tried to get through the gate, but the bull caught me and struck me down. I felt no pain then or afterwards though he had me down on the ground punishing me for half an hour. . . . No one came to help me or to drive the bull away. . . He "punned" me with his head mostly, but he ran his horn into my side and into one of my legs. . . . When I came to myself and stumbled into the house I was bruised all over and covered with blood, almost naked, with my clothes torn nearly off me. . . . I have never been so strong or well since. I have gatherings on my side and the bull hurt something within me. . . . After I got well I went back to [the farm] and finished my time. . . . I never liked to break my time.[84]

Solitariness in Emma's case had proved to be a bane and not a blessing, as Kilvert stressed in several ways. There was no-one to help her when she was being attacked by the bull. Poverty, her isolated home, and the work she had to start when she was ten had robbed her of childhood and education. The result was that she was 'wise by sad experience . . . that sorrowful touching thing, a grey head on green shoulders'. Kilvert made a point of visiting her on Good Friday 1872 precisely because she lived remote from others and when he revisited her in March 1873, he pointedly referred to her home as 'the *lone* cottage in the Chapel Dingle'. In the portrayal of Emma's attitude to her suffering, influences from Evangelicalism, from sentimentalism and from Wordsworth's poetry can be seen to merge.[85] Evangelicals inclined to the notion that to be visited with a large measure of sorrow was a sign of God's favour. Permeating the *Lyrical Ballads* and other Wordsworth poems is the theme of compassion and the belief that people were capable of rising above their suffering in order to give thanks for such blessings as they had. Evangelicals were counselled to do the same, as well as to show understanding of others' sorrow. Emma was grateful to Kilvert for his kindness; he in turn was grateful to her for her example of fortitude in the face of suffering, and for the way the pathos of her situation had aroused his compassion.

Note has been taken of Kilvert's awareness of the literary character of the tales of suffering that were told to him. One aspect of this is the way in which he lets the character involved tell most or a part of his or her own story. Another aspect is the use frequently made of the actual speech of participants, which sometimes includes dialect words or expressions. Kilvert could have learned these techniques from a number of writers but it is noticeable that they are marked features of Barnes's work and of Wordsworth's *Lyrical Ballads*. Kilvert showed good judgement in employing these techniques because the result is entries which have great vitality because they seem true reflections of the personalities involved, increasing their intensity and 'presentness'.[86] In the last of the accounts of suffering to be considered the techniques are well to the fore. It is relevant to underline the fact that, as is true of the Jones and Ferris accounts, it concerns a person whose story had literary and religious implications he found fascinating. Mary Meredith had died on 16 February 1858, seven years before Kilvert came to Clyro and her story was told him by Hannah Jones, the teller of tales of fairies who was introduced in chapter four.

> Hannah Jones lighted her pipe, began to smoke, and told me the tragic story of Mary Meredith's suicide. She lived at New Barn and a son of Juggy (Joan) Price, Bill Price, lived close by at Sunny Bank. They went together and he got her with child. She had a little money of her own in the bank but she could not draw it out without her brother John's consent for their money was mixed up together. Mary thought that if she could get her money her lover would marry her for the sake of the money. But her brother would not yield to let Mary draw her money. Moreover he and his father were very angry with Mary for being with child and disgracing them. Whereupon poor Mary seeing no hope of marriage became melancholy mad. 'Often,' she said to Hannah Jones my informant, 'often I have gone out on

moonlight nights and sat down by the spring and cried for hours, thinking that I would drown myself in the river.'

Mary had a very close counterpart, in terms of her basic situation and the nature of her suffering, in Martha in Wordsworth's *The Thorn* (another *Lyrical Ballad*). Martha, like Mary, was courted by a young man and became pregnant. Her hopes of marrying were dashed not by the opposition of relatives but because her lover married another. Six months later, unable to hide her secret, she began to haunt a mountain top: 'What could she seek? —or wish to hide? / Her state to any eye was plain; / She was with child, and she was mad'. At the spot Martha haunted is a mysterious stunted thorn bush, lacking both leaves and thorns, that 'looks so old, / In truth, you'd find it hard to say / How it could ever have been young. . . .' Beside the Thorn is a little mound of moss resembling 'an infant's grave in size'. And just as Mary Meredith 'sat down by the spring and cried for hours', so in Wordsworth's poem 'A woman in a scarlet cloak' sits by the pond next to the Thorn 'And to herself she cries / "Oh misery! Oh misery!"' Highlighting further parallels must wait until all of Mary's story is told:

Then her father died and she grew worse and worse. At last there came an outbreak. One day she suddenly declared she would do no more for her brother, left the bacon half salted and the meat was spoilt. Not long after she was seen walking and 'prancing' about down by the river on Boatside. But she left the river and in the evening she was seen 'prancing' about in the Bron. John her brother went down and brought her up home to New Barn. He suspected she was up to something, for she asked him to let her little boy who always slept with her sleep with him that night, and when they went to bed he locked the front door and put the key in his pocket forgetting that the backdoor had no fastening but a bolt on the inside. In the night Mary got up and left the house and was seen by people who were abroad very early in the morning dodging and ducking behind the hedges and going down the Cwm. The carter boys at Boatside were at plough that morning when they saw a woman coming up from the river with her head

buried in her breast. She was a long way from them
and they thought it was Mary Pugh who lived then at
the Tump House. They called out, 'Mary, you are out
early this morning'. They thought she had been down
gathering wood by the river. The woman lifted her
head, looked at the teams, turned and ran down to the
river as hard as she could go and plunged headlong
in. It was a fortnight before she was found, and then
a flood cast her body up near Whitney Court. It was
surmised that she would be buried as a suicide without
any service on the 'backside of the Church', but she was
buried by Mr Venables with the usual ceremony.[87]

A particularly interesting and important parallel between
the two stories concerns their narratives. *The Thorn* is narrated
through the character of a retired sea captain, a crusty, obtuse
man whom Wordsworth requested readers to see as bored,
under-occupied, and consequently inclined to be 'credulous
and talkative' and superstitious. Wordsworth said he intended
to show thereby how 'superstition acts upon the mind'.[88]
Thus, he was concerned, as Kilvert was in reproducing the
account by Hannah Jones (another superstitious character)
of Mary's story, to show the way a story reflected its teller.
We are given Hannah's emphases, the homely detail of 'she
left the bacon half salted and the meat was spoilt', and her
actual words: the use of 'prancing' (twice), she was 'up to
something', her nickname for Joan Price and her use of 'the
backside of the Church'. Hannah's sympathies are clearly
with Mary for she shows herself critical of the way her brother
blocked her marriage and of the way he and her father felt she
had disgraced them. One terrible result of their actions, apart
from Mary's suicide, is that her little boy was left motherless.
The failure to empathise with another's suffering is the theme
also of *The Thorn*: Martha's neighbours are eager to judge
her, to bring her before a magistrate, to dig up the mound to
find her baby's body. There are hints of superstitious belief
in Hannah's account: in the detail of sitting by a spring on
moonlight nights, in the chilling description of her running
to the river 'as hard as she could go' and plunging 'headlong'
in, as though able to find solace only in Nature.[89] (The idea
of suffering producing isolation from humankind is strong in
both stories.) Martha is also identified with Nature — 'She is

known to every star, / And every wind that blows.'

Kilvert was as interested as the Romantic poets were in the sheer power of people's feelings that could make the impressions received by their senses emerge as superstitious beliefs. It is another way in which Mary's story and its teller are made to appear intrinsic parts of their landscape, just as the stories of William Jones, Henry Ferris, and Emma Griffiths are. That Kilvert viewed the story as having the quality of a ballad or a Romantic poem is made very plain by the way he isolated his image of its essence: 'What a picture. The solitary figure of the weeping girl sitting by the well in the moonlight. The many bitter tears shed on many a cold night by the moonlit well.' To Garber, the characteristically romantic poem is the one in which the observer's vision moves from 'outward gaze', focusing on things, to an 'inward gaze', in which the reality or meaning of an experience resides finally in images. 'For Wordsworth there is a close relationship between his sense of the presence of a thing . . . and the truth of the experience in which it partakes . . . experiences centred on objects do tend, for him, to have various kinds of irrevocable truth about them'.[90] In his encounters with individuals Kilvert was trying to break through to the truth about them, their lives, and their suffering.

The image Kilvert retained of Mary Meredith's story is an image, above all, of feeling. Her story had particular poignancy for him because it illustrated how a suffering individual could be driven first into the most profound isolation and finally into death, whereas his whole effort, as a man and as a priest, was directed towards making real the notion that the meaning of suffering lay chiefly in its potentiality for bringing people together in sympathy. Mary's tragedy, like Martha's in *The Thorn*, was that she was cut off from feeling — from the love of her family and the love of the man she wanted to marry. To Kilvert, it was of the utmost importance to feel; not to feel was synonymous with sinfulness, as the case of Peter Bell exemplified. Kilvert's 'religion of the heart' was bound to exalt the capacity to feel above all other capacities. He believed with Wordsworth that suffering was not only a moral force within a community, but also a significant factor in the individual's pilgrimage through life. The *Diary* entries that grew out of encounters with suffering parishioners and with travellers whose paths he crossed often have a meditative quality that has been likened to that of the *Lyrical Ballads,* poems which present experience but, by revealing its complexity, go on to draw a meaning from it. This understanding led Wesling to observe of Wordsworth's method: 'to Wordsworth poems about ways of knowing objects and landscapes are also poems about how to live.'[91] Together, the stories of lives that Kilvert featured make his *Diary* like Wordsworth's *The Excursion,* in which 'history ... becomes a network of narratives ... the cumulative "biography" of a community'.[92]

Preceding chapters have demonstrated that the literary influences on Kilvert's writing were as much religious as secular in their impact because he read books largely for their capacity to enhance his sense of himself as a Christian. Thus, it was possible for him to obtain similar satisfaction from an Evangelical tract and a Romantic poem, provided that they dealt in the kinds of experience and feeling which were of spiritual significance for him. At the same time, he had a keen appreciation of the literary qualities of books and could be highly discriminating in his response to them.[93] The present chapter has noted that the themes underpinning certain entries are his beliefs in the need for a feeling response to human suffering and in the way suffering, and people's ability to cope with it, are integral to the landscape in which they were raised. His interest in biography has been further exemplified in this chapter by the accounts he gave of lives he deemed worthy of his readers' notice. They were his 'annals of the poor.'

Chapter 7
Mountain Beauties

The work of the Romantics . . . celebrates the fact of
love.

> [John Jones, *The Egotistical Sublime.*
> *A History of Wordsworth's Imagination*]

> God has given . . . a power of love,
> A spark of His own nature that pure flame, —
> An earnest of a close relationship,
> A likeness of the Father in the child. . . .
> > [Francis Kilvert, *The Pilgrimage*]

Kilvert was extraordinarily sensitive to physical beauty
whether in men or women, though particularly in
girls.

> [A.L. Rowse, *The English Spirit*]

> She had a rustic, woodland air,
> And she was wildly clad:
> Her eyes were fair, and very fair;
> — Her beauty made me glad.
> > [William Wordsworth, *We Are Seven*]

The Wordsworthian child is a "quiescent" border figure
moving lightly, unselfconsciously . . . between Nature
and Spirit.

> [Judith Plotz,
> *Romanticism and the Vocation of Childhood*]

———

Chapter one noted that Kilvert's uncle Francis registered his
love of Wordsworth by copying into one of his notebooks the
lines from his *A Poet's Epitaph* which told how the true poet
could see beyond 'The outward shows of sky and earth' to the

'deeper impulses' that they concealed. Francis also showed his reverence for Sedgwick's *Discourse* in which Sedgwick had been very careful to underline that the Christian poet saw beyond mere sense impressions. He noted that Rousseau, though a great advocate of Nature, was 'sensual and impure' whereas Wordsworth was 'one of the purest of mankind'. Sedgwick had therefore a warning for his readers: 'Let no academic student ... forget the Poet's faith; or dare to draw from his noble lessons the materials of an idolatrous or pantheistic dream'. The danger for worshippers of Nature was that they would live entirely for the life of the senses and 'sensuality is the bane of all that is good and hopeful in our nature'.[1] It was the worst, most sordid, kind of living for oneself, whereas Christianity was about living for others. Earlier chapters have illustrated Kilvert's feel for the sheer physicality of natural forms. This chapter explores the conflict inherent in Sedgwick's warning — between Christianity and paganism — as it concerned Kilvert.

It seems certain that he was showing his awareness of this conflict when he wrote 'An angel satyr walks these hills', which implies that he pictured his own self as composed of a sympathetic, caring part and a corrupt, lustful part. The statement has always been problematic for Kilvert readers. As Grice noted, it was 'apparently a single diary entry', though given undue emphasis because Plomer may have removed what preceded and followed it; Kilvert rarely wrote one sentence entries.[2] Grice offered an explanation of it after reviewing a number of 'disturbing' *Diary* entries in which Kilvert wrote of mysterious moral struggles, of 'evil thoughts' he said he had in church when observing a beautiful girl, and of the episode when, lifting a young girl onto a swing, he got her dress caught up, revealing her naked bottom and he commented: 'her flesh was plump and in excellent whipping condition'. Such entries, Grice thought, exemplified the 'satyric elements in [Kilvert's] make-up ... impulses which the Victorian consciousness labelled as guilty and bestial, and of which, in his role as parson, he is expected to be exceptionally censorious'. Grice accounted for these 'lapses' by pointing to 'the effect of prolonged celibacy on an unusually passionate nature', a Victorian 'sense of sin', and an 'immature romantic strain' on him.[3]

However, Grice distanced himself from some points made

in a talk to the Kilvert Society by Mr H.S. Scarborough in support of his thesis that there are 'peculiar features of [Kilvert's] writing, all of which I take to be signs of a violently repressed character'. These features were Kilvert's dreams (which, Grice observed, were 'no more bizarre than most dreams'), the fascination that nakedness had for him ('an absurdly mild fascination' in Grice's view when 'put alongside our twentieth century obsession with pornography'), Kilvert's interest in flagellation, and finally his 'passionate fondness for girls'. Scarborough went on: 'When he met little girls he poured out on them emotion which was rather his repressed sexual feeling than unsatisfied parental affection. He delighted to romp with girls, to fondle them, to nurse them, to kiss them'.[4] Grice noted that Scarborough's concern was shared by many readers and that others 'suspected that Kilvert was the victim of a psychological disorder'. Anxious to reject this last suggestion, Grice acknowledged that 'It is true that Kilvert was inordinately attracted by little girls, but he was not alone in this respect: paedophilia was almost as fashionable an eccentricity in the 1870s as homosexuality in the 1970s'.[5] Thus, in his effort to establish Kilvert's 'normality', Grice had virtually admitted that Kilvert was typical of his time in being a paedophile. Other commentators have touched on these issues whilst at the same time insisting on Kilvert's essential innocence (as Grice tried to do).[6] Aware of conflict within the Clyro curate, Ivor Lewis sought 'a psychological unity behind his diverse behaviour-patterns' and concluded:

> I see Kilvert as basically a sensualist, in no disparaging sense of that word. This might give as his leading thought something like "a feeling for the beauty of Creation". Here the final phrase allows us to include his deeply held religious convictions, though with a stress upon the world of appearances, or what strikes the five senses.[7]

Kilvert was quite used to seeing these issues discussed in Brooke's life of Robertson, the Brighton preacher. For example, in his 1849 letter to his friend Moncrieff, Robertson had struggled to define his theological position. His aim, he said, was to get inside 'the mind of Christ; to feel as He felt'. The essence of Christ's teaching he saw as 'benevolence', loving your brother, and Christ's commandment that we did so rested on 'eternal principles which are recognisable by the human heart', in other words, on human sympathy. Kilvert had been raised to respect this principle in the literary and religious teaching of his uncle Francis, as well as to recognise that God's goodness manifested itself in the beauty of the world. Robertson was perfectly aware of the danger that Sedgwick had seen of placing too much emphasis on the sensuous appreciation of natural beauty: 'I know that pantheism occupies this ground; and I think that pantheism is, for the most part, sentimental trash'. It offered only the immediate reality of 'what is pleasant'. However, Robertson declared that he was not 'afraid of a truth' because pantheism had caricatured it. He went on:

> Besides, even pantheism ... has its true side.... I think some pantheists are nearer the truth than most evangelicals. Many — most — make this world a machine, at a great distance from which a Superintendent sits, guiding and interfering but totally disconnected ... from the said machinery, which is in itself composed of quite base and gross materials. Now I believe that the pantheist is right in saying, there is something much more divine in God's universe than that ... God is a spirit ... the universe is localised Deity. ... The universe is the body, of which God is the Spirit.[8]

In addition to Robertson's general endorsement of the 'true side' of pantheism, Kilvert had his searching examination of the particular issue of sensuousness:

> *Perhaps no man can attain the highest excellence who is insensible to sensuous beauty.* A sense of earthly beauty may, and often does, lead to softness, voluptuousness, and defilement of the heart; but its right result is to lead on as a stepping-stone to the sense of a higher beauty. Sensuous beauty leaves the heart unsatisfied; it gives conceptions which are infinite, but it never gives or realises the infinite. ... Still it *leads* on to the infinite.

Robertson found a positive value in the unsatisfied craving in that the 'true objective' of it was 'moral beauty', the 'supersensuous' that was glimpsed beyond the merely sensuous, the 'invisible loveliness' beyond the visible. Thus, he was quite confident in asserting the value of physical beauty for 'No man knows the highest goodness who does not feel beauty. The beauty of holiness is its highest aspect'.[9] It was all very well for him to defend his view of Nature in this way but there was always the likelihood that it would be interpreted simply as paganism. The Romantic emphasis on the primacy of the feelings and on responsiveness through the senses to the beauty of Nature and of women was seen by some Victorians as an acknowledgement of the primacy of sex. For Romantics, it all came down to the 'creative energy of the imagination. No matter how carnal the Romantic in his inclinations or his expression, he trusted his imagination to purify his sensuality'.[10] It was this outlook that enabled Victorians like Kilvert to love children passionately but innocently.

Perhaps the most important section of a community for Kilvert was its children. He yearned to be a parent himself and his deep feeling for them came partly from that source. As he contemplated other people's children a note of envy crept in: 'At Wye Cliff I found the Crichtons at home with all their children, a lovely happy family group'.[11] In the view of children and women with which Kilvert was brought up, there was a conflict that paralleled the angel/satyr one. Evangelicals believed in the holiness of the natural affections, which meant love between men and women, the family, and love of children. Kilvert read in Mrs Charles's *Chronicles* that 'The kernel of the State and the type of the Church is the Family'.[12] His aunt Sophia paid tribute in her *Home Discipline* to the home 'where dwells . . . a household united by the law of kindness. . . .'[13] This law, however, clashed with another concept that had the force of law — original sin — which was 'the linchpin of the Evangelical creed'.[14] Kilvert was caught in a conflict between one strand of Christian thought that portrayed the child as innocent[15] and another which emphasised its original sin and its origin in depraved sexual instincts.

In Victorian society purity could be held up as women's prime virtue because their sexuality was denied, while men's was assumed to be natural and uncontrollable. Thus, as regards sex, there was one rule for men and another for women, which led to the categorising of women into the 'pure' and the 'fallen'.[16] Victorian women were supposed to play a moral role in which sexual desire played virtually no part.[17] 'On the other hand, the more woman's moral mission was emphasised, the clearer it became that the "nature" essential to this mission had to be protected against or even constructed in defiance of the sexual assertiveness also feared to be innate in women', themes which Tennyson had explored in *Idylls of the King*.[18] Kilvert's mentor, Frederick Robertson, accepted 'the sublime truth of the adorableness and heavenliness of female purity'.[19] Evangelicals were especially prone to emphasise the importance of bringing up girls with a deep sense of purity because they believed that women had a greater tendency to sins of the flesh than men.[20] According to Houghton, Evangelicals were 'the primary source of the ethic of purity . . .',[21] a judgement endorsed by Bradley: 'Like all Puritans, [Evangelicals] were obsessed with loose and immoral behaviour . . .' and were particularly interested in sexual morality.[22] This picture of the Evangelical conscience fits Kilvert. He acknowledged being 'greatly troubled' by the licentiousness of some Langley Burrell schoolgirls[23] and showed a similar concern over cases of unmarried mothers. With regard to a woman whose son was born three months after her wedding, he commented: 'This has been a great scandal and grief to us'.[24] He regularly recorded other cases of illegitimate births.[25]

It should not be assumed that these attitudes of Kilvert constituted a rejection of sex; it is evident he not only had a very strong sexual drive himself and was attracted to the 'wildness' of sensual passion, but that his religion taught him that such passion was natural and right. Mason emphasised that the most militant Christian opinion — that of nonconformist and Low Church sectors — actually opposed sexual self-control and that Anglican Evangelicals were, if anything, in favour of sexual freedom.[26] On the surface, the latter were more anti-sensual than other Anglicans but this can lead to a misguided view of the Evangelical position. The most obvious way in which this can be recognised is in their condemnation of celibacy as practised by religious communities of monks and nuns. 'With the Protestant majority, clerical and monastic sexual codes . . . remained an insurmountable objection to Catholicism'.[27] This is a very strong theme in books that Kilvert read, especially in Mrs Charles's *Chronicles*, which he read to his Langley Burrell Church working party. At one point, it is noted that monks condemn 'fleshly lusts' and that the character Fritz, who has entered a monastery, has renounced his. The question is then posed: 'if all our natural affections are to die in us, what is to live in us?'[28] Kilvert himself condemned as 'morbid and unnatural' the life of the Capel y Ffin monks.[29] He was one of those whom Mason called the 'more thoughtful Anglicans' who embraced both hostility to celibacy and anti-sensualism; the sensuality he opposed was that which lay outside marriage.

Kilvert was much taken with the notion of the angel-child, which emerges in the episode in which he saw 'a barefooted child, a little girl' watching him as he sat in a Bristol confectioner's shop eating a bun. She had 'shapely limbs' and 'fair hair tossed and tangled wild' and 'a winning beseeching look . . . Christ seemed to be looking at me through the beautiful wistful imploring eyes.'[30] He found those eyes irresistible and so he gave her a bun. The angel-child concept is embodied in the character of Eva in Mrs Charles's *Chronicles* but was given its finest expression in Wordsworth's *Ode Intimations of Immortality from Recollections of Early Childhood* (usually referred to as the *Immortality Ode*), but it was a concept 'totally incompatible with the Evangelical vision of the child'.[31]

As both clergyman and artist Kilvert was interested in child consciousness because he believed it had a specially important quality. His curiosity about it was in line with that which he showed in relation to other unusual states of consciousness. This allegedly un-profound man was always seeking exper-iences in which his sense of himself, of humankind, and of the universe was deepened. Dreams fascinated him. Being amongst passionately singing crowds moved him to tears. He exposed himself to savage Nature and to ancient ruins in order to experience awe and sublimity. He felt he couldn't draw close enough to natural forms unless he had solitude. He explored the mystery of the life experiences of other individuals by means of 'encounters'. He probed the significance of memory and the acts of perception involved in it. His obsession with memory was driven partly by the desire to enter into the closest possible relationship with the living and the dead. He tried to journey into the heart of Tennyson's *Idylls of the King* and to merge himself totally with Aberedw's rocks and river and Yaverland's mansion because he knew they were the sources of his artistic and religious imagination. Behind his diary-keeping lay an autobiographical impulse which at bottom was a desire to delve into the mystery of his own consciousness. And he could think of no better way of drawing close to God than being on a mountain top with only a child for company.

His guides for the exploration of child consciousness were
Robertson and Wordsworth. Robertson had written:

> I wish that nature could do her own healthy work upon
> all our hearts. I could conceive a marvellously healing
> power to come from opening the soul, like a child's, to
> receive spontaneously, without effort, the impressions
> of the unliving — and yet how living! — world around
> us with all the awe that accompanies them.
>> One impulse from a vernal wood
>>> Will teach you more of man,
>> Of moral evil and of good,
>>> Than all the sages can.[32]

The quoted poetic lines are from Wordsworth's *The Tables
Turned*, which with *Expostulation and Reply*, contain the
essence of the poet's ideas about Nature as teacher. An
extended version of them, particularly in relation to child
consciousness, is to be found in his *Immortality Ode*, a poem
about the process of maturity, the transition from childhood
to adulthood, and the changes in consciousness that occur. It
begins with a statement of how the world looked to the poet
as a child:

> There was a time when meadow, grove, and
>> stream,
> The earth, and every common sight,
>> To me did seem
>> Apparelled in celestial light,
> The glory and the freshness of a dream.

However, he is conscious that the childhood vision has faded;
the beautiful forms of Nature are still beautiful but he cannot
view them in the same way: 'The things which I have seen I
now can see no more. / . . . there hath past away a glory from
the earth'. The movement away from the joys of infancy is seen
as a movement away from divine origins:

> Our birth is but a sleep and a forgetting:
> The Soul that rises with us, our life's Star,
>> Hath elsewhere had its setting,
>> And cometh from afar:
> Not in entire forgetfulness,
> And not in utter nakedness,

> But trailing clouds of glory do we come
> From God, who is our home:
> Heaven lies about us in our infancy![33]

That Kilvert had fully assimilated Wordsworth's account of childhood vision is apparent in his poem *Paradise Clyro*, which begins: 'I met within the village street / A cottage maiden, shy and sweet; / "Whence do you come," I said, "fair child?" / "From Paradise," she said, and smiled.' He was playing with a double meaning that 'Paradise' had for him: in addition to the heaven that in Wordsworth's poem lies about us in our infancy, it also meant for Kilvert Paradise Farm where the Williams family lived, and the 'cottage maiden' was Eleanor Williams.[34] Eleanor of course knew nothing of the Wordsworthian meaning of 'Paradise'; it was 'a truth beyond what she could guess / In her sweet unconsciousness'. Nevertheless, Kilvert could glimpse her divine origins:

> For there still lingered in her eyes
> Gleams from the light of Paradise,
> And through her features yet did shine
> A likeness of the Face Divine.

She exemplified for him a two-way traffic: she was one of the 'blest spirits' who passed 'downward . . . to earth from heaven / To tell how sin might be forgiven'; the soul cleansed from sin then could pass 'heavenward — as with a new birth'.

In the *Immortality Ode*, the child grows as the years pass further and further away from the primal bliss of infancy, yet 'the Youth, who daily farther from the east / Must travel, still is Nature's Priest'. Nature serves as a second mother to the young child, preserving its joy in natural forms and the radiance surrounding them. However, all the time he is forgetting 'the glories he hath known'. He retains some memory of them but he is haunted by a profound sense of loss. Nevertheless, his 'shadowy recollections', dim and imperfect as they are, 'Are yet the fountain-light of all our day, / Are yet a master-light of all our seeing'. Immortal themselves, they are our link with our first divine consciousness and sustain us through the 'noisy years' of our mortal life. Kilvert's determination to recall with as much clarity as possible the exact features of the landscape surrounding his Hardenhuish birthplace was informed by these understandings from Wordsworth's poem. Wordsworth

expressed the mature adult's relationship with his primal
consciousness in the image of a sea shore:

> Though inland far we be,
> Our Souls have sight of that immortal sea
>   Which brought us hither,
> Can in a moment travel thither,
> And see the Children sport upon the shore,
> And hear the mighty waters rolling ever-more.

Several Victorian writers who embraced Wordsworth's
account of childhood took up this image of children sporting
on the shore. Keble, in his poem *Pebbles on the Shore*, pictured
children as 'some joyous crew / Glittering with ocean dew'.[35]
Kilvert, too, incorporated this image of the children of Nature
sporting at the edge of the ocean of immortality in his poems
To Some Little Friends at Aberystwyth and *The Tanybwlch Beach*,
both of which are about the need to remember. In the former,
he asked the children to recall the love and friendship 'that
should hallow each fair scene beside that western sea', while
he himself recollected their 'merry voices' blending with the
'ceaseless roar' of the waves 'along the shingle shore'. He
wanted the children he met on Tanybwlch beach to remember
as he did their friendship and the promise they had made that
evening, when they all felt 'nearer to Heaven', to pray that
God would wash them 'whiter than snow'. And, as in *Paradise
Clyro*, he envisaged these children, who had come from heaven,
meeting him there when life was over, by the immortal sea:

> And oh! for the shores of that crystalline sea,
> Where these sorrowful partings no longer shall
>   be.[36]

What is lost, according to Wordsworth, by the maturing
adult as he grows away from the immortal sea from which
he came is the ecstatic joy of existence manifested by the
young child, a joy which, in essence, is the continuity the
child senses between himself and the universe. This is what
the poet meant when he talked in the *Immortality Ode* of the
child having an 'immensity' of soul, being 'a Mighty Prophet!
Seer blest! / On whom those truths do rest, / Which we are
toiling all our lives to find, / In darkness lost. . . .' The darkness
is adult intellectual consciousness, as opposed to the infant's
emotional/intuitive consciousness; the adult form lacks the joy

and spontaneity of the child vision. The recovery or sustaining of that vision was for Wordsworth linked to poetic creativity, an aspect of the theme of his poetry as a whole, which concerns the establishment of a sense of relationship, of wholeness, between man and Nature. The organic continuity, the sense of belonging to the universe, must be recaptured by the man of imagination. 'For the Imaginative Man, the powers of the child are available through recollections, which are in themselves "the master-light of all our seeing".'[37] To 'see' in this sense was to see God and thus the child was

> the true centre of our religion. . . . The child is the new minted coin of life, its freshest currency, stamped with the impressure of the latest signature of paradise . . . its very being is a light and a vision. The child is the new eye of life. In later years we sleep. But in poetry, religion, music, love, in all ecstatic experience, we may wake to essential life. . . .[38]

Attention has been drawn earlier to Kilvert's interest in all these states of consciousness. In one particular *Diary* entry, his concern with child consciousness is very evident. His friend, Mrs Henry Dew, had shown him one of Dorothy Wordsworth's letters which mentioned Wordsworth's sonnet, *The Infant M- M-*, about Mary Monkhouse, Mrs Dew's name before she married. Kilvert declared that he was 'very much interested' in this information and that 'The sonnet is very beautiful'.[39] The poem is a pure expression of the Wordsworthian child, the image of which dominated some of Kilvert's most characteristic experiences of landscape.

Plotz noted that the Victorians hailed Wordsworth as the 'discoverer' of childhood and that this Victorian claim of Romantic discovery of childhood was widespread.[40] Lewis Carroll was one Victorian who owed much to this 'discovery' and regularly quoted Wordsworth in his writing.[41] According to Plotz, 'This Quintessential Child is the product of a Romantic Discourse of Childhood that is drawn from a few Romantic writers, notably Wordsworth, the Coleridges, Lamb and De Quincey'.[42] It was Rousseau who addressed childhood directly, 'rejecting outright the Calvinistic principle of original sin' and replacing it with 'the notion of inborn divinity. The child for Rousseau was a primitive in the grandest sense, unblemished and noble, uncorrupted and pure'.[43] Another writer on Carroll,

Karoline Leach, underlined the importance of the virtue of purity for Victorians. She referred to:

> the strange Victorian child-cult, the Blakean worship of the child as innocent ... for the Victorians innocence was expressed ultimately through an affected and devotional love of children. If you wanted to show a man's good heart, you said that he loved the society of little ones more than adults. ... Purity was the Victorians' favourite virtue, and it was purity that they derived from their image of children. It is no coincidence that the "patron saint of childhood" [i.e. Carroll] was born into the era of Blake and lived through the period of our history that invented childhood innocence as a new expression of religion.[44]

Kilvert was heavily involved with children's spiritual, moral and emotional development in his dual role as priest and teacher. When he recorded 'Bought *Phenomena of Nature* in Piccadilly at the SPCK Repository' on 28 January 1870, he no doubt thought of it as a practical handbook for his work.[45] That he bought the book early in his diary-keeping may also indicate that he saw it as connected with his responding to and recording of the natural forms of the landscape around Clyro. The book's full title, *The Phenomena of Nature Familiarly Explained. A book for parents and instructors, and especially adapted to schools* (1832), by Wilhelm Von Türk (1774-1846), indicates something of its aims.[46] He gave up his work as a lawyer and spent three years with the Swiss educationist Pestalozzi at his Yverdon school, studying his methods, after which he set up a school for orphans and became known as 'the Prussian Pestalozzi'. He was obviously a Wordsworth disciple because his preface paraphrases ideas from the *Immortality Ode*. The predicament of the adult whose consciousness has been damaged by 'the uncertainty of human affairs, misfortune and toil' is first sketched in. Then we are told that 'the study of nature will restore his mind to equilibrium' especially if 'by a moral life he have preserved the purity of his heart and its susceptibility to her beauties'. What follows is a picture of the Wordsworthian child, pure and ever responsive to Nature:

> This susceptibility is possessed by children in common with innocence and purity —nothing escapes their

observation — every worm, every pebble, every murmur of the brook and echo of the hill speaks visibly to the child, and it ought to be an object with parents and instructors to cherish this susceptibility. . . .

It is not only the adult who can be worn down by worldly cares and corruption: the child too is beset by 'luxurious pleasures, imaginary wants . . . affectation . . . and deceit, . . . low pleasures, indifference to religion . . . on his first emerging from the paradise of childhood and innocency'. In the preface of the book is to be found the spiritual view of Nature that Kilvert found and followed in Wordsworth. Nature, we are told in its opening paragraph, is God's Book and the wise man is he who understands how to read it because it contains 'an inexhaustible source of the purest, most exalted pleasures. . . .'[47] In the idea of everyone learning together from Nature's book Wordsworth could see an aspect of man's essential relationship to man. Kilvert's poem, *Undivided*, reflects this understanding:

> At once in Nature's page we look,
> As sitting eye to eye,
> And daily read the self-same book
> Of earth, and sea, and sky.

An element in Kilvert's purchase of Von Turk's book was no doubt awareness of himself as a teacher.[48] Von Türk said he proposed using the child's powers of observation to develop understanding of natural objects and natural laws, a method that placed him firmly in the Pestalozzian tradition. Pestalozzi's approach began with familiarising the child with his own environment, studying its particular features and examining in the classroom the experiences and the natural objects so gained. Kilvert had been taught this way himself. The schools of his father and of his uncle Francis featured study of natural objects collected by pupils themselves or by others on 'field trips'. The British pioneer of infant education, Samuel Wilderspin (1791-1866), another Pestalozzi disciple, had urged that Nature should be studied 'in the garden, in the lanes, in the fields', and that 'museums' of natural objects should find a place in schools.[49] Kilvert's father built this element into his school, as Hare recorded: 'From 12 to 1 we were taken out for a walk, when we employed the time collecting all kinds of rubbish—bits of old tobacco pipe etc—to make "museums".'[50] For Pestalozzi, geography and natural history, taught in this empirical way, were the foundation of most other subjects, including science.[51] It is noticeable that Kilvert had a reputation at Clyro school for being a geography specialist: 'Mr Kilvert do come and tell us about all parts,' said one boy.[52] The school prided itself on its geography teaching, including Kilvert's contribution to it. He showed particular concern for the older pupils' performance during an HMI inspection in their 'special subject' — geography.[53] No *Diary* entry has survived showing Kilvert using in school the approach of Von Türk (and Pestalozzi) to geography and natural history. However, in his own Sunday School, we see him following their approach to the letter.

In the summer of 1875, he noted a pattern of conducting these classes on the lawn of Langley Rectory on sunny days. On 8 August, he referred to his 'little scholars' being amused at what he called the 'green drawing room' under the shade of the lime trees. He had taught them outside two weeks before, though the lessons were on conventional religious subjects, and this was the case on 8 August too. However, on Sunday 5 September, he recorded that he taught them on the lines laid down in Von Türk's manual: 'I taught them lessons from the nuthatch tapping in the tree overhead, the woodpigeon cooing in the elm and the flowers that grew around us'.[54] His approach here had an exact counterpart in Pestalozzi's own. The latter recorded in his diary that 'children should learn to read first in the Book of Nature', adding 'Lead your child out into nature, teach him on the hill tops and in the valleys . . . should a bird sing . . . [the bird] is teaching him'.[55] Kilvert was also following George Fox's advice that wisdom was not to be found in libraries of human knowledge but in the study of God's handiwork.

The children who appear in Wordsworth's Lucy poems receive the greater and the best part of their 'instruction' from Nature itself without human intervention. If the *Immortality Ode* is the blueprint for his concept of Nature as it relates to childhood, the Lucy poems are its working models. They appear in the *Lyrical Ballads* collection and are a mysterious, highly ambiguous set of poems, comprising *Lucy Gray, Strange fits of passion have I known, Three years she grew in sun and shower, She dwelt among the untrodden ways,* and *A slumber did my spirit seal.* They centre on Lucy, a child of Nature, whose death all the poems record in various vague, oblique ways; the exact circumstances of her death are never established. Jones referred to the poems' 'extreme spirituality of tone and lack of literal content'.[56] They are concerned basically with Lucy's death and the reactions to it of those who knew her. As a group, the poems reiterate some of the themes of the *Immortality Ode*. In all of them, there is continual emphasis on Lucy's isolation. This is a strong theme of *Three years she grew,* in which, at the age of three, she is taken over by Nature:

> Three years she grew in sun and shower,
> Then Nature said, "A lovelier flower
> On earth was never sown;
> This Child I to myself will take. . . .
> Myself will to my darling be
> Both law and impulse. . . ."

The child is shaped, both internally and externally, by contact with natural forms. We are told that 'in rock and plain, / In earth and heaven, in glade and bower' she would experience 'an overseeing power / To kindle and restrain', and that her 'form' would be moulded into graceful shape by the 'motions of the Storm' through the agency of 'silent sympathy'. 'Vital feelings of delight / Shall rear her form to stately height, / Her virgin bosom swell'. And all the while, Nature would supply her thoughts.

In *Lucy Gray*, her isolation is not as complete as in *Three years she grew* but she is characterised as the 'solitary child' who knew 'no mate, no comrade' and she 'dwelt on a wide moor, — / The sweetest thing that ever grew / Beside a human door!'[57] We are immediately presented with a mystery because though in the first stanza the poet / narrator says that he 'chanced to see . . . the solitary child', the third stanza records that the 'sweet face of Lucy Gray / Will never more be seen'. Her loss is seen as the result of parental neglect. Her father, knowing that a snow storm was expected, sent Lucy out with a lantern to guide her mother, who is in the town, back through the snow.

> The storm came on before its time:
> She wandered up and down;
> And many a hill did Lucy climb:
> But never reached the town.

All night her parents searched for her but in vain. When the poet/narrator glimpsed Lucy it was 'at break of day'; dawn is again presented as the critical time in her existence because 'At

day-break' her parents stood on a hill overlooking the moor
to see if they could see her. They notice a wooden bridge and
discover that Lucy's footprints lead to it but stop in the middle
of it — 'And further there was none!' Her 'in-between' quality,
that is caught in the two references to the time between night
and day, is stressed again by her disappearance in the middle
of the bridge. It is not made clear how she died or even that
she is dead.

> — Yet some maintain that to this day
> She is a living child,
> That you may see sweet Lucy Gray
> Upon the lonesome wild.
>
> O'er rough and smooth she trips along,
> And never looks behind;
> And sings a solitary song
> That whistles in the wind.

The emphasis on her still being alive suggests that she is not
a ghost but occupies some middle ground between life and
death. This suggestion helps to account for the survivors'
response to her loss because, though it provokes sadness, there
is also resignation. The final picture of her tripping along, never
looking back, singing and whistling in the wind, suggests that
she at least is happy in her new existence.

The idea that Lucy is a happy child of Nature over whom
death has no power is strong in *A slumber did my spirit seal*.
There is calm acceptance of her 'death', as though it is part of
Nature's inevitable cycle of change:

> A slumber did my spirit seal;
> I had no human fears:
> She seemed a thing that could not feel
> The touch of earthly years.
>
> No motion has she now, no force;
> She neither hears nor sees;
> Rolled round in earth's diurnal course,
> With rocks, and stones, and trees!

In the second of these two stanzas (which comprise the whole
of the poem), Lucy has become part of Nature itself, just as
Lucy Gray merged into the very snow in which she was lost.
Lucy in *She dwelt among the untrodden ways* is also identified

with natural forms, being described as 'A violet by a mossy stone' and as 'Fair as a star'. She is likened to a flower in *Three years she grew* and to 'a rose in June' in *Strange fits of passion*. The passing of flowers cannot be regretted like the passing of human beings, but more emotional shock is registered in *Strange fits* — ' "Oh mercy!" to myself I cried, / "If Lucy should be dead!" ' — and in *She dwelt* — 'But she is in her grave, and, oh, / The difference to me!' However, in *Three years she grew*, the note of calm acceptance is sounded again:

> She died, and left to me
> This heath, this calm, and quiet scene;
> The memory of what has been,
> And never more will be.

Lucy has left a mood of stillness that contrasts with the 'motion' she once had.

Liveliness and changeability, as well as wildness, underlined in most of the Lucy poems, are characteristic features of the Wordsworthian child and, coupled with the intermediate position Lucy occupies between life and death, they have led several critics to see her, not as a real human being with a history, but as a poetic object or symbol. The poems represented for Ferguson 'a Wordsworthian quest for a poetical object', a sort of private language of imagery.[58] (It is significant that the sub-title that Wordsworth gave to *Lucy Gray* is *Or, Solitude*.) For Hartman, her essential quality is that she is 'a boundary being', on the edge of the human and the natural world; she is 'nature-sprite and human', living an intermediate life between different realms of existence.[59] Watson summed up the Lucy poems in this way: 'They deal with the growth of the poet's love for a pure young girl, and the loss of the beloved'.[60]

It is very evident that Kilvert, both in his poems and in his *Diary*, was fascinated by the poetic image that is Lucy and was keen to make his own explorations of it. He referred to the young girl, Florence Little, as 'The Flower of Slaughterford', and emphasised her purity and her star-like eyes: 'not a star in all bright heaven / Shines with a purer light / Than those twin stars. . . .'[61] In his description of Katie, daughter of his sister Emily, there are distinct elements of Lucy:

> She is a pretty, delicate, exquisitely made child . . .
> Her face is a very remarkable one, variable as shade

and sunshine, sometimes dimpled with a mischievous
smile, sometimes stern and frowning with a severe
determined look upon the mouth. When smiling it is a
beautiful bewitching fascinating face with an espiègle
spirituelle look. Katie is plainly a very uncommon child,
exceedingly clever and original, changeable, sudden
and full of moods. You never know what is coming next,
or what she will say or do under given circumstances.
She is somewhat of an elf and a sprite excitable very
and apt to be wild, as playful as a kitten.[62]

Nothing stands out more clearly as a parallel to Lucy Gray
that Kilvert consciously developed in his writing than his
relationship with Emmeline Vaughan, daughter of his close
friend, Rev David Vaughan of Newchurch, near Clyro. When
he visited the Vaughan home on 26 February 1870, 'At tea there
were Sarah, Emmeline with her Geneva brooch and fair curls
and saucy Jinny (i.e. Janet) with her dark eyes. She gave me
a kiss at parting'.[63] Visiting again in May 1870, he confessed
that he 'travelled ten miles . . . over the hills . . . to kiss that
sweet child's face'. It was Janet's face he meant, Janet who kept
looking at him 'saucily with her mischievous beautiful grey
eyes'.[64] By the time of his visit on 5 September 1871, Emmeline
was dead (she had died from consumption in early May that
year) and in the entry he wrote she is identified, as she is in
subsequent entries, with a 'little lonely tree':

> The little lonely tree bowed on the mountain brow, and
> below lay the tiny village deep in the valley among the
> trees embosoming the little church with its blue spire
> and Emmeline's grave.

As the months of 1872 went by, *Diary* entries concerning
Emmeline are increasingly marked by a concern with mourning
and remembering her that is strongly reminiscent of the Lucy
poems, the steady theme of which is preserving her memory.
He can be seen constructing for her the kind of poetic reality
possessed by the nature-sprite of Wordsworth's poems. Parrish
said that the most important thing about Lucy is that she is
presented as living in local memory and in the imagination
of the poet.[65] Similarly, Ferguson referred to the Lucy poems
as 'memory poems — or poems in memory of Lucy'.[66] Kilvert
began to make increasing use of poetic means to enhance his

memory of Emmeline. A few days after the journey to the Vaughans he recorded: 'Writing at night late "Emmeline's Grave" '.[67] On 8 August 1872, the time for him to leave Clyro only a month away, he wrote: 'It was perhaps my last journey . . . to the sweet Vale of Newchurch . . . and Emmeline's grave. Seldom have I seen more lovely the beautiful hills and vales which I shall now see no more'.[68] The impulse to make her part of a landscape, as Lucy was, had now become insistent:

> I paid a last visit to the storm blown hawthorn on the mountain top, "the little lonely tree" among the fern and carved upon the trunk about two feet from the ground a little cross on the Eastern side of the tree. . . .[69]

He began the journey back to Clyro but not before he 'cut a cross in remembrance on the stem of one of the silver birches near the Great Cayan, the next tree but one to Newchurch'.

He always made maximum effort to remember his child lovers, as we have seen, and four months after leaving Clyro he went through those rituals of remembrance that helped to confirm her as a permanent part of his consciousness:

> Today I have laid away the lock of our dear Emmeline's hair, with my other such memorials, in the secret drawer in my new desk. It seems but yesterday since I saw the beautiful golden-haired child for the first time. She was dancing down the steep meadow brow from Gilfach y Rheol to Newchurch village. . . .

'*Our* dear Emmeline's hair. . . .' In his imagination, he had become her father. In this memory of their first meeting, her spriteliness is the dominant impression, another link to Wordsworth's Lucy: 'Emmeline with a merry parting word danced away down the hill', recalling the 'dancing Shape' that is Lucy in *She was a Phantom of Delight* and the Lucy in *Three years she grew* where she is 'sportive as the fawn'. At the end of this entry, which emphasises Emmeline's physical liveliness, Kilvert contrasted it with her lack of 'motion': 'she now sleeps in the God's Acre at Newchurch'. On subsequent revisits to the scene of Emmeline's life and death, the emphasis on mourning increases and entries reiterate the sense, very powerful in the Lucy poems, that Nature's child has returned in death to her native element. With Emmeline, too, the circle of sympathy encompasses a variety of natural phenomena. On 14 March

1873, when Kilvert came in sight of the church, 'snow began to fall heavily in large flakes'. This sign that Nature was mourning is reinforced by what follows:

> As I stooped over the green grave ... placing the primrose bunches in a cross upon the turf the large flakes of snow still fell thickly upon us, but melted as they fell, and the great yew tree overhead bent weeping upon the grave.[70]

It is especially in *Three years she grew* that Nature is shown having the special care for Lucy that it has here for Emmeline. We are told in Wordsworth's poem that for Lucy 'the willow bends' and that all of Nature is in 'silent sympathy' with her. 'Sympathy' here is more than a response to her death; it is the affinity that other beautiful forms feel for her. The snow in which Lucy Gray disappeared is associated in Kilvert's description with the landscape of which Emmeline has become a part. (He made it very clear that the story of Lucy Gray had taken a firm hold on his imagination by the poem called *Snow* that he wrote in which a girl 'as pure as the snow' is lost in a snow storm 'so long ago'.) The mountain and Emmeline and Kilvert seem as one in 'The mountain was full of memories of sweet Emmeline Vaughan', which he wrote in April 1876. The echo of 'sweet Lucy Gray' is very strong here, especially when he recollected Emmeline's 'light elegant delicate form so bright and fairy-like and the quick tiny feet as she danced ... down the steep green hill ... ,' reminding us of the final image of her counterpart: 'you may see sweet Lucy Gray / Upon the lonesome wild. / O'er rough and smooth she trips along. ... '

After Emmeline's death, the account of Kilvert's return visits to mourn at her grave presents her as a spirit of the Newchurch landscape, her 'bright and fairy-like' liveliness transformed now into a still, melancholy, brooding presence. She became 'a living spirit of landscape', in the phrase used by Bloom to sum up the meaning of Lucy Gray,[71] or, in Averill's view, a 'genius loci'.[72] And Kilvert's writing about the dead Emmeline took on the part-love poem, part-epitaph quality that Ferguson found dominant in the Lucy poems.[73] The Clyro sections of the *Diary* contain a series of Lucys, of whom Emmeline is the most highly developed. Sarah Smith is represented by Kilvert as the archetype of those young girls he designated 'mountain beauties'. She was born at New Barn farm:

> And this is the birthplace of Sarah Smith. Sarah of the
> Cwm. To me there seems to be a halo of glory round this
> place. Yet in what poor mean dwellings these wild rich
> natures, these mountain beauties, are born and reared.
> Many sweet and sacred memories hover about these
> hill homes and make the place wherever one stands
> holy ground.[74]

The characteristic singled out here — the girls' 'wild rich
natures' — was the key one for him and the one that linked
them to Lucy Gray. Wild scenery and relative remoteness from
human society were their required environment, as is made
clear in the Lucy poems.[75] The other thing that stands out in
the description of Sarah Smith, who was nine at this time, is the
extravagant religious language, which relates to Wordsworth's
presentation of childhood. 'Halo of glory' recalls the infant
vision of Nature as 'the glory and freshness of a dream' in the
Immortality Ode; 'holy ground' would have reminded Kilvert
of Wordsworth's *Prelude*:

> it shall be my pride
> That I have dared to tread this holy ground,
> Speaking no dream, but things oracular.[76]

Memories of the 'holy ground' and the wild mountain beauties
who inhabited it would inevitably be 'sacred' for Kilvert as
the source of his artistic creativity, just as the memories of
Emmeline were.[77] To Victorians like him, for whom poetry
and religion served the same ends, religious language would
have seemed entirely appropriate to describe beautiful young
girls, who themselves belonged to the Victorian cult of the
pure maiden. He was expressing this understanding when he
described Pussy as 'spirituelle': 'Pussy looked very spirituelle
this morning and wore a breastknot of primroses'.[78] He also
used the word in relation to Katie, daughter of his sister
Emily.

A group of girls formed in Kilvert's mind a distinct entity
that he associated with the hills behind Clyro, girls whose
beauty and wildness, like that of the Clyro hills themselves,
made him 'glad' (cf. the verse of Wordsworth's *We are Seven*
that provides one of this chapter's epigraphs). These 'beauties'
were 'Eleanor and Florence Hill and Gipsy Lizzie and Esther
and Pussy of New Barn'. Florence Hill, in particular, had all

the right credentials for inclusion in this select group: 'She was indeed as Mrs Vaughan said "beautiful and wild and stately, a true mountain child" '.[79] Gipsy Lizzie's 'wildness' resided chiefly in her looks that he saw as gipsy-like. He contrasted her dark hair and skin with Pussy's blond looks:

> The two shy beauties, Pussy with her fair curls and bright quick blue eyes, and Gipsy Lizzie with her dark curls and complexion, blue eyes and delicate regular features, were sitting side by side, a pretty sight, the fair child quick in eye and movement, restless and timid as a fawn easily startled, ceaseless in her quick shy glances, the dark child earnest thoughtful, sometimes smiling but often lost in rapt observation or reverie.[80]

The overtones of Wordsworth's Lucy are very evident here — her changeability in 'quick in eye and movement' and 'restless', and in the comparison with a fawn, while Gipsy Lizzie by contrast is 'earnest thoughtful' and 'often lost . . . in reverie'. Kilvert was utterly captivated by Gipsy's looks:

> How is the indescribable beauty of that most lovely face to be described — the dark soft curls parting back from the pure white clear transparent brow, the exquisite little mouth and pearly tiny teeth, the pure straight delicate features, the long dark fringes and white eyelids that droop over and curtain her eyes, when they are cast down or bent upon her book, and seem to rest upon the soft clear cheek, and when the eyes are raised, that clear unfathomable blue depth of wide wonder and inquiry and unsullied and unsuspecting innocence. Oh, child, child, if you did but know your own power. Oh, Gipsy, if you only grow up as good as you are fair. Oh, that you might grow up good. May all God's angels guard you, sweet. The Lord bless thee and keep thee.[81]

It was passages like this that Scarborough found unpalatable because they provided evidence of Kilvert's 'repressed sexual feeling'.[82] Plotz, too, acknowledged this element in the mixture of elements contained in the passage:

> This astonishing tribute to a little girl's "power" is clearly a self-serving justification of Kilvert's prohibited desire. This is a transparent example of the way in which the

claim of the child's *power* answers the adult's wish for self-justification or comfort.[83]

Kincaid saw the passage as an illustration both of Kilvert's 'obsession with the "pure" and his slipping and sliding between the call of the wild and the call of God'.[84] Gipsy's power lay, according to Plotz, partly in the 'devastating erotic and emotional authority' he attributed to her, which was linked to the innocence he saw in her and sought for himself. The way this link operated Leach explained thus: 'To worship [the pure child] was to worship purity; more importantly perhaps, to be seen to worship her was to be seen to possess that all-important purity by association'.[85] Ironically, the heavy stress placed on the purity of children and of women by Christianity in fact gave rise to paedophilia in that, by associating purity with children, it made a connection between purity and the sexually prohibited child. Thus, 'purity was . . . defined by and riddled through with sexual desire in Victorian England'.[86] Similarly, Kilvert's interest in seeing naked children, deemed highly suspect by some *Diary* readers, has this ambivalent quality. Far from feeling guilty about such episodes, he treated them with hearty relish. One Saturday night in April 1871, when visiting the Sackville family, he was cheered when Polly, their young daughter, prepared herself for the bath:

> Polly with great satisfaction and celerity stripped herself naked to her drawers before me and was very anxious to take off her drawers too for my benefit, but her grandmother would not allow her.

It is evident that he took the child's unselfconscious behaviour as delightful proof of her innocence; if she had appeared modest, it would have indicated sexual awareness.[87] When bathing naked or observing others naked, he believed that he was innocent and was pursuing innocence.

His susceptibility to child innocence is clear from his response to Le Jeune's painting, *Innocence*, which he saw at the Royal Academy on 25 June 1874:

> It was the face of a lovely child who had been unjustly blamed and punished for a fault of which she was Innocent, innocent. Her little hands were clasped and her flushed cheek laid against them. Indignant tears were brimming in the sad imploring eyes which told

their own tale. 'Innocent, innocent, oh indeed, indeed
I am innocent.'

At the same exhibition, Millais's *North-West Passage* was on
display and Kilvert admired it, but insisted that *Innocence* was
the one he would have most liked to own. Millais's reputation
had been built partly on the *North-West Passage, The Huguenot*
and *The Black Brunswicker*, but partly also on his child pictures
that presented beautiful, innocent children,[88] which would be
labelled 'sentimental' today but registered with the Victorian
public. 'The public were ready to draw narrative interest and
moral significance not only from the anecdotal subjects [*The
Huguenot, The Black Brunswicker*] but also from portraits of
children'.[89] It is clear that Kilvert was much taken with Millais's
work since he made several references to his child studies. On
24 May 1875, he called at the Lanhill farm where he knew he
would find the beautiful child, Florence Little. Amy Little sat
in the garden 'in a pretty ivy arbour with some crumbs for a
tame robin' with Florence standing beside her in a landscape
cameo:

> it was a beautiful picture, the pretty golden-haired girl
> sitting on the rustic seat in the green gloom of the arbour
> calling to the robin while the beautiful child stood at
> her knee. What a subject for Millais.

Millais's child paintings made a large contribution to the
child cult of the time and Kilvert responded to it. His illicit
response to child beauty in paintings was, however, never far
away. About Millais's *Picture of Health*, a portrait of his daughter
Alice, Kilvert wrote: '[It] was so like Georgie Gale that I could
have kissed the blooming face and ruddy lips'.[90]

A significant aspect of the Victorian child cult concerned
what Plotz called 'sequestering' of children and it is relevant
to Kilvert's involvement with the cult. She noted that the idealisation of the child in the nineteenth century was accompanied
by a deliberate detaching of it from the family circle: 'It is a
being outside of the social and familial net'.[91] This isolation
of the child was the result of identifying it with Nature. The
special psychological powers of children needed, Wordsworth
believed, separation from society in order to grow because their
unitary mode of thinking, their faith in 'the meaningfulness of
the world', was threatened by society. 'Wordsworth habitually

focused on solitary children assimilated to landscape — Lucy, the Idiot Boy, Ruth. . . .'[92] Their unitary minds are in tune with the unitary landscape, but they need solitude if they are to harmonise properly. While Kilvert lived in Clyro, he identified a number of solitary children, daughters of parishioners, who approximated closely to Wordsworth's figures, and he made them into semi-poetic objects who excited his special care. His concern for Gipsy Lizzie and for some of the other 'mountain beauties' was occasioned by what he knew of their backgrounds. In a significant number of cases the girls lacked one or more parents, a fact which had several important implications for him. Firstly, it made them interesting and challenging in that he himself could to an extent fill the place of the missing parent. Secondly, he could recognise that they all stood in an increased degree of moral danger. Thirdly, that danger was increased by the fact of the girls' particular beauty. And fourthly, the girls more fully met the key criterion of the Wordsworthian child by being 'sequestered', partly because they were mountain children and partly because they were half outside the conventional family unit. Kilvert was therefore more able to romanticise them in accordance with the Wordsworthian model.

The 1871 Clyro census shows that Gipsy Lizzie had been born in Pontypool and was living, not with her parents, but with her grandfather, John Harris.[93] She was 10 at this time and her particular moral vulnerability lay in the fact that living in the same house were Harris's 26-year-old unmarried son and two other sons aged 16 and 13. Then there was Sarah Bryan, whom Kilvert recalled first meeting on 29 May 1865.[94] When he met her sister on 8 April 1875, the mention of her name 'took me at once as in a dream and a vision to the top of Coed y Garth . . .' where he first saw her. The former date indicates that she would have been associated with the children in the party he had seen at the Rocks of Aberedw, the magical place where his poetic creativity had been aroused as never before, when he viewed landscape in the way that the infant of Wordsworth's *Immortality Ode* did and it became for him too the 'master-light' of all his seeing. Sarah had much in common with Lucy Gray: she lived in the wild with only her father, who had a 'little keeper's hut in the woods', and he was old, 'grey-moustached'. Emphasised repeatedly is Sarah's 'wildness': she had 'clear wild grey eyes', 'She was like a beautiful wild spirit of the hills', and she lived 'the free open wild life of the hills'. And very significantly, when 'obliged to go to service, and confined to the house and indoor work, she seemed to languish and sicken and pine away' to the extent that she died. Social constraints, even of this modest kind, destroyed her. Kilvert mourned her but felt united with her in memory and prayed they would meet again in heaven, pictured as a landscape, 'a more beautiful hill than the Coed y Garth and by the shore of the crystal sea. . . .' She epitomised perfectly the dangers that threatened young girls lacking proper protection: 'She left one child behind her, Marianne. Over the birth of the child let us draw a tender veil'.[95]

Wildness was a powerful concept for Kilvert but it had negative as well as positive aspects. In its positive form it stood for vitality, spontaneity, freedom and naturalness but its dark side was the sensuality which, as was noted at the start of this chapter, was feared by Sedgwick because it could lead to a pagan love of Nature. Kilvert used 'wild' with this latter connotation when speaking of Hannah Williams who had been sexually promiscuous: 'The poor wild beautiful girl is stopped in her wildness at last. . . .'[96] He hinted at this danger on 27 February 1874 with regard to the pubescent Louisa Dew who, he noted, had the qualities of a child of Nature — 'quick bright blue eyes and a merry lively manner', with 'dancing spirits' — but a little note of anxiety crept in: 'She is growing very pretty . . . and as *wild* as a hawk but as good as gold. . . .'[97] His innocent, semi-erotic 'romps' with girls were often overlaid by his fear that sometime in the future the girls would be seduced and corrupted, their innocence destroyed. It was an inevitable, tragic and Romantic tension. One way out of it was to project their primal beauty and innocence into a poetic/imaginative ideal such as Lucy Gray.

Nowhere in the *Diary* is the tension more powerfully expressed than in the episode of the Mouse Castle girls. It is an entry that enacts aspects of the *Immortality Ode* and has a Spring setting as does Wordsworth's poem. 'A stout elderly man in a velveteen jacket . . . sat or lay upon the dry turf' of the earthwork known as Mouse Castle. A figure less like a spirit of Nature could hardly be imagined. Initially, he resembles the adult of Wordsworth's poem on whom 'earthly freight' and custom lay with such 'a weight, / Heavy as frost and deep almost as life' that he had been compelled to lie down! But the appearance is deceptive. Around him frolic his children, mainly girls, 'about 12 or 14 years old', who 'climbed up the steep rocks ... quite regardless of the shortness of their petticoats and the elevating ... powers of the wind'.

> The man lay down in the grass on his face and apparently went to sleep. The girls called him 'Father'. They were full of fun and larks as wild as hawks, and presently began a great romp on the grass which ended in their rolling and tumbling head over heels and throwing water over each other and pouring some cautiously on their father's head. Then they scattered primroses over him.

The girls' 'wildness' is repeatedly emphasised. They are a 'wild group' and become ever more 'wild and excited' (as Kilvert himself did); the one in the red frock was the 'wildest'; water was 'wildly dashed' at each other; they had 'wild saucy eyes' and were 'a wild troop of girls'. Their resemblance to Bacchantes is increased by their being compared (as Lucy Gray is) to animals — to 'young antelopes or fawns', 'young wild goats'. Insistent stresses suggest that the girls are creatures of instinct, half human and half spirits of Nature. As Lucy, in *A slumber did my spirit seal*, became after death as one with rocks and trees, so these girls are identified with water, which they obtain from a spring in the wood. They also push each other into the spring, seeming like the spirits who haunt springs. Eventually, their repeated applications of water to their father enable him to recover the child consciousness within himself and soon he is sporting Pan-like with the other nature-spirits: 'the father began to roll down the hillockside to amuse his younger children. . . . Next he went to hide himself in the wood. . . .'

The Mouse Castle passage has a visionary quality to it that Kilvert was careful to create:

> I could not make the party out. . . . They were perfectly nondescript, seemed to have come from nowhere, but just to have fallen from the sky. . . . I cannot think who the wild party were. They were like no one whom I ever saw before.

He implied their non-human nature by referring to them as 'spirited' and 'high-spirited', and towards the end of the passage he expressed their essence: 'they were the *genii loci* and

always lived there'. These emphases are very redolent not
only of Lucy Gray but also of Howitt's enthusiastic comments
on the thatched cottages of the New Forest: 'They seem . . .
erected in the spirit, and under the influence, of the genius
loci.' And he spoke of the Forest inhabitant who 'has walked
through the spirit-land with power' and who was honoured
'by all true lovers of pathos and imagination.'[98] For Kilvert, the
Mouse Castle girls were border-spirits and part of the border
landscape of Wales. The fact that the girls were on the verge
of puberty, on the border between childhood and adulthood,
innocence and knowledge, is significant and explains the
passage's erotic overtones. He drew attention to the Bacchantes'
leader, the girl in the red frock: 'In the romp her dress was
torn open all down her back . . . showing vast spaces of white,
skin as well as linen'. And he, while 'envying the father his
children', was also very aware of their 'young supple limbs,
their white round arms . . . red sweet full lips. . . .'[99] These
children of Nature were plainly only part spirit; there was also
a very earthy, sensual quality to them and he was aware at that
moment of the conflict within himself, and potentially within
the concept of the Wordsworthian child of Nature, between
angel and satyr. He was aware of it too when, in his clergyman
role, he strove to protect pretty girls in moral danger while
simultaneously acknowledging their sexual attractiveness.

For Kilvert, an important aspect of Pan and of the mountain
beauties who made the landscape above Clyro 'holy ground',
was *unselfconsciousness*. He saw it in the spontaneity and
naturalness of the Mouse Castle girls and of the women and
girls of the Radnorshire farms and cottages. The Hill women
(Florence, Eleanor and their mother) of Noyadd's Farm were
'simple, natural, and at their ease, . . . courteous, considerate,
. . . and unaffectedly happy'. He found these qualities too in
Carrie Gore, the miller's daughter who played hymn tunes
for him 'without any false shame or false modesty',[100] and
in Mrs Jones of Harbour farm, whom he surprised 'in the
midst of her Saturday cleaning but quite unconscious of
herself' welcomed him 'simply and naturally'.[101] He made it
one of the features of 'The Highest of Women' in his poem
of that name: 'She wears that brightest, loveliest dress / The
robe of unselfconsciousness. . . .' Florence Hill had many of
the attributes of this ideal woman but was pre-eminent in
unselfconsciousness: 'there came over her lovely face a rapt

far-away look, self-forgetful, self-unconscious, a look as of one divinely inspired'.[102] Such naturalness was linked to purity because, as he often made clear, excessive concern on women's part with their looks, clothes and hair signified vanity and awareness of male admiration: 'I do think the way the Vaughan girls wear their short curling hair is the most natural . . . in the world'.[103]

The matter of girls' hair presented him with a conflict. Evangelicalism recommended short hair (and plain clothes) for women: '[Girls] were expected to have straight hair and not curls or ringlets, eschewed gauze bonnets ornamented with bows and wore straw bonnets without bows, preferred green and grey colours to red and lilac'.[104] It will be recalled that the leader of the Mouse Castle girls wore 'a red frock' and that Martha Ray in *The Thorn* wore 'a scarlet cloak'. Kilvert, however, was as powerfully drawn to the red frock as he was to abundant tresses. He enthused over Gertrude Headley's 'luxuriant wealth of beautiful brown hair'.[105] His angel-children often had long golden curls but, importantly, were unselfconscious about them and their other charms. However, in the Wordsworthian child of Nature, unselfconsciousness went beyond mere appearance; it was a matter of sensibility, which manifested itself in a spontaneity indicative of its harmony with Nature.[106] In particular, it was the antithesis of the deflating rationality, the analytical tendency of adults that Wordsworth criticised by saying 'We murder to dissect'.

Kilvert met the epitome of the child of Nature, somewhat paradoxically on a Wootton Bassett train, in what he described as 'this *seemingly* chance crossing of paths', signifying that it was one of those 'encounters' heaven sent for his spiritual benefit. 'It was a singularly beautiful child . . . with . . . flaxen curls' and it exhibited Lucy Gray traits — 'eyes that expressed a thousand emotions, by turns arch and laughing, sweet, reproachful and grave'. She is both 'sequestered' and mysterious to an extent by being bereft of family, seeming 'not to belong to the lady who was taking care of her'; she also remained nameless because he omitted to ask her name.[107] However, that was immaterial because, as with Mary Williams of Penllan and Florence Hill, there was immediate sympathy between her and him:

From the moment the child was in my arms a sudden and great happiness came over me. I had thought

my heart was growing hard and that I was no longer
capable of such emotion. But . . . once more there was
only one thing in the world and that was love.

The idea of Love as the principle of the universe had been
inculcated into Kilvert as a central element of his religious
upbringing. Both his uncle Francis and his aunt Sophia
were disciples of Fénelon, the seventeenth-century divine.[108]
Fénelon's writings had a great influence on eighteenth-century
Quakers and the leaders of the Evangelical revival.[109] It is clear
that Kilvert knew something of these writings because he
was gratified to find one of his Langley Burrell parishioners
'studying Fénelon'.[110] Fénelon preached the doctrine of 'Pure
Love' that counselled abandonment of the self to God and the
embracing of a life of simplicity, like that of a child.[111] Flew
described Fénelon's 'Pure Love' as 'a state of perfect charity'
which has the power of overcoming evil.[112] Kilvert could
imagine no heart, however hard or sinful, being able to resist
the innocence and beauty of the angel-child whose appearance
before him had been ordained.

Kilvert's celebration of Love as the principle of the universe
and of his own responsive heart may be contrasted with his
desire to be shut off from all feeling, following the abortive
encounter with the Miss Halls that was focused on in chapter
six. The rest of the angel-child passage represents his response
as an ecstatic experience: 'I knew a man — Such an one caught
up to the third heaven, and saw and felt unspeakable things'.
The Biblical allusion Kilvert made helps us to understand what
this experience meant to him. He was quoting St Paul's second
Letter to the Corinthians: 'I knew a man in Christ . . . such an
one caught up to the third heaven. . . . How he was caught up
into paradise, and heard unspeakable words, which it is not
lawful for a man to utter'.[113]

We have come full circle here — to the child waif Kilvert saw
in the Bristol street through whose eyes he could see Christ, to
the farm girl Eleanor Williams who came from 'Paradise', to
the essence of Christ's teaching which Robertson saw as love, to
Eva, the 'angel-child' of Mrs Charles's *Chronicles*. And of course
to the *Immortality Ode* because Kilvert, though far 'inland', had
had a glimpse of 'that immortal sea' which is Paradise, and
he had been vouchsafed it by the angel-child. That Paradise
was in part perfect love and he had been reassured that he still

had a 'human heart'. 'The angel child looked into my eyes and soul' and he knew 'that she had a message'. He knew he was in the presence of the kind of child whom Wordsworth called a 'Mighty Prophet' and a 'Seer blest'. But, even in this moment of spiritual exaltation, there is the familiar hint of sensuality:

> As the beautiful child lay in my arms and lifted her fearless blue eyes laughingly to mine and clasped her baby hands round my neck, sending a thrill of inexpressible delight through me, I saw she was no ordinary child. . . . I relinquished her sorrowfully with a shower of kisses. . . .[114]

Kilvert's Wootton Bassett train entry poses problems for the modern reader because it yokes together the spiritual and the erotic, the sacred and the profane, and the suspicion that he was a paedophile, as Grice seemed ready to admit, still lingers. The key to the problem lies in understanding the Victorian child cult and its origins. Leach's summing up of it helps us to recognise what the experience was that Kilvert had on his train journey:

> The Child, as invented by Victorian sentimentality, was an extraordinary symbol, in which many of the images of Christianity were united with a curious quasi-paganism . . . her soft beguiling image, sacrificial as the Cross, redemptive as the Madonna, innocently sensual as an earth-sprite, took the place of the Crucifix as the towering emblem of Christian sacrifice. . . .[115]

The impression we have of Kilvert's sexuality can partly be attributed to William Plomer, the editor of the *Diary*: 'he included almost every passage indicative of [his] passion for young girls . . . it made Kilvert more like his editor: less interested in God and more concerned with sex'.[116] Plomer himself said that because he had to bear in mind the general reader in his selection of *Diary* passages, it would be found that 'I was not able to do full justice to Kilvert's preoccupation with his priestly functions'.[117] In his poem, *Angel Satyr*, Plomer not only showed considerable insight into Kilvert's Clyro ministry, but also provided a sensitive assessment of the relationship between religion and sex in his life. Plomer depicts Kilvert as a dynamic force, walking through the landscape, engendering power in others and in turn absorbing power from them and the landscape itself. The poem demonstrates what this chapter has sought to show, namely that Kilvert's concerns with God and sex were not only compatible but inseparable. He singled out, according to Plomer, 'the child, the virgin, and the wise' because he knew that it was they who possessed the 'fitness' to 'bear the vision and receive the seed' from his 'life-giving hand'. Plomer's use of 'vision' and 'seed' indicates that Kilvert was concerned with creativity as well as religion and sensuousness.

The result of the wandering curate's contact with the three groups of his parishioners was an enhancement of their capacity for life, initially in the theological sense of conveying to them the means of achieving eternal life. In addition, there is the notion that in his 'angel' capacity he was able to convince children to have faith in their own childhood experience, to 'Hold fast to your dream', not to mind if they were ridiculed for believing 'Inanimate things [were] alive'. In this way, he gave them 'strength'. He shared Wordsworth's belief that the freshness and spontaneity of the child's primal vision, preserved into adulthood, became the creativity of the poet. Plomer was acknowledging the part *that* belief played in Kilvert's attitude to children when he wrote 'You, child, are already a man', a reference to 'The Child is Father of the Man', the epigraph to Wordsworth's *Immortality Ode*. Kilvert recognised that the creativity released in him by the landscape of Aberedw owed something to the children who shared his joy on that first visit in May 1865, and to their joy simply in existence.

There was also mutually beneficial contact with the second of his parishioner groups that Plomer identified — virgins. They sensed Kilvert's sexual desire for them, a desire indistinguishable from, or confusingly blended with, his evangelising role: the virgin, suddenly meeting him in a lane, found that her heart 'madly drums / At the double revelation of the sacred and profane'. And, as a result, found herself 'locked in a more than mortal embrace / Which un-locks the strength in her', strength that is both her sexuality and spirituality (her affective, sympathetic capacity and her purity). In his autobiography, Plomer pointed to the connection between Kilvert's honesty in setting down his 'supercharged rhapsodisings over young girls' and his success as a parish priest: 'At least his feelings may have helped him, as a priest, to understand and perhaps allow for the little weaknesses of others'.[118] He brought inspiration, as well as understanding, to Plomer's third group, the 'wise', the experienced, who had 'known the worst, seen hope degraded'. To these disillusioned ones, he represented perfect Christian love so that they may 'take heart again, escape / Sterilities of knowing'.[119]

'There was something magnetic in [Kilvert]', Plomer wrote.[120] The power that Plomer sensed in him was partly his ability to excite love (which Kilvert called his 'strange and terrible gift'), and partly his success at drawing people to Christ. It was a perceptive insight by Plomer into a man who was fascinated by the power which drew strangers together into intimacy, the means by which 'hearts are linked to hearts'.[121] Plomer's conclusion is that the angel and the satyr facets of Kilvert were interdependent and inseparable and together represented the best and worst of his ministry, but that 'worst' was essentially innocent. And that seems to have been the judgement also of Kilvert's friend Helen Dew, the daughter of the Mrs Henry Dew mentioned earlier. Helen was once asked by a clergyman, worried about Kilvert's 'inordinate affection' for young girls, whether she thought he was 'a really good man'. After a moment's thought she replied: 'Yes, he was a good man; if he had not been a good man he would have been a very dangerous man'.[122]

Chapter 8
Superstition and Dreams

Scratch the Christian and you find the pagan —
spoiled.

[Israel Zangwill, *Children of the Ghetto*]

The 'domains of dreamland' are those within which
we either deceive or liberate ourselves, in which we
have the opportunity to explore the past, present and
future, to discover the forces of will and energy within
us, and to use power and knowledge for good or evil
ends.

[Fred Kaplan, *Dickens and Mesmerism.*
The Hidden Springs of Fiction]

It is probable that Radnorshire is the richest mine of
folklore in England and Wales.

[H.J. Massingham, *The Southern Marches*]

Romantic poets were taken with the notion of life as
most fully lived in special states of consciousness to be
best rendered through dream and imagery. . . .

[Fred Kaplan, *Dickens and Mesmerism.*
The Hidden Springs of Fiction]

We may define Romantics as all who do not believe in
the Fall of Man.

[T.E. Hulme, *Speculations.*
Essays on Humanism and the Philosophy of Art]

There is no going so sweet as upon the old dreams of
men.

[Edward Thomas, *The South Country*]

———

The wild girls of the last chapter, who crowded Kilvert's
world and imagination, filled his senses and his spirit, had
a supernatural dimension; they seemed half human and half
nature-sprites. So much of his apprehension of landscape
contains this supernatural dimension and this chapter will
explore it. He can be seen not only blending elements of
superstitious folklore with descriptions of places and people,
but also blending himself with natural forms in much the same
way as did the ancient peoples who once inhabited the locations
in which he walked. One feels that he came close to joining the
vernal revels of the Mouse Castle girls; that *Diary* entry closes
with a vigorous statement of the power of Spring:

> The air blew sweet from the mountains and tempered
> the heat of the sun. All round the brow of the hill the
> sloping woods budded into leaf, the birds sang in the
> thickets and the afternoon sun shone golden on the
> grassy knolls.[1]

Kilvert's sensuous feel in this passage for the sun will be
examined later. It is worthwhile recalling here what has been
said earlier about his response to landscape. It has been said
that he *felt* landscapes rather than simply saw them, that he
gave himself up entirely to the spirit of place (as Wordsworth
and Robertson did), that he deliberately cultivated awareness of
landscape in terms of memories structuring his consciousness,
that places registered themselves unusually sharply on his
senses, that he sought intensification and extension of awareness
of people and things through landscape 'encounters', and
that he believed Nature was permeated by a divine spirit. His
characteristic blend of the sensuous and the spiritual, those
twin strands of Romanticism, will be particularly apparent
in this chapter, which examines *Diary* entries concerned with
the supernatural, another aspect of his interest in unusual or
heightened forms of consciousness.

His father recorded that one of his first memories was being
told by a malicious girl older than himself that the reflection
of the sun on a polished door handle was 'the eye of a spirit'
watching him, and how similar stories told him by servants
'wrought havoc in [his] timid sensitive nature'. Even at the
age of thirteen or fourteen, he remembered sitting alone in
the house in the dark 'in an agony of terror at the thought of
supernatural surroundings'.[2] Robert was also impressed by a

story told him by a parishioner whose husband was dying. She heard, while sitting downstairs, 'solemn music' coming from her husband's bedroom. Robert said he questioned her closely as to whether there could be a natural cause for the music but she was convinced it was a supernatural event. He indicated he was disposed to agree with her, for though he had not been able to prove her story, 'yet we know there are attendant angels . . . , that there is celestial music and . . . there is nothing to forbid exceptional communications from the other world'.[3] Kilvert's mother had a similar susceptibility and gave credence to a vivid dream she had when young:

> It was about her first cousin Thersie Ashe. She dreamt that Thersie Ashe was going to be married. The wedding party drove up to the north door of Langley Church in a hearse. John Chambers was driving. The hearse stopped with a jolt and they all fell to dust. Then Death appeared and closed with my Mother in a mortal struggle. They wrestled all about the churchyard over the graves and among the tombs especially by Lessiter's tomb and the little child Warrilow's grave, and at last she conquered Death.[4]

Kilvert's recording of this dream, among many that appear in his diary, is indicative of the importance he had been encouraged to attach to them. Chapter three noted that Wesley defended superstition and found wisdom in it and that his evangelising flourished among the Celtic peoples of Cornwall because magic and folklore were especially strong there. He believed that it was possible to have spiritual experience of God through 'a new class of senses opened in your soul, not depending on organs of flesh and blood'. The senses made it possible to perceive the 'spiritual objects' of the 'invisible world'.[5] There is also evidence to suggest that Kilvert inherited a tendency to experience supernatural events. One commentator thought that his diary shows that he was psychic: 'His senses are abnormally acute. He was occasionally overwhelmed by psychic invasions'.[6] This could explain the following passage:

> After dinner today I was seized with a strange fit of nervous restlessness such as I never felt before. I should think it must have been something like the peculiar restlessness that comes shortly before death. I could not

sit still or rest for a minute in any posture. The limbs all kept jumping and twitching and I should have liked to set to a run only I felt so weak and wretched. It was a strange uncomfortable feeling. . . .[7]

The nurturing of a personality already given naturally to psychic experiences included a massive exposure to the Waverley novels of Sir Walter Scott. Kilvert was very familiar with Scott's work[8] but he has not been identified as a major influence on the diarist, though, in the matter of superstitious belief (as well as in other matters), he very probably was one. Kilvert's sister Emily suggested that the Kilvert children had many of Scott's novels read to them by their father: 'Papa used to tell us such splendid stories round the fire on winter evenings. I think he knew all the Waverley novels by heart'.[9] Evangelicals distrusted fiction in general but Scott was an exception because his fictional world was safe.[10] Kilvert (and Scott and Wordsworth) generally preferred landscapes to be inhabited.[11] In his work as a young lawyer, Scott made excursions into Liddesdale in the Scottish Borders[12] and acquired 'intimate acquaintance with the living manners of these unsophisticated regions', which provided material for his writing later. Wherever he went, he gathered 'songs and tunes, and occasionally more tangible relics of antiquity'. . . .[13] It was from Scott in this mode that Kilvert learnt to create a landscape that lived in terms of the traditions, legends, superstitions, songs and dialect of its inhabitants. Virginia Woolf underlined how closely Scott's peasants are identified with their landscape: 'Images, anecdotes, illustrations, drawn from sea, sky and earth, race and bubble from their lips'.[14] Her comment indicates the way some modern critics, as well as nineteenth-century ones, have drawn attention to the importance in Scott's work of landscape as an integrated entity — locations and their inhabitants. Basic to his vision of landscape was sympathy with Scottish peasants, a quality which Carlyle recognised: the novels had, he said, 'a sunshiny freshness and picturesqueness, brilliant paintings of scenery and figures . . . a wide sympathy with man'.[15] Ruskin made this ability to create living landscape a central element in his evaluation of Scott: he didn't look at scenery as a dead thing but 'as having an animation and pathos *of its own* . . . an animation which Scott loves and sympathises with, as he would with a fellow creature, forgetting himself altogether . . . before what seems to him the power of landscape'.[16] He singled out Scott as a man 'who feels [landscape] most deeply'.[17]

Scott located the story of *The Antiquary* in 'the class of society who are the last to feel the influence of that general polish which assimilates to each other the manners of different nations'. His reason for this concerned his perception of the language used by people of this class who, he said, were 'less restrained by the habit of suppressing their feelings'. They were inclined to express 'the higher and more violent passions . . . in the . . . most powerful language'. This was especially true, he said, 'of the Scottish peasantry'. 'The antique force and simplicity of their language . . . , in the mouths of those of an elevated understanding, gives pathos to their grief, and dignity to their resentment'. He acknowledged that he was indebted for these ideas to Wordsworth, which must have meant the latter's *Preface* to the *Lyrical Ballads*.[18] The profound significance of these poems for Kilvert (many of which are marked by a supernatural dimension) has been explored in previous chapters. Thus, from both Wordsworth and Scott he developed a perspective on landscape that valued peasant traditions, including importantly the ballads and the folklore in which peasant life was distilled. When he collected ballads and dialect words he was following Scott's example.[19] Kilvert's diary is dominated by memory and his folklore collection can be seen as part of his effort to memorialise the way of life of a peasantry for whom the passing down of stories was a vital activity. It was particularly important for him to record the oral culture of his Clyro community because it reflected the passionate, mystical involvement of the Celts with Nature. The Celts were, above all, for him a people in harmony with Nature.

He came to recognise that one of the deepest roots of peasant life, especially for those that lived in remote regions, was superstition because it was of ancient origin and reflected man's basic response to natural forms.[20] He would have sympathised with Wordsworth's statement in *The Wishing-Gate*: 'Yet how forlorn, should *ye* depart, / Ye superstitions of the heart, / How poor were human life.' The stories told Kilvert by parishioners often fascinated him exactly because they expressed superstitious understandings. One *Diary* entry of disturbing power and sheer strangeness seems to be connected to his attitude towards superstition. The entry describes what he called the 'grey old men of Moccas', the ancient oak trees in the Moccas Park of Sir George Cornewall (Kilvert's squire when he was Vicar of Bredwardine on the Wye). These trees 'stand waiting and watching century after century, biding God's time with both feet in the grave and yet tiring down and seeing out generation after generation. . . .' Here the oaks stand for the ineradicable, irresistible force of the past that intrudes on and shapes the present, a force of Nature in comparison with which human beings are powerless. Faced with such power, the inevitable response of people is to do what the ancient Celts did and that is to make the oaks into deities and to regard them with the fear and awe they showed to other natural forms (the word 'Druid' means 'oak-knowers').[21] That Kilvert conceived of the oaks' power as essentially pagan and primitive is seen in his characterisation of the oaks as 'low-browed, . . . huge, strange, long-armed, deformed [and] misshapen', and always *'with such tales to tell [which] make the silver birches weep . . . and the long ears of the hares and rabbits stand on end'.*[22] The italicised words show that Kilvert habitually saw landscape as charged with stories, many of which were superstitious and frightening. At the same time the stories (often the same ones) could be romantic, pathetic and alluring.[23] Scott's novels bear witness to a similarly ambivalent attitude. For example, as Edie Ochiltree and Dousterswivel in *The Antiquary* dig for treasure at midnight in a ruined abbey, while the wind moans in the trees, Scott commented: 'In these sounds, superstition might have found ample gratification for that state of excited terror which she fears and yet loves'.[24] Kilvert showed himself willing to be simultaneously terrified and amused by superstitious stories: 'Joe Phillips entertained me with the terrors of the Llowes road at night, the black dog, the phantom horses etc which made my hair stand on end'.[25] Cottom emphasised the importance of superstition in Scott: 'Superstition is a major element in almost all of the Waverley novels. . . . Its significance goes beyond the fact that it is a characteristic topic in Scott's fiction', as well as in other Romantic works.[26] A debate goes on throughout *The Antiquary* about the supernatural, with Scott putting both sides of the question.

Superstition is given this dual aspect throughout Kilvert's *Diary*. He knew and respected the fact that the uneducated of his parishes paid serious attention to it. James Jones of

Clyro, the man Kilvert called 'the old wizard', 'had emerged from the atmosphere of charms, incantations, astrology and witchcraft' to embrace Christianity. In this passage, there is genuine tenderness towards Jones, partly because the old man was dying but importantly too because Kilvert recognised how it was that a human being could harbour belief in magic in order to come to terms with life's mysterious, frightening aspects. And this is because he acknowledged that part of him betrayed the same response, even though he, as an educated man, was quite conscious of the relationship between past and present as it concerned magic, that its irrationality was a stage in human development, that, as he put it, 'the days of magic and necromancy had gone by'.[27] It is generally accepted that the Enlightenment, the increased belief in reason and science in the eighteenth century, ushered magic out. Jones was born in 1793 so was 83 in 1876 when Kilvert was saying that he had put magic behind him. Another Clyro Jones — Thomas — was, however, still practising magic at this time and so was his wife, who was 30 years younger than he (he was 62 and she was 32). She suspected a neighbour of stealing her washing from the hedge:

> She and her husband consulted the ordeal of the key and the Bible (turning the key in the Bible). The key said 'Bella Whitney'. Then Jones the jockey went to the brickyard and got some clay which he made into a ball. Inside the ball he put a live toad. The clay ball was either boiled or put into the fire and during the process . . . the toad was expected to scratch the name of the thief upon a piece of paper put into the clay ball along with him.[28]

Kilvert was repelled by this practice, noting that 'Some other horrible charm was used to discover the thief, the figure of a person being pricked out on a piece of clay. It is almost incredible'. On the other hand, he was not disposed to reject what he was told by an old Langley Burrell parishioner, William Halliday, who had been treated as a child to 'strange tales of ancient times [when] the world was once full of "witches, weasels (wizards) and wolves".'[29] Kilvert clearly found credible the story the Langley Burrell schoolmistress, Miss Bland, told him about how her brother's death was predicted by a vision she had of a young man who passed her in the dusk, running swiftly without a sound and his feet not [touching] the ground. . . . A day or two afterwards she heard that on the day and at the hour when she saw the young man running her brother was struck for death.[30]

Kilvert took seriously belief in fairies partly because he knew peasants whom he admired did. Hannah Whitney listened as a child to her grandparents telling 'their old world stories and tales of fairies *in whom they fully believed.'*[31] That Kilvert was prepared to repose some belief in fairies is evident from the entry he wrote at the time of the Franco-Prussian war: 'Today it was rumoured that Paris was about to capitulate. How prophetic was the old Welsh country dance taught to men by the fairies and called (why?) "The Downfall of Paris".'[32] It is evident, too, that he respected what David Price had to say about his experience of fairies: 'We don't see them now because we have more faith in the Lord Jesus and don't think of them. But I believe the fairies travel yet'.[33]

The way in which Kilvert scrupulously recorded these statements of belief in fairies indicates not only that he respected them, but that he himself recognised that fairies existed, or had existed. Chapter three showed his susceptibility to the mysterious and magical in Nature, his relish for the Arthurian legends and Bottrell's legends of ancient Cornwall, and his admiration of the imaginative Celt. If any doubt remains that he himself was a highly superstitious person, there are more *Diary* passages which dispel it. He had the characteristically evangelical belief in bibliomancy — the belief that whatever passage a person happened to open the Bible at had special significance for him. He had this experience one September morning in 1872 when he was about to embark with his mother on a sea journey down the Bristol Channel to Ilfracombe:

When I opened the Testament this morning, the first passage my eye fell on was this, "And falling into a place where two seas met they ran the ship aground. . . ." The next passage I lighted on was this, "There came down a great storm of wind . . . and the ship was filled with the violence of the waves". When my Mother heard of this ominous conjunction she doubted whether we had better go.[34]

The manner in which Kilvert can be seen entertaining both superstitions and Christian beliefs simultaneously is also illustrated in several entries that concern the Holy Thorn.[35]

The fusion of pagan and Christian in Kilvert's imagination corresponds to their fusion, as he saw it, in landscape, which for him was saturated with stories from the past that persisted into the present. Nowhere is this pervasiveness of the ancient past more powerfully conveyed than in his descriptions of landscape monuments of various kinds. The former pagan inhabitants of Wiltshire are recalled by 'the great silent White Horse on the hillside at Cherhill. . . .'[36] And there is Old Sarum: 'the strange sad mysterious deserted city, silent but for the voices of children at play amongst the bushes within the desolate mounds and broken walls'.[37] The similar phrasing here is important: the emphasis is on mystery that should remain mystery, on monuments rightly withholding their secrets. Kilvert's imagination was deeply stirred by the standing stone of Cross Ffordd, near Clyro, which was referred to in chapter one. One entry about the stone presents it starkly against 'a sheet of dazzling snow a solitary silent witness of some deed covenant or boundary'.[38] In its silence is an implication that to probe its origin would be an intrusion. In a powerful description, he also linked the stone, by means of the 'rude ancient stony road' that led from it, to a ruined cottage with the most unpleasant associations (ruined cottages usually elicited his sympathy):

> The hindmost of these hovels has now gone idle, being now and having been for a long time before it was deserted unfit for human habitation. It has fallen into ruin, the window is gone and the roof has broken its back. The dirty white walls of the cabin look as if they had the leprosy, being straked with green stripes of moss and damp. The little old garden, neglected and grass-grown, lay along the margin of the rushing brook and dreary swamp. The little old garden gate still hung on its hinges over a waste of mud and a stagnant pool.[39]

It is as though he was unwilling to dwell *overtly* on the stone's pagan past and chose instead to express his repugnance by implication. What stands out in a third entry is his preoccupation with time and memory:

Turned aside into the meadow to look at the great stone
of Cross Ffordd. It is a long time since I stood beside
it, and I had forgotten that the stone was so large. I
suppose no one will ever know now what the grey silent
mysterious witness means, or why it was set there.
Perhaps it could tell some strange wild tales and many
generations have flowed and ebbed around it. There
is something very solemn about these great solitary
stones which stand about the country, monuments of
some one or something, but the memory has perished
and the history is forgotten.[40]

The stone is a repository of stories in which the lives of
'many generations' are distilled but, because no-one possesses
the key to unlock it, the stone remains a mystery. A Britton or
a Warner would have offered some conjecture as to its origins
and purpose, but Kilvert was content that its secret remained
inviolate.[41] It is an attitude that sharply differentiates his antiquarianism from that of others. Explanations derived from
history and archaeology would for him be a profanation of
something sacred. Hence, 'there is something very *solemn*
about these great solitary stones'. He employed 'solemn' about
other ancient landscape monuments to indicate his sense of
their sacredness, another thing he had learned from Robertson.
It was noted in the introduction that Robertson juxtaposed the
words 'solemn', 'awful' and 'holy' to designate experiences
which provided insight into Nature's *mystery*. Stonehenge,
Kilvert said, was 'a solemn awful place'.

The words he used to describe the barrows around Silbury
Hill give the clearest evidence of his stance: 'Soon we came
in sight of the first outlying barrow rising over a shoulder of
the down, solemn, mysterious, holding its secret in unbroken
silence and impenetrable mystery'.[42] The feeling here is one
of relief that the barrow's secret is untold. Other features of
the entry reveal more of his stance. A succession of details
reiterate notions of stillness, solitude, virtual absence of all
motion, as though he was consciously reproducing the effect
of the passage in Wordsworth's *Peter Bell* (quoted in chapter
six) in which the 'fair prospect' gave to the observer the sense
that 'moving time had been / A thing as steadfast as the scene'.
'There was a ceaseless singing of larks in the vast empty
expanse of the sky and down'. 'The monotony of the downs'

is relieved only by 'lonely clumps of trees'. The surrounding downs present the usual routines of agricultural life but there is a suggestion that time has almost stopped, a notion beloved of Victorian viewers of landscape. 'Teams of horses and oxen were crawling slowly along the great slopes at plough and harrow, and one team of four white oxen harrowing in the distance seemed scarcely to move at all'. The echo of Cowper's description in *The Task*, Book I, 159-162, is very strong. Cowper wrote: 'Thence with what pleasure have we just discerned / The distant plough slow-moving, and beside / His labouring team that swerved not from the tracks, / The sturdy swain diminished to a boy!.' The later details of Kilvert's passage reinforce the idea that both human and natural things come together in quiet veneration of the long dead incumbents of the barrows: 'The keen wind hummed a melancholy song among the telegraph wires and each post had its own peculiar measure and mournful song'. The theme of remembering the dead is given a final emphasis by 'The grey tower of Yatesbury Church [that] rose among the grove of trees . . .', linking earth and sky. The spirits, fairies, and ghosts that haunt Kilvert's landscapes may be seen as connected to this theme.[43]

The passage illustrates Kilvert's best and most characteristic writing, presenting as it does a landscape whose features seem to glow with the strange intensity of dream images. It was his intention to present it that way rather than in the conventional way of other writers with antiquarian interests.[44] He was not concerned to delve into the history of the barrows or of the Cross Ffordd stone. At Restormel Castle, one of his party hinted at a desire to know more of its history, and part of Kilvert concurred: 'So little is known of it, no one to show it, or explain it. . . .' But his dominant feeling was that he was an intruder there, that 'the old giant or king who lived there' had trustingly left his castle gate open and might at any moment return, so that Kilvert felt 'awe, expectation, a feeling almost of fear'. Nor did he want to probe Tintagel's history with antiquarian questions but simply to accept its mythic reality, its 'dream', that with his visit had 'come true'. He used the word 'solemn' on this occasion only about the graveyard nearby, but the castle too had solemnity because of its 'fabulously ancient, time-worn, rude weather-beaten masonry' that appeared indistinguishable from, and therefore as old as, the surrounding rock. The theme here is that such ancientness demands veneration for its own sake:

time itself is a sacred mystery. In all these passages, there is an element of the mourning, elegiac note that was commented on in chapter one.[45]

'The devout Christian lives the life of the Saviour in microcosm each year by acting out its main events'.[46] It is clear from headings to *Diary* entries that this applies to Kilvert and that to an extent he was influenced by Keble's *The Christian Year*, but at the same time he was something of a primitive in his response to the passage of the seasons, ever sensitive to changes in Nature's moods.[47] His approach to the seasons, as to natural forms, is an animistic one, feeling in his imagination and senses a spiritual presence in supposedly inanimate things. In this and in his belief in dreams and 'Providences', he displayed a pronounced sympathy towards the superstitious mind. In the headings to many *Diary* entries, he can be seen marking days and seasons significant in Celtic times, as though his nature demanded that he kept in touch with the original impulses of ancient peoples. He was obviously aware that many of our most hallowed festivals predated Christianity. 'Long ago, they marked the key dates of the Celtic rural year — for example, the days when planting began or when harvesting was completed'.[48] He was also aware that the Christian Church, recognising the hold that these festivals had on people from time immemorial, had wisely retained them while overlaying them with its own.[49] Thus, we find Kilvert recording Lammas Day, a corruption of 'Loaf Mass', which was 1 August and originally signified the festival of Lugnasad, when the Celts would make propitiatory offerings to the god Lugh in the hope of a good harvest. He also recorded Michaelmas (29 September), the end of harvest;[50] All Hallowmas (1 November), the date that marked the Celtic festival of Samain, when ghosts and fairies roamed abroad and bonfires were lit to ensure the return of the sun;[51] Childermas (28 December), which occurred in a season when several pagan festivals were celebrated, many honouring the rebirth of the sun after the winter solstice;[52] Candlemas (2 February), which was the Celtic festival of Imbolc, the beginning of the lambing season.[53] The recognition Kilvert gave to key dates in the Saxon agricultural and pastoral year is seen most clearly in his use of 'monat' headings for *Diary* entries: Wolf Monat (New Year's Day), Lenat Monat (1 March), Barn Monat (1 August), Barley Monat (1 September), Wine Monat (1 October), Wind Monat (1 November).[54] He showed his awareness of the origin of these

Rhos Goch Mill (with William Powell on the left)

terms when he wrote in the entry for 1 November 1871: 'And true to its old Saxon name the month has come in howling. A wild wind is blowing tonight over valley and mountain'. He had an impassioned response to wind[55] and it can be shown that he evinced the same response to other elemental forces in Nature as they were marked in calendar dates and in folklore. Another way of expressing what is characteristic about his stance towards the seasons is to say that he was acutely conscious, as ancient peoples were, of *weather*.

A number of *Diary* entries indicate that he was drawn to water. One 'delicious day' in spring 1870, he decided to explore the lane parallel with the brook towards Painscastle and to 'discover the old Rhos Goch Mill'. He was drawn to it partly because it was 'picturesque' (he twice used that word about it).[56] He was as pleased with the Mill's inhabitants as he was with the Mill itself. In front of the house was 'a handsome young man with a fine open face, fresh complexion and dressed as a miller. . . .'[57] This was William Powell, who later married Caroline (Carrie) Gore of Whitty's Mill, Clyro. Kilvert was pleased by Powell's 'perfect politeness and well-bred courtesy'. The main reason for Kilvert's visit is then revealed. Apart from there being 'something very fascinating . . . about an old-fashioned flour mill on a brook' (it and its inhabitants were part of an ancient past, integral elements of

Carrie Gore

the landscape), the Mill came complete with legends: it was 'the place where the old miller sleeping in the mill trough used to see the fairies dancing of nights upon the mill floor'.[58]

Supernatural associations characterise most of the *Diary* passages concerning water and Kilvert's feeling about it takes us back to ancient times: 'As far back as the Bronze Age, . . .

people regarded water as one of the prime sources of life, rivers, springs and wells were frequently believed to be the dwelling places of the gods',[59] and became sacred places. The Wild Duck Pool that Hannah Whitney told Kilvert about was one of these places. Rituals were observed at this pool which very probably dated from ancient times, though they possessed a Christian overlay: 'To this pool the people used to come on Easter morning to see the sun dance and play in the water and the angels who were at the Resurrection playing backwards and forwards before the sun', Kilvert wrote.[60] On Easter Day 1870 he showed his awareness of the 'relics of doings and beliefs not belonging to the Christian religion [that clung] even to this, the greatest day in the church year'. One of these ancient rituals was to get up very early and climb a hill 'to see the sun dance on Easter morn'.[61] On this occasion, he forgot the water ritual: 'The mill pond was full, but I forgot to look at the sun to see if he was dancing as he is said to do on Easter morning'. He was honouring the traditional significance of sunlight on water when he wrote, in the middle of the entry celebrating the overwhelming meaning for him of the river Wye at Aberedw: 'the morning sun [was] shining like silver upon Llanbychllyn Pool'.[62] This pool had significance also because the nearby Rocks of Pen Cwm were 'the last haunt of the fairies'.[63] The Wye itself had very strong supernatural associations for local people and Kilvert had assimilated these, building them into his image of the river. Palmer noted that the Wye was 'feared for its power' and had the reputation of 'wanting at least one human victim a year'.[64] In what he called a 'vision' one sleepless night, Kilvert saw himself as Builth's vicar, 'to the accompaniment of the rushing and roaring of torrents of rain'.[65] The untamed aspect of the Wye, which flows through Builth, fascinated him, as emerges in the talk he had with Edward Williams of Clyro: 'We talked of the extraordinarily wet weather and the floods. He said the Wye was a *wild river* (Kilvert's italics) and the valley was frequently flooded in the winter.[66]

Even the Dulas, the little brook that flowed through Clyro, impressed him with its changeable nature. On 4 March 1870, he wrote: 'A wild stormy night. The Dulas, Clyro, roaring red, and the Wye surging broad yellow and stormy'.[67] He knew and felt deep in his own being why 'In ancient and pre-Christian times wells, springs, lakes and rivers were worshipped as gods . . . and associated with them were purification ceremonies, sacrifice, ... healing'.[68] Part of the aura of purity that surrounded 'the fatherless girl' of Penllan stemmed from his image of her going out after she had 'prayed towards the east ... to draw water from the holy spring of St Mary's Well'.[69] There is a distinct element of water worship in the entries in which he described sea bathing. On 5 September 1872 he wrote: 'There was a delicious feeling of freedom in stripping in the open air and running down naked to the sea. ...' His love of bathing naked was accompanied by fierce resistance to encumbering himself with drawers. While bathing at Shanklin, the waves were in harmony with him and 'stripped them off'.[70] Bathing at Seaton (Devon), he was insulted at being offered 'rags ... a pair of very short red and white striped drawers to cover my nakedness'. However, 'unaccustomed to such things', he bathed naked.[71] Such determined nudism seems to have been founded on some principle and it may be found in his Quaker background. Stark noted 'how deeply the first Friends shocked the respectable part of society ... through their nudism.'[72] (Kilvert showed something of this motive, taking delight at Seaton that he had 'set at nought the conventionalities of the place', while at Shanklin he argued: 'If ladies don't like to see men naked why don't they keep away from the sight?') To seventeenth-century Friends, going naked in the manner of the Hebrew prophets was a sign of faith and was recommended by Fox. He described how William Simpson 'went three years naked ... as a Sign' to Cromwell and to priests, 'showing how God would strip them of their power.' Such behaviour was seen by Friends as testimony to God's 'naked truth' and as proof that they could deny their own will.[73] The ascetic aspect of this and its simple symbolism would have appealed to Kilvert.

The celebration of water and of spring that he saw enacted at Mouse Castle[74] took place, so he noted, on Easter Tuesday, as though he was conscious of the way the Christian season was grafted onto an older tradition. The spirits of the spring he saw on this occasion were benign, but supernatural forces attendant upon water also had a malign aspect for him. The Rhos Goch bog, where the cutting of peat left pits that filled with water, was an evil place. In the following passage, the superstitious element in his nature comes out strongly: 'Below lay the black and gloomy peat bog, the Rhos Goch, with the dark cold gleam of the stagnant water among its mawn pits, the graves of children. This place has always had a strange singular irresistible fascination for me. I dread it yet I am drawn to it.'[75] He visited a family who were mourning the death of a boy drowned in one of the pits. The episode deeply affected him because the original *Diary* concerning it was, Plomer tells us, 'a long account'. Throughout the surviving entry runs a superstitious thread reflecting in part the mind of Mrs Watkins, who told Kilvert the story. He wrote extensively about the Rhos Goch in his manuscript about Radnorshire legends and superstitions on which Mrs Essex Hope later based an article.[76] In his manuscript, he said that 'Rhos Goch always seemed to me a place of magic and marvel'. It was such statements, plus the affinity which he displayed with the superstitious Welsh people he knew, that led Mrs Hope to state: 'There must have been in him some touch of the Celtic spirit, some strain of mysticism. . . .'[77] He wrote admiringly of Radnorshire folk: 'everywhere they are credulous, highly imaginative and superstitious'.[78]

He had a mystical stance towards the sun as well as to water. The two elements came together on Midsummer Day (24 June), a date he usually marked in his diary, sometimes noting that it was also the day of St John the Baptist.[79] Just as there was always something physically and emotionally thrilling for him about contact with water and an awareness of its power for good or ill, so he was never happier than on days of glorious sunshine. As soon as the sun had acquired power at Easter, he became excited, seeing it as a form of rejoicing at Christ's resurrection. Thus, on Easter Day 1870 he wrote: 'As I had hoped, the day was cloudless, a glorious morning. My first thought was "Christ is Risen".'[80] No doubt some of his feeling here derived from Malachi (4.2): 'The sun [son] of righteousness shall rise with healing in his wings.' Like Wordsworth and Robertson, he was very responsive to sunrises and sunsets, as for example on 20 September 1870 when he 'watched the sun set in a crimson ball behind the hills. . . . It was like seeing a sunset over the sea'.[81] Quite often *Diary* entries simply reflect the fact that he was a sun-worshipper and exhibited something of the response to it that we associate with people of ancient cultures for whom it was a central fact in their existence. The absence of it dashed his spirits, but not on Good Friday 1870 when he was delighted there was sunshine because 'so many Good Fridays [have been] dark and gloomy'. He then went to Hay

John Constable, 'Stonehenge', 1820-35

— 'The walk across the fields in the glowing hot sunshine'.[82] It is noticeable too that he steadily recorded the longest day in the summer, as though revelling in the luxury of having the maximum amount of light to enjoy and in the knowledge that the maximum amount of nurturing was taking place. When the longest day coincided with sunshine, he was ecstatic, as in 1873: 'A splendid summer's day, burning hot. . . .' In 1876, he was happy to note simply: 'Burning heat', while the entry for 1875 links sunshine with seasonal work: 'The longest day and a beautiful haymaking day'. In 1871, the absence of sun was deeply felt: 'The longest day, and one of the darkest dreariest coldest Junes that I ever remember'.[83] The pagan that lay just below the skin of his Anglican clergyman self becomes most visible in the passage commemorating Midsummer Day 1875:

> The sun went down red under a delicate fringe of gold laced cloud, the beautiful Midsummer evening passed through twilight and gloaming into the exquisite warm soft Midsummer night, with its long light in the north slowly, softly lingering as Jupiter came out glorious in the south and flashed glittering through the tresses of the silver birches softly waving, and the high poplars rustled whispering and the Church clock at Draycot struck ten and I longed to sleep out of doors and dream my "Midsummer night's dream".

Midsummer was the season particularly associated with women because their fertility was identified with crop fertility: 'feminine love magic culminates during the solstice season. It is aimed exclusively at proliferating the species'.[84] Midsummer night was therefore the night when women would dream of their lovers and when supernatural beings — witches, fairies and mischievous spirits — were abroad.

His paganism is evident in the entry dealing with what is probably the most spectacular pagan landscape in Britain — Stonehenge, which he visited on 27 August 1875 with his friend Arthur Morres.[85] Among various influences that pushed Kilvert into making a 'pilgrimage' to this ancient site was Howitt, who had declared that it was 'worth a long pilgrimage to see' because of its 'lonely grandeur' and 'savage and mysterious antiquity.' [86] Though it was a hot, sunny day, there is a melancholy oppressive air to Kilvert's description of it. The Plain 'heaved mournfully with the great and solemn barrows' (one theme of the description is Kilvert's fellow-feeling with the dead). The main theme centres around his awareness that Stonehenge was a Temple to the Sun: 'The Sun was present at the service in his Temple and the place was filled with his glory'. Kilvert, too, was present as a sun-worshipper. His awareness was informed by the knowledge that the pagan urge to worship a force of Nature had been superseded by Christianity: 'a purer faith' which had com-pelled the stones into 'reluctant acknowledgement and worship of One Greater than They'. He nevertheless showed respect for what he evidently saw as a profoundly religious impulse on the part of the pagans whose shrine it was:

> It seemed to be holy ground and the very Acre of God. . . .[87] It is a solemn awful place. As I entered the charmed circle of the sombre Stones I instinctively uncovered my head. It was like entering a great Cathedral Church. A great silent service was going on and the Stones inaudibly whispered to each other the grand secret.

His sense that the stones were alive is reinforced by his likening them to 'ancient giants who suddenly became silent and stiffened into stone directly anyone approached'. That he felt at this moment in close touch with the whole tradition of ancient belief, with historical memory immanent in landscape, is clear from what follows: the giants 'might at any moment become alive again at certain seasons, as at midnight and on Old Christmas and Midsummer's Eve. . . .' There are signs that his description was influenced by his uncle Francis's poem, *Stonehenge*, which speaks of 'rocks Cyclopean, as by Giants' hands / In a rude Temple's forms disposed'. Francis also stressed that pagan worship involved 'rites impure' (human sacrifices) but that their 'false Religion' had been superseded by 'the Sun of Righteousness'. However, like Kilvert, he acknowledged his religious inheritance since we are, he said, 'the progeny of Pagan Sires'.[88]

It is in the Radnorshire sections of the *Diary* that Kilvert's preoccupation with superstitious stories is most intense and this is because its people were Celtic in origin and, like their Cornish cousins, particularly superstitious. It is worthwhile to examine his view of accidents in relation to superstition. There is a clear suggestion in the entry in which he recorded two tragic accidents in Radnorshire that some mysterious, malign power in Nature lay behind them, and he added meaningfully: 'There have been many dreadful accidents and strange adventures on these hills'.[89] One measure of the importance he attached to accidents is the large number of entries (39) that appear under this heading in Plomer's index, to which must be added 9 and 13 respectively under the headings Floods and Shipwrecks. Kilvert clearly felt a compulsion to record such events and this is because he saw a meaning in them. However, it was also Evangelicalism that taught him to see God's hand in 'accidents', or in what religious people call 'Providence'. The concept of Providence denotes the 'continued community between God, humanity and world'.[90] 'It was a belief of nearly every Evangelical that even the slightest happenings . . . are acts of an immanent God protecting or chastising his people'.[91] 'Evangelicals could discern a special providence in the most trivial occasions'.[92] In a discussion of Providence by a number of London-based Evangelical clergymen, the Rev John Newton observed: 'A knock at a door, or a turning a corner, may be events which lead to important consequences. There is no such thing as an accident'.[93] Kilvert confirmed he had assimilated this doctrine when he wrote: 'God . . . plans every little incident of life'.[94]

To those like Kilvert with a strong religious faith, the attribution of daily events to divine Providence would not have seemed a surrender of rationality, which might be said to be the basis of superstition, but rather a religiously orthodox version of pre-Christian attitudes. Belief in the significance of dreams, another of his preoccupations (29 references in Plomer's index), was a more problematic area of experience. In Christian thought, dreams are regarded ambivalently because they stand between rationality and inspiration. In the Old Testament, prophets and patriarchs receive messages through dreams, while the New Testament has a tradition of revelatory dreams. The Church was in a dilemma over dreams, on the one hand valuing the revelatory kind but on the other condemning those that encouraged superstition and diabolical practices.[95] It is useful to know what other *Evangelical* clergymen thought of dreams as a guide to Kilvert's thinking. The issue came up for discussion — framed as 'What is the morality and use of dreams?' — by the influential London group on 29 October 1798. The Rev Goode began with this couplet: 'My waking dreams are best concealed; For little good, much ill they yield'. The Rev Patrick thought that if what was dreamed was 'consonant with God's word', it should not be despised and that dreams were not evil if dreamed by good men. The Rev Cecil stated: 'Dreams are one of God's witnesses in the world . . . a witness to his being and providence. . . . A sort of half-way house to the other world: a porch to the spiritual world'. From the Rev Clayton came this statement to close the discussion: 'Dreams are not to be despised. There is much in Scripture about them. God avails himself of every avenue'.[96]

Like the Romantic poets, Kilvert was drawn to symbols because they were a feature both of dreams and poetry. The period in which he was being educated by his uncle Francis in poetic literature no doubt saw the beginning of his preoccupation with the Romantic view of dreams. Uncle Francis grew to maturity in the early 1800s when dreams were of great interest to writers, scientists and philosophers[97] and was likely, especially with his interest in antiquarianism, to have been influenced by this movement. It was Coleridge in particular who saw links between dreaming and poetic, imaginative creativity, as part of his concern with different levels of consciousness. Byron, too, shared this interest and Kilvert was always quoting Byron's poem *The Dream*,[98] which reflects many of the controversial opinions about dreams of the early 1800 period. A further indication of the seriousness of Kilvert's interest in dreams is that when writing of them he carefully distinguished between different kinds. It has been noted that he habitually used 'dream' and 'vision' in the Romantic manner to denote the imaginative apprehension of landscapes such as the ancient mansion of Yaverland, rugged Cornish scenes and the Rocks of Aberedw. The most powerful memories had the quality of intensity that existed, so Romantics (and Kilvert) believed, in the child's perception of natural forms, the perception Wordsworth characterised as 'the glory and freshness of a *dream*'. The memories Kilvert had of his Hardenhuish childhood, described in chapter five, had this intensity, clarity and vibrancy, as did his perception of the 'glowing roses of the Vicarage lawn'. He used both 'dream' and 'vision' in connection with an experience he had in Dolgelly on 12 June 1871: 'I have always had a vision of coming into a Welsh town about sunset and seeing the children playing on the bridge and this evening the dream came true'. In moments like this he was fully awake but also strongly aware of a persistent memory. A memory of something he had been told probably overshadowed the *Diary* entry in which he had a vision of 'a crew of dead men . . . kicking football and my great-grandfather, who has been in his grave nearly a hundred years, was looking on'.[99]

Coleridge considered that dreaming, superstition and witchcraft were connected complementary phenomena and he sought, as Kilvert did, explanations for the appearance of ghosts, visions and supernatural occurrences.[100] Coleridge's poem, *Frost at Midnight*, focuses on dreaming, particularly the state of consciousness between waking and dreaming. Examples of *waking* dreams, some of them precisely defined as such, are to be found in *Kilvert's Diary*. On 15 September 1871, for example, he recorded: 'Lying in bed this morning dozing, half awake and half asleep, I composed my speech of thanks at my wedding breakfast'. The dream recounted to him by John Hatherell was, Kilvert noted, a 'waking' one.[101] And to confirm that distinctions between dreams meant something to Kilvert, he underlined in the case of another parishioner's experience 'It was not a dream, she said, she was broad awake'.[102] The experience of his own, when he 'seemed to see' pretty girls sitting at the windows of his grandfather's house three hundred years, before was another waking dream. Sometimes, it is evident that Kilvert knew that some of his dreams originated from evil sources.[103]

It was noted at the end of chapter three that Kilvert conceived of his diary, in part, as a journey into his own inner landscape; it is appropriate to see his intense preoccupation with dreams and superstition as complementary to this search for self. The Romantics sought insights into their own identity by studying various modes of consciousness, one of which was dreams. Their distrust of the rational led them naturally to study and to respect so-called 'primitive' consciousness, and superstition and dreams are concerned with the submerged, irrational elements of the mind. Certainly dreams were one of the states of consciousness that interested Kilvert because they seemed to offer insights into a reality that would otherwise remain hidden. (Mesmerism interested him for similar reasons.)

This chapter has covered further aspects of Kilvert's view of the internal and external landscape of the past, particularly with its inheritance of superstition, the supernatural 'stories' symbolised by the Moccas oaks and the monuments of ancient, pre-Christian people, both of which exercised mysterious power over him. His attitude to the relation between past and present owes a lot to Scott, who demarcated them clearly while simultaneously blurring them.[104] He blurred them, as Kilvert did, by showing how, through superstition, folklore, ballads, ruins and dialect, the past persisted into the present.[105] For Kilvert, the key to the mystery of the individual self and of the land lay in the web of memories which constituted the eternal landscape of the past. Although he declined to probe the deepest sources of his own personality,[106] his concern with the superstitious dimension of the life of the Wiltshire and Radnorshire peasants indicates a willingness to probe them in others' lives. It was the Radnorshire ones who had the 'rich folklore and deep vein of superstition' which, as chapter three noted, he found specially fascinating in their Celtic brothers of Cornwall. He entirely concurred with his father's belief that 'there is nothing to forbid exceptional communications from the other world'.[107] Superstition was an important channel by which the living were united with the dead and with the ancient past in bonds of sympathy and recognition. This concern with what Kilvert liked to call the *primitive* past[108] was essentially Romantic, as was his tendency to portray the ancestors of the peasants he knew as 'Noble Savages' living free, simple and natural lives. To journey back imaginatively into their beliefs, their consciousness, was part of Kilvert's 'passion for the past' that was seen earlier as a strong element in his depiction of landscape, a journey into the heart of mystery.

Chapter 9
Mountains and Mystery

The power of hills is on thee.
[Wordsworth, *To — On Her First Ascent to the*
Summit of Helvellyn]

I am seeking wildness.
[The Hon John Byng, *A Tour of North Wales 1793*]

What a multitude of adventures . . . may be grasped . .
by those ramblers who have the spirit to investigate;
curiosity to enquire; and attention to observe; who
interest their hearts in everything.
[The Rev Richard Warner, *A Walk through Wales*
in August 1797]

O, the wild hills of Wales, the land of old renown and of
wonder, the land of Arthur and Merlin.
[George Borrow, *Wild Wales*]

The Christian faith continued to flourish in those parts of
the land that were still held by the Britons. Almost their
last refuge was the high mountain country west of the
Wye. Here, in what is now Wales, the Britons stubbornly
lived their own lives for many centuries, waging
continual war, sometimes offensive and sometimes
defensive, against the Saxons on their borders. Here
they kept alive their ancient Christian tradition; here in
song and in legend they recorded the heroism of their
leaders and the bravery of their fighting men.
[Beram Saklatvala, *The Christian Island*]

———

In the spring of 1865 Kilvert left the curacy of Langley Burrell, Wiltshire, where he had served his father for two years and where all was comfortable and familiar, for Clyro, a village across the river from Hay-on-Wye. Although Clyro was very much border country and Radnorshire, especially its eastern end where Clyro lies, was highly anglicised, he must have been apprehensive about the way an English curate would be received by its predominantly Welsh inhabitants. After almost seven and a half years in Clyro, he was pleased to pay tribute to the kindness its people 'have showed to the stranger'.[1] This chapter will show that he made himself less of a stranger to Wales by reading guide books about it, which helped to shape his understanding and image of Wales.

Until the eighteenth century, English tourists had been content to regard Wales as a foreign country and to leave it to itself. 'The fame of Wales developed late; in the middle years of the eighteenth century the impression made upon travellers was still almost a totally unpleasant one'.[2] From the late seventeenth century to the early eighteenth, they regarded mountains, waterfalls, rocks and precipices as disturbing and terrifying: 'The starkness of Welsh scenery had long been imagined in London as the epitome of barbaric rudeness, and the language spoken by the natives the phonetic equivalent of the landscape.'[3] A dramatic shift of taste had occurred by the end of the eighteenth century: 'Wild barren landscape had ceased to be an object of detestation and became instead a source of spiritual renewal' and appreciation of it 'had been converted into a sort of religious act . . . mountains had become the highest form of natural beauty and a reminder of God's sublimity'.[4] The moral sentiments that figured so prominently in Kilvert's education with his uncle Francis had a part to play in this cultural shift because the eighteenth-century cult of feeling also extended to scenery: 'Sentimentalism lay . . . behind a new cult of rude, wild and authentic nature which . . . put the margins of the nation — the Scottish Highlands and the Welsh hills — at the centre of its taste'.[5] The revival of Welsh life early in the eighteenth century made its culture both better known and more worthy of admiration. Learned societies sprang up that treasured the Principality's history and culture. The Cymmrodorion Society was founded in London in 1751 by Welshmen for whom British culture seemed too London-based and too English, with the aim of reviving authentic Welsh culture. Ancient Welsh manuscripts were rediscovered and documented, as well as ancient Welsh poets. New poets, such as Goronwy Owen (1722-1769), were celebrated and national Eisteddfods, which had lapsed since 1568, were revived in 1819.

There are grounds for believing that uncle Francis helped to introduce Kilvert to this movement, known as the Celtic Revival, that set out to enhance the status of Wales by drawing attention to its history, literature and music. Among English scholars who showed interest in it was Richard Hurd (1720-1808), Bishop of Worcester, whose life story was actually being written by uncle Francis while Kilvert was his pupil (it was published in May 1860). Hurd was first cousin to Richard Kilvert, elder brother of Francis, Kilvert's coachbuilder grandfather; Richard Kilvert became Hurd's Chaplain in 1786.[6] Hurd's letters show that he was involved with a group of literary-minded friends in explorations of Welsh culture. (The Bath literary club, of which uncle Francis was the leading light, may be seen as an attempt to recreate the Hurd coterie.) William Mason (1725-1797) became a friend of Hurd and Gray at Cambridge. Passionately fond of poetry, music and drama, Mason was the author of the verse drama *Caractacus* (1759), dedicated to Hurd, about the British chieftain who led resistance to Roman invasion in AD 48-51.[7] It was Gray, however, who was the driving force behind the interest in Welsh culture that united the group of friends: 'Gray was early recognised as an authority on Celtic matters, especially on the history of the Welsh bards'.[8] It was Gray who advised Mason on the background to *Caractacus*. It was Gray who studied Welsh history, examined the part played by Arthurian romance in Welsh culture, and analysed Welsh poetry, particularly its verse forms (the alliteration typical of traditional Welsh poets is to be found in Gray's poetry).[9]

Uncle Francis underlined that Hurd's was one of the 'hidden lives' (see chapter one) which needed to be rescued, like the lives of the poor and humble in Gray's *Elegy*, from obscurity: 'no account deserving of a life has appeared even though he had higher claims to one than many whose biographies have been written'.[10] Echoes of Gray and his *Elegy* are everywhere in Francis's account of Hurd. He not only noted Hurd's grief at the poet's death but paid his own tribute to the 'grace and elegance' of his writing.[11] He also stated that the biographical model he had adopted for his life of Hurd was that used by

Mason in his life of Gray.[12] Furthermore, it would have been of considerable importance to a Wordsworthian like uncle Francis that Gray had written a guide book, *Journal in the Lakes* (1775),[13] which the Lakeland poet himself had praised in his own *Guide to the Lakes* (1810) for its 'unaffected simplicity'. (In this context, we may recall Hoskins's observation about the latter work: '[it is] one of the best guide-books ever written, for poets make the best topographers'.)[14] Kilvert was familiar with Wordsworth's *Guide to the Lakes* and brought its criteria to bear in his evaluation of landscape, as will be demonstrated later in this chapter, which will also show that, long before he went to live in Clyro, he had developed an *idea* of Wales as a place of poetry, romance, tradition, simplicity and innocence — symbolised by the figure of the Bard, immortalised in Gray's poem, *The Bard*.[15] Schama recounts the well-known story of how Gray attended a recital given in Cambridge by the blind Welsh harpist, John Parry, and returned with fresh inspiration to work on his poem, *The Bard*. 'Thanks to the ode', Schama wrote, 'there was a sudden rage in fashionably sublime circles for druidical harpists, preferably blind'.[16]

In the poem's opening lines, the Bard shouts defiance at Edward I and his English army as they retire across Snowdonia after subjugating Wales, and warns that not even the king's virtues will save him from 'Cambria's curse, from Cambria's tears'. Gray wrote the poem in the belief that Edward had ordered the execution of any captured bards. The Bard on his mountain top embodied, therefore, Celtic independence as well as Celtic visionary and poetic tradition:

> Robed in the sable garb of woe
> With haggard eyes the Poet stood;
> Loose his beard, and hoary hair
> Stream'd like a meteor, to the troubled air,
> And with a Master's hand, and Prophet's fire,
> Struck the deep sorrows of his lyre.[17]

The poem calls on Wales's mighty mountains — Snowdon and Plinlimmon — to remember the slaughtered bards. This image of the spirit of ancient Wales, doomed but defiant, caught the public imagination and artists were eager to represent it in paint. The 1774 version by Thomas Jones (1742-1803) is perhaps the most famous[18] and Kilvert very probably knew it, so taken was he with the romantic image of bards

it represents. The Kilvert children were brought up looking at topographical prints; it was an interest that stemmed
originally from uncle Francis, who passed his veneration of
the topographical engraver/antiquary, John Britton, on to
his younger brother, Kilvert's father. It was the latter who
spent happy hours perusing Britton's *The Beauties of England
and Wales*. The connections between Britton, Jones and that
supreme painter of (particularly Welsh) landscapes, Richard
Wilson (1713-1782), are close and it is likely that Kilvert came
across all three artists, either in uncle Francis's study or at
home. Jones was brought up from 1750 at Pencerrig, near
Builth Wells in Radnorshire and became Wilson's pupil in 1763.
Britton was clearly an admirer of Wilson because he wrote *On
the Paintings and Merits of Richard Wilson* (1842). The references
in *Kilvert's Diary* to paintings of landscape are few and they
indicate a predilection for the domestic kind of rural scene. He
wrote, for example, that a hillside in Radnorshire reminded
him of William Collins's picture, *Come Along*, which shows
'two barefooted gleaning girls fording the brook on stepping
stones'.[19] Kilvert also liked the paintings of Cuyp, commenting
on some beautiful ones he saw among other 'old masters' at
the Royal Academy on 20 January 1870.[20]

Cuyp was an influence on Wilson, though a minor one;
Wilson's pictures are much more in the 'Grand Style' of landscape
painting, the masters of which are Claude, G. Poussin and Rosa.
(Kilvert would have noted Cowper's reference to Rosa and
Richard Wilson in *The Task*, Book I, 420-1.) Wilson was heavily
involved in the Celtic Revival partly through being related to
Thomas Pennant, whose *Tour in Wales* (1784) was important in
the rediscovery of Welsh landscape. Wilson was also a friend
of Paul Sandby, who worked with Wilson's patron, Sir Watkins
Williams-Winn, to popularise views of Wales and Welsh culture. One type of work that Wilson did was topography, in
the sense of paintings intended to represent specific known
views.[21] 'Williams-Winn's own house at Wynnstay, set in an
arcadian vale, became a favourite subject of Welsh Romantic
painters like Richard Wilson, who drenched it in improbable
Italian sunlight'.[22] The blending of classical Italian with sites of
ancient British culture was another of Wilson's habits: 'besides
classicizing landscapes. . . . Wilson symbolically equated antique Italy with Ancient Britain'.[23] The way in which Jones too
took liberties with his subjects is well illustrated by *The Bard*,

in which Stonehenge is visible in the background, showing the leaning column that Kilvert highlighted — 'the great leaning stone' — in his description of the monument. Believing that this 'Stupendous Monument of Remote Antiquity' was Druidic, Jones relocated it to the top of a Welsh mountain in order to accentuate the Bard's Druidic origins.[24]

Kilvert's visit to Stonehenge was mentioned in the last chapter in the context of his fascination with superstition. Note was taken of the echoes in his account of the monument from his uncle Francis's poem on the subject, notably the comparison of the stones with giants. However, it is evident that Kilvert was also remembering Gilpin's pronouncements, which are of considerable importance for understanding Kilvert's feel for the Druidic ancestors of the Welsh. There are similar phrasings in both writers' descriptions of Stonehenge's setting. Kilvert's statements that 'the Plain heaved mournfully' and 'the Plain swelled into bolder hills' match Gilpin's '[the plain] is continually heaving in large swells'. The harping on the 'solemn' nature of the monument and the comparison of it with 'a great Cathedral Church' corresponds to Gilpin's 'it is the *grandeur of the idea* [of the construction] that strikes us' (his italics). But the chief similarity between the two accounts resides in their basic viewpoints. Both men assume that the structure owed its origin to the Druids. Gilpin was convinced that the antiquarian, Dr Stukeley,[25] was right in tracing it 'into Druid times'. Kilvert, too, though he mentioned Druids by name only once, makes the central feature of his account the idea of a pagan people worshipping the sun in their temple of stones. This is also Gilpin's basic stance and both he and Kilvert expressed it by dwelling on the particular notion of worshipping *outdoors*. To Kilvert

> It must be a solemn thing to pass a night among the shadows of the awful Stones, to see the Sun leave his Temple in the evening . . . , and to watch for him again until at morning he enters once more. . . .

Gilpin formulated the same idea thus:

> [The Druids] always worshipped under the canopy of the sky. . . . I have known the idea taken up by pious Christians, who have confessed they found their minds most expanded when they worshipped in the open air.

   The respect Gilpin had for Druids is seen most clearly in
his equating of them with 'pious Christians'. Kilvert was
just such a 'pious Christian' and was very prone to worship
God in the midst of landscapes. His respect for Druids' piety
is seen in his comparing the fallen stones to worshippers
'prostrate with adoration before the lamp of Heaven'.
Gilpin spoke for Kilvert when he wrote: 'The Druid, though
savage in his nature, had the sublimest idea of the object of
his worship, whatever it was'.[26] Kilvert had no doubt what
it was — the Druid worshipped the sun, as he did. He also
had Wordsworth's sympathetic account of the Druids of
Stonehenge to help to shape his own. The poet wrote of seeing
on 'Sarum's Plain . . . Our dim ancestral Past in vision clear'.
He described how he was 'charmed / Into a waking dream, a
reverie', which presented 'a work . . . / Shaped by the Druids,
so to represent / Their knowledge of the heavens' and 'long-
bearded teachers, with white wands / Uplifted pointing to
the starry sky'.[27]
   Kilvert does not refer to the role of guide books in shaping his
outlook on landscape. Nevertheless, they were vital as sources
by which to set his own responses to landscape and uncle
Francis's library must have provided most of them.[28] Kilvert
certainly knew some of the 'spate of publications', recording
tours of Wales, which flooded the market in the 1790s.[29]
The highly sympathetic view that he had of ancient British
culture was largely derived, as we have seen, from Britton's
topographical volumes. Britton's *Introduction* begins with a
lengthy examination of the origins of the British, identifying
them with the inhabitants of Gaul, who consisted of two tribes,
the Cymry (i.e. the Welsh) and the Celtae. We cannot be sure
that Kilvert knew George Borrow's *Wild Wales*, published in
1862 but based on a tour in 1854.[30] In 1872, Borrow became
a friend of Theodore Watts-Dunton, in whose introduction to
the 1906 edition of *Wild Wales* we find the following rhapsody
on the land of the Druids:

   Now every peak and cliff of Snowdonia, and every
   matchless valley and dale of the land of the Druids, is
   very specially beloved by the Spirit of Antiquity — the
   land of that mysterious poetic religion which more than
   any other religion expresses the very voice of Nature,
   is the land painted in this delightful volume — Wild

Wales. . . . The scenic witchery of Wild Wales is great, no doubt, but it is enormously intensified by the memory of the heroic struggle of the unconquerable remnant of the ancient Britons with the brutal, physical power of Roman and Saxon.

Watts-Dunton (1832-1914) was another Wordsworthian, devoted to life in the open air and to the recognition of mystery — 'the mystery of man's life and the mystery of nature's theatre on which the human drama is played'.[31] It was mystery in this sense that Kilvert was seeking in the unusual states of consciousness he explored, especially in relation to the experience of Nature, the mystery lying at the heart of life (see end of chapter three). To him, as to earlier travellers in Wales, such mystery was to be found in the culture of its ancient Britons, a culture that received significant shaping from Wales's mountainous landscape, which was chiefly responsible for the preservation of the Arcadia which eighteenth-century travellers found there. Tourists were particularly impressed by colourful scenes of country folk on their way to market, Moir noted, just as Kilvert was by the Breconshire people at Neath market when he commented how pleasant, courteous, obliging, quiet and sober they were. 'It was difficult,' Moir said, for travellers 'not to find the sight of such a life an occasion for moralising and pious reflection'.[32] The admirable moral character of the people 'was deemed to be due in part to surroundings which demanded a hardy way of life. . . .'[33] This is the theme of the Rev Warner's observations in 1798 on entering the mountainous North of Wales: 'the native simple manners of the people yet maintain their ground'. He couldn't expect it to last, however, because turnpike roads were opening up the country so that its 'wildest and most beautiful parts' were open to travellers in carriages. This would inevitably please the 'lazy traveller' but 'subtract from the pleasure of the speculative one':

> To him, the lofty mountain, the deep valley, the thundering cataract, and the beetling precipice, are but secondary objects; for he is not so much in pursuit of *natural* curiosities, as of *moral* singularities, original manners, ancient customs, local traditions . . . which gradually fade away and disappear, when intercourse with other countries becomes easy.[34]

The 'singularities' that Warner identified were those deemed important by Sir Walter Scott in his Waverley novels and by Kilvert in his collection of Radnorshire folklore, as was made clear in the last chapter.

Among the 'moral singularities' identified among the Welsh by eighteenth-century travellers was piety. Byng, for example, touring Wales in 1784, saw near Welshpool 'numbers of people going to, and returning from church, cleanly dressed and civil', and after dinner he went to hear a field preacher, 'surrounded by the most attentive congregation'. At Dolgelly, he commented on 'a very devout congregation'.[35] Similarly, Kilvert was pleased to endorse what a clergyman said about the Welsh being 'a religious nation'.[36] The qualities of courtesy, kindness, hospitality and naturalness which, as earlier chapters have shown, Kilvert found pre-eminent in Welsh people, were all heavily underlined in the guide books of earlier English travellers. Byng commented on the civility of the staff at an inn at Dinas-Mawddwy and 'the lusty, cheerful inhabitants' of nearby cottages.[37] Moved by so many instances of courtesy in his encounters with the people, Warner paid this tribute to the quality: 'Oh! courtesy, how wonderful is thy power', adding, in a remark that indicates his awareness of the operation of the moral sentiments, 'Thy gentle influence stealing to the heart, smooths every asperity, subdues each unkindly emotion. . . .'[38] This was the general impression made on Borrow too: 'Wherever I have been in Wales, I have experienced nothing but kindness and hospitality'.[39] We have seen how Kilvert was particularly impressed by the naturalness and grace of the women of his borderland region. The close similarity between the tributes paid by him and by Warner to Welsh women confirms that the former knew the guide books of the latter. Warner found Welsh girls especially charming:

> A round, candid, open countenance, illuminated by a brilliant complexion, dark eyes, and teeth of dazzling whiteness; and a certain indescribable naiveté (which happily blends archness and simplicity, a great deal of intelligence, with an equal share of modesty) give an air peculiarly agreeable . . . to the Welsh girls.[40]

Kilvert's descriptions of 'mountain beauties' such as Gipsy Lizzie and Florence Hill are built up of the emphases that characterise Warner's tribute to Welsh girls. In Kilvert's

statement about the Clyro people's habit of strewing flowers
aimlessly on graves — 'one does not like to interfere too much
with their artless, natural way of showing their respect and
love for the dead'[41] — there are clear echoes of a passage in
Warner's 1797 tour account. He too was delighted by the custom
'of ornamenting the graves of the deceased with various plants
and flowers ... by the surviving relatives because it speaks
directly to a principle deeply rooted in the mind of man. To live
in the remembrance of those we love ... is a natural wish'.[42]
A desire to remember 'the unhonoured Dead' of Gray's *Elegy*
lay behind Warner's sentiments, as he made clear on another
occasion when he walked through a churchyard reminding
himself of Gray's poem while examining the headstones of
the poor.[43] Warner's desire to honour the humble dead with
proper epitaphs is of a piece with the general desire many
eighteenth-century travellers had to recognise the worth of
living Welsh peasants as well as departed ones, which links
to Wordsworth's belief that country people, especially those
in mountainous regions, exhibited a superior morality as a
result of living close to sublime natural forms.[44] In dwelling
so repeatedly on the excellence of Welsh moral character, as
so many of the guide books did, they were confirming the link
between people and their landscape.

The idea that Kilvert had of the beauties of Celtic culture
was expanded further, it seems, by reading he did just as he
was taking up his post as curate of Clyro. Matthew Arnold
was elected Professor of Poetry at Oxford in May 1857, a post
that carried the duty of delivering three lectures per year. Prior
to Arnold, only clergymen had held the position and, apart
from Kilvert's love of poetry, Arnold's appointment had the
added interest that his predecessor was John Keble. The other
innovation with regard to Arnold's appointment was that his
lectures were delivered in English — Keble's had been in Latin.
While Kilvert was a student at Wadham, Arnold had given
lectures on translating Homer, which the former probably
attended.[45] The lectures Arnold gave at Oxford between December 1865 and May 1866 were on Celtic literature and, appearing
in the *Cornhill Magazine* under the title of *On the Study of Celtic
Literature* throughout 1866, they must have attracted Kilvert's
attention, particularly as it was his first year in a Welsh curacy.
Furthermore, he regularly saw the *Cornhill Magazine*, as he
demonstrated when he wrote on 5 October 1874 '*This month*

there is in the *Cornhill Magazine* an article on Crabbe's poetry'
(my italics. The general disparagement of Kilvert's literary taste
and the consensus that he was not a 'serious' reader ignore the
fact that he consistently read a number of literary periodicals).[46]
Arnold's name does not appear in the list of poets known to
Kilvert, most probably because his poetry expressed religious
doubts.[47] What he had to say about Welsh people and culture
was a different matter, and the new curate of Clyro might
well have regarded the *Cornhill* articles as timely, preparatory
reading for the challenge facing him.

The issue of Celticism was in vogue in various intellectual
fields at this time: 'Celtic was a word to juggle with in mid-
Victorian Britain',[48] partly because of Renan's *Sur la poésie des
races celtiques* (1860), which Arnold described as 'a beautiful
essay'.[49] An anonymous article on 8 September 1866 in the *Daily
Telegraph* attacked Welsh eisteddfods, which Arnold had praised
as representing 'something spiritual, something humane' in the
Welsh people.[50] To the *Telegraph* journalist, an eisteddfod was
simply an excuse to 'recite songs, and sing ballads, and read
essays, and talk patriotism, and eat leeks'. Arnold had declined
an offer to speak at the Chester eisteddfod in 1866 and wrote a
letter to the *Times* instead, which prompted the *Telegraph* article.[51]
Eisteddfods were important to Arnold because they meant that
the culture of Wales was a living force among its people:

> Wales where the past still lives, where every place has its
> tradition, every name its poetry, and where the people,
> the genuine people, still knows this past, this tradition,
> this poetry, and lives with it, and clings to it, while, alas,
> the prosperous Saxon on the other side [of the Dee] has
> long ago forgotten his.[52]

What Arnold was doing in his articles was using this notion
of a living Welsh culture to show the limitations of the English
who, in their successful pursuit of industrial/technological
progress and of Empire, had become shallow, materialistic and
Philistine. He outlined a contrast in general terms between the
Celts (by which he meant the Welsh, Irish, Scots, Cornish and
Bretons) and the Saxons (English and Germans). Because of
their lack of 'reason, control, steadfastness and discipline', the
Celts were failures at 'dealing with the great world', whereas
the Saxons as a result of being 'phlegmatic, disciplined' and
'steadily obedient' were successful at it.

The close correspondence between Arnold's and Kilvert's
view of the Celtic character can be seen by setting the one
against the other. We have seen that when Kilvert was visiting
Cornwall, one Celtic territory, he explicitly identified six
main Celtic qualities. Every one of them is found in Arnold's
account of Celticism, usually in precisely the same terms, or
synonymous ones. The first mark of the 'genuine Cornish Celt'
for Kilvert was impulsiveness, a quality formulated by Arnold
as 'quick feeling', responsiveness to 'emotion', and being
'soon up and soon down', which the 'impressionable' Celt
was. It was this last quality that Kilvert emphasised so heavily
in his account of meeting Irish Mary, noting how from 'merry
laughter' she changed to being 'quiet and pensive', from 'swift
rich humour' to 'sudden gravity and sadness'.[53] Arnold, too,
had made a particular point of the fact that the Celtic nature
was 'keenly sensitive to joy and sorrow'. It is a significant fact
that Kilvert sought explanation for Irish Mary's changeability
in her racial origins: 'You are not Welsh are you?' He knew
he had detected a Celtic quality in her but (presumably
because of her accent) could not locate it precisely. (She told
him she was half Irish and half English — from Yorkshire.)
He found the same quality in Welsh girls such as Florence
Hill and Daisy Thomas. The second Celtic quality identified
by Kilvert was 'warm-hearted', which existed for Arnold in
Celtic 'sentimentality' and emotionality. There is some overlap
between Kilvert's third quality — 'excitable' — and his first
(most of the qualities identified by Arnold overlap to a degree).
Arnold expressed the excitability of the Celt in such terms as
'lively' and 'attracted by emotion'. The demonstrativeness that
was Kilvert's fourth quality Arnold called 'expansiveness',
'eagerness', being 'sociable'. The particular behaviour that
it resulted in for Arnold was hospitality, one of the qualities
which Kilvert paid tribute to in Welsh people.[54]

Arnold concurred with the sixth quality — eloquence —
highlighted by Kilvert as typical of Celtic people because it was
an aspect of another quality (Kilvert's fifth) in which both men
found the Celt pre-eminent — imagination. Inevitably, they
were going to attach considerable importance to imagination
because they were both writers and were concerned with
national responsiveness to the cultural traditions of music and
poetry. For Arnold, the positive side of the Celt's disinclination
to seek worldly success was his tendency to turn inwards to

the realm of feeling and creativity. He talked of the 'perpetual straining after mere emotion' that was the mark of 'Celtic genius' and of the Celt's achievement in the 'spiritual arts of music and poetry . . . poetry which the Celt has so passionately, so nobly loved'. He praised Celtic sensibility — 'the power of quick and strong perception and emotion' — which (and here we come very close to the basis of Kilvert's affinity with the Welsh and Welshness) 'gives him a peculiarly near and intimate feeling of nature and the life of nature'. This feeling was characterised by a responsiveness to *mystery*, 'the secret of natural beauty and natural magic', which manifested itself in reverence for 'the bard'. By 'magic', Arnold meant one of the prime qualities that we associate with the Romantic imagination: the feel for the supernatural dimension of natural forms. He referred to Nature's 'fairy charm' and the 'fairy-like loveliness of Celtic nature', of Nature's 'weird power' and its 'mysterious life'.

Significantly, his illustrations came from Arthurian legend;[55] one will show what he had in mind. He said that the landscape in the following passage is 'suddenly magicalised by the romance touch': 'And they saw a tall tree by the side of the river, one half of which was in flames from the root to the top, and the other half was green and in full leaf'.[56] To Samuel, the essence of Arnold's lectures on Celtic literature was 'a plea for the re-enchantment of the world, counterposing the mysteries of the past to the vulgar materialism of the present'.[57] We have seen how Kilvert too was drawn to magical transformations, to landscapes experienced in terms of *magic* and *enchantment*, especially the 'beautiful enchantment' that hung over the town of Builth and nearby Aberedw, with which he associated the release of poetic energy within himself.[58] According to Arnold, it was the quality of magic in Celtic poetry, as well as its melancholy, yearning tone ('this vein of piercing regret and passion')[59] that English poets sought to copy. Kilvert's evocation of the weird, haunting atmosphere of the ruined farmhouse of Whitehall perfectly illustrates the extent to which he had assimilated these qualities.

Although he lived and worked for several years in the Welsh borderland, there are indications in his diary that he wanted to draw closer to the Celtic soul, to its 'severe and exquisite Christianity,'[60] and decided that one means to this end was to undertake journeys to particular locations in Wales that would provide him with authentic experiences of it. One example of this is his trip to St David's in mid-October 1871. The whitewashed roofs of St David's houses particularly caught his attention because he harped on them: 'Like most of the houses in these parts the . . . roofs were all whitewashed and I kept on fancying that snow had fallen and whitened the roofs'. He seemed to object to this feature without making his reason clear: 'At a little distance this peculiarity gave the village city a strange appearance. It looked like a snowy city. . . .' Later, he returned to this feature, referring to 'the weird ghostly-looking city with its roofs white. . . .' The explanation for his disquiet may lie in Wordsworth's *Guide to the Lakes*, in which the poet dwelt at length on the principle that the colour of a house 'must harmonise with the surrounding landscape'. The best colour is 'something between a cream and a dust-colour, commonly called stone colour'. 'A small white building . . . may be . . . delightful' but only 'in solitary circumstances'. 'The objections to white, as a colour, in large . . . masses in landscape . . . are insurmountable'.[61] Kilvert's vague discomfort over St David's white roofs is another instance of the way in which 'rules' for viewing landscape lingered in his mind and affected his experience, as they did in Cornwall. He was remembering Cornwall as he toured around St David's. As he approached St David's Head, he noted: 'And then we came in sight of the famous headland, the Land's End of Wales'.[62] Furthermore, his descriptions at this point take on the overtones typical of picturesque landscape writing that were strong in his account of his Cornish holiday. The emphasis is all on the awesome power and savagery of Nature:

> The cliffs were rent and eaten into great caves and chasms, with perpendicular sides. The tide was going out but the sea still roared and plunged booming among the cliff chasms, and ran up and foamed into the recesses of the little coves.
>
> St David's Head is littered with huge boulders and wildernesses of grey stone.[63]

Here he is the picturesque tourist, described by Brewer, for whom Nature 'became an exotic', of which he had to collect 'specimens' that he had hunted down and trapped. These specimens were then brought together in guide books and books of prints and engravings for others to enthuse over. 'The enthusiasm for the picturesque was all about this translation of what at a distance seemed wild into something more orderly and civilised. . . .'[64] To Brewer, the picturesque tourist was inevitably a border figure, 'on the boundary between cultivated and wild nature', and demanding the softer lines of pastoral landscape as well as the wild, craggy mountain tops.[65]

There are some signs that Kilvert sought to meet both demands in his descriptions of landscape. Thus, before he recorded the wild picture presented by St David's Head, he had noted 'the road over the hill past a white-roofed farm house and steading well plenished with neatly built corn ricks'.[66] In the *Diary* entry dealing with his journey to St David's, the balancing of the two kinds of landscape is very clearly marked:

> Then we came into a wild bare region of mountain and deep desolate valleys, with waterfalls leaping down the steep hill sides. The mountains loomed in gloomy grandeur, dark, grey, indigo and purple under a heavy cloudy sky. As we drew near Brecon again we got into a beautiful rich woodland country highly cultivated, with lovely dingles and deep green meadows, and a fine gleam of sunshine at sunset lit the dingles and hill slopes and set the gorgeous woods aflame.[67]

In this description of the landscape around Rhayader, wild scenes modulate into more gentle ones:

> Soon after leaving Rhayader the railway leaves the valley of the Wye and enters the sweet vale of Marteg by a wild and narrow gorge which soon opens, broadens and settles down into a winding valley shut in by gentle hills about which are dotted lone white cottages and farms.[68]

He was in upper Radnorshire reconnoitring St Harmon's parish (where he spent a brief time as vicar) when he wrote the following description of another Welsh landscape. Again, mountains are seen giving way to a more pastoral landscape:

> When I alighted at Tylwch I found myself among the mountains, at the mouth of a gorge. . . . The beautiful little river Clwrdag came rushing down the gorge on its way to the Severn and in a curiously picturesque manner it was carried over and across the course of another stream. . . . This other and smaller stream came wimpling down a pretty little dingle. . . .[69]

The entry containing this passage is notable for the reference
it makes (one of many in the Welsh parts of the *Diary*) to Welsh
history. Kilvert was only five or six miles above Clyro when
he encountered the landscape described in the following
passage:

> The beautiful Glasnant came leaping and rushing down
> its lovely dingle, a flood of molten silver and crystal
> fringed by groups of silver birches and alders, and here
> and there a solitary tree rising from the bright green
> sward along the banks of the brook and drooping over
> the stream which seemed to come out of a fairy land of
> blue valley depths and distances and tufted woods of
> green and gold and crimson and russet brown.[70]

It is a landscape that recalls to mind Watts-Dunton's phrase
(quoted earlier in this chapter) about the 'scenic witchery of
Wales', as well as the capacity that the Celtic imagination possessed, according to Arnold, for 'magicalising' landscape with 'the
romance touch'. Kilvert was very fond of that mysterious quality
of 'blueness' in hilly landscapes that was the result of distance
and the particular light through which they were viewed. He
wrote, for example, of the hills surrounding Llanthony Abbey in
the Black Mountains: 'the tender blue haze that veiled the hills
made the happy valley look like fairyland.'[71] This unearthly blue
effect, which was neither the actual colour of the hills nor of the
light, was able, with the help of a little imagination, to transform
the natural scene into something strange and compelling, an
effect he was always alert to, probably having had his attention
drawn to it by Robertson, who had written: 'Poetry represents
things, not as they are, but as they seem'; his illustration of this
truth was 'The painter [who] represents his distant mountains
blue. . . .'[72]

The eighteenth-century movement to revive Welsh culture
was romantic in character. While there were attempts to seek out
genuinely historical material, there was also a strong emphasis
on the 'mythical stories and legendary heroes . . . brought in
to fire the imagination and to create national sentiment'.[73] An
even older version of Welsh history consisted of three elements:
a set of fables proving the Welsh to be the earliest inhabitants
of Britain; the claim that British Christianity was introduced
first in Wales and was defended by King Arthur against pagan
Saxons; and a concern with the descent of a line of princes

from figures like Cadwallader the Blessed, last Welsh king to claim lordship over Britain in the seventh century, down to Llewellyn II in 1282.[74] These three elements, along with others, came together in the heroic, romantic figure of the Bard in Thomas Jones's painting. In the account that follows of further explorations made by Kilvert in the culture of Wales, it will be seen that his vision was influenced mainly by the mythical and the legendary, by Howitt's notion of 'landscape poetry,' although both men took some cognisance of real historical facts. When Kilvert wrote, about his entry into St David's, 'And so we came to the end of the world where the Patron Saint of Wales sleeps by the western sea', the sonorous, elegiac, Tennysonian phrasing is one indication that he envisaged his journey as an attempt to recapture the romantic past of Wales, to raise what Watts-Dunton called 'the Spirit of Antiquity'. Just as Kilvert had viewed Cornwall through the lens supplied by Rev Warner, so he followed the agenda Warner announced at the beginning of his account of his 1797 tour of Wales. Warner stated that he was going to seize the opportunity

> to visit the country of the ancient Britons; . . . to climb the steeps of Snowdon and Cader Idris; to listen to the thundering cataracts of Mawddach and Dol-y-Myllyn; to admire the variegated landscapes of Festiniog, Clwyd, and Llangollen; and to breathe the inspiring air where liberty made her last stand in these kingdoms, against the strides of Roman power.[75]

Kilvert was aware of a Celtic civilisation extending westward from Wiltshire, where evidence of it existed in the landscape monuments of Stonehenge, Silbury Hill, Old Sarum, Avebury and the barrows of Salisbury Plain, into Wales and down through Somerset to Cornwall. He was deeply influenced by the tendency for the West to be associated with the spiritual, the mysterious and the Celtic.[76] An understanding of Celticism came to him via Gray and Hurd, Britton, Bottrell, Tennyson's *Idylls of the King*, Arnold's articles on Celtic literature, and Warner's guide books about Cornwall and Wales.[77]

In Kilvert's account of his visit to St David's, he stressed that the Cathedral was 'the object of our *pilgrimage*'. The word is a vital clue to his stance towards this and similar experiences. Throughout this account of his depiction of landscape, it has been felt necessary to identify the ideas and images in his mind

in order to understand why he wrote of it as he did. St David's
was one of several linked locations which were to him shrines
associated with missionaries, prophets and churchmen. One
legend that he subscribed to — and it forms a prominent theme
in Welsh tradition — is

> the hope for a saviour who would lead the Welsh
> from the state of oppression by their neighbours ...
> The hopes of the Welsh focused on names with the
> sound of military and political strength like Arthur and
> Cadwaladr ... hopes expressed in bardic poetry. ....[78]

John Morris summed up thus Arthur's general significance
for people in every age: 'The core of the story has always been
melancholy regret for a strong and just ruler who protected
his people against barbarism. ....' For those living in Kilvert's
time, 'He is the pattern of the Victorian hero, just, benevolent,
protective to his inferiors of any class or colour, so long as they
keep their station'.[79] One of the legends about King Arthur,
with which Kilvert was very probably familiar, was that he was
present at the battle of Badon around AD 517, when an army
of Britons (i.e. Welsh)[80] defeated the Saxons. That such events
were real and important to Kilvert is clear from the interest
he showed in 'a tall white tower, battlemented' he saw near
Castle Combe, which commemorated 'the Battle of Ethandune
between King Alfred and the Danes'.[81] Edington, 25 miles south
of Castle Combe, is the actual site of the battle of Ethandune,
in which Guthrum and his Danes were utterly routed by
King Alfred, with the result that Guthrum was baptised into
the Christian faith.[82] Such battles symbolised the defence of
Christianity against paganism.[83] In Kilvert's mind, St David
was identified with this struggle, and hence his pilgrimage to
the place where he slept 'by the western sea'. Born in the early
6th century, David founded a monastery where he lived a quiet,
studious life. Welsh tradition pictures him as the defender of
early British Christianity and of the Britons against Saxon
domination: '[St David's] primacy was an office within the
vital heartland of the British people and British Christianity'.[84]
Richter also emphasised that St David's was one of the 'cultural
centres of late Celtic civilisation',[85] while Greswell wrote of the
Celtic Church: 'It combined mission work with its monastic
system, and especially the gift of preaching'.[86] The significance
for Kilvert of St David's Cathedral as the resting place of other

men who, though bishops, nevertheless remained simple men of God, emerges in his comments on them, which recall those of his uncle Francis on Bishop Hurd. Of Bishops Anselm, Jorweth, Giraldus Cambrensis, and Gower, Kilvert wrote: 'All these great men are content with simple tombs'. These figures (and the holy men who were the focus of the other Kilvertian pilgrimages that are dealt with later in this chapter) constituted a veritable 'Communion of Saints'.

Alan Bull has drawn attention to Kilvert's relative lack of interest in the architectural features of churches in which he ministered, and suggested it was because they were too familiar. Though he had 'an artist's eye for the minutest detail in the world of nature', he was, in Bull's view, 'heedless toward the beauty of the church as a building'.[87] The only exception Bull found was Kilvert's admiration for Malmesbury Abbey. It is true that he didn't write much about church architecture, but this makes his praise of St David's Cathedral the more remarkable. The fact that he singled out the Cathedral of the man whom he called 'the great *Welsh* Saint' (my italics) and Malmesbury Abbey for praise is significant. They are two in a whole network of shrines of early Christianity in the west and south-west of Britain that receive particular emphasis in the *Diary*, and the key to their meaning is the British Church (i.e. the Church of the ancient Britons) at Gwythian that attracted so much of his attention on his Cornish holiday. Then he was in the role of a latter-day defender of early Christianity, following the sixth century example of St David and King Arthur. Loyn's definition of the 'British Church' enables us to understand why Kilvert venerated it so much: 'the church that survived in unbroken descent from the Christianity that existed in these islands in Roman days'.[88] He also had Britton's tribute to reflect upon: 'The British Church . . . had been remarkable for strict adherence to the genuine doctrines of the gospel'.[89] Kilvert's mother's Moravianism and his own Evangelicalism had, as their main objective, the recovery of those original doctrines.

Although most of Kilvert's information[90] about the early Bishops of St David's came from the commentary of his guide, Canon Thomas, it is also evident that he had enough knowledge of the history of Christianity in Britain for a number of sites to have formed a pattern in his mind (that is why he made a pilgrimage to St David's in the first place). He also knew that Wales, with its mountain fastnesses, played a crucial part in that history: 'The real clue to the history of British Christianity in the fifth and sixth centuries' lies in the refuge afforded by the mountainous parts of the country that guaranteed 'highland religious continuity within Roman Britain'.[91] According to legend, the Druids were in the forefront of British resistance in the Welsh mountains to invaders — Romans, Saxons, Danes.[92] Kilvert's sympathetic feelings towards Stonehenge and other standing stones that represented Druidic power derived from such legends. The 'outdoor' religion they represented appealed to him, as did that of the 'more or less unhoused Celtic Church.'[93]

Malmesbury's role in early British Christianity was played out in the century following St David's primacy. When Kilvert went there on foot on 12 October 1874 it was another pilgrimage. Though autumn, it was a particularly hot day and he 'walked slowly on account of the heat', taking three hours. He lovingly praised the architecture of the Abbey Church — 'the grandest Norman doorway in the world, arch within arch sculptured richly with pictured medallions of the history of the Bible'. And he entered into a reverie about its past that included its sacred landscape — the 'grey-buttressed high-gabled Abbot's house' and below it 'the golden heads of chestnuts and limes and the reflections of the trees glassed in the quiet water. . . .' He sought help from a guide, Mrs Jennings, but, as seemed to be the case at St David's, he clearly knew about the site beforehand and sought to supplement his knowledge. Mrs Jennings, he said, 'took me out into the garden [of the Abbot's house] *at my request*' (my italics), in order that he could see the private entrance by which the Abbot entered the church and also the 'site of King Athelstan's grave'.[94] The Abbot whom Kilvert came to revere was Aldhelm, who became Abbot *c.* 675 and remained there thirty years. He was 'one of the leading Anglo-Saxon churchmen' and endeared himself to his flock, it was said, by playing music to entice them to church. Under him, Malmesbury became a centre of Christian learning and piety.[95] Kilvert intended his pilgrimage to the shrine of Malmesbury to cost some effort (as pilgrimages were designed to do) and he was gratified when friends expressed incredulity at his walking there from Langley Burrell and back in the heat in one day (the total distance was 26 miles).[96] The reason for his interest in the 'site of King Athelstan's grave where the High Altar used to stand' becomes clear from what is known

of this king of Wessex. Not only was he as illustrious a son of
Malmesbury as Athelstan, but was related to the abbot. Britton,
who was probably Kilvert's main source of information about
Athelstan, had written: 'So great was Athelstan's veneration
for the memory of Aldhelm, that he chose him for his tutelar
saint'.[97] Furthermore, he was a worthy grandson to King Alfred,
being involved in what his biographer, Paul Hill, called 'the
crusading nature of the English struggle against the pagan
Danes'.[98]

Aldhelm is one factor connecting Malmesbury to another
holy site in the landscape of south-west Britain to which
Kilvert made not one but two pilgrimages on the evidence of
the *Diary* (6 September 1872 and 24 September 1873), for it was
Aldhelm who urged King Ine (AD 688-726) of Wessex to build
Glastonbury Abbey, according to the twelfth-century William
of Malmesbury. But a Celtic monastery almost certainly predated it, making it 'venerated by all the Christian British
peoples as a place of awesome and holy antiquity'.[99] The great
Abbey of St Mary developed from a small wattle church built
before AD 633. Two main legends dominate the Glastonbury
story, one of which concerns Joseph of Arimathea who was,
on the testimony of St John, a secret disciple of Christ; all four
Evangelists agreed that he buried Christ. Other claims about
him stem from William of Malmesbury,[100] who stated that
Joseph came to Glastonbury at the head of twelve missionaries
sent by the Apostle Philip. Joseph was alleged to have thrust
his staff into the ground at the foot of Glastonbury Tor where
he stopped to pray and it miraculously sprouted leaves. This
staff became the famous Glastonbury Thorn. Kilvert's visit to
Glastonbury has the same pattern as his visits to St David's
and Malmesbury: he came armed with some knowledge,
was determined to find out more, but above all was there to
venerate the place for the part it played in the history of the
British Church.[101] He was very interested in the Holy Thorn
'which is said to have sprung from the staff of St Joseph of
Arimathea which he struck into the ground in his wanderings
when he first caught sight of Glastonbury and determined to
end his journey in the isle of Avalon'.[102] The reference to Avalon
introduces the second main strand of Glastonbury legend
— that King Arthur came to Glastonbury and that he and his
Knights dedicated themselves to recover the Holy Grail, the
cup which Christ used at the Last Supper. Allegedly, Joseph

had buried it at the foot of Glastonbury Tor and the 'Chalice Well' was its location.[103] This was the 'Holy Well, St Joseph's Well' which Kilvert asked the Glastonbury guide to show him. Glastonbury is identified in legend with Arthur's Isle of Avalon and his city of Camelot with Cadbury Castle.[104] To make the Arthurian associations even richer, the bodies of Arthur and Guinevere were allegedly discovered at Glastonbury in 1191, when the abbot of the time ordered his monks to dig between two stone pyramids.[105] If that were not enough, John Hardyng in his *Chronicle* (1457) stated that the heart of Sir Galahad was buried at Glastonbury.[106] These associations made Glastonbury's fame 'pre-eminent throughout the Celtic world'.[107]

Recent scholars are agreed that the claims on which this fame rests are largely spurious. Rhatz, for example, stated: 'Most, if not all, of the myths associated with Glastonbury are a compendium of invention of medieval and later centuries'.[108] He nevertheless considered the myths important because they reflect the religious/spiritual aspirations of earlier times. This is their significance in Kilvert's life; it was a whole series of mutually reinforcing religious and literary myths that sent him on pilgrimages to various shrines from Tintagel, to St David's, to Old Sarum.[109] It was the myth of Joseph of Arimathea bringing the Holy Grail to Glastonbury that really fired his imagination, as a number of *Diary* entries make plain, and his love for Tennyson can be explained partly by the fact that he was the poet who made the Arthurian tradition come alive. Kilvert had not only read Tennyson's *The Holy Grail* but was ready to lend his copy of it to his Clyro literary friend, Lewis Williams, on 1 June 1870, only months after its publication. Just over a month later, Kilvert noted: 'I had some pleasant talk with Barton, who is a clever well-read man, about Tennyson . . . [and] the Holy Grail'.[110] (The phrase 'a clever well-read man' indicates Kilvert's criteria for a good conversation; they are not the criteria of the utterly unbookish man portrayed by the principal commentators on the diarist.) It is clear that he eagerly made the Holy Grail the subject of conversations within a short time of the publication of Tennyson's poem, which was one of four new *Idylls of the King* that appeared in 1869. (The others were *The Coming of Arthur*, *Pelleas and Ettare*, and *The Passing of Arthur*.) The poet's comments on *The Holy Grail* are some indication of why it had interest for Kilvert:

> Faith declines, religion in many turns from practical
> goodness to the quest after the supernatural and
> marvellous and selfish religious excitement. Few
> are those for whom the quest is a source of spiritual
> strength. . . . *The Holy Grail* expresses my strong feeling
> as to the Reality of the Unseen.[111]

Early in the poem, Sir Percivale tells how he was driven
from all worldly concerns by the 'sweet vision of the Holy
Grail', which 'the good saint Arimathean Joseph' brought to
Glastonbury (50-1). 'The Victorians did not consider the *Idylls*
as merely a poem, but an event, a cultural phenomenon',
according to Eggers. He went on: 'It helped to define the
mentality that we called Victorian. . . . The age saw in the
Idylls an exalted reflection of itself as the second coming of
the Round Table'.[112] *The Holy Grail* is a reflection on how the
Grail meant different things to the different men who sought
it,[113] according to the quality of their own character and faith.
It suggests Christ's Second Coming but the knights, except
perhaps for Sir Galahad, prove themselves unworthy of it.
Earlier chapters have shown how Kilvert was drawn to the
religious and literary representations of *mystery* lying at the
centre of Nature and of human life. The quest for the Grail is
portrayed in Tennyson's poem as an exploration of mystery.
Arthur's origins and final destination are mysteries. The
landscapes of the poem often have the quality that Arnold
called 'magicalised', so that the knights' journeys are made,
not through recognisable earthly landscapes, but through
landscapes of dream or, indeed, nightmare.

Mystery was the key element in an important passage that
occurs in another of Kilvert's Welsh excursions. He went on 15
April 1872 to the Gower peninsula in south Wales to stay at Ilston
Rectory with the Rev Westhorp and his wife. His five-day visit
was not overtly a pilgrimage to a significant holy place such as
St David's but it nevertheless took on a religious meaning and
has a place in the story of his encounters with Welsh landscape
and people. Aspects of his descriptions of Gower suggest that
he thought of it as a kind of earthly Paradise.[114] The important
passage referred to above concerns his visit to neolithic graves
and it is relevant here to examine closely the phrase he used
about them: 'the graves of the children of the people'. It is
evidently a quotation (it appears in inverted commas) and

comes from 2 Kings 23.6 — one indication that for him the site
had religious significance. The second book of Kings deals with
the last kings of Judah, one of whom was King Josiah. He was
so horrified when he learned of the idolatrous practices of his
father, Amon, and his grandfather, Manasseh, that he ordered
that all objects used for the worship of the pagan deities Baal
and Asherah to be burnt and he suppressed the priest cults
associated with them. He took the sacred pole of Asherah, burnt
it and scattered the ashes 'upon the graves of the children of the
people' (in the words of the Authorised Version). The phrase's
meaning becomes clearer in the NEB's rendering of the original:
'over the common burial ground'.

After a detailed, accurate description of the burial chambers
known as the 'Giant's Grave',[115] Kilvert noted that in some
chambers 'were found ... skeletons sitting upright. ...' He
then added: 'It was a strange weird place — how old, no one
could tell — and no one knew who was buried there. No man
knoweth anything about their sepulchres to this day'. These
words, with their slight Biblical overtones, reiterate the sense of
deep respect for the graves that informs his earlier reference to
them as 'Graves of the Unknown' - 'the graves of the children
of the people'.[116] It is evident that these phrases, especially
perhaps the latter one, produced an imaginative response in
Kilvert, disposing him to reject the idea that a burial ground of
common people was in any way a shameful place. He valued the
graves of common people exactly because they were the graves
of the humble, and even more if they were the graves of the
pious humble. The 'graves of the children of the people' passage
belongs with other mourning, elegiac passages in the Diary. The
respect he had for their tombs was composed of three elements:
he felt sympathy with the dead per se; he was impressed by
their enormous age;[117] and he identified their occupants with
the ancient Britons who had cherished Christianity in the Dark
Ages.

The entry recording Kilvert's visit to the Church of Llan
Madoc suggests that it too was a place that had significance
for him before he went to Gower, and it seems that he had
requested his hosts to take him there (having heard from them
about Llan Madoc's incumbent no doubt increased his interest,
as will become clear). The Church itself and its history fitted
admirably well into his mental picture of Wales as a place of
Celtic shrines and of piety. The saint to whom the Church is

The Giant's Grave, Gower (showing the author)

dedicated — St Madoc — possessed all the qualities to attract him. He was the early seventh-century Irish saint, St Aidan (his Welsh name — Maedoc — is a variant of Aidan),[118] who travelled to the monastery at St David's in order to study the Scriptures. He lived there a long time and performed many miracles, according to legend; the history of his miracles 'leaves a general impression of kindliness and charity'.[119] Legend also said that he played an important part in preserving British Christianity from the invading Saxons.[120]

Kilvert's hosts of course knew Llan Madoc's vicar, John David Davies (1831-1911), and went into the Rectory to see him. It is when they returned to the Rectory for lunch that the references to 'cleanliness' begin, which permeate the account of Kilvert's first visit to Gower. 'We were waited on by a tall clean old woman', Davies's housekeeper, who 'is so clean that she washes the kitchen four times a day'. Kilvert's prior knowledge of the history of Gower appears in his suggestion to Davies that the housekeeper 'might be of Flemish blood which would account for her cleanliness'.[121] The very heavy stress on the housekeeper's cleanliness, which appears as an aspect of her godliness,[122] is reinforced by Kilvert's depiction of Gower's coast as having a cleanness bordering on perfection: 'This is the cleanest coast I ever saw — no seaweed, no pebbles, hardly a shell — not a speck for miles along the shining sand, and scarcely even any scent of the sea'.[123] It is as though he was trying to put himself in the place of the neolithic people who

inhabited Gower thousands of years before, the 'children of
the people', and to see its landscape as they saw it when it
was fresh and new. Ideas of bareness, spareness and freshness
multiply, and there are frequent emphases on the perfect
quality of the weather and the purity of its elements — wind,
water and sun. Near Mumbles, he saw 'the greenest sea I ever
saw'. Llan Madoc itself sits on the top of 'a windy bare hill',
looking across 'sands and blue water'. In all of his descriptions
of the landscape of Gower (he visited it three times), the wind
is ever present. On 17 April 1872, we hear of 'the sighing of the
wind through the gorse and dry heather' and of the tolling of
the bell on the buoy moored off Mumbles, borne 'upon the lift
of the wind'. As he walked to the Westhorps's home on 10 June
1878, he commented on the 'strong wind blowing from the
sea'.[124] During the visit in autumn 1878, he wrote of 'a merry
windy luncheon' he enjoyed, 'An E wind blowing fresh and
strong' and of 'white seagulls . . . in a splendid sunburst. . . . A
wild merry happy day'. Wind was also the dominant element
in the weather on the longest day (11 June) in summer 1878:

> Barnaby Bright, but the weather wild, cold and wet
> and stormy. Walked with Westhorp to Penmaen. We
> went down to the Three Cleeves (Cliffs) Bay through
> the foxgloves and the fern, among which white fantail
> pigeons were walking. The fern and foxgloves clothe the
> hillside down to the sandhills. The storm at Penmaen
> high on the hill looking seaward was tremendous. We
> sat on the rocks as the tide came in and watched the wild
> grey sea and the waves breaking white with foam and
> the surf dashing high against the black cliffs and falling
> back in showers of spray while a solitary deserted boat
> with a bare mast rode tossing at anchor in the bay.[125]

(The eye that Kilvert had for the telling detail denoting singularity is seen in the 'solitary deserted boat'.)

Because he always liked the longest day to be sunny, he was
disappointed on this occasion, but there is enjoyment of the
sheer wildness of the weather in the passage that one Diary
reader very appropriately characterised as 'a delight that
owed much to grandeur that had its origin of primeval beauty
and the impressiveness of its terror in Kilvert's appreciation
of the Garden of Eden'.[126] Kilvert himself did link Gower's
landscape to the Garden of Eden on his first visit there in April

1872, significantly in the entry in which he described its coast as the 'cleanest . . . I ever saw', by quoting Genesis 3.8: 'They heard the voice of the Lord God walking in the garden in the cool of the day'. (The landscape of Aberedw also represented Paradise to Kilvert – see chapter five.) The theme of Gower as Paradise reaches a peak in the entry of 17 October 1878:

> The morning was perfectly glorious, a brilliant cloudless blue sky, a tender blue haze hung over the green and golden woods like a gauzy veil, and the gossamers shot and twinkled into green and gold in the grass which in the shade of the woods was still hoary with the night's frost.

Kilvert's emphasis on green and gold is notable here and it is a feature of many of his landscape descriptions (for example 'the richness of green and gold meadows' seen on his visit to Chieflands farmhouse — see next chapter). This was his last visit to Gower; in less than a year he was dead and beyond all earthly landscapes. His last experience of Gower's landscape was, however, a perfect one.

The picture of Kilvert in Gower is incomplete without his response to Llan Madoc's vicar, the Rev John Davies. Although Kilvert was a little disturbed by his appearance — 'he looked like a Romish priest' — he was greatly impressed by his asceticism, piety and learning. He had devoted his bachelor existence to furthering the interests of the Church in Gower. He had not only restored both of his churches[127] (Cheriton was in his care too), but was a very skilled wood-carver and his work adorned local churches. He was also an antiquarian ('chiefly remembered for his monumental *History of West Gower, 1877-94*').[128] 'He is very clever and can turn his hand to anything,' wrote Kilvert. 'Besides which he seemed to me an uncommonly kind good fellow, a truly simple-minded, single-hearted man'. Kilvert could pay him no bigger tribute: Davies was a man of simplicity and sympathy; he was, like Gower itself, the epitome of *innocence*, a worthy successor to St Madoc.

Kilvert's other main excursion into 'Welshness' — a visit to Snowdonia that began on 12 June 1871[129] — had the exploration of mystery as its central objective, because it was to the wild mountainous north of the country which, as the early part of this chapter noted, had been regarded by tourists since the

eighteenth century as the place where the real spirit of the
ancient Britons was to be apprehended:

> The beauties of south and central Wales . . . paled before
> the prospects offered [to tourists] by the north. . . .
> Caernarvonshire was the main goal of every tourist, for
> here they found themselves face to face with the savage
> and majestic face of untamed nature, precipitous,
> rugged, gloomy.[130]

What the Rev Richard Warner had written about North
Wales would have had particular significance for Kilvert. In
its landscape, Warner and his companion had 'looked through
nature up to "nature's God"; the sublimity of the objects . . .
fills our souls with sentiments of wonder and adoration. . . .'[131]
Warner's list of the qualities of North Wales people — 'openness
and candour, hospitality, quickness of feeling, national pride, a
religious spirit, superstition, decency of manners' — is almost
identical with those that Kilvert identified in Celts and Welsh.[132]
The way Warner developed his thesis about Welsh national
character brought him even closer to Kilvert. Welsh character
was as it was, he said, because 'little variation has taken place in
it, during the lapse of eighteen centuries'; it was, in other words,
the ancient British character that he was encountering. He noted
that the Welsh, like other Celts, attributed to mountains spiritual
presences and the reason for this was not simply the credulity of
ignorant people, but the 'circumstances of the *scenery* wherein
they reside', its gloom and desolation (his italics). He hastened
to add that he did not at all condemn this superstition: 'It is a
principle that arises from the feelings and affections of nature',
and was a welcome contrast to the 'cold philosophism' of
the age, 'which disbelieves everything, which contracts and
petrifies the heart, deadens the affections . . .', a statement in
which eighteenth-century sentimentalism and Romanticism
are blended, as they are characteristically in Kilvert's writing.
As both men travelled through Wales, they liked to record their
awareness of links between certain locations and Welsh heroes.

The Welsh harper not only sang of heroes but was himself
a hero and Kilvert, perhaps stimulated by Gray's *The Bard*
and by paintings of this most romantic of Welsh figures, was
determined to find a harper and to hear him play. Arriving in
Llangollen, he headed straight for the Hand Hotel because 'This
is the only hotel in Wales where a Welsh harper can be heard'.[133]

Richard Warner, 1774

His imagination had been stirred early by the Welsh harp when, on a visit to London in 1851 to see the Great Exhibition, he and the other Kilvert children were taken by their mother 'to hear some beautiful harp playing, especially that of John Thomas, Queen Victoria's Welsh harpist'.[134] In Wordsworth, Kilvert was able to find numerous tributes to bards and harpers,[135] and the poet referred to himself as 'a youthful Druid taught . . . primeval mysteries, a Bard elect. . . .'[136] Mrs Hemans's poetry, which Kilvert evidently knew, also contains many celebrations of harpers.[137] The harper symbolised for him all the passion, poetry and heroic past of Wales, which is why he wrote: 'I would have come all the way to Llangollen on purpose to hear the Welsh harp'.[138] Eighty years before Kilvert's visit, the tourist trade had provided a whole crop of Welsh harpers to fulfil the dreams of English travellers:

> The passion for touring filled the pockets of the many (ostensibly blind) Welsh harpers, dressing picturesquely and with flowing locks, who cashed in on Gray's famous poem of *The Bard* by performing in Wales' main tourist towns.[139]

Kilvert's Llangollen harper was not 'ostensibly blind' but suffered another disability that increased his attractiveness to tourists: he was a cripple, Kilvert noted, and 'his crutch rested by his side against a chair'. He added to the knowledge he already had of harps and harpers by quizzing this harper.[140] 'While he played Llwyn-on and the Roaring of the Valley, I stood by him *entranced*,'[141] he wrote in a passage reminiscent of one in Warner's account of his 1797 tour. While staying at the Bull at Conway, a young man asked Warner and his companion whether they would like to hear a harp: 'C- and I were electrified at the word. . . . The idea of the ancient bards, who animated the hero to fight . . . rushed into our minds'. Warner went on: 'Mr Jones, a venerable old man, totally blind, with grey locks, was introduced to us'. He played, on his three stringed harp, Welsh airs characterised by 'extreme simplicity, and a wild originality . . . and the pathetic'.[142] Warner was clearly infatuated, as Kilvert was, by the legendary Wales that had been created during the eighteenth-century revival in order to bolster national pride.[143]

   Kilvert summed up his experience of harp music at the Hand Hotel thus: 'It was a great and *strange* delight to listen to the music of this Welsh harp'.[144] 'Strange' has been italicised to show the continuity between this experience and an even stranger one, which supplied the main motive for his visit to North Wales — he intended to climb one of its great mountains in order to explore mystery. Generations of tourists before him had had the desire to savour the most extreme picturesque experiences of awe and terror by risking their lives on some dangerous mountain: 'most of those who had faced Snowdon went on to climb Cader Idris. . . .'[145] Kilvert was aware of mountains because they were chiefly what he came to see.[146] He was set on experiencing awe and fear in the manner of picturesque travellers but he had a deeper purpose, which can be understood by recalling his reverence for what he called 'the great mountains'. (His love of mountains was partly stimulated by his knowledge of the

Victorian physicist and populariser of science, John Tyndall.)[147]
He continued: 'A man can hardly be a beast or a fool on a great
mountain. There is no company like the grand solemn beautiful
hills ... one had a feeling and a love for them which one has
for nothing else', adding that it was perfectly understandable
that Christ went up a *mountain* to pray.[148] Since this passage was
written on 29 May 1871, only two weeks before his ascent of
Cader Idris, it is likely that he was anticipating the latter event.
The experience to which he intended to expose himself in his
search for the deepest insight into Welsh consciousness can best
be grasped by reference to Mrs Hemans's poem, *The Rock of
Cader Idris*, that he mentioned in the middle of the entry dealing
with his ascent of the mountain (he called it 'Mrs Hemans's fine
song').[149] There are distinct parallels between the wording of
the two texts. He couched the legend about what happened to
anyone who spent a night on the mountain's summit in almost
identical words to those used by Mrs Hemans. He wrote:

> It is said that if any one spends a night alone on the top
> of Cader Idris he will be found in the morning either
> dead or a madman or a poet gifted with the highest
> degree of inspiration.

She wrote:

> It is an old tradition of the Welsh bards, that on the
> summit of the mountain of Cader Idris is an excavation
> resembling a couch; and that whoever should pass a
> night in that hollow, would be found in the morning
> either dead, in a frenzy, or endowed with the highest
> poetical inspiration.[150]

The physical/emotional aspects of the challenge of Cader
Idris are contained in the shocking story told to Kilvert by his
guide 'old Pugh'[151] of a Mr Smith, who attempted the mountain
alone and without a guide from the Machynlleth side. Pugh
went up twice that day but saw no sign of Smith. Six weeks
passed and Smith's relatives became uneasy.

> Mr Smith disappeared in September, and in the
> following May a man was up on Cader Idris looking for
> a quarry. He heard his dog bark suddenly and looking
> over a precipice he saw a dead body. He hurried back
> to Dolgelly and fetched a doctor and policeman and the

coroner, and Pugh came along with them. When the
body was turned over Pugh was horrified. He said he
never saw such a sight and he hoped he should never
see such another. It was what had been Mr Smith. It was
a skeleton in clothes. The foxes and ravens had eaten
him. His eyes were gone. His teeth were dashed out by
the fall and lay scattered about the mountain. His head
was bent double under him and crushed into his chest
so that his neck was broken. The only piece of flesh
remaining on the bones was where the coat buttoned
over the chest. One leg was gone and one boot.[152]

Pugh rounded off this gruesome tale by adding that Smith must
have fallen over a precipice in the dark, and that 'the body must
have fallen 440 yards'. To Kilvert, who, as has been shown,
relished stories of 'dreadful accidents' among the Radnorshire
hills, the tale would have appeared almost as intrinsic a part
of the landscape of Cader Idris as its terrifying precipes. It was
important to Kilvert to respond imaginatively to stories of this
kind;[153] it was part of eighteenth-century sentimentalism.

Smith's fate must have rushed back into Kilvert's mind as
he found himself briefly without a guide when Pugh lagged
behind and told him to 'go on alone to the top of the mountain'.
Kilvert's description of the landscape on the way up depicts
Cader Idris as a truly forbidding place: 'The head of Idris, which
had been cowled in cloud, had cleared for a while, but now an
impenetrable dark cloud settled down upon it and the mist came
creeping down the mountain'. All around were 'vast tracts . . .
of large stones lying so close together that no turf could be seen
and no grass could grow between them'. All these impressions
were combined in his conclusion that 'Cader Idris is the stoniest,
dreariest, most desolate mountain I was ever on'.

Having established Kilvert in a stone hut just below the
summit and provided him with some sustenance, Pugh 'van-
ished' and the diarist was alone once again. It is after picturing
himself sitting there eating a hard-boiled egg, that Kilvert's
account mentions the legend about what happened to the
individual who passed the night on the top of the magic
mountain.[154] He added that 'The same thing is said of the top of
Snowdon. . . .' He had not intended to spend the night on top of
Cader Idris (although Pugh's disappearances threatened that he
might have to); perhaps he hoped that even a brief exposure to

Richard Wilson, 'Cader Idris', 1774

the mountain's terrors might result in a small augmentation of poetic inspiration. The similarity between his account and Mrs Hemans's suggests that he was imaginatively projecting himself into the full nocturnal experience. She imagined herself lying at midnight on the rock where the solitary watcher would have the visions that would leave him dead, a madman, or an inspired poet. Around the rock, the 'voice of the mountain-wind' made 'deep music'. Through the shifting shadows she glimpses 'dim shrouded stars', as she faced 'the dread gloom of its grandeur alone'. Enchanted by a 'spirit', she experienced unearthly visions that were so 'glorious' that she 'almost fainted with rapture and awe'. Combined with the beauty of these visions, however, was horror, because she was forced to look on 'dread beings' and called on darkness to hide them in order to reduce the turmoil within that threatened 'madness and death'. The next verse gives more detail of the visions. They were the mighty forms of Nature, 'the powers of the wind and ocean', forms she felt rather than saw. There were also great figures from the past, from whose eyes darted 'a cold radiance' that produced in her spiritual insight but also a dreadful coldness that chilled her very heart.[155] They were visions that normally kill those that look upon them but she was the favoured one: 'my spirit / Was strong, and triumphantly lived through that hour'.

The feeling of triumph with which the poem ends takes on more markedly religious overtones, hinted at earlier. She experiences a new birth, 'as from the grave, I awoke to inherit / A flame all immortal, a voice, and a power'. The phrasing here, and especially the idea that 'There was light on my soul', is very suggestive of religious conversion. The effect of the experience on the subject of Mrs Hemans's poem was that she was able to perceive spiritual meaning in Nature: 'But oh! what new glory all nature invested, / When the sense which gives soul to her beauty was won!' The explanation of this seems to be that the sensuous impressions she had of natural forms were so transformed by her ecstatic, visionary experience that they ceased to be merely things of sense and 'won' their way to a perception of the 'soul', or spiritual dimension, in Nature's beauty. Mrs Hemans's lines provide the answer to the problem the Christian worshipper of Nature faced that was posed at the beginning of chapter seven: how worship of Nature was to escape the charge of pantheism or even paganism. And her answer was the same as Robertson's: the good person could find the 'supersensuous' beyond the sensuous, the 'invisible loveliness' beyond the visible, the infinite beyond the finite. This is the essence of Kilvert's attitude to Nature.

His experience on Cader Idris, limited though it was, represented another exploration of those heightened forms of consciousness that he was always seeking. He must have known Wordsworth's account, in *The Prelude*, of a visit to the top of Snowdon. The climb begins in the evening and his aim and that of his companions is to be 'In that wild place . . . at the dead of night', in order to test the myth about experiencing madness or poetic inspiration, although no such myth is in fact mentioned. They climb up through mist and suddenly emerge into clear air and Wordsworth sees the moon in a cloudless sky. The walk seems like an exploration of the power of imagination. Hartman suggested that the ascent through mist is a kind of entering upon 'imagination's landscape', and added: 'Snowdon is a magic mountain. It is a place of enchantment and danger. . . .'[156]

The ability to converse with the spiritual world through the senses Kilvert regarded as the particular gift of the Celts, and hoped and believed that it was a gift which he too possessed. He favoured Celts because they lived so close to Nature that natural forms became part of their consciousness. At the other significant Welsh locations he visited — Aberedw, Llewellyn's cave, St David's, the Llangollen inn where he heard the harper, Llan Madoc, and the Giant's Grave — he was able to feel something of this inspiration, some replenishing of the religious and literary springs within him. It is of huge importance, therefore, that he declared himself to be Welsh: 'I believe I must have Welsh blood'.[157] In his journeys into the hinterland of the real, authentic Wales (the borderland around Clyro was half English), he was trying to draw closer to the Welshness in him, to his own true, or best, self, and thus it is another aspect of the journey of self-discovery that the *Diary* represents. His interest in racial origins, which was a reflection of the contemporary interest in such matters, fed into this self-exploration.

The desire he had to realise the Welshness in his nature was so strong that he felt moved to attack certain aspects of English national character. For example, it was for him nothing less than a blasphemy to respond to Nature's beauty, in the form of a fine autumn day, by riding through the countryside with the sole intent of hunting down a terrified animal: ' "What a fine day it is. Let us go out and kill something." The old reproach against the English.'[158] He sought to dissociate himself from that behaviour as he did from English 'social life, cumbrous, stiff, vulgarly extravagant, artificial, unnatural'.[159] The social life with which he contrasted his own in this entry was in fact French but the Welsh kind had the same 'elegant ease'. But the principal drive behind his desire to identify with the Welsh derived from his belief that their Christianity was older than that of the English, that they were the heirs of the ancient British Church founded by Joseph of Arimathea, and were therefore closer to Christ.

This chapter has shown that Kilvert's idea of Wales was heavily influenced by sources that held to the thesis that the country's geography had over centuries nurtured a people who were imaginatively and spiritually deep. The Welsh landscape reflected for him the life of the ancient Britons, who had saved early Christianity from barbarism. In his diary, he sought to reanimate forgotten memories of important Welsh people and places in a circle of sympathy, as a tribute to what the past had achieved and to bring the power of those memories to bear on his own ministry in the present and the future and on his own capability as an imaginative writer.

Chapter 10
The Spirit of the Dream

From Nature doth emotion come, and moods
Of calmness equally are Nature's gift:
This is her glory. . . .
Hence Genius, born to thrive by interchange
Of peace and excitation, finds in her
His best and purest friend.
                    [Wordsworth, *The Prelude*, Book XIII]

the visible scene
Would enter unawares into his mind,
With all its solemn imagery. . . .
                    [Wordsworth, *The Prelude*, Book V]

A maiden knight — to me is given
        Such hope I know not fear.
I yearn to breathe the airs of heaven
        That often meet me here.

I muse on joy that will not cease,
        Pure spaces clothed in living beams,
Pure lilies of eternal peace.
        Whose odours haunt my dreams.
                    [Tennyson, *Sir Galahad*]

———

In this study of Kilvert and landscape, his journey has been represented as a search for unusual states of consciousness that gave access to different kinds of *power*, creative and spiritual power shaping individuals and communities. He was fascinated by the mysterious force that drew 'heart to heart', that forged bonds of sympathy among the living and the dead. He was persuaded that particular landscapes nurtured not only kindness and piety, but imagination too; he knew that the landscape of Aberedw had fostered his own creativity. Landscape's power to shape consciousness lay partly in its mythic and superstitious associations, an aspect of his search which confronted the mystery of time itself. He experienced awe at the power of Nature that could rear up mountains as well as smash them into fragments. He was driven to record instances of power residing in single objects and people. He was drawn to the ecstatic experiences that could be found in music, love, dreams, poetry, the beauty of young girls, religion and Nature because they were experiences of power that ultimately derived, in his view, from God. As an Evangelical, he was especially alert to moments of 'conversion', common to such experiences, in which individuals were taken over by non-rational forces, seen as the intervention of supernatural grace, and he continually exerted himself to be the means by which others were brought to God. His search for a deeper spirituality involved probing the mystery of his own identity, the role played in its formation by the memory of particular objects and particular landscapes. The search naturally led him to the solitude of mountain tops, the 'favoured haunt' of God's 'eternal Voice', the literal *pinnacle* of landscape's moral power. This chapter's final image of Kilvert is an individual in quest of a mystical symbol of power.

It was when Kilvert was due to leave Clyro that the full measure of his love for Wales was displayed. The *Diary* entry of 26 March 1872 was special because the journey it recorded marked a seventh anniversary. He had called at the Wernewydd farmhouse on his way down what he called his 'favourite Cwm' on a March evening in 1865 too, but then he had had before him the prospects of many more delightful walks and warm welcomes from the hospitable farming folk. In 1872, the opportunity for more of those pleasures was limited and knowledge of it weighed heavily on him. The entry begins: 'Today I wrote to the Bishop of St David's to give notice that I intend to resign the Curacy of Clyro on the 1st of July next'. He had been able to respond to the warmth of people at the farms where he called. He liked the girl 'with a merry arch rolling eye' at Bryn y garth and the way that the farmer there shook hands 'heartily' with him and thanked him for his visit. Mrs Lloyd of Wernewydd, 'with her sunbonnet and her eager handsome honest face', made a fuss of him as usual. She cut some 'sweet home-made bread and butter and made some tea into which I am sure she put some spirit, rum I think. . . .' It was as though nothing had changed. It was after the visit to White Ash farm that Kilvert referred to 'the spirit of my dream', the dream he had when he first came to Clyro and the Welsh hills seven years before. Then, he said, he was in 'a transport of delight and enthusiasm', in which he saw himself as a Welsh poet: 'The "awen" was upon me and I composed a poem on that "Dingle of Cwm".' The Welsh word 'awen' means inspiration or muse (Borrow noted that to the Welsh, Snowdon was the hill of the 'awen' or muse).[1] Kilvert was reminded of the earlier occasion and of the poem because, now as then, he was descending the Cwm at dusk. He recalled that a lone blackbird was singing. The fanciful melancholy of the two poems[2] he wrote about the earlier occasion is replaced by the profound grief of the later one: 'Now all is changed. But much of the change is in my own spirit. Years have done their work and a change has come o'er the spirit of my dream'. It is another moment when he highlighted the importance of the landscape of memory.

The entry in which the moment is recorded gives details of changes that saddened him. He noted 'my beautiful favourite Cwm is devastated and laid waste' because so many of the ancient ash and beech trees had recently been felled. By far the saddest event for him was that his courtship of Daisy Thomas had come to an abrupt end the previous September because her father, disturbed at Kilvert's lack of prospects, had forbidden him to talk to her of his affection and their affair had since languished. However, though these factors were of significance in the change that had come over the spirit of his dream, he stressed that 'the change is in my spirit'; it was a matter less of external factors than of internal ones. The one had, of course, affected the other but it is clear when he said 'the years have done their work' that he meant changes occurring over a long period within his own personality, his own sensibility, which had sapped his creativity. Relevant here is Dunham's view of Kilvert as a figure, not only continually on the move (Dunham spoke of his 'inherently "restive" quality'), but always in need of experiences whose 'freshness' or vitality he could capture in writing.[3] That freshness had now gone.

In Kilvert's *Diary* entry of 26 March 1872, in which he compared his first visit to his favourite Cwm with his later one, there is the same melancholy, elegiac quality that informs

J.M.W.Turner, 'The Chancel and Crossing of Tintern Abbey,' 1794

Wordsworth's *Tintern Abbey*. The poet compared a visit to the Abbey on the Wye five years earlier with the present one, registering a 'sad perplexity' amid his endorsement of the positive force of the memories he had treasured of the scene ever since.[4] He saw again the 'steep and lofty cliffs' whose 'beauteous forms' had, over the years, been for him sources of 'sensations sweet, / Felt in the blood, and felt along the heart; / And passing even into my purer mind, / With tranquil restoration'. The memories had been a source of regenerative power, of emotional, poetic and moral energy. (Jacobus observed: *Tintern Abbey* is about 'a saddened self-searching

for renewal'.)[5] Wordsworth also noted that his attitude to
Nature at the earlier time was simple, spontaneous and joyful,
which corresponds closely to the 'delight and enthusiasm' that
Kilvert remembered experiencing when he first visited his
beloved valley. He, too, experienced a surge of creative power,
the 'awen' that produced the 'Dingle of Cwm' poems. And just
as Wordsworth owed to the memories of the Wye's 'beauteous
forms' a disposition towards 'little, nameless, unremembered,
acts of kindness and of love', so Kilvert, as he wandered from
one 'pastoral farm' (Wordsworth referred to such in his view
of the river valley) to another on his way down the Cwm, was
involved with acts of kindness, his own to the farming families
or theirs to him, as for example Mrs Lloyd's hospitality.

Kilvert was fond of using the phrase 'a change came over
the spirit of the dream' and, apart from one instance, used it in
relation to the 'work' wrought by the passing of time in changing
his perception of important landscapes or relationships, an
aspect of his steady concern with self-awareness. This concern
is seen at its most intense in his effort to recapture the particular
feel of his earliest childhood memories and to identify himself
as closely as possible with suffering individuals encountered
in his travels. The phrase 'a change came over the spirit of
the dream' appears in his account of revisiting his old Oxford
college in May 1874, when he noted that the scene it presented
was unchanged, 'But all else was altered'. He loved and revered
Oxford; it was to be expected, therefore, that Oxford was a
'dream' landscape to him, replete with notions of expectation,
love, fulfilment,[6] and to feel that he no longer had any place
in that dream caused him intense anguish. Another occasion
when he experienced a sense of a fatal disruption of a vision
of belonging, of wholeness, and used 'a change in the spirit of
the dream' to convey it, was apropos an actual dream — his
dream of killing Venables. After describing his murderous
assault on his friend and master, he noted: 'Then the spirit of
the dream changed. Mrs Venables became her old natural self
again',[7] that is, she became kindly and reproached Kilvert for
his shocking betrayal of their friendship. That friendship was
as much a part of the 'dream' of Clyro, of its fulfilment and
beauty, as Kilvert's favourite Cwm Dingle. When he used 'A
change came o'er the spirit of the dream' again, it was for comic
effect, with reference to the boat passengers who had set out
with Kilvert and his mother, 'laughing, talking, joking', on a

trip down Bristol Channel to Ilfracombe. However, seasickness made them 'serious, silent, melancholy, white, yellow and green'.[8] His use of the phrase here was an ironic comment on the importance it normally held for him. In the other three instances, it registered significant moments in his picture of his developing self against a background of continuity. It is only in the Ilfracombe entry that inverted commas appear around 'A change came o'er the spirit of the dream', signifying a quotation.

The poem that contained the line that Kilvert found so memorable and that expressed crucial understandings for him was Byron's *The Dream* which, like *Tintern Abbey*, is an autobiographical poem recording changes in consciousness. (Garber referred to it as 'an act of taking stock'.)[9] Kilvert's knowledge of it is a further indication of his concern with dreams and their relationship to the self that was explored in chapter eight. Furthermore, what Byron had to say about the nature of dreams corresponds with the way Kilvert thought of them. The lengthy analysis of them at the start of the poem shows why they held a powerful fascination for Byron, as for other Romantic poets. What follows is the story of his doomed love affair with Mary Chaworth, who enjoyed his attentions while loving another.[10]

The really important link between *Tintern Abbey* and Kilvert's twilight in the Cwm entry is that, in both, physical scenes and the human spirit are shown to be mysteriously involved in the way things are perceived. *Tintern Abbey* begins with the poet seeing once again 'these steep and lofty cliffs / That on a wild secluded scene impress / Thoughts of a more deep seclusion; and connect / The landscape with the quiet of the sky'. The effect of these lines is to blur conventional distinctions. Cliffs are said to be impressing 'thoughts' on the physical scene instead of the more familiar idea of the scene 'impressing' the mind. That the mind is capable of connecting physical objects together whose different qualities make them distinct, is shown in the way the landscape is merged with 'the quiet of the sky'. The epithet 'quiet' invests the sky with additional meaning. How can a sky be 'quiet' or noisy? The sense of sight is thus connected with that of hearing. The notion of dissolving categories is increased further by the reference to 'thoughts of a more deep seclusion', which might indicate thoughts of a more inward, personal nature or thoughts about a seclusion deeper than the secluded physical scene. Isobel Armstrong stated that 'thoughts of a more deep seclusion' is Wordsworth's 'most paradoxical expression of the power of thought to dissolve categories'.[11] The implication is that the mind is moving into new, deeper dimensions of experience. There is more emphasis on physical objects merging into each other in the latter half of the poem's opening section: 'Plots of cottage-ground, these orchard tufts, / . . . are clad in one green hue, and lose themselves / 'Mid groves and copses' and the 'little lines' of hedge-rows lose their distinct shape and become a 'sportive wood run wild'. Fruits in the orchards are 'unripe', half way between first budding and maturity.

The *Diary* entry about Kilvert's changed landscape of Cwm Dingle does not have such a profusion of dissolving physical forms, though it does not lack them. Devastated trees appear alongside those showing spring growth. A farm dog rushes at Kilvert as though 'about to tear me in pieces. . . . Then he immediately became a lamb'. We are constantly reminded too of the ever-changing light that is twilight, as day mysteriously merges into night. Early in the passage, 'sunny hill sides' and 'distant woods' can be seen. Later, we are told that the setting sun lit up the kitchen and was 'glowing upon the warming pan hanging on the wall'.[12] Later still, Kilvert is guided by a farmer across a meadow in 'the fast darkening dusk'. It is as though Kilvert was half-consciously remembering particular details and especially the general tone of the early part of *Tintern Abbey*, while composing his own account of a momentous change in his vision of the hills and valleys behind Clyro.[13] Here he is the 'borderland' figure characterised by Dunham whose writing 'repeatedly unsettles the distinctions between past and present (yet another "borderland"), and which chronicles a succession of unfolding "double moments" of writing and remembered experience.'[14] The moment of Kilvert's awareness of change has considerable poignancy in that it encapsulates the agony of a man who always sought closer communion with the God-like in people and Nature yet experienced frustration either because he was a 'stranger' or because the reality often fell short of the ideal.

Wordsworth had spoken in his poem of 'another gift, / Of aspect more sublime', in addition to the urge towards acts of kindness, which stemmed from his memories of beautiful landscapes. This gift was

>   that serene and blessed mood,
> In which the affections gently lead us on, —
> Until, the breath of this corporeal frame
> And even the motion of our blood
> Almost suspended, we are laid asleep
> In body, and become a living soul:
> While with an eye made quiet by the power
> Of harmony, and the deep power of joy,
> We see into the life of things.

The mystical experience of calm that appears in this passage recurs frequently in Wordsworth. In *The Prelude*, he wrote of experiencing from landscapes not only 'feelings of delight' at the 'latent qualities / And essences of things', but also of

>   such a holy calm
> [That] would overspread my soul, that bodily eyes
> Were utterly forgotten, and what I saw
> Appeared like something in myself, a dream,
> A prospect in the mind.[15]

The opening lines of *Tintern Abbey* show the mind apprehending and unifying a variety of experiences and producing others of greater depth, and the key to this process is 'the eye made quiet' for it represents the mind's capacity to find relations between itself and the external world.[16] What the mind was perceiving was not simply the physical form of natural objects but their spiritual essences. It was the perception of these essences, this 'seeing into the life of things', that produced the 'harmony' and its accompanying feeling of 'deep joy'. When the eye became 'quiet', it meant that sense impressions and thought were one. In the state of consciousness where sense and thought become one, the normal distinctions between inner and outer reality are broken down, and landscapes pass into the mind and feelings. Beautiful natural scenes could, Wordsworth believed, pass by means of 'the inward eye' into the consciousness, extending and deepening it, becoming part of the landscape of the mind.

Kilvert showed unmistakably that he had absorbed Wordsworth's ideas about the deepest experience of landscape and they provided a framework for his own. The *Diary* entry that records his visit in May 1876 to the farmhouse of Chieflands, close to his Wiltshire home of Langley Burrell,

is one of the most sustained and carefully elaborated he
ever wrote. It contains a passage that represents his own
understanding of *Tintern Abbey* and his attempt to use it to
convey his experience of landscape. As he walked towards
Chieflands he was overwhelmed by the fresh beauty of
spring. 'I thought I had never seen the country arrayed in
such dazzling beauty and such richness of green and gold
meadow and foliage'. In the next sentence he strove to
express more explicitly the pattern made by the variety of
sense impressions and the way they combined into a unified
whole:

> The afternoon was glorious and as the sunlight streamed
> in splendour upon the oaks and the elms and the larches
> and beeches and the meadows, each with its peculiar
> tints of green yet blending into one bright harmonious
> whole, the Sun seemed to me to be a mighty minstrel
> playing upon a beautiful instrument a sweet melody
> and harmonious air, bringing out as clear distinct notes
> the variegated colours of the trees and softly blending
> them through exquisite variations into one melodious
> tune.

Kilvert's best descriptions are notable for communicating
with exactness the physical quality of objects, whereas here
there is a prevailing vagueness and generality. He harps on
'peculiar tints', 'variegated colours', 'exquisite variations'
without giving precise details of the various greens, and
he reiterates 'harmonious whole', 'harmonious air', and
'melodious tune' in order to stress the blend of the landscape's
greenery.[17] The image of the sun as a 'mighty minstrel' seems
forced (he was probably recalling Wordsworth's 'minstrelsies
of rural scenes').[18] However, he was attempting Wordsworth's
philosophical writing in which, arguably, precise detail
is inappropriate, though it is sometimes criticised for its
vagueness, its reiteration of large abstractions. Of special
interest here is the way he underlined the significance of the
sun by giving it a capital letter.

In his description up to this point Kilvert had tried with
mixed success to express the Wordsworthian sense of total
correspondence between mind and Nature that produced 'the
quiet eye', the spiritual calm. The climax of his effort comes in
the next sentence: 'The heavenly alchymy of a quiet eye and a

contented mind turned all it saw into gold, a better gold and a more glorious transmutation than any which the alchymist philosophers and gold-seekers knew'. Here he had recourse to virtually the identical wording of Wordsworth's evocation of the 'serene and blessed mood' in order to convey the sense of blending and of harmony that he felt. Where Wordsworth referred to 'an eye made quiet', Kilvert had 'a quiet eye' and for Wordsworth's 'purer mind', Kilvert used 'contented mind'. Kilvert knew the power of the mind's 'inward eye' to transform sense impressions and to merge physical and mental ideas into spiritual realities. His analogy between this process and that of the philosopher's stone has some force in emphasising the miraculous superiority of the one to the other.

The idea of vision that was capable of transforming ordinary things into experiences of extraordinary worth so appealed to him that he used it frequently. It is central, for example, in his poem *Honest Work*, linked to the concept of sacrament. There we are told that as long as an individual possesses the 'magic wand'[19] and can say the 'magic word', 'All [he] touches is turned to gold'. In *A Pageant*, 'the world, to some so common and so drear', can be 'transmuted . . . to Paradise' by 'Heaven's alchemy' for one who is 'wise'. *Little Things* insists that ordinary objects can be turned 'to jewels golden'. Again, as has so often been noted in this study of Kilvert and landscape, his inheritance from Wordsworth is striking. The lines from the latter's *A Poet's Epitaph* which Kilvert's uncle Francis found so important referred to 'truths', capable of being imparted by a poet, which lie all around us in 'common things', and which are 'The harvest of a quiet eye'. (It is in such instances that we see just how much Kilvert owed to his uncle's teaching.) What he was incapable of reproducing in his poems and in his diary was Wordsworth's capacity, never surpassed, of expressing the mysterious communion with the 'presences', the deep, unchanging, infinite realities of Nature, of which the sensitive, imaginative mind is capable.

Throughout this exploration of Kilvert's portrayal of landscape, it has been continually emphasised that his vision of landscape was always an imaginative one, working more through image and symbol, legend, folklore, the supernatural and the visionary than through realistic or naturalistic detail. Barth underlined the difference between the two approaches when he observed that Wordsworth's 'new' poetry, in spite of the 1801 *Preface* to the *Lyrical Ballads*, is not primarily about a change in technique but a change in *vision*. What is important is not that he focused on 'low and rustic life' but that 'in that situation the passions of men are incorporated with the beautiful and permanent forms of nature'. He was concerned with environment — the bond that connected man with the world about him. The *Lyrical Ballads* signified a revolution in poetic vision, 'a vision of the deep and inherent inter-relationships of thought and feeling, of mind and nature, of nature and the transcendent'.[20] Thus, his poetry is a poetry of *wholeness* and its theme is the mystery of the self. His poetry also contains a vision of mystery, and mystery is expressed best, though never completely, by symbol.[21] Previous chapters have illustrated the various ways in which Kilvert sought spiritual, creative power, and the mystery of power. The bond of unity between man and Nature was the essence of it and he sought it in experiences of solitude, poetry, mountains, time and beauty which produced heightened forms of consciousness. His visits to Cornwall, St David's, Gower, Snowdonia and a variety of ancient sites have exemplified this search.

That symbol always played a prominent role in the search is clear from the enormous meaning he attached to such symbols as home, the landed estate, the stone of Cross Ffordd, churchyards, mountains, the 'book' of Nature, an eternal crystalline sea, the Holy Grail, memorials, Chieflands and Gaston's Farm. It is an essentially imaginative and poetic view of landscape that relies so heavily on symbol. He was brought up by his uncle Francis to recognise the importance of *imagination*, to see in Wordsworth the exemplar of the 'Romantic Genius ... whose imagination was an oracular organ of truth'.[22] Kilvert later learned for himself to appreciate a group of writers — Cowper, Barnes, Mrs Hemans, Robertson, Kingsley, Macdonald, Tennyson — for whom imagination represented the prime means of perceiving the spiritual reality lying behind natural forms. Their approach to Nature found a ready response in one in whom the imaginative faculty was highly developed, one who loved dramatic and touching stories, who was drawn to the unusual, the mysterious, the supernatural and the poetic, who saw landscape as instinct with spirit. The editors of *Kilvert's Cornish Diary* expressed the essence of his imaginative approach to landscape when they wrote: 'Kilvert loved to project himself imaginatively into a scene of old ruins or natural beauty'.[23] Perhaps the epitome of his approach to landscape is his response to the poetic image that is Lucy Gray. Insofar as *Kilvert's Diary* is an account of self-development, which it substantially is, it is importantly a record of his *imaginative* life, just as *The Prelude* is (Wordsworth noted in Book XIII of it that imagination was its theme). And a crucial element in both works is a sustained monitoring of changing responses to familiar scenery. Abrams saw this as

> The major lyric innovation of the Romantic period. . . .
> the extended poems of description and meditation, are
> in fact fragments of reshaped autobiography, in which
> the poet confronts a particular scene at a significant
> stage of his life, in a colloquy that specifies the present,
> evokes the past, and anticipates the future and thereby
> defines and evaluates what it means to have suffered
> and grown older.[24]

The writers Kilvert favoured, for whom the imagination was the means of perceiving spiritual truths behind natural forms, were ones whose work combined poetry with piety. Earlier chapters have shown that he, like them, was able to combine his Evangelicalism with his fondness for Romantic poetry, an outlook closely reflected in the following statement by George Macdonald:

> God is the God of the beautiful, Religion the love of
> the Beautiful, and Heaven the home of the Beautiful,
> Nature is ten-fold brighter in the sun of Righteousness,
> and my love of Nature is more intense because I am a
> Christian. . . .[25]

Throughout this study of Kilvert and landscape, his tendency to designate particular landscapes as 'holy ground' has been noted. He actually used the phrase about the landscapes of his 'mountain beauties', of his love affair with Ettie Meredith Brown, and of Stonehenge, but clearly other of the landscapes that have been focused on, which we know passed into his inner landscape of memory, qualified for the term. He expressed a similar understanding when he wrote, during a return visit to Clyro, 'Every foot of Clyro ground is classical and sacred and has its story'.[26] The idea of landscapes with stories to tell has been a theme of this enquiry and it has been shown that when Kilvert deemed the stories to be important, from a religious, literary or personal perspective, he made a point of visiting and commemorating the landscapes that bred them. This was true of other Celtic shrines in addition to Stonehenge, neolithic barrows and standing stones, St David's, the 'Paradise' of Gower, Cader Idris, Tintagel and other Arthurian sites, his Hardenhuish birthplace, Yaverland, Godrevy, the British Church at Gwythian, Penllan, Aberedw, Oxford, Cwm Dingle and Tintern Abbey. It has been noted that he preferred that the stories of some landscapes remained untold because they involved mysteries that it was irreverent to pry into, even if the mystery was simply ancientness, the mystery of time itself. It has been said that the *Diary* is full of mini-biographies, that it is his own autobiography, a record which measured changes in identity, especially in its spiritual and imaginative dimensions, against unchanging landscapes. It has been shown that he was born into a family that had an unusual preoccupation with writing lives, those of the worthy, the humble and pious departed, as well as their own, a preoccupation driven partly by literary aspiration and partly by the Evangelical motive of 'watchfulness', the impulse to account for every day of one's life, in order to measure spiritual progress and 'usefulness'.

In Kilvert's story of the land and its people, there was a strong tendency to look backwards, which earlier chapters of this study have recognised. The reading of Scott's novels early in Kilvert's youth encouraged a romanticisation of the past. The novels of Grace Aguilar that were read to the Kilvert children were set in the 1820s and focused on traditional rural society. Furthermore, the Kilvert children were steeped in antiquarianism from their earliest years. The characteristic elegiac note in the *Diary* has been linked both to the culture of mourning, the remembrance of forbears, and to the 'passion for the past', which much Victorian writing displays. Also reflected in the *Diary*'s picture of the countryside is the unease Victorians felt about the new urban/industrial society that was emerging. According to Houghton, they were 'lonely for a lost companionship, human and divine; nostalgic for an earlier world of country peace and unifying belief'.[27] The sentimentalism on which Kilvert was reared was inevitably going to recoil from the new society's dominant values of competitiveness, utilitarianism, acquisitiveness, materialism and worldliness. Kilvert's idealisation of the landed family and its estate is a clear example of a harking back to earlier values.

His conception of a rural community retained its traditional rulers and envisaged the classes beneath them living together in a harmony based on the idea of involvement in a shared enterprise, in which charity and love of neighbour prevailed. To revere the country house was, however, to revere an institution that had had its day, because, as a result of enclosures and the poverty that followed the Napoleonic War, 'the social image of the estate as an ideal' was collapsing.[28] From the late eighteenth century onwards, capitalist agriculture made farming into a competitive business like any other and the traditional social relations that Kilvert valued were reduced to 'a crude moneyed order'.[29]

His picture of the farm of Chieflands (it is another of the 'stories' the *Diary* tells; the description of it and its history, in which Kilvert's own family was involved, occupies six pages) contains idealised social relations that belong to an earlier, kinder age. Chieflands is an 'old-fashioned farmhouse', which is 'half-veiled by and embosomed in trees' (Kilvert was fond of underlining feminine qualities of landscape).[30] Though it had 'evidently seen better days', it was 'a tall fair mansion . . . once apparently the residence of a gentleman and lord of the soil'. It had 'a strange quaint old world look which took one back a hundred years' and appears like something 'out of a fairy tale'. And, in a typically Kilvertian way, the surrounding landscape is presented as a dream image, in which time has slowed and virtually stopped: 'life had gone sleepily on and the people of the farm had moved about the yards and fields and ploughed and sowed and milked and mowed like figures in a dream'.[31] It is evident that Kilvert's description of Chieflands was influenced by Tennyson's *The Day-Dream*, which deals with the Sleeping Beauty story. Kilvert wrote: 'The Sleeping Beauty might still be sleeping there and waiting for the magic touch and kiss of the Prince'. Tennyson's poem mentioned a peacock and 'terraced lawns' of the palace and Kilvert made much of 'a magnificent peacock which would have adorned the terraced lawns . . . of a palace'. The people of Chieflands themselves are figures from a fairy tale — with 'beaming smiles', 'weather-beaten good-humoured faces' and old world courtesy. They live a 'quiet plaintive peaceful uneventful monotonous life . . . with the few cares, the simple anxieties, the narrow interests, the limited horizon'.[32]

To Kilvert in this mood, these apparent restrictions on human possibility were entirely positive; urban society might offer greater fulfilment but was plagued by doubt, conflict, and stress. He could, however, put the alternative case as, for example, when in Dorset and looking for the 'ruined ivied tower' of Holditch Court, he met a labourer who 'regretted that he had never travelled or been far from home' and described himself as 'a slave'. A boy Kilvert met at the same time had no idea where nearby Hawkchurch lay and had never heard of the tower, even though it was 'within a stone's throw'.[33] Here, the innocence enjoyed by the Chieflands folk has become lamentable ignorance, and Kilvert's awareness of the fact indicates that there was complexity in his vision of landscape: he could be realistic as well as sentimental. His vision has been characterised earlier as, at bottom, a search for, or a celebration of, innocence. The rural bliss of Chieflands, Gaston's Farm and Wernewydd, the Cwm Dingle farm of Mrs Lloyd, had a form of innocence at its core. Kilvert's beloved cottagers and benign, dutiful patriarchs — John Morgan, George Jefferies, John Hatherell and Simon Lee — were innocents, as were the solitary 'half-hermits, half-enchanters' John Price of Llanbedr and William Barnes of Winterbourne Came. The 'mountain beauties' and the Mouse Castle girls, those close relatives of Lucy Gray and the Wordsworthian child, were innocents. The landscape of Wales, the landscape which more than any other quickened Kilvert's desire to write, epitomised a traditional way of life in which innocence still thrived. His praise for the naturalness of Welsh women and girls was in essence a celebration of innocence. Even the neolithic agriculturalists who raised the standing stones were a species of innocents.

Kilvert was not ignorant of the harsh realities of rural life, as is clear from *Diary* entries recording visits to homes of his poor parishioners, and he did all he could to relieve hardship. Nevertheless, he was less interested in the poor's living and working conditions than in their moral and spiritual state. In this, he was very much the disciple of Frederick Robertson, who was, as has been noted, very sympathetic to working men and their need for independence but was opposed to socialism. This was the position adopted by Kingsley in *Alton Locke*, which we know Kilvert greatly admired. When the news of Kingsley's death was announced on 31 January 1875, Kilvert wrote: 'So Charles Kingsley is dead. . . . We could ill spare him'. His admiration for Kingsley may have owed something to Robertson, who paid him this tribute:

the Church of England will endure no chivalry, no *dash*, no effervescing enthusiasm. . . . [It] bears nothing but sober prosaic routine, and the moment anyone with heart and nerve fit to be the leader of a forlorn hope appears, we call him a dangerous man. . . . I suppose God will punish us . . . by banishing from us all noble spirits . . . like Kingsley.[34]

Robertson followed Kingsley by challenging the status quo in his writing and preaching but refused to ally himself with any political faction, believing he was following Christ in urging sympathy and relationship between all classes instead of hostility. In this lay his radicalism, as he himself recognised. Similarly, when Kilvert sided with the poor, dependent and dispossessed, it was motivated not by political conviction but by the recognition that their souls and their sensibility mattered as much as those of their masters. He also believed that the morality of humble folk was often superior to that of the rich and grand. Both convictions were radical enough in their way at that time, and reflected his Quaker, Moravian, and Evangelical background. His religious outlook found a parallel in his stance towards the countryside. Politically, he was a Conservative and one feels that it was largely his love of the land that made him so. His attitude to the extension of the franchise, to trade unions, to socialism seems to have been that those issues belonged to the urban, industrial world and had no place in the countryside.[35] It was there that he could more easily hold to his conception of community. Behind the landed interest lay centuries of tradition, which was not the case with industrialism; it was Kilvert's nature to hark back to older ways. In this respect, he was the rural writer identified by Keith: 'Politically, he may belong to any party, but his attitudes will usually be, in the non-party sense, conservative'.[36] Kilvert possessed all the other traits which, in Keith's view, distinguished the countryman — suspicion of innovation, nostalgia, an overwhelming love of country life, and a tendency to envisage it as a Golden Age. Only small signs of the radicalism that often surfaces in rural writing[37] are to be found in *Kilvert's Diary*, but they are there: his support for the independent smallholder, opposition to the aggregation of small farms into larger ones, censure of landowners' extravagance, of game laws, of neglect of tenants

and destruction of woodland.[38] And, of course, he displays the
radicalism that the young Wordsworth displayed in choosing
to celebrate the lives of ordinary country folk.

Speaking up for the rural poor was never going to be
Kilvert's way. The core of his being can be glimpsed in some
remarks Robertson made about how a person's character 'may
be measured, both in depth and quality, by the poet who is
the chosen favourite'. Robertson used the metaphor of a river
to stand for the particular quality of each poet. Wordsworth's
was the kind of river that travelled 'many miles underground',
representing the 'lost power of life', deep and immeasurable.[39]
One of the major themes of this exploration of Kilvert and
landscape is that he was never more Wordsworthian than in
the impulse which his writing exhibits towards recovering this
'lost power', establishing the unity between his imaginative
and his spiritual self. His poetry and his *Diary* are all about
establishing or re-establishing *relationship* — with the 'dream'
of beauty, of love, of creativity, of community, of the spiritual
presences lying beyond natural forms, of the mysterious
affinity between people by which 'hearts are linked to hearts'.

It has been repeatedly emphasised in this study that Kilvert
might never have become a writer at all if he had not gone to
live, in spring 1865, in the *border* country of Wales, and one of
the ways in which 'border' as an idea has been shown to have
resonance with regard to his writing is in the poetic image of
Lucy Gray, the genius loci that signified the union of Earth and
Spirit — the most important and most comprehensive form of
relationship for him. Scott's influence has been seen as a critical
influence on Kilvert's writing because the border life pictured
in the Waverley novels had much in common with that of the
Welsh-English border. In both cases, the border was a wild
area giving rise to colourful history, conflict, rich folklore and
legend. These elements stirred Kilvert's imagination almost
as much as did the area's outstanding beauty. In addition to
providing him with the stimulus to write, it has been suggested
that his 'border' position socially gave him the *freedom* to write,
that his 'in-between' position as a parish priest, existing on the
margins of various social groups but not really belonging to
any, enabled him the better to observe people and their ways
in 'fluid' encounters.[40] And the close resemblance between
his mode of writing and Wordsworth's poetry of encounter
have been noted. Of course, he did his best as the 'stranger'

in Clyro to connect himself with the region and its culture, not only by involving himself closely with people through his parochial work, but also by imaginatively identifying himself with Wales. It ought to be remembered, in this connection, that his roots were in the Welsh–English border, a fact that emerges strongly in the entry in which he met an unemployed hatter from Bridgnorth in Shropshire. The man was destitute, his clothes soaked by the rain and, moved by his condition, Kilvert gave him a shilling, 'For the sake of the old county'.[41]

It is appropriate to close this study of a man who thought and wrote in images with an image which had outstanding significance for him. It occurs very early in the *Diary*, before the change came over the spirit of his Clyro dream. Before going to bed, he looked through his curtains and indulged in a brief romantic reverie. He saw 'one of the magnificent sights of the world, the crescent moon setting', and it reminded him of the following lines from Tennyson's *Sir Galahad*:

> When down the stormy crescent goes,
>   A light before me swims,
> Between dark stems the forest glows,
>   I hear a noise of hymns.

In this poem of 1834, one of three lyrics written as an introduction to the *Idylls of the King*, Tennyson idealises Sir Galahad, whereas in the *Idylls* his dedication to the Holy Grail is an example which brings destruction to the other knights who follow it. Eggers summed up the essential quality of Sir Galahad thus: 'his is the way of the mystic — to make no terms with the world but to condemn it by leaving it for a better'.[42] Kilvert must have liked to believe that his own spiritual aspirations and abhorrence of worldliness gave him at least some sort of entitlement to follow Sir Galahad's path. This was how he pictured himself in the motto he chose for himself: an alien in a foreign country, a stranger and a pilgrim on earth. He could identify closely with the 'just and faithful Knight of God', of Tennyson's poem, whose heart is above earthly things, including beautiful women. The Knight, like Kilvert, was drawn to their charms — 'How sweet are looks that ladies bend / On whom their favours fall!' — but his heart is 'drawn above. . . . I never felt the kiss of love, / Nor maiden's hand in mine'. He is moved by 'mightier transports' and keeps himself pure 'through faith and prayer / A virgin heart in work and will' and in his quest for the Grail, his purity gives him 'the strength of ten' when facing dangers.

The poem pictures magical landscapes that he encounters in his journeys. The uncertain moonlight he follows takes him among the 'dark stems' of a forest, where he hears 'a noise of hymns'. He rides by 'secret shrines' where he hears a disembodied voice, because 'none are there' and the choir stalls are empty, yet candles burn, bells ring, and the 'solemn chaunts' continue to be heard. 'Sometimes on lonely mountain meres / I find a magic bark; I leap on board: no helmsman steers: / I float till it is dark', and suddenly he has a vision of the Holy Grail. Buoyed up by hopes of eternal life, yearning for the 'airs of heaven' and musing on 'joy that will not cease', the last landscape seems to tell him that his final goal is at hand: 'the clouds are broken in the sky, / And through the mountain walls / A rolling organ-harmony / Swells up . . . the prize is near.' And so the 'maiden knight' that is Kilvert rides on through his dream Welsh landscape, passing 'hostel, hall, and grange; / By bridge and ford, by park and pale'. Beautiful young women do figure in this landscape and he is their champion: 'For them I battle till the end, / To save from shame and thrall'.

The fact that the crescent moon *Diary* entry contains Kilvert's statement, 'I have . . . a peculiar liking for a deserted road', reinforces the sense that he was picturing a Christian hero whose hard and lonely road he could follow. Reviewers of Tennyson's *Idylls*, as well as the general public, 'had tended to see Galahad's purity . . . as the finest ethical message' of the work.[43] Its message was to reject worldliness and to seek spiritual and moral strength by pursuing the mystery, the perfection, symbolised by the Holy Grail. That in truth was the Spirit of the Dream. (We may recall the fact that when Kilvert dreamt he saw his own grave, growing beside it was a laurel bush —that symbol of Christian purity.) He, like Frederick Robertson, was drawn to the Knight who stood for the Christian ideal of pure, selfless Love and believed he had experienced it in his encounter with the angel-child on the Wootton Bassett train. As he walked through his landscapes, he hoped that he represented, without claiming he personally had achieved it, the 'Love in a perfect form', referred to by William Plomer in *Angel Satyr* and idealised by Fénelon.

References

Introduction

1. F. Grice, *Francis Kilvert Priest and Diarist 1840-1879*, Leamington Spa, Kilvert Society, 1975, p. 52.
2. *Ibid.*, p. 52.
3. Ira Bruce Nadel, *Biography. Fiction, Fact and Form*, London, Macmillan, 1984, p. viii.
4. Simon Schama, *Landscape and Memory*, London, Harper Collins, 1995, pp. 10, 14 and 18.
5. David Matless, *Landscape and Englishness*, London, Reaktion Books, 1998, p. 12.
6. M. Andrews, *Landscape and Western Art*, Oxford, Oxford University Press, 1999, p. 8.
7. Louis James, 'Landscape in Nineteenth-Century Literature', in *The Rural Idyll*, G.E. Mingay (ed.), London, Routledge, 1989, p. 64.
8. Raymond Williams, *The Country and the City*, St Albans, Paladin, 1973, p. 149.
9. W.J. Keith, 'The Land in Victorian Literature', in Mingay (ed.), *op. cit.*, pp. 80-1.
10. Chapter two cites particular works by Howitt and his wife Mary that we know Kilvert read.
11. W. Howitt, *The Rural Life of England*, third edition (1844), London, reprinted by Irish University Press (Shannon), 1971, p. 315.
12. *Ibid.*, pp. 333-4. Howitt repeatedly emphasised the 'genuine characteristics . . . , real scene and circumstance . . . poetical landscapes' of Bewick's work. Two of Bewick's engravings grace Howitt's *Rural Life of England*. Cf. David Dimbleby: 'Animals were for Bewick the truly legitimate figures in the landscape' (*A Picture of Britain*, London, Tate Publishing, 2005, p. 50).
13. Randal Keynes, *Annie's Box. Charles Darwin, his Daughter, and Human Evolution*, London, Fourth Estate, 2002, p. 159.
14. Howitt, *op. cit.*, p. 16 and pp. 8-9.
15. *Ibid.*, p. 249.
16. *Ibid.*, p .269.
17. Kilvert was probably influenced also by his uncle Francis, who had charge of his literary education and was fascinated by Byron. Howitt's book also contained an account of his visit to Byron's home of Newstead Abbey.
18. W. Howitt, *Visits to Remarkable Places*, Philadelphia, Carey and Hart, 1842, p. 2.

19. *Ibid.*, p. 93. Later chapters show that the antiquaries who figured prominently in Kilvert's life and reading – his uncle Francis, Rev Richard Warner, William Gilpin, and (to a lesser degree) John Britton – were all in the Scott mould.

20. *Ibid.*, p. 298 and p. 300.

21. Cf. Kilvert's responses to Wordsworth's *Extempore Effusion upon the Death of James Hogg* (Kilvert referred to it as the 'Graves of the Poets'): it is a 'beautiful poem,' he wrote (*Kilvert's Diary*, vol. I, 1938-40 (reprinted 1971), p. 318). Wordworth's poem also commemorates the deaths of Coleridge, Lamb, and Crabbe. Kilvert's frequent visits to St Mary Redcliffe Church, Bristol, and his reverential feel for it perhaps owe something to Howitt's description of it in *Homes and Haunts of the Most Eminent British Poets*, vol. II, London, Richard Bentley, 1849, pp. 234-5, where he called it 'the finest parish church in England' and said it 'awoke the soul of one of its lovers' i.e. Chatterton (cf. *Kilvert's Diary*, vol. III, p. 89).

22. W. Tyte (*A History of Lyncombe and Widcombe*, Bath, William Tyte, 1898, p. 45) gave its date as 1502.

23. E. Wyndowe, 'Rambling Recollections', in *More Chapters from the Kilvert Saga*, Leamington Spa, Kilvert Society publication, n.d., p. 110.

24. *Ibid.*, p. 89. She also showed familiarity with publications of the Wiltshire Archaeological Society (*ibid.*, p. 113).

25. *DNB* entry on Howitt. The *DNB* spoke of his 'three highly influential books that form a piece: *The Rural Life of England* (1838), *The Boy's Country Book* (1839), and *Visits to Remarkable Places* (2 vols., 1840 and 1842).' All of them sold widely, going through several editions each.

26. Keith, *op. cit.*, p. 80.

27. James, *op. cit.*, p. 70. It is an interest that Kilvert shared, emerging most clearly in his excursions to Cornwall (see chapter three) and to Wales (see chapter nine).

28. Howitt, *Rural Life of England*, p. 37. He gave the example of 300 tourists, 'just landed from a London steamer,' competing fiercely for accommodation around a Scottish loch.

29. He described them as 'loathsome' and 'vermin' (vol. I, p. 79), 'a noisy rabble' (vol. I, p. 196).

30. James, *op. cit.*, p. 71. He noted that idyllic country scenes were often associated with childhood. Cf. Kilvert's evocation of his childhood landscapes in chapter five.

31. Keith, *op. cit.*, pp. 87-8.

32. For example, Lady Verney's *Fernyhurst Court* and *Lettice Lisle*, Annie Keary's *Castle Daly*, Trollope's *Is he Popenjoy?*, Macdonald's *Malcolm* and *The Marquis of Lossie*.

33. Rosemary Treble, 'The Victorian Picture of the Country', in Mingay (ed.), *op. cit.*, p. 53. Kilvert's taste in paintings shows this love of idealised pastoral subjects, typified by such pre-Victorian painters as Morland, Wilkie, and Collins.

34. Leonore Davidoff, *Worlds Between: Historical Perspectives on Gender and Class*, Cambridge, Polity Press, 1995, p. 9 and p. 42.

35. Wordsworth wrote of the unnaturalness 'An inventive Age / Has wrought.... To most strange issues.... From out the labours of a peaceful Land / Wielding her potent enginery to frame / And to

produce. . . .' One 'issue' was 'the huge town, continuous and compact' where 'Abodes of men [were] irregularly massed' and 'O'er which the smoke of unremitting fires / Hangs permanent' (*The Excursion*, Book 8, 87-93 and 117-126). The city he had in mind was Manchester.

36. Howitt, *Rural Life of England*, p. 201 and p. 196.

37. *Kilvert's Diary*, vol. II, p. 202. Cf. the hero of Kingsley's *Alton Locke* (a novel much admired by Kilvert) expressing his joy at escaping from London's 'ceaseless roar of the human sea' (*Alton Locke, Tailor and Poet. An Autobiography*, (1850), Oxford, Oxford University Press, 1987, p. 116).

38. W.E. Houghton, *The Victorian Frame of Mind, 1830-1870*, New Haven, Yale University Press, 1957, pp. 79-80.

39. Howitt, *op. cit.*, p. 318. 'God is Love,' Howitt explained, 'all natural forms have beauty as they are contemplated in love.' (p. 322).

40. See L. Le Quesne, 'Suggestions for Further Research', in *A Kilvert Symposium*, Hereford, Kilvert Society publication, 1975.

41. F. Grice, *Francis Kilvert and his World*, Horsham, Caliban Books, n.d., p. 17.

42. L. Le Quesne, *After Kilvert*, Oxford, Oxford University Press, 1978, p. 40.

43. Brenda Colloms, *Victorian Country Parsons*, London, Book Club Associates, 1977, p. 179. She also attributed his 'conventional literary taste', which she declined to examine, to his father's reading aloud 'the literary classics' (*ibid.*, p. 170).

44. A little arithmetic proves the extent of his reading. In the index to Plomer's edition of the *Diary*, there are references to over seventy publications with which Kilvert was familiar. The NLW editions and the Cornish holiday edition of unabridged *Diary* material yield nine and fourteen more literary references respectively. Add to these Brooke's life of Robertson and a handful of unidentified references and the total is over 100. Two additional facts need to be taken into account. Firstly, Kilvert's original *Diary* was three times as large as all the published portions. Thus, the total number of literary references could well have been three hundred. Secondly, the *Diary* covers just seven years of his life (though ostensibly ten years, 1870-9, are covered, there are gaps in it of two years – September 1875 to February 1876 and June 1876 to December 1877 – and only two months of 1879 are represented). Even allowing for the fact that not all the books referred to were read in those seven years (about 75% of the prose works were), it is quite evident that Kilvert was always reading something and furthermore that his was a consciousness consistently informed by books.

45. D. Lockwood, *Francis Kilvert*, Bridgend, Seren Books, 1990, pp. 68 and 33.

46. L. Le Quesne, *op. cit.*, p. 112.

47. L. Le Quesne, 'Kilvert and Woodforde— the Diarists Compared', *Kilvert Society Journal*, No. 12, September 2003.

48. A.L. Rowse, *The English Spirit. Essays in History and Literature*, London, Macmillan, 1945, p. 233. Rowse added that Kilvert 'does not appear to have been a great reader'. Pivotal in this assessment of Kilvert's mental powers is the fact that he obtained a fourth-class honours degree at Wadham College in 1862. However, that result needs to be seen in the context of Oxford education at the time: fewer than half of its students then took an honours degree at all and a mid-Victorian fourth is the

equivalent of a modern third. This is the view of the current keeper of Wadham's archives (letter of 1 October 2004 from Dr C.S.L. Davies to the author). He also noted that though Kilvert's father regarded the third-class degree he himself achieved as deplorable, his contemporaries would not have seen it that way. In a recent *Kilvert Society Journal* article, 'Kilvert's Degree' (number 17, June 2005), Davies stated: . . . to get high honours really needed four years. Kilvert did his degree in three years and a term . . . to do well in the (honours) schools required private coaching to supplement the inadequate teaching. . . . it may be that he could not afford it. Measured by the standards of his peers, Kilvert's results were above average, in that most of them took pass degrees . . . His performance was by no means disreputable.' In any case, it seems unwise to damn a man forever simply on his degree result obtained at the age of 22. Far more importance should be attached to the evidence of his intellectual capacity as it appears in subsequent sources; that evidence has so far not been available.

49. *Companion to Welsh Literature*, Stephens (ed.), Cambridge, Cambridge University Press, 1986, p. 333.

50. Fred Kaplan, *Sacred Tears. Sentimentality in Victorian Literature*, Princeton, Princeton University Press, 1987, p. 3. Kaplan traced the way the Victorian ideal of the individual with the 'feeling heart' developed from the eighteenth-century 'man of sentiment'.

51. *Kilvert's Diary*, vol. I, p. 32.

52. The *DNB* stated: 'There is perhaps no parallel in English Church history to the influence of Robertson's six years' ministry at a small proprietary chapel. . . . The extraordinary thing was that . . . he should acquire so much influence and celebrity far beyond its limits.'

53. Stopford A. Brooke, *Life and Letters of the Rev F.W. Robertson*, vol. I, London, Kegan Paul, Trench and Trübner, 1891, p. 97. Between 1865, when it was first published, and 1868, the *Life* went through four editions. Kilvert's *Friendship* poem also has echoes of the Robertson passage: both refer to true friends vouching for each other's honour. The Rev Augustus Stopford Brooke (1832-1916) was born in Donegal, the son of an Evangelical minister. He admired Kingsley for his 'robust liberal Christianity and social commitment' and worked for the benefit of the poor in the working-class parish of St Matthew's, Marylebone. He became disillusioned with a Church he saw as essentially illiberal and aristocratic. He was an accomplished literary critic and a devotee of Wordsworth.

54. Evangelicalism was responsible for encouraging 'practical charity' (Richard E. Brantley, *Wordsworth's "Natural Methodism"*, New Haven, Yale University Press, 1975, p. 7). It was part of the ideal of Pure Love, 'that kind of perfection or moral excellence that may be reached through charity or love of one's neighbour' (*ibid.*, p. 103).

55. Kaplan, *op. cit.*, p. 79.

56. Brooke, *op. cit.*, vol. I, p. 262.

57. *Kilvert's Diary*, vol. I, p. 309. It is not hard to imagine a scenario in which he, as a young priest and poet, deliberately undertook the same journey undertaken by Robertson (and Wordsworth) when they too were young and inexperienced, as a kind of homage to these heroes, a dedication of himself to their ideals and their memory. Kilvert's itinerary included

other places — Geneva, Strasburg, Heidelberg — that Robertson had visited. Robertson was minister for a time at Heidelberg's English chapel. Heidelberg may also have been significant for Kilvert because William and Mary Howitt lived there in the early 1840s.

58. *Brighton and Hove Herald*, 20 August 1853.
59. '[W]e must consider Wordsworth's Evangelicalism as it contributes to his view of nature; for . . . we cannot study the man for whom "poet of nature" is an apt if somewhat vague and general label . . . without seeming to ignore what is both obvious and centrally important' (Brantley, *op. cit.*, p. 141).
60. For an analysis of some of them, see J. Toman, *The Books that Kilvert Read*, Kilvert Society publication, 2002.

Chapter 1: To Mind the Living of the Dead

1. *Kilvert's Diary*, vol. I, p. 13. My italics.
2. *Ibid.*, vol. II, p. 428.
3. *Ibid.*, vol. III, p. 159. Kilvert was quoting Ecclesiastes 7.2.
4. *Ibid.*, vol. I, p. 269.
5. *Ibid.*, vol. I, pp. 314-5. Frederick Robertson also had a liking for churchyards and the sense they gave him of communing with the dead: 'After a walk I bent my steps to . . . the churchyard at Hove. It was quite dark, but the moon soon rose up and shed a quiet light upon . . . the white tombstones. . . . I went to the tomb, and stood beside it quietly for some time. I felt no bitterness — infinite pity and tenderness — that was predominant.' He then mourned over a young soldier's death and recalled that it blighted the prospect of marriage to a young woman who was one of his parishioners (Brooke, *Life and Letters*, vol. I, p. 269).
6. *Kilvert's Diary*, vol. I, p. 329.
7. *Ibid.*, vol. II, p. 363. Kilvert most probably knew that Wesley had often preached around Builth Wells and that Marmaduke Gwynne of Garth was Charles Wesley's father-in-law. Wesley conducted the marriage of his brother to Sarah Gwynne on 7 April 1749.
8. *Ibid.*, vol. I, p. 307.
9. *Ibid.*, vol. III, p. 74. My italics.
10. *Ibid.*, vol. III, p. 86. The details of the hearse, mourning coach, and horses with black plumes are a reminder of how elaborate the Victorian cult of mourning was.
11. *Ibid.*, vol. III, pp. 131-2.
12. *Ibid.*, vol. III, p. 42. Cf. vol. II, p. 159: 'I had left [Clyro] bright and sunny and green smiling under a blue sky. Now . . . it lay apparently deep in snow. . . . And over the village stooped low the terrible black leaden sky like a pall. . . .'
13. *Ibid.*, vol. II, p. 145. The landowner who ordered their 'murder' was Walter de Winton of Maesllwch.
14. *Ibid.*, vol. I, p. 118.
15. David De Laura, 'The Allegory of Life: the Autobiographical Impulse in Victorian Prose', in *Approaches to Victorian Autobiography*, George P. Landow (ed.), Athens, Ohio University Press, 1979, p. 334. The second and third quoted phrases are from Wordsworth's *Tintern Abbey*.

16. Paul Turner, *Victorian Poetry, Drama and Miscellaneous Prose 1832-1890*, Oxford, Clarendon Press, 1989, p. 10.

17. *Kilvert's Diary*, vol. I, p. 71.

18. *Ibid.*, vol. III, p. 223. The quoted phrase is from Tennyson's *Tithonus*.

19. *Ibid.*, vol. I, pp. 121-2. The NLW edition of the *Diary* (April-June 1870, 12 May entry) records that Kilvert's parishioners, old Morgan and his wife, told him about the Quarterly Dances. It is another example of the way in which his perception of Clyro landscapes was permeated by stories from the past. Whitehall was the property of Walter de Winton.

20. As a member of Bath's Literary and Philosophical Association, he took a lead in exploring and presenting the city's history and published works on such influential citizens as Ralph Allen and Richard Graves.

21. His early schooling was undertaken by his father at their Hardenhuish home, near Chippenham. Kilvert was one of the signatories in a book presented to his uncle by 17 of his pupils in 1851, when Kilvert was 11 (*Kilvert Society Newsletter*, spring 1974, p. 8). 'The younger Francis Kilvert's most formative years were passed in close association with his learned and literary uncle, and this may be the explanation of his remarkable familiarity with a wide range of English poets' (F. Grice, *Francis Kilvert and his World*, p. 17).

22. 'The older Francis's literary sympathies were Augustan' (T. Williams and F. Grice, *The Other Francis Kilvert: Francis Kilvert of Claverton 1793-1863*, Hay-on-Wye, Kilvert Society publication, 1982, p. 11).

23. Jean H. Hagstrum, 'Description and Reflection in Gray's *Elegy*', in *Pre-Romanticism in English Poetry of the Eighteenth Century*, J.R. Watson (ed.), Basingstoke, Macmillan Education, 1989, p. 150.

24. *Ibid.*, p. 152.

25. Mary Jacobus, 'Nature, God, and the Imagination — From Thomson to Wordsworth', in J.R. Watson (ed.), *op. cit.*, pp. 218 and 220.

26. Introduction to *William Cowper. The Task and Selected Other Poems*, James Sambrook (ed.), London, Longman, 1994, p. 27.

27. *Ibid.*, Book VI, 84 and 184-5.

28. According to F.C. Gill, it would have been found in most genteel homes (*The Romantic Movement and Methodism: a study of English Romanticism and the Evangelical Revival*, London, Epworth Press, 1931, p. 72). James Hervey (1714-58), the son of a clergyman, had Wesley as his tutor while at Oxford. His writings are filled with an awareness of the beauties of Nature and its evidence of God's 'diffusing benevolence', which formed the basis of the religion of gratitude to which he was giving voice long before Wordsworth: 'I have always looked upon gratitude as the most exalted principle that can actuate the heart of man' (Hervey, *Reflections on a Flower Garden, The Works of the Rev J. Hervey A.M*, Edinburgh, Thomas Nelson, 1843, p. 32). For the importance of gratitude to Kilvert, see chapter four.

29. Hervey, *Meditations among the Tombs*, pp. 1-2. His description of the tomb of a medieval knight has much in common with Kilvert's description of the tomb of Sir Reginald de Fresne (*Diary*, vol. III, p. 165). Kilvert preferred Burns's lighter touch with regard to Gothic horrors to Hervey's overblown style: see *Diary*, vol. II, p. 194, where Kilvert said he wanted to write his own version of Burns's *Tam O'Shanter*, 'the scene to be laid in the ruined Church of Llanbedr Painscastle. . . .'

30. *Edward Young. Night Thoughts*, Stephen Cornford (ed.), Cambridge, Cambridge University Press, 1989, p. 17.
31. *Ibid., Night IV*, 689-90.
32. *Ibid., Night IV*, 966-7, 1565-7.
33. *Extracts from Unpublished parts of Kilvert's Diary relating to the Dew and Bevan Families*, Hereford, Kilvert Society publication, n.d., p 8.
34. Kilvert wrote a poem in which a church bell boomed 'To mind the living of the dead', a phrase reminiscent of 'mindful of the unhonoured dead' in Gray's *Elegy*.
35. Esther Schor, *Bearing the Dead. The British Culture of Mourning from the Enlightenment to Victoria*, Princeton, Princeton University Press, 1994, p. 39.
36. *Ibid.*, p. 46.
37. This development is discussed in Houghton, *The Victorian Frame of Mind*, pp. 273-6.
38. Quoted in Schor, *op. cit.*, p. 35. The passage is from Smith's *Theory of Moral Sentiments* (1813), which Kilvert may have read at Oxford. We know that Smith's *Wealth of Nations* was a set text in the Law and Modern History course that Kilvert took. The former work by Smith may have appeared in his reading list because the range of books recommended was 'surprisingly wide' (F.H. Lawton, *The Oxford Law School, 1850-1965*, Oxford, Oxford University Press, 1968, p. 21).
39. Schor, *op. cit.*, p. 40.
40. To McCarthy, the *Elegy* is primarily about relationships: he noted that it contains them from the beginning because the narrator describes the village, the village dead, the nature of their lives and deaths, the worldly people of towns and cities. He added that for him, the 'speaker's sense of himself is the key relationship since he changes' in the course of the poem (Eugene McCarthy, *Thomas Gray: the Progress of a Poet*, Madison, Farleigh Dickinson University Press, 1997, pp. 129-30).
41. *Kilvert's Diary*, vol. III, pp. 258-9. It exemplifies perfectly the 'community of feeling between sophisticated and simple, literate and illiterate' that Jacobus saw as a key quality in Wordsworth's poetry (M. Jacobus, *Tradition and Experiment in Wordsworth's Lyrical Ballads*, Oxford, Oxford University Press, 1976, p. 185). Michael Baron noted that there was a tradition of using images of churches and churchyards to denote community relationships (*Language and Relationship in Wordsworth's Writing*, London, Longman, 1995, pp. 54-5).
42. Hatherell was ten years old at the time.
43. 'It is a happiness to have, in an unkind World, one Enclosure where the voice of detraction is not heard'. However, he acknowledged that some of the dead must have had 'vices and rancorous dispositions' and that thought held him back from seeing a village churchyard as 'the central point of some rural Arcadia'. Nevertheless, he was persuaded that it was a reasonably 'faithful representation of homely life . . . among a Community' (*Essay upon Epitaphs, Prose works of W. Wordsworth*, vol. II, W.J.B. Owen and Jane Smyser (eds.), Oxford, Clarendon Press, 1976, pp. 63-4).
44. Kilvert's notion of a 'mother' who gave birth to all the churchyard dead is very similar to lines 922-6 of Wordsworth's *Excursion* Book V: 'And blest are they who sleep . . . / That all beneath us by the wings are covered / Of motherly humanity, outspread / And gathering all within their tender shade'.

45. *A New Dictionary of Christian Theology*, A. Richardson and J. Bowden (eds.), London, SCM Press, 1983.
46. *New Dictionary of Theology*, S. Ferguson and D. Wright (eds.), Leicester, Inter-Varsity Press, 1988.
47. *Kilvert's Diary*, vol. I, p 317. The church was at Whitney-on-Wye.
48. Cornford (ed.), *op. cit.*, pp. 20-1.
49. The *Gentleman's Magazine* obituary of Francis, November 1863, noted that he kept adding names to his books of inscriptions because 'few eminent public men or friends of the writer went to their graves without some grateful memorial in the same form from his pen'.
50. Schor, *op. cit.*, p. 6.
51. F. Kilvert, *Pinacothecae Historicae Specimen*, London, G. Bell, and Bath, J. Sims, 1848. The title roughly means 'figures in an historical portrait gallery'.
52. E. Monro Purkis, *William Shenstone. Poet and Landscape Gardener*, Wolverhampton, Whitehead Brothers, 1931, p. 44. In his *Essay on Elegy*, Shenstone stated that the rich and famous would always be adequately memorialised but he favoured a poetry that 'endears the honest delights of love and friendship, that celebrates the glory of a good name after death' (*ibid.*, p. 131).
53. Wordsworth, *Essay upon Epitaphs*, p. 56. The *Essay* appeared in Wordsworth's *Poetical Works* (1849-50). *Essays* II and III appeared only in 1876.
54. *Bath Chronicle*, 2 December 1858. My italics. A cutting of the obituary, signed 'F.K.', was found among his papers. George Stothert was the son of George Stothert senior, who settled in Bath with uncle Francis's father.
55. Wordsworth, *Essay upon Epitaphs*, p. 64. This essay has as its epigraph two stanzas (lines 77-84) from Gray's *Elegy* about epitaphs supplying for the poor 'the place of fame and elegy'.
56. Wordsworth subsumed his poems under such headings as Epitaphs and Elegiac Pieces, Inscriptions, and Poems of Sentiment and Reflection. It is evident that these headings held a lot of meaning for uncle Francis.
57. It is possible that Kilvert chose this verse (beginning 'the outward shows . . .') as the epigraph to his *Musings in Verse*, the collection of his poems privately printed in 1882 by Edward C. Alden. If the epigraph was chosen by someone else (which seems unlikely), it was a very apt choice, as Bernard Jones emphasised: 'no one can doubt that it indicates the level of the attempt in Kilvert's poetry and however well or ill he succeeded in his attempt, such was his aim' (*Francis Kilvert's Poetry. A Study*, Kilvert Society publication, 2004, p. 3). The *Collected Verse* by Kilvert, cited in subsequent chapters, is *Musings in Verse*, plus some previously uncollected poems.
58. Uncle Francis perhaps intended his poem *Je Pense Plus* as his own epitaph. It has been widely recognised that the poem is an accurate representation of Kilvert's personality too.
59. Francis Falkner came to Bath in 1778 and set up a wine business. On his death in 1797, it was carried on by his son Francis Henry. Frederick was a younger brother of Francis Henry and the cousin of Kilvert's father.
60. Its full title was *A Discourse on the Studies of the University of Cambridge* (1832), Cambridge, John Deighton, 5th edition, 1850. It was delivered

first as a sermon in the Chapel of Trinity College, Cambridge. Sedgwick agreed with those like Lyell who showed that the earth's rocks were very ancient but he steadily refused to accept the idea of evolution, which threatened to undermine religious belief. According to Sedgwick's biographer the book 'made a sensation at the time'. Sedgwick's work as Professor of Geology at Cambridge naturally led him into contact with Charles Darwin and Sedgwick's reaction to *The Origin of Species* (1859) — another book that made a sensation — provides the clearest evidence of his beliefs. He was anxious to see God in Nature, a divine intelligence causing the changes in natural forms that had taken place over time: 'I call causation . . . the will of God', he wrote on 24 December 1859 to Darwin, who had sent him one of the first copies of *The Origin of Species*, 'and I can prove that He acts for the good of His creatures'. Sedgwick was appalled by the idea that there was no moral dimension to Darwin's theory: 'There is a moral or metaphysical part of nature as well as a physical. A man who denies this is deep in the mire of folly . . . the glory of organic science is that it links material to moral' (John Willis Clark and Thomas Hughes, *The Life and Letters of the Reverend Adam Sedgwick*, vol. I, Cambridge, University Press, 1890, p. 357). In his reply, Darwin expressed regret 'to have shocked a man whom I sincerely honour'. In what has survived of *Kilvert's Diary* there is no mention of *The Origin of Species*, which appeared during his first term at Oxford, but it is reasonable to suppose that his uncle had acquainted him beforehand with Sedgwick's (and his own) view of Nature and that this helped him to withstand the thrust of Darwin's thesis.

61. His admiration of Shenstone and Pope are underlined, each of whom was, like Kilvert, an 'adorer of Nature's God' and wrote extensively about gardens and life in the country.

62. *Kilvert's Diary*, vol. II, p. 383. Noticeably he did not say he wanted to *read* the novel, but to *possess* a copy. There is evidence that he had read it before he bought it on 11 October 1874 in the form of phrases he used that appear in it, e.g. keeping the table/company 'in a roar' (*Gil Blas*, p. 54/*Diary*, vol. I, p. 194); 'working double tides', meaning working twice as hard as usual (*Gil Blas*, p. 56/*Diary*, vol. I, p. 371). *Gil Blas* came out in four volumes between 1715 and 1735.

63. 'The lessons which *Gil Blas* teaches are the common virtues: honesty, gratitude, generosity, and patience' (E. Showalter, *The Evolution of the French Novel 1641-1782*, Princeton, Princeton University Press, 1972, p. 278).

64. A.R. Lesage, *The Adventures of Gil Blas of Santillane*, trans. by T. Smollett, London, George Routledge, n.d., p. 37. The *Diary* entry Kilvert wrote on 15 May 1874 might have come from *Gil Blas*: 'Called at the Langley Lodge and found old Mrs Dallin . . . a cheery chatty chirruping old lady, who like a true philosopher insisted on looking on the bright side of things.' Cf. Robertson: 'A sunny cheerful view of life — resting on truth and fact, coexisting with practical aspiration ever to make things, man and self, better than they are — that, I believe, is the true healthful poetry of existence' (Brooke, *Life and Letters*, vol. I, p. 298).

65. At 'touching expressions' from Dona Mencia, Gil's 'tears flowed in torrents. I felt and expressed as much affection as the human heart is capable of containing' (Lesage, *op. cit.*, p. 30). Gil Blas himself generally

shows little feeling but 'there is clearly some attempt to achieve effects of deep emotional stress and pathos. . . .' (Vivienne Mylne, *The Eighteenth Century French Novel*, Manchester, Manchester University Press, 1965, p. 53).

66. Peter Ackroyd, *Dickens*, London, Minerva, 1990, p. 47. Such works as *Don Quixote*, *Gil Blas* and *Gulliver's Travels* and Fielding's novels made Wordsworth's school days 'very happy ones' (Juliet Barker, *Wordsworth: a life in letters*, London, Penguin, 2003, p. 5). It is important to recognise that Kilvert's fictional choices followed the same path of connections and influences that linked these and other writers. Smollett, who translated *Gil Blas*, acknowledged that his *Roderick Random* was based on Lesage's work (see R. Gidding, *The Tradition of Smollett*, London, Methuen, 1967, p. 38); *Gil Blas* is greatly influenced by Cervantes' *Don Quixote*, to which Lesage wrote a sequel; Kilvert's uncle Francis wrote a biography of Richard Graves, who wrote *A Spiritual Quixote*; *Tristram Shandy* owed much to *Don Quixote*; the poet Gray was a great admirer of *Tristram Shandy*. Kilvert also showed an interest in, and a familiarity with, *Don Quixote*. On 20 January 1870, while in London at a picture gallery, he remarked that there were 'some wonderful illustrations of *Don Quixote* and *Gulliver's Travels*'. At a ball at Clifford Priory on 5 April 1872, he encountered some very tall dancing partners, adding 'Certainly there were giants in the dance as Sancho Panza said.'

67. 'I brought *Tristram Shandy* down from Llysdinam to read' (*Kilvert's Diary*, vol. I, p. 338, 20 May 1871). He had probably read it before. Llysdinam was the country mansion belonging to Kilvert's Clyro vicar, Richard Venables.

68. John Mullan, *Sentiment and Sociability. The Language of Feeling in the Eighteenth Century*, Oxford, Clarendon Press, 1988, p. 91. In his introduction to the novel, Ian Campbell Ross pointed out that 'for all Sterne's delight in bawdy, it is a genuinely moral work' (L. Sterne, *Tristram Shandy*, I. Campbell Ross (ed.), Oxford, Clarendon Press, 1983, p. x).

69. Mullan, *op. cit.*, p. 159. Kilvert liked sentimentalism in painting too. The eighteenth-century concern with social relations is reflected in the novels of Richard Graves that were much admired by Kilvert's uncle Francis. Lower-class country people are always presented in those novels with sympathy and affection (Clarence Tracy, *A Portrait of Richard Graves*, Toronto, University of Toronto Press, 1987, p. 17). Graves was formerly (1750-1804) Rector of Claverton.

70. *Kilvert's Diary*, vol. III, p 285. His hearers were Florence Hill and her brother.

71. Mullan, *op. cit.*, p. 29.

72. R. Kilvert, 'Memoirs of the Rev. Robert Kilvert', in *More Chapters from the Kilvert Saga*, p. 28. Robert emphasised that, with the river in front and canal at the back of their home, 'How it was that any of us escaped drowning is a mystery. . . .'

73. *Ibid.*, p. 26.

74. *Ibid.*, p. 42.

75. Schor, *op. cit.*, p. 197. One chapter of her book is devoted to a study of these documents, over 200 of which have survived. Kilvert himself knew all about Princess Charlotte's story and it informs his visit to her former home of Claremont in Surrey on 18 January 1871.

76. R. Kilvert, *op. cit.*, pp. 41-2.
77. Schor, *op. cit.*, p. 197.
78. R. Kilvert, *op. cit.*, p. 42.
79. Schor, *op. cit.*, p. 149.
80. *Ibid.*, p. 224.
81. *Ibid.*, p. 210.
82. R. Kilvert, *op. cit.*, p. 42.
83. Schor, *op. cit.*, p. 221.
84. F. Kilvert, *The Loving Heart*, dated 28 December 1851.
85. One of several Quaker elements in Kilvert's background. Grice and Williams (*op. cit.*, p. 6) cast doubt on Sophia's Quaker allegiance by pointing out that she was never 'admitted' to the Society of Friends. However, considerable importance must attach to the fact that she was brought up from 1793, when she was only four, to 1822 in a Quaker household. She also paid a very large tribute to Quakers in her book. Emily, Kilvert's sister, stated unequivocally about Sophia: 'She became a Quaker'. Grice and Williams stated misleadingly that her husband was 'even less evangelical than his brother Robert'. Uncle Francis *was* evangelical and his brother even more so. His sermons not only have a decidedly Evangelical tone but reiterate all the basic Evangelical doctrines and continually cite St Paul, who was revered by Evangelicals. See, for example, his *Sermons Preached at Christ Church, Bath, before the National Schools*, London, John Taylor, 1827.
86. S. Kilvert, *Home Discipline, or Thoughts on the Origin and Exercise of Domestic Authority*, London, Joseph Masters, 1847, p. vii.
87. *Ibid.*, p. 35.
88. *Ibid.*, p. xii.
89. *Ibid.*, pp. 99-100.
90. *Ibid.*, pp. viii-ix.
91. *Ibid.*, p. 105. Wordsworth may have been one source of these sentiments. In *The Excursion* (Book V, 381-4) he wrote:
    >   Turn to private life
    > And social neighbourhood; look we to ourselves;
    > A light of duty shines on every day
    >   For all. . . .
92. A.S. Kilvert, *op. cit.*, p. vi.
93. *Ibid.*, p. x.
94. *Ibid.*, p. 39.
95. Wordsworth, *The Excursion*, Book V, 650-7. His italics. Two entire books (VI and VII, both entitled *The Churchyard among the Mountains*) are devoted to remembering the dead.
96. *Ibid.*, 661-3.
97. *Kilvert's Diary*, vol. I, p. 56. My italics. Tybella was a farm near Clyro. The quotation is from Hebrews 11.4 and refers to Abel's power to speak after his death because of his faith.
98. Wordsworth, *The Prelude*, Book 13, 162-7.
99. *Kilvert's Diary*, vol. I, pp. 41-2. Maria Lake died on 18 December 1868 and Kilvert had conducted her funeral. Cf. Wordsworth, *The Excursion*, Book 1, and the description of Margaret's ruined cottage: 'She is dead, / The light extinguished of her lonely hut, / The hut itself abandoned to decay, / And she forgotten in the quiet grave' (507-10).

100. *Kilvert's Diary*, vol. III, p. 148. Emma lived in the village of Langley
     Burrell. Kilvert underlined that she was closely involved with both birth
     and death, on one occasion laying out the body of an old man in the
     morning and acting as midwife to a baby in the evening (*Diary*, vol. III,
     p. 235).
101. Quoted in Schor, *op. cit.*, p. 268.
102. Over the 60 years of the Kilvert Society's existence correspondents have
     submitted to its journals material expanding the lives of the scores of
     individuals mentioned in the *Diary*.
103. Later chapters explore this aspect. It is interesting that the reaction to the
     Diary of Kilvert's Oxford friend, Anthony Mayhew (the only person, as far
     as we know, to have read any of it before its publication), was to comment
     particularly on a *biographical* element — the accounts Kilvert gave of
     'three remarkable men', as Kilvert put it, 'The Solitary of Llanbedr, Father
     Ignatius and William Barnes'. The stories of these men's lives (and of others
     such as Wordsworth, Kingsley and Frederick Robertson) *were* of profound
     significance for Kilvert. What stood out for Mayhew was the element of
     personality, captured in all its strangeness and uniqueness, in Kilvert's
     mini-biographies. Perhaps it is an indication of the class consciousness
     of the time that Mayhew didn't find impressive the stories Kilvert told
     in the *Diary* of lives of humble people. Evangelicals *did* find such stories
     interesting. It is worthwhile noting, too, that Kilvert says proportionately
     very little of the inner lives of gentry people in the *Diary*.
104. Uncle Francis noticeably emphasised George Stothert's 'good heart'
     in his obituary of him: 'Mr Stothert had received from nature a sound
     and vigorous understanding, a correct taste, and a kind and benevolent
     heart'. And after his retirement, he devoted himself to 'the duties of
     active benevolence'.
105. De Laura, *op. cit.*, p. 338. For Tennyson, memory was 'the foundation
     of human personality' (R. Reed, *Victorian Conventions*, Ohio, Ohio
     University Press, 1975, p. 411). The melancholy quality of so much
     Victorian autobiographical writing came in part from personal factors,
     as Houghton recognised, but he too envisaged a general cause: 'a mood
     so widespread was indebted to the general environment — in particular,
     to the breakdown of traditional thought. It was in truth the *mal du siècle*'
     (W.E. Houghton, *The Victorian Frame of Mind*, p. 65).
106. It is there also in the *Memoirs* of Kilvert's father (p. 17) where he wrote of
     the 'triviality' of the events he recorded of his childhood. In that period
     'we are none of us responsible for [its] circumstances'. After that, the
     story of lives assumes a more serious moral dimension because 'we act
     a part and occupy a place of our own' and then 'our retrospect becomes
     a matter of humiliation that we have not higher and better things to
     record about ourselves'.
107. A.S. Kilvert, *op. cit.*, p. 34.
108. J. Hervey, Religious Letters no. CXI, *op. cit.*
109. E.S. Phelps, *The Gates Ajar*, London, Milner, 1868. Roy, the young
     man Mary mourns, appears in the story as her brother for the sake of
     propriety.
110. She herself is the widow of a missionary.
111. The story, *Dream Children*, in Lamb's *Essays of Elia*, is praised for its 'pathos
     and symmetry' (Phelps, *op. cit.*, p. 30). With a professor of theology as a

father and the daughter of one of the most redoubtable New England theologians as a mother, it is not surprising that Phelps herself was intellectually gifted. The *American DNB* stated that she had 'a brilliant mind, nervous temperament, and intense susceptibility to artistic and spiritual impressions.' Her book sold in even greater numbers in Britain than in the USA.

112. *Ibid.*, p. 76. Winifred added: 'Roy [Mary's dead lover] tries to speak to you through the blessed sunshine and flowers.'

113. *Ibid.*, p. 246. She also referred approvingly on p. 152 to Rev Stopford Brooke, Robertson's biographer.

114. It seems inevitable that Kilvert would have obtained a copy of the *Lecture* as he had obtained copies of other books by the Brighton preacher. The *Lecture* was given to the members of the Brighton Athenaeum on 10 February 1853. It appears in F. Robertson, *Lectures and Addresses on Literary and Social Topics*, London, Smith and Elder, 1858, along with his *Address at the Opening of the Working Man's Institute* and his two *Lectures on the Influence of Poetry on the Working Classes*. The Brighton Athenaeum aimed at extending education to the working class (its full title was Brighton Athenaeum and Young Men's Literary Union) but it, unlike Robertson's Institute, was dominated by gentry.

115. *Lecture on Wordsworth*, p. 248.

116. Kilvert wrote on 13 January 1872: 'bought a book ... by Margaret Fuller Ossili, *Summer upon the Lakes*, an autobiography with a life of the authoress.' Though it provides insights into Ossili's spiritual development, it is not really an autobiography. When Robertson referred to reading Ossili's *Life*, he probably meant the *Memoirs of Margaret Fuller Ossili*, edited by Emerson (2 vols., 1852). Initially put off her by reviews of the book, he came to admire it and its author, largely because of its moral sentiments: 'I have read her life with increasing depth of interest, with respect, admiration and — no! not with tears, but — a certain moisture on the eyelids, the result of reading by a bad light — nothing else! ... she was a woman, whose brain was all heart.' (Brooke, *op. cit.*, vol. II, p. 131). Kilvert's reading of Mrs Gaskell's *Ruth* was also likely to have been prompted by Robertson's reference to it, as was his purchase of Margaret Ossili's 'autobiography'.

117. Wyndowe, 'Rambling Recollections', p. 93.

118. *Kilvert's Diary*, vol. II, pp. 105-6. Presumably the two fishermen were there because of Lord Lansdowne's generosity.

119. Stags are said to 'bell' at rutting time.

120. Scott, 'Marmion' (stanza 15, Canto IV) in *The Poetical Works of Sir Walter Scott, Bart.*, vol. VIII, Edinburgh, printed for R. Cadell, 1833.

121. L. Sterne, *A Sentimental Journey through France and Italy, (1768)*, London, Oxford University Press, 1968, p. 84.

Chapter 2: Spirit, Song and Sacrament

1. Introduction to *Approaches to Victorian Autobiography*, George P. Landow (ed.), Athens, Ohio University Press, 1979, pp. xiii-xvi.

2. The phrase comes from Elizabeth Helsinger's essay, 'Ulysses to Penelope: Victorian Experiments in Autobiography', in Landow (ed.), *op. cit.*, p. 15.

3. These are summarised in J. Toman, *Kilvert: The Homeless Heart*, Almeley, Logaston Press, 2001, pp. 138-9.
4. Landow (ed.), *op. cit.*, p. xviii.
5. His *Memoirs* reflect his deference to rank, his love of the country house, his fears of the mob, of democratic movements, of the power of newspapers. He appears not to have told his son that he was writing the story of his life.
6. Toman, *op. cit.*, (p. 15) noted: 'Kilvert was one of many who, living in the country and loving its ways, tried to believe that it hadn't changed. . . . The possibility . . . of being able to hold back time receives general expression in the *Diary* as a whole.'
7. *Ibid.*, p. 2.
8. Wyndowe, 'Rambling Recollections', p. 122. Emily also noted her mother's 'horror of what she called "Bathy" people', i.e. idle, frivolous people (*op. cit.*, p. 120).
9. *Kilvert's Diary*, vol. II, p. 297.
10. *Ibid.*, vol. II, p. 400.
11. *Ibid.*, vol. II, p. 281.
12. *Ibid.*, vol. III, p. 306.
13. The Colemans, while they professed the religion of Quakers, were buried in the Quaker burial ground at Stanton St Quintin. Prior to that they were buried at Kington Langley. Walter Langley was at first buried in the churchyard of Kington St Michael then reinterred in the grounds of his private chapel (WRO 873/161).
14. Quaker meetings in Wiltshire had fallen from 13 in 1775 to 7 in 1800. The total number of Quakers nationally declined by one third between 1799 and 1861 (O. Chadwick, *The Victorian Church*, Part 1, London, Adam and Charles Black, 1966, p. 430).
15. W. Stark, *The Sociology of Religion. A Study of Christendom*, vol. II, London, Routledge, Kegan Paul, 1967, p. 18.
16. David L. Edwards, *Christian England From The Reformation To The Eighteenth Century*, vol. II, London, Collins, 1981, p. 345.
17. Some strict clergymen even declined to regard Quakers as Christians for rejecting the sacraments (Chadwick, *op. cit.*, Part 1, p. 423).
18. *Kilvert's Diary*, vol. III, p. 249. On a visit to Brinsop Court, Herefordshire, he met 'a grand old Quaker lady' (*Ibid.*, vol. III, p. 456).
19. A very favourable opportunity occurred in the entry for 16 December 1872 when Mrs Banks was telling him of his tyrannical great-grandmother and went on to refer to local Quakers who journeyed regularly to the Quaker meeting house at Calne.
20. Kilvert's dilemma is seen in a clergyman's story passed on to him. One of the clergyman's parishioners had given his own church a miss in order to attend a Baptist meeting-house. The preacher had chosen to illustrate his text – 'They that honour me I will honour' (obviously a hit at the Church's ministers) – by declaring that Church parsons were fond of being honoured, but his advice to his brethren was that if they honoured parsons, they would go to hell. It is evident that Kilvert approved of what the parishioner did on hearing this – he picked up his hat and left (*ibid.*, vol. II, p. 424). The fact that the Meeting House was Baptist, not Quaker, is irrelevant; a Quaker minister's attitude would have been identical.

21. See chapter on Nonconformity in Wiltshire, *A History of Wiltshire*, E. Crittall and D.A. Crowley (eds.), London, Oxford University Press, 1953.

22. 'John Cennick's Diary', 1738-52, ETAMCC, AB/130/Packet I. 'Aquae fortis' is nitric acid. For further information about Cennick, I am indebted to 'Whither John Cennick?' by Rev Peter Gubi, unpublished M.A. thesis, Cheltenham and Gloucester College of Higher Education, 1998.

23. *Kilvert's Diary*, vol. II, p. 238.

24. R.A. Knox, *Enthusiasm. A Chapter in the History of Religion*, Oxford, Clarendon Press, 1950, p. 402. Communities on this pattern were established in England in the eighteenth century and in 1749 the Moravians were recognised by Parliament as 'an ancient Protestant Episcopal church'.

25. *The Oxford Companion To Christian Thought*, Hastings, Mason and Pyper (eds.), Oxford, Oxford University Press, 2000, entry by Trond Enger on Pietism.

26. *Oxford Dictionary of the Christian Church*, F.L. Cross (ed.), Oxford, Oxford University Press, 2001. Rack noted that Pietists generally emphasised good works more than Lutherans did (Henry D. Rack, *Reasonable Enthusiast. John Wesley and the Rise of Methodism*, London, Epworth Press, 1989, p. 162).

27. These numbers are given in 'Some Account Of The Life Of The Single Sister Ann Grigg Who Departed At Tytherton, Dec. 11th 1814, Written By Herself', 1814, on which these notes on the school's beginnings are partly based (ETAMCC). Clair Figes (*250 Years of the Moravian Settlement at East Tytherton, 1743-1993*, privately printed, 1993, p. 17) says there were six boarders and seven day scholars. Money to start the school (£370) was raised by public subscription.

28. 'Tytherton Congregation Diary', September 1st 1813-December 31st 1824 (ETAMMC).

29. Their missions in size and character were the first modern missions (Towlson, *Moravian and Methodist*, London, Epworth Press, 1957, p. 180).

30. Frank M. Turner, 'The Victorian Crisis Of Faith and the Faith That Was Lost', in *Victorian Faith in Crisis. Essays in Continuity and Change in Nineteenth Century Religious Belief*, Richard J. Helmstadter and Bernard Lightman (eds.), London, Macmillan, 1990, p. 14.

31. John Henry Newman, *Lyra Apostolica*, London, Mozley, 1849.

32. Forty-five years old when she died (17 August 1868), she was the adopted daughter of the Irish peer, Lord Molesworth and, according to the 1861 Census, lived with him at 43 Grand Parade, Brighton. She published *A Stumble on the Threshold: a story of the day*, London, 1848; *Claude, or the Double Sacrifice* (2 vols.), London, 1850; and *The Great Experiment* (3 vols.), London, 1860.

33. It is likely that entries for each of these occasions contained an example; some have been lost in Plomer's editing.

34. *Kilvert's Diary*, vol. III, p. 94. His sense of isolation in Clyro, where he found few other Evangelical clergymen and where he lacked the support of his family, must have been very great. His *Diary*, in the role of confidant, was one means of easing this isolation.

35. E. Prentiss, *Stepping Heavenward*, London, Sunday School Union. Another

book that Kilvert was in the habit of passing on to others was Oxenden's *The Pathway of Safety*, which steadily reiterates the life-as-a-journey metaphor. Ashton Oxenden, after education at Harrow and Oxford, held livings in Kent before becoming Bishop of Montreal in 1869. *The Pathway of Safety* (1859), London, Macintosh, 1870, sold 350,000 copies. He also published numerous tracts, 'cottage' readings and sermons.

36. *Kilvert's Diary*, vol. II, pp. 279-80.
37. Isabel Rivers, '"Strangers and Pilgrims": Sources and patterns of Methodist narrative', in *Augustan Worlds*, J.C. Hilson, M.M.B. Jones and J.R. Watson (eds.), Leicester University Press, Harper Row, 1978, p. 189. When Kilvert was journeying to Canterbury, he was pleased to refer to himself as a medieval pilgrim (*Kilvert's Diary*, vol. III, p. 337). He also habitually referred to the lives of his parishioners as 'pilgrimages'.
38. For example *The Pilgrimage, The Foregoing Footstep, The Pilgrim of the Eternal*, all in *Collected Verse by the Rev Francis Kilvert*, Hereford, Kilvert Society publication, 1968.
39. Peter Alexander, *William Plomer: A Biography*, Oxford, Oxford University Press, 1990, p. 217.
40. Wyndowe, *op. cit.*, p. 122. Grace Aguilar (born 1816), although Jewish in origin, wrote highly Evangelical books: *Home Influence* (1847), *A Mother's Recompense* (1851); *Women's Friendship* and *Home Scenes and Heart Studies* came later.
41. 'Religion of the heart' was a phrase 'beloved of the Brethren' (Towlson, *op. cit.*, p. 174).
42. The tender hymns of the Moravians encouraged emotion in their services. Knox (*op. cit.*, p. 410) referred to music being drowned by weeping in Moravian services. At East Tytherton, we hear of 'a general emotion' taking place among the girls of the boarding school ('Tytherton Congregation Diary', 1 Sept. 1813-31 Dec. 1824).
43. G. Aguilar, *Home Influence*, London, Evans, 1852, preface p. vii. The importance of maintaining bonds of sympathy between the dead and the living through memory is the theme of the song sung by Emmeline to the dying Mary in Aguilar's *A Mother's Recompense* (London, Evans, 1853):
    Remember me! though upward flying,
    Still I wait love's last fond kiss,
    Then, oh, farewell; my spirit's sighing
    To behold its home of bliss.
44. Thus, Eleanor owes her vanity, selfishness, and worldliness to her upbringing by Lady Lascelles, 'a woman of the world, utterly heartless . . . and supremely fashionable' (Aguilar, *Home Influence*, p. 24).
45. *Ibid.*, p. 217. It is one of the themes of Gray's *Elegy*.
46. Aguilar, *A Mother's Recompense*, pp. 69-70.
47. Quoted in Bonnelyn Young Kunze, *Margaret Fell and the Rise of Quakerism*, London, Macmillan, 1994, p. 199.
48. Towlson, *op. cit.*, p. 103.
49. 'Some Account Of The Life Of The Single Sister Ann Grigg', (ETAMMC).
50. Preface to Legh Richmond's *Annals of the Poor* (1814), London, Nelson, 1859. His son, who died young of T.B., was named Wilberforce. In 1801, Richmond was appointed to preach the annual sermon at Bath on cruelty to animals. He became a national figure because of that

publication and his preaching and promoting of the CMS. The original readership of *Annals* (estimated at over 1,354,000 — E. Jay, *The Religion of the Heart. Anglican Evangelicalism and the Nineteenth Century Novel*, Oxford, Clarendon Press, 1969, p. 151) were middle-class Evangelicals, of which the Kilvert family was a typical example. It was 'one of the Evangelicals' favourite books' (O. Chadwick, *The Victorian Church*, Part 1, p. 451).

51. Richmond, *op. cit.*, p. 27.
52. Cf. Kilvert's poem *The Pilgrimage* in which he wrote of 'Mounting till noon the highest pitch of life, / Or entering down the slope into the vale'.
53. R. Kilvert, 'Trevellyk', in *More Chapters from the Kilvert Saga*, p. 74. The full title of *Aids to Reflection* by Coleridge is *Aids to Reflection in the Formation of a Manly Character on the Several Grounds of Prudence, Morality, and Religion*, London, Taylor and Hersey, 1825. Robert Kilvert was at Oriel College when it was published. In his preface, Coleridge wrote that reflection was the key to self-knowledge.
54. Charles Elliott in *The Oxford Companion To Christian Thought*, pp. 421-2.
55. Aguilar, *Home Influence*, p. 78.
56. Spangenberg, *Idea Fidei Fratrum* (1779), third English edition, Moravian Church USA, 1959, section 27, p. 49. Kilvert encountered a similar passage early in Mrs Charles's *Kitty Trevylyan*: 'it seemed as if the sun, and the sea, and the green earth, and I were all young together, and God like a father was smiling on all' (p13).
57. 'Quakers generally had few pictures in their houses, unless it were an engraving of George Fox preaching or William Penn treating with the Indians' (Amice Lee, *Laurels and Rosemary. The Life of William and Mary Howitt*, London, Oxford University Press, 1955, p 190).
58. Mary Moorman, *William Wordsworth. A Biography. The Early Years 1770-1803*, Oxford, Clarendon Press, 1969, p 275.
59. John Williams, *William Wordsworth. A Literary Life*, Basingstoke, Macmillan, 1996, p 29.
60. Moorman, *op. cit.*, p 29.
61. Williams, *op. cit.*, p 30
62. Letter 305, *The Letters of William and Dorothy Wordsworth. The Middle Years*, Part II, 1812-1820, A.G. Hill (ed.), Oxford, Clarendon Press, 1969.
63. *Ibid.*, Letter 341.
64. W. Howitt, *The Homes and Haunts of the Most Eminent British Poets*, vol. II, The Modern Poets, London, Richard Bentley, 1849, p. 280.
65. Its full title is *A Portraiture of Quakerism taken from a View of the Moral Education, Descriptions, Peculiar Customs, Religious Principles, Political and Civil Economy and Character of the Society of Friends*, 3 vols., London, 1806. For the Wordsworths' sustained interest in it, see Letters 10, 67, 87 and 117, in A.G. Hill (ed.), *op. cit.*, Part I, 1806-1811.
66. Charles Lamb also commented ('Review of Wordsworth's "The Excursion, 1814"', in *Quarterly Review*, Oct 1814, vol. xii, p. 98) that Wordsworth's faith in Nature had 'the character of an expanded and generous Quakerism.'
67. *A Portraiture of Quakerism*, vol. II, pp. 146-150, quoted in Robert Woof, *Wordsworth: The Critical Heritage*, vol. I, 1793-1820, London, Routledge, 2001, pp. 94 –5.

68. The book is a reflection of Mrs Kilvert's Quaker upbringing. Emily underlined that it was her mother's gift by differentiating it from other books provided by her godmother (Wyndowe, *op. cit.*, p 89).

69. M. Howitt, *The Children's Year or The Story of a Happy Home*, (1847), London, Nelson, 1892, p. iv and p. 117.

70. The book was first published in 1831. The edition called *Pictorial Calendar of the Seasons* (London, Bohn's Illustrated Library, 1854) used by the author is credited to Mary Howitt.

71. *Kilvert's Diary*, vol. I, p. 318. Cf. Howitt (*Homes and Haunts*, vol. II, pp. 286-7): 'Rydal Mount ... is as perfectly poetical in its location and environment as any poet could possibly conceive'.

72. Cf. *Kilvert's Diary*, vol. II, p 195: he had come across a blackbird dead in a trap and wrote: ' "The whole creation groaneth and travaileth in pain. . . ." I felt as if some sin of mine had brought [the suffering creature] there'. His statement is a reflection of Fox's notion of the unity of all creation. For Kilvert's attitude to field sports, see chapter seven of Toman's *Kilvert: The Homeless Heart*.

73. C.R. Young, *Music of the Heart. John and Charles Wesley on Music and Musicians*, Carol Stream, Illinois, Hope Publishing, 1995, p. 20. The Congregation Diary of Mrs Kilvert's Moravian school noted in 1813 that some scholars could play the organ and this made possible the more frequent use of liturgical hymns. Mrs Charles's *Chronicles of the Schönberg-Cotta Family* (1862: 1895, London, Nelson), which Kilvert had read, links Huss's hymns to those of Luther and underlines the importance Moravians attached to hymn singing (p. 493).

74. *The New Grove Dictionary of Music and Musicians*, vol. XVII, Stanley Sadie (ed.), London, Macmillan, 2001, p. 97. The first Moravian hymnal appeared in 1505. John Cennick published in 1741 his *Sacred Hymns for the Children of God in the Days of their Pilgrimage*.

75. In his poem *The Skylark*, the bird's voice links earth and sky and men's praise of God, 'our highest thoughts and loftier airs', finds perfect expression in it.

76. *Kilvert's Diary*, vol. II, p. 356. His reading gave back the same ideas. In Mrs Charles's *Chronicles*, 'the whispering grasses, the trembling wild flowers . . . all seemed to take up the chorus [of praise]' (pp. 396-7).

77. See *Kilvert's Diary*, vol. I, pp. 46-7 and vol. II, pp. 312-6.

78. Wordsworth felt that, among the great works of literature, the worth of humble ballads 'as Power / Forever to be hallowed' should be asserted (*The Prelude*, Book V, 207-219).

79. Mary Jacobus (*Tradition and Experiment in Wordsworth's Lyrical Ballads*, pp. 111-2) observed that 'the traditional ballad seems to have had little direct influence on Wordsworth's experiment [in the *Lyrical Ballads*]. . . . The colloquial vigour and flamboyance of Wordsworth's ballad experiment has no real counterpart in the traditional ballad'. His approach in the *Lyrical Ballads* was indirect but 'the impulse was the same'. Kilvert favoured other poets — Burns, Barnes, Chatterton — who had links to the ballad tradition. He was also interested in traditional songs sung by children, noting a wassailing song, *Old Jeff and Nelly Ray*, performed by some Chippenham boys, the children of Pentwyn singing *Ding Dong Bell*, and Teddy Evans of Clyro singing *My mother said that I never should* (*Kilvert's Diary*, vol. II, p. 398; vol. II, p. 123; vol. I, p. 149).

He encountered some children giving voice to a song with scriptural content: 'Where is now the prophet Daniel? Where are now the Twelve Apostles', they sang (vol. II, p. 134). Other *Diary* entries confirm this sensitivity to song, his readiness to respond to experiences of good singing and to ensure that they were recorded, especially if there was some magic in the moment, as on 20 January 1872. 'A party of young men of the village have just gone past my window in the clear bright frosty moonlight with an accordion well played and sweet voices singing "Though hardy Norsemen" ' (vol. II, p. 122).

80. Nicholas Temperley, *The Music of the English Parish Church*, vol. I, Cambridge, Cambridge University Press, 1979, p. 208. Evangelicals like Kilvert valued the strong *feeling* they found in both Methodist hymns and in Wordsworth. Between the *Lyrical Ballads* of Wordsworth and the hymns of the Wesleys there is some overlap as regards the objective of imparting Christian doctrine (as well as in their subjective feeling and lyricism): 'Wordsworth's lyric writing is essentially doctrinal, and in this it owes something to the hymns of the evangelical period' (Jacobus, *op. cit.*, p. 91). Jacobus also traced Watts's influence on Wordsworth and noted: 'What both poets share is their concern to make belief accessible — to carry it out of the church and the book and into the heart'.

81. *Kilvert's Diary*, vol. II, pp. 437, 440-1.

82. Robert Kilvert was hostile to Tractarians (Wyndowe, *op. cit.*, p. 99). Tractarians in turn were deeply critical of Evangelicalism (Knox, *op. cit.*, p. 73).

83. Mary Moorman, quoted in Brian W. Martin, *John Keble: Priest, Professor and Poet*, London, Croom Helm, 1976, p. 75. In G.B. Tennyson's opinion, it was 'the most popular and influential volume of religious poetry that the Victorian age would know' ('The Sacramental Imagination', in *Nature and the Victorian Imagination*, Berkeley, University of California Press, 1977, p. 371). It was 'Keble's passport to the hearts of his generation' (G. Battiscombe, *John Keble. A Study in Limitations*, London, Constable, 1963, p. 110); Knox said 'it rejoiced the hearts of the devout' (E.A. Knox, *The Tractarian Movement 1833-1845. A Study of the Oxford Movement*, London, Putnam, 1933, p. 154).

84. Paul Turner called it 'a kind of verse commentary on the Prayer Book', *Victorian Poetry.*, p. 159. Mary Howitt's *The Children's Year* was clearly intended to echo the title of Keble's book.

85. Amy Cruse (*The Victorians and their Books*, London, Allen and Unwin, 1936, p. 48). In Cruse's typical Victorian family, it was natural that the daughter should receive as presents both *Lyra Apostolica* and *The Christian Year*. Martin stressed how much the latter became 'a family book' which aroused in its readers a 'sentimental glow of affection for the Church' while at the same time encouraging them to think more deeply on matters of faith (*op. cit.*, pp. 31-2).

86. R. Kilvert, *Memoirs*, p. 60. Isaac Williams said that Keble's double first 'invested him with a bright halo in the eyes of an undergraduate' (*Autobiography of Isaac Williams*, edited Sir G. Prevost, London, Longmans Green, 1893, p. 16).

87. Wordsworth said of *The Christian Year*: 'It is very good; so good that if it were mine, I would write it all over again' (quoted in Brian W. Martin, *op. cit.*, pp. 73-4). There was a hint of criticism in Wordsworth's remark:

he admired the content of the poems but objected to their artificiality and archaic diction.

88. In Lecture IV he stated that the best poets were 'those who, spontaneously moved by impulse, resort to composition for relief . . . of a burdened or overwrought mind' (*Keble's Lectures on Poetry*, translated by E.K. Francis, vol. I, Oxford, Clarendon Press, 1912, p. 53).

89. *Ibid.*, Lecture XL, vol. II, p. 481.

90. The *Lectures* were originally in Latin and appeared in English only in 1912. 'The pervasive appeal of *The Christian Year* disposed many Victorian minds to view Nature as Keble and the Tractarians viewed it, as God's book which [was] . . . a means . . . of experiencing through the visible world that contact with the invisible one that is normally effected through the sacraments' (G.B. Tennyson, *op. cit.*, p. 379). The theme of Nature as sacrament appealed to Mrs Charles and it appears in the following passage which Kilvert read in her *Chronicles of the Schönberg-Cotta Family* (pp. 553-4). Luther's wife is describing the way he talked of Nature:

> It is delightful, she says, to listen to the heavenly theology he draws from birds and leaves and flowers. . . . At table, a plate of fruit will open to him a whole volume of God's bounty. . . . Or, taking a rose in his hand, he will say, "A man who could make one rose like this would be accounted most wonderful; and God scatters countless such flowers around us!" . . . God writes His gospel, not in the Bible alone, but in trees, and flowers, and clouds, and stars.

91. J. Keble, *The Christian Year: Thoughts in Verse for the Sundays and Holydays throughout the Year*, Oxford, Henry and Parker, 1863, p. 68.

92. Tennyson, *op. cit.*, p. 373.

93. *Ibid.*, p. 388. In this statement Tennyson was following E.D.H. Johnson, *The Poetry of Earth: a Collection of English Nature Writing*, New York, 1974, p. 361.

94. Keble, *op. cit.*, p. 2.

95. From Kilvert's poem, *Little Things*.

96. *Kilvert's Diary*, vol. III, p. 285.

97. The Oxford Movement contributed, partly through the impact of *The Christian Year*, to the Choral Revival in the English Church.

98. *Kilvert's Diary*, vol. III, p. 50. Herbert would have had particular significance for Kilvert because he married into the Danvers family of Dauntsey, near Chippenham. Moreover, his mother was from Eyton in Shropshire.

99. See Cristina Malcomson, *George Herbert. A Literary Life*, Basingstoke, Palgrave Macmillan, 2004, p. 21. In his Dedication to *The Temple* group of sacred poems, Herbert wrote: 'Lord, my first fruits present themselves to thee'. None of Kilvert's poems is concerned with *romantic* love; the fact that they are all, in a general sense, devotional indicates that, like Herbert, he saw poetry as 'part of his calling' (Harold Toliver, *George Herbert's Christian Narrative*, Pennsylvania, Pennsylvania University Press, 1993, p. 11).

100. Ronald Blythe, *Divine Landscapes. A Pilgrimage through Britain's Sacred Places*, (1986), Norwich, Canterbury Press, 1998, p 178.

101. Kilvert's poem *The Skylark* has echoes of Wordsworth's two poems on

this subject but the specifically Easter/resurrection theme of the former may derive from Herbert's *Easter Wings*.

102. Blunt, in his *Duties of the Parish Priest*, London, John Murray, 1857, p. 144, which we know Kilvert read, alluded to 'the excellent Herbert' and quoted *The Country Parson*.

103. *George Herbert. The Country Parson, The Temple*, edited John Wall, London, SPCK, 1981, p. 84.

104. Keble's original poem had '*would* furnish'. The close similarity in theme and wording between Keble's lines and Kilvert's suggests that the latter was influenced by the former.

105. Keble's *Lectures on Poetry*, 1832-1866, vol. I, Oxford, Clarendon Press, 1912, Lecture XIII, p. 257.

106. *Ibid.*, p. 257.

107. For the Fourth Sunday in Lent.

108. Isaac Williams said that the poem was inspired by the scenery around Devil's Bridge, near Aberystwyth (*op. cit.*, p. 12).

109. For the Twentieth Sunday after Trinity.

110. *Kilvert's Diary*, vol. I, pp. 349-50.

111. Since Keble was a disciple of Wordsworth, it is unsurprising to find that this idea has a precise counterpart in a Wordsworth poem. The Wanderer in *The Excursion* had learned early in his life 'To reverence the volume that displays / The mystery, the life which cannot die; / But in the mountains did he *feel* his faith' (*The Excursion*, Book I, 223-6 — his italics). By 'the volume', Wordsworth meant the 'book' of Nature.

112. W. Howitt, *Homes and Haunts*, vol. II, p. 276 and pp. 282-3.

113. Brooke, *Life and Letters*, vol. I, p. 186.

114. *Ibid.*, vol. II, p. 261.

115. *Kilvert's Diary*, vol. I, p. 349.

116. *Ibid.*, vol. III, p. 336.

117. Brooke, *op. cit.*, vol. I, p. 187.

118. *Kilvert's Diary*, vol. III, p. 319.

119. In Kilvert's 'the heart of the great city lying in its Sabbath rest' there is an echo of 'all that mighty heart is lying still' (Wordsworth's sonnet *Composed upon Westminster Bridge, September 3, 1802*).

Chapter 3: The Cornish Dream

1. *Kilvert's Cornish Diary*, edited by Richard Maber and Angela Tregoning, Penzance, Alison Hodge, 1989, pp. 22-3.

2. M. Shaw, 'Tennyson and his Public 1827-1859', in *Tennyson, Writers and their Background*, D.J. Palmer (ed.), London, Bell, 1973, p. 82.

3. By 'Sense' he meant sexual indulgence. It is ironic that Emma's own family background had its scandalous aspect in that she herself was conceived before her parents were married. Her father, John Borlase Baines, son of the Rev Baines, Vicar of Burwell, Cambridgeshire, made a marriage that was probably considered beneath him with Mary Ann Eastwell, daughter of Thomas Eastwell, a cooper by trade, on 16 February 1840. The newly-weds set sail for New Zealand where John Baines was to participate in a pioneering survey and Emma was born at sea on 11 September 1840, seven months after her parents' marriage.

4. Houghton, *The Victorian Frame of Mind*, p. 359.

5. Brooke, *Life and Latters.*, vol. I, p. 4. Another major influence on Kilvert, Charles Kingsley, was, according to his wife, just like his hero, Lancelot in *Yeast*, 'a bold thinker, a hard rider, a "most chivalrous gentleman"....' (Mrs Kingsley, *Charles Kingsley. His Letters and Memories of his life*, London, C. Kegan Paul, p. 12). Alice Chandler, in *A Dream of Order. The Medieval Ideal in Nineteenth Century English Literature*, London, Routledge and Kegan Paul, 1971, explored Victorian interest in medievalism. Because it was bound up with Romanticism, it shared that movement's concern with nature, the supernatural and creative processes. 'Medievalism, like the worship of nature, was part of the yearning for a more pastoral England that was rapidly disappearing ...' (p. 52). The society medievalists were seeking was essentially emotion-based and hostile to calculating rationalism. It was supposed that in medieval times people were closer to their feelings.

6. M. Girouard, *Return to Camelot. Chivalry and the English Gentleman*, New Haven and London, Yale University Press, 1981, pp. 169 and 173.

7. R.D. Altick, *Victorian People and Ideas*, London, Dent, 1973, p. 106.

8. Houghton, *op. cit.*, pp. 371-2 and 354-5.

9. *Kilvert's Cornish Diary* contains allusions to Macaulay, Milton, Tennyson, Shakespeare, Burns, Hood, Gray, Coleridge, Cowper and Wordsworth. To half of these poets there are several, sometimes four or five, allusions. There are two allusions to unknown poets. In addition, there are allusions to Bottrell and the Bible.

10. *Kilvert's Diary*, vol. I, p. 208. My italics. Kilvert's use of 'mourning' here reflects the entry's elegiac tone.

11. *Ibid.*, vol. III, p. 107.

12. Christopher Salvesen, *The Landscape of Memory. A Study of Wordsworth's Poetry*, London, Edward Arnold, 1965.

13. The full title is *The Beauties of England and Wales: Or, Delineations Topographical, Historical, and Descriptive of Each County*, by John Britton and Edward Brayley, London, various publishers, 1801-1818.

14. *Ibid.*, vol. XV, p. 357.

15. *Ibid.*, vol. II, p. 509. Britton's remark occurs in a passage dealing with Carn Brea hill in Cornwall. The antiquarian William Borlase had, erroneously in Britton's view, considered Carn Brea 'as the grand centre of Druidical worship in this county'. Borlase had found Druidical circles, cromlechs and platforms which, according to Britton, 'must all have been conjured into shape from the rude heaps of stones and crags that occupy the surface of the hill'. Kilvert passed Carn Brea but didn't go to its summit.

16. Warner wrote it up in *A Tour through Cornwall in the Autumn of 1808*, Bath, Richard Cruttwell, 1809.

17. *Ibid.*, pp. 335-6.

18. *Kilvert's Cornish Diary*, pp. 90-1. (Proof that Kilvert was well versed in Tennyson's *Idylls* before he came to Tullimaar resides in the fact that this line from *Guinevere* did not come from the Doré edition belonging to Mrs Hockin but from another.)

19. Its full title was *Observations, Relative Chiefly to Picturesque Beauty, made in the year 1772 of Several parts of England, Particularly the Mountains and Lakes of Cumberland and Westmorland*, London, printed for R. Blamires, 1786.

20. A.R. Humphreys, *William Shenstone. An Eighteenth Century Portrait*, Cambridge, Cambridge University Press, 1937, p. 103.

21. *Ibid.*, p. 6.
22. *The Guardian*, 29 September 1713, *Selected Prose of Alexander Pope*, Paul Hammond (ed.), Cambridge, Cambridge University Press, 1987, pp. 57-8. Pope went on to say that Virgil's account of the garden of Corycian exemplified this view of Nature.
23. *Kilvert's Diary*, vol. III, p. 94.
24. C. Tracy (*A Portrait of Richard Graves*, Toronto, Toronto University Press, 1987, p. 138) noted that Graves tended towards a more Romantic view of Nature: 'For him . . . the fine thing about nature was that it is natural, not the product of a scene-painter's art', and did not teach 'little copy-book maxims'. He did not outline in his novels the 'semi-mystical philosophy of Nature' we associate with the Romantics but implied it in many passages in *The Spiritual Quixote* and *Eugenius*.
25. Esther Moir, *The Discovery of Britain. The English Tourists 1540-1840*. London, Routledge Kegan Paul, 1964, p. xiv.
26. K. Woodbridge, *Landscape and Antiquity. Aspects of English Culture at Stourhead 1718-1838*, Oxford, Clarendon Press, 1970, p. 170.
27. Gilpin, *op. cit.*, pp. 121-2
28. Warner, *op. cit.*, pp. 336-7.
29. Gilpin, *op. cit.*, p. 120.
30. *Kilvert's Cornish Diary*, p. 91.
31. John Brewer, *The Pleasures of the Imagination. English Culture in the Eighteenth Century*, London, Harper Collins, 1997, p. 582.
32. *Kilvert's Cornish Diary* , p. 92.
33. James H. Averill, *Wordsworth and the Poetry of Human Suffering*, Ithaca, Cornell University Press, 1980, p. 23.
34. Britton, *The Beauties of England and Wales*, 'Introduction' (1818), pp. 76-7. Kilvert also had the opinion of Borlase, quoted by Warner, on the meaning of 'Logan': in the ancient British tongue, it signified a pit or hollow of the hand, while 'Leagan' meant a high rock. Borlase surmised that it might be a corruption of the Welsh 'Llygadtyn', meaning 'bewitching', an indication that the Stones' uncanny balance was due to witchcraft (Warner, *op. cit.*, p. 171).
35. *Kilvert's Cornish Diary*, pp. 64 and 66.
36. *Ibid.*, p. 117. The editors suggested that he may have intended to add to this reference later and forgot.
37. Britton, *op. cit.*, p. 76. He added in a note: 'Although many rocking stones may be entirely the works of nature, there is little room for doubting but that art was employed in completing the effect of others'. Some stones bore the mark of tools.
38. Bottrell did not make a great deal of logan stones, although he did refer to the story of the giant of Carn Galva using one as a rocking chair (T. Bottrell, *Traditions and Hearthside Stories of West Cornwall*, Newcastle-on-Tyne, Frank Graham, 1980, p. 48).
39. That day he was on his way to Phillack to visit the branch of the Hockin family who lived there.
40. Warner, *op. cit.*, p. 129. Cf. Edward Thomas: 'On every hand lie cromlech, camp, circle, hut and tumulus of the unwritten years. They are confused and mingled with the natural litter of a barren land. It is a silent Bedlam of history, . . .' (*The South Country* [1909], London, Everyman, 1993, p. 122).
41. His dilemma — of reconciling a respect for idol-worshipping pagans with

Christian belief — had been shared by a number of eighteenth-century clergymen, John Toland, William Stukeley, William Borlase, who became obsessed with Druids (see *The Romance of the Stones*, by John Payne and Rosemarie Lewsey, Fowey, Alexander Associates, 1999, p. 42).

42. *Kilvert's Cornish Diary*, p. 67.
43. Some of Kilvert's references to giants include mention of Bottrell. Kilvert likened the stones of Stonehenge to giants.
44. Bottrell, *op. cit.*, p. 9.
45. *Kilvert's Cornish Diary*, p. 47.
46. Bottrell, *op. cit.*, p. 12. A cromlech consists of several upright stones on which rests a flat capstone. A number of passages in Bottrell represent ancient stones as objects to stir the imagination, as for example 'a loadstone (sometimes spoken of as the stone of knowledge, stone of virtue) [which] was regarded as . . . a kind of divinity, or at least it was venerated as the shrine of a deity' (*ibid.*, p. 42). Kilvert had read similar passages in Warner.
47. Gilpin, *op. cit.*, p. 123.
48. *Kilvert's Cornish Diary*, p. 68.
49. Warner, *op. cit.*, p. 229.
50. *Kilvert's Cornish Diary*, p. 99.
51. *Ibid.*, pp. 65-6.
52. *Ibid.*, p. 48.
53. R.E. Brantley, *Locke, Wesley and the Method of English Romanticism*, p. 25.
54. F.C. Gill, *The Romantic Movement and Methodism*, London, Epworth Press, 1937, p. 50.
55. *Wesley's Journal*, 12 August 1771 (his italics).
56. Howitt, *The Rural Life of England*, p. 328.
57. Norman Nicholson, *William Cowper*, London, John Lehmann, 1951, p. 11.
58. E.L. Tuveson, *The Imagination as a Means of Grace. Locke and the Aesthetics of Romanticism*, Berkeley, University of California Press, 1960, pp. 68-9. I am indebted to Tuveson's detailed account of the links between the religious revival and Romanticism.
59. *Kilvert's Diary*, vol. I, p. 264.
60. David H. Solkin noted: 'The practice of meditating upon ancient ruins . . . was assiduously cultivated by the genteel sector of eighteenth-century British society' (*Richard Wilson. The Landscape of Reaction*, London, The Tate Gallery, 1982, p. 28).
61. R. Montgomery, *The Omnipresence of the Deity*, London, Samuel Maunder, 1828, pp. 36-7. The poem went through eight editions in as many months in spite of being bombastic and self-indulgent.
62. Montgomery's conversation was noted for its warmth and feeling and his character for its 'naïve simplicity' (Eliza Fisher, *Sketches and Souvenirs*, Bath, privately printed, 1839, pp. 84 and 86).
63. *Kilvert's Cornish Diary*, p. 27. Kindness was for Kilvert the key social virtue as later chapters show.
64. See Solkin, *op. cit.*, p. 70.
65. *Kilvert's Cornish Diary*, p. 77.
66. *Ibid.*, p. 85.
67. Mrs Charles, *The Diary of Mrs Kitty Trevylyan. A Story of the Times of Whitefield and the Wesleys*, New York, M.W. Dodd, 1864, p. 404.

68. A.K. Hamilton Jenkin, *Cornwall and its People*, Newton Abbot, David and Charles, 1990, p. 125.

69. Richard Pearse, *The Land beside the Celtic Sea. Some aspects of ancient, Medieval and Victorian Cornwall*, Redruth, Truro, 1983, p. 98.

70. Writing under the pen name of Don Manuel Alvarez Espriella, 'Letters From England', in *Early Tours in Devon and Cornwall*, R. Pearse Chope (ed.), Newton Abbot, David and Charles, 1967, p. 302.

71. Pearse, *op. cit.*, pp. 100-1. Rapid expansion of tourism to Cornwall began only in 1876.

72. One late eighteenth-century tourist, the Hon. John Byng, showed a fairly typical stance when he instructed the housekeeper of Raby Castle, Durham: 'show me anything ancient' (*The Torrington Diaries. A selection from the tours of the Hon. John Byng between the years 1781 and 1794*, C.B. Andrews (ed.), London, Eyre and Spottiswoode, 1954, p. 414).

73. Introduction to *Kilvert's Cornish Diary*, p. 6.

74. Keith Thomas, *Man and the Natural World. Changing Attitudes In England 1500-1800*, London, Allen Lane, 1983, p. 253.

75. Warner, *op. cit.*, p. 10.

76. Andrews, *Landscape in Western Art*, p. 167.

77. Moir, *op. cit.*, p. 97.

78. Mentioned in Woodbridge, *op. cit.*, p. 166.

79. *Kilvert's Diary*, vol. II, pp. 215-6. He was keen to visit an iron works in Glamorgan (*ibid.*, vol. I, p. 54).

80. *Kilvert's Cornish Diary*, p. 33.

81. *Ibid.*, p. 32.

82. Warner, *op. cit.*, p. 131 and pp. 105-6.

83. *Ibid.*, pp. 132-3.

84. Not a serious antiquarian or archaeologist himself, Kilvert usually mocked those who were, as, for example, when he saw in Taunton 'two Antediluvian parsons, who [were] making a steeple chase towards Trull Church to fall in with the rest of the Archaeologists' (*Kilvert's Diary*, vol. II, p. 267).

85. See Brewer, *op. cit.*, pp. 621-2. R. Williams (*The Country and the City*, pp. 147-8) noted that with Gilbert White's *A Natural History of Selborne*, we get a new scientific mode of observation of country things.

86. *Kilvert's Cornish Diary*, p. 53.

87. Quoted in introduction to William Bottrell's book. Bottrell transcribed the stories from native 'droll-tellers'. Tennyson was a subscriber to the first edition of Bottrell.

88. For an account of this cult of feeling, simplicity and rural retreat, see Brewer, *op. cit.*, pp. 115-120. Cf. Keith Thomas, *op. cit.*, p. 175: 'The mid-eighteenth century saw a cult of tender-heartedness. . . . Kindliness and tenderness became official ideas'.

89. John Pearce, *The Wesleys in Cornwall*, Truro, Bradford Barton, 1964, p. 10.

90. *Kilvert's Cornish Diary*, p. 98. Kilvert was bound to recognise that there were a lot more believers in Cornwall among ordinary working people than was the case in his native Wiltshire. It was estimated that by 1852 one in three Cornish people were Methodists (R.E. Brantley, *Locke, Wesley and the Method of English Romanticism*, p. 120).

91. *Kilvert's Cornish Diary*, p. 96

92. Maximin Piette, *John Wesley and the Evolution of Protestantism*, London, Sheed and Ward, 1937, p. 334.

93. Gwythian parish had also been the centre for many years of a thriving Methodist community. A Methodist society was formed in the parish in 1782, established its chapel in 1810, and by 1851 had a morning congregation averaging 60 and an evening one of 80 (Barry Smith, *The Hockins and the British Church*, Kilvert Society Newsletter, February 1989, p. 9).

94. *Kilvert's Diary*, vol. III, p. 243. 'Trevelyan' is an error, it should be 'Trevylyan'. Tennyson, on a visit to her uncle, read some of Mrs Charles' early poems. She achieved considerable fame in 1862 with *Chronicles of the Schönberg-Cotta Family*, a story set in Reformation times, another book which Kilvert read to his adult church working group in Langley Burrell.

95. Mrs Charles, *The Diary of Mrs Kitty Trevylyan*, p. 212.

96. Pearce, *op. cit.*, pp. 18-19. Pearce also emphasised that Wesley himself found congregations much less responsive in eastern Cornwall.

97. Hamilton Jenkin, *op. cit.*, p. 166.

98. Wesley, *Journal*, vol. IV, p. 375.

99. Rack, *Reasonable Enthusiast*, p. 432 and p. 435.

100. Thomas McFarland, *Romanticism and the Forms of Ruin. Wordsworth, Coleridge and Modalities of Fragmentation*, New Jersey, Princeton University Press, 1981, p. 7.

101. J. Robert Barth, SJ, *The Symbolic Imagination. Coleridge and the Romantic Tradition*, New Jersey, Princeton University Press, 1977, p. 78.

102. *Ibid.*, p. 72.

Chapter 4: The Religion of Gratitude

1. Frederick Garber, *Wordsworth and the Poetry of Encounter*, Urbana, Chicago, University of Illinois Press, 1971, p. 104.

2. Michael Mason, *Lyrical Ballads*, London, Longman, 1992, p. 18.

3. W. Howitt, *The People's Journal*, 24 January 1846, printed in R.H. Horne, *A New Spirit of the Age*, vol. I, London, Smith and Elder, 1848, p. 45.

4. John E. Jordan, *Why the "Lyrical Ballads"?*, Berkeley, University of California Press, 1976, p. 99.

5. *Ibid.*, p. 150.

6. William Cowper, letter of 17 January 1782 to William Unwin in *Letters and Prose Writings of William Cowper*, J. King and C. Ryskamp (eds.), vol. II, Oxford, Oxford University Press, 1981, p. 10.

7. Robert Burns, preface to *Poems, Chiefly in the Scottish Dialect* (1786), Donald Low (ed.), London, Dent, 1985.

8. Quoted in *Wordsworth's Poetical Works*, vol. III, E. de Selincourt and Helen Darbishire (eds.), Oxford, Oxford University Press, 1944, p. 442.

9. S.T. Coleridge, *Biographia Literaria*, vol. II (1907), J. Shawcross (ed.), Oxford, Oxford University Press, 1969, p. 5.

10. W. Wordsworth, *Essay, Supplementary to the Preface* to the 1815 edition of his poems.

11. S.T. Coleridge, letter to William Wilberforce, January 1801, quoted in Mason, *Lyrical Ballads*, pp. 45-6. When the *Lyrical Ballads* was published, Wordsworth made a gift of a copy to Wilberforce. Wordsworth's sister,

Dorothy, had a very close friendship with Wilberforce (R.E. Brantley, *Wordsworth's "Natural Methodism"*, New Haven, Yale University Press, 1975, p. 3 and p. 24).

12. Averill, *Wordsworth and the Poetry of Human Suffering*, p. 13. While noting that Wordsworth's roots lay in eighteenth-century sentimental writing, Averill underlined the 'quite different pathetic mode of the *Lyrical Ballads*'.

13. William Wilberforce, *A Practical View of the Prevailing Religious System of Professed Christians, in the Higher and Middle Classes in this Country, Contrasted with Real Christianity*, London, printed for T. Cadell, pp. 84, 225 and 246.

14. *Kilvert's Diary*, vol. I, p. 56. This was how he reassured himself as he laboured one cold March day up a muddy lane on a visit to outlying farms and he recalled guiltily how years before he had neglected to visit a dying child 'for a long time' and discovered, when he did eventually visit, that he had died ten minutes earlier.

15. William Wordsworth, *Preface* to the *Lyrical Ballads*, 1801.

16. *Kilvert's Diary*, vol. II, p. 439.

17. W. Barnes, *Thoughts on Beauty and Art*, Macmillan's Magazine, June 1861. It seems that Kilvert regularly read this journal.

18. R.A. Forsyth, 'The Conserving Myth of William Barnes', in *Romantic Mythologies*, Ian Fletcher (ed.), London, Routledge and Kegan Paul, 1967, p. 141. Forsyth stated that Barnes's 'backward-looking habit of mind . . . did not result from a sentimental evasion of contemporary issues . . .' (*ibid.*, p. 138).

19. The *DNB* lists his admirers as Matthew Arnold, Browning, Edmund Gosse, Gerard Manley Hopkins, Coventry Patmore, Tennyson and Hardy. Largely self-taught, he became something of a polymath, boasting highly developed skills in wood and copper engraving and in music, as well as scholarship that embraced history, folklore, economics and particularly philology (Kilvert noted that he 'is said to understand seventeen languages'). He was also one of the first joint secretaries of the Dorset County Museum. He interested himself in the social and economic injustices of the times: the rise in crime rates, treatment of offenders, enclosures, provision of allotments, and emigration of labourers. Barnes took a leaf out of Robertson's book by founding with Rev Henry Moule, the friend of Kilvert's father, the Dorchester Institute of Adult Education for working-class students in 1850.

20. Quoted in Dugdale, *William Barnes of Dorset*, London, Cassell, 1953, p. 113.

21. W. Barnes, *Views of Labour and Gold*, London, Routledge / Thoemmes Press, 1996, p. 71. Barnes rejected the argument that smallholders could not work their land as efficiently or as economically as large holders. 'Why could not a man with £800 work a hundred acres as productively as another with £8,000 could till a thousand acres?' And a group of smallholders could share threshing and drilling machines.

22. *Kilvert's Diary*, vol. III, p. 199. Wordsworth's *Guide to the Lakes* seems to have fed into this understanding. Wordsworth stated that because of economic pressure and their own lack of adequate capital, small proprietors and farmers were 'no longer able to maintain themselves upon small farms, several are united in one, and the buildings go to

decay and are destroyed' (p. 91). Howitt, in *Rural Life of England,* praised the small farmer (pp. 103 –6) and hated the system 'by which a dozen moderate farms are swallowed up in one overgrown one' (p. 101).

23. W. Barnes, *Humilis Domus: some Thoughts on the Abodes, Life and Social Conditions of the Poor* (1849), London, Routledge/Thoemmes Press, 1996, p. 19. Cowper, too, insisted that domestic life enjoyed in 'rural leisure' was the foundation of morality (see *The Task,* Book III, p. 292 and pp. 298-304).

24. *Kilvert's Diary,* vol. II, p. 444.

25. Hylson-Smith, *Evangelicals in the Church of England 1734-1984,* Edinburgh, Clark, 1988, p. 102. This picture of the typical *Record* reader accords closely with the portrayal of Kilvert's father in J. Toman's *Kilvert: The Homeless Heart,* chapter one.

26. 'For it alone set a supreme value on the emotional exaltation in which the greatest art is produced, it alone made the imagination the centre of its system. . . . The Evangelicals may have disliked poetry, but their sublime conception of the universal plan is the most imaginative poem of its day' (Lord David Cecil, *The Stricken Deer,* London, Constable, 1929, p. 83).

27. W. Wordsworth, *Essay, Supplementary to the Preface* (of the 1815 edition of his poems).

28. Quoted in Moorman, *William Wordsworth: A Biography,* p. 106.

29. W. Wordsworth, *Essay, Supplementary to the Preface.*

30. *Kilvert's Diary,* vol. II, p. 384.

31. W. Wordsworth, *The Prelude,* Book XIV, lines 346-7 and line 293.

32. Geoffrey Hartman, *Wordsworth's Poetry 1787-1814,* London, Yale University Press, 1971, p. 153 (my italics).

33. *Kilvert's Diary,* vol. II, p. 440.

34. J. Jones, *The Egotistical Sublime. A History of Wordsworth's Imagination,* London, Chatto and Windus, 1970, p. 48. Cowper's descriptions of natural forms are often more detailed than Wordsworth's and Kilvert may have learned more from him in this respect. Cf. F.C. Gill, who said that Cowper is more compressed than Wordsworth — 'His edges are always sharp' (*The Romantic Movement and Methodism,* p. 145).

35. S.T. Coleridge, *op. cit.,* p. 118.

36. W. Wordsworth, 'Preface to the 1815 Edition of the poems', in Hutchinson (ed.), *The Poetical Works of William Wordsworth,* Oxford, Oxford University Press, 1920, p. 954.

37. Robin Jarvis, *Romantic Writing and Pedestrian Travel,* London, Macmillan Press, 1997, p. 2 and p. 12.

38. In Warner's *Literary Recollections* (London, Longman, 1830, vol. II, p. 136) he claimed that the popularity of his two books on his Wales walks 'originated a taste . . . for pedestrian tours into the principality'.

39. Jarvis, *op. cit.,* p. 21, pp. 27-8.

40. Wordsworth's early poetry is described by Jarvis (*ibid.,* p. 90) as a kind of 'textual pedestrianism'; he also referred to Wordsworth's 'itinerant poetic mode' (*ibid.,* p 96).

41. *Ibid.,* p. 68.

42. *The Rural Life of England,* pp. 80-1. Howitt also extolled walking in his *Ruined Abbeys and Castles of Great Britain,* (London, Bennett, 1862, pp. 78-9, 82): 'I told him of the advantages people drew from walking; of

the acquaintance it gave them of people passing the same way, . . . of the many poems Wordsworth wrote from materials picked up in walking.' He also stressed that 'the finest estate which God and Nature had given [people] was a vigorous pair of legs'. Cf. Cowper (*The Task*, Book I, pp. 112-3): 'I have loved the rural walk / O'er hills, through valleys, and by the river's brink.' He was pleased to possess, as Kilvert did, 'Th' elastic spring of an unwearied foot.'

43. Brooke, *Life and Letters*, vol. II, p. 78 and p. 80.

44. Frank, *The Memory of the Eyes. Pilgrims to Living Saints in Christian Late Antiquity*, Berkeley, University of California Press, 2000, pp. 68-9.

45. *Ibid.*, pp. 12-13 and p. 16. The issue highlighted by Frank has much in common with the idea of sacrament which we know had a central place in Kilvert's apprehension of landscape. It is also involved with the 'problem' of his response to female beauty that is discussed in chapter seven.

46. *Kilvert's Diary*, vol. II, p. 444. (Cf. Kilvert's comments on one of his father's sermons: 'It was like a spirit preaching without the body.' *Ibid.* vol. III, p 148.)

47. *Ibid.*, vol. I, pp. 81, 119, 234, 318-9.

48. W. Wordsworth, *The Prelude*, Book III, 195-6.

49. *Kilvert's Diary*, vol. I, p. 257.

50. W. Wordsworth, Preface and Appendix to *Lyrical Ballads*, 1801, in *Wordsworth's Literary Criticism*, W.J.B. Owen (ed.), London, Routledge, Kegan Paul, 1974, pp. 72-3.

51. Mason explained that the word 'ballad' was rare in titles of collections of poems around 1798 when the *Lyrical Ballads* appeared. It was used then to denote poems for lower-class people (defined thus in the *Encyclopedia Britannica* of 1797). 'Lyrical' was added by Wordsworth to signify that more than simple stories would be found in the poems and that other kinds of verse would be found. *Simon Lee* is one such poem.

52. In June 1840, Frederick Robertson was at Oxford, one of a vacation reading party of students and they were visited by a group of ladies. When the happy group broke up, he was feeling a 'friend to no one' but he received lots of invitations, forcing from him a grateful response which saddened him. He quoted the last verse of *Simon Lee* and added: 'That is the genuine, manly feeling of dear old Wordsworth' (Brooke, *op. cit.*, vol. I, p. 44). When Kilvert wrote 'dear old Wordsworth', he was also paying tribute to Robertson.

53. W. Wordsworth, letter of 28 May 1825 to Sir George Beaumont, *The Letters of William and Dorothy Wordsworth 1821-1830*, E. de Selincourt (ed.), Oxford, Oxford University Press, 1967, p. 204.

54. J. Jones, *op. cit.*, p. 185.

55. M.H. Abrams, *The Correspondent Breeze. Essays on English Romanticism*, New York, Norton, 1984, p. 71.

56. J.F. Danby, 'Simon Lee and The Idiot Boy;, in *Wordsworth's Lyrical Ballads*, Alun R. Jones and William Tydeman (eds.), London, Macmillan, 1972, p. 197.

57. W. Wordsworth, *The Prelude* Book XIII, 266-9 and 271-8.

58. Kilvert also showed his kindness and gratitude to Morgan by arranging for him to receive a pension of 9d a day (about half the wage of an agricultural labourer) from Chelsea Hospital.

59. *Kilvert's Diary*, vol. II, p. 182. Robertson had a parishioner whose

situation resembled that of old Price and Kilvert's response to the latter may well have been modelled on Robertson's to his old man. One of Robertson's friends wrote (Brooke, *op. cit.*, vol. I, p. 86):

> I recollect his calling on me . . . as late as ten o'clock at night, and taking me with him a distance of three miles, through such a storm as Lear was out in, to visit a poor, disconsolate old man, who seemed to have shut himself out from human sympathies, and therefore all the more enlisted his. I never knew one whose care and constant kindness to the poor could compare with his.

60. *Kilvert's Diary*, vol. II, p. 331.
61. *Ibid.*, vol. I, p. 302.
62. Alistair Moffat, *The Sea Kingdoms. The story of Celtic Britain and Ireland*, London, Harper Collins, 2001, p. 36.
63. *Kilvert's Diary*, vol. I, pp. 246-7.
64. J. Jones, *op. cit.*, p. 67.
65. *Kilvert's Diary*, vol. I, p. 252. In several of the *Lyrical Ballads*, people are shown achieving calmness through suffering. Jordan (*op. cit.*, p. 6) observed that the poems' tragic figures experience a joy that might better be called peace or calm. Crabbe and Cowper present rural suffering in this way.
66. *Ibid.*, vol. I, p. 84.
67. Chandler (*A Dream of Order. The Medieval Ideal in Nineteenth Century English Literature*, London, Routledge and Kegan Paul, 1971, p. 98) noted that the *Goody Blake* poem is 'a tragedy of a dying culture' in that she tried to assert her traditional right of wood-gathering but was opposed by a hard-hearted farmer with no sense of inter-dependence. Kilvert made a point of underlining such traditional rights: 'It is an old custom in these parts [i.e. Clyro] for the poor people to go about round the farm-houses to beg and gather milk. . . .' (*Diary*, vol. I, p. 246).
68. Abrams (*op. cit.*, p. 71) observed: 'The archetypal figure, among Wordsworth's many solitaries, is the humble shepherd . . . the Good Shepherd himself.'
69. *Kilvert's Diary*, vol. III, p. 442.
70. The occasion (*ibid.*, vol. III, p. 67) when Kilvert gave his coat to Katharine Heanley to keep her warm and she looked 'so sweet and grateful' is a special case because of their shared interest in pursuing piety, which reinforces the point being made here.
71. It is evident that Kilvert had very strong feelings about such cases. The case of John Hatherell is dealt with fully in J. Toman, *Kilvert: The Homeless Heart*, pp. 261-2. Other cases are George Killing (*Kilvert's Diary*, vol. III, p. 252), and the labourer who committed suicide rather than be put on the parish (*ibid.*, vol. I, pp. 282-3) — see chapter six.
72. L. Claridge, *Romantic Potency: The Paradox of Desire*, Ithaca, New York, Cornell University Press, 1992, p. 107.
73. J. Jordan, *op. cit.*, p. 186.
74. J.R. Watson, *English Poetry of the Romantic Period*, London, Longmans, 1985, p. 185.
75. This view is expressed succinctly in *To Joanna* where he referred to 'the sympathies of them / Who look upon the hills with tenderness.' The poem is one of the *Lyrical Ballads*.
76. *Kilvert's Diary*, vol. III, p. 413.

77. G.W.E. Russell, *The Household of Faith. Portraits and Essays*, London, Hodder and Stoughton, 1903, p. 232.
78. *Kilvert's Diary*, vol. III, p. 274.
79. *Ibid.*, vol. I, p. 156.
80. *Ibid.*, vol. II, p. 246.
81. *Ibid.*, vol. I, p. 231.
82. *Ibid.*, vol. III, p. 167 (my italics).
83. Evangelicals were uneasy about the lack of emphasis in Wordsworth's poetry on Christ as the means of salvation, though they were prepared to recognise its general tone of piety. The Evangelical *Christian Observer*'s reviewer stated in 1850 that he would confine his remarks to 'the religion of Wordsworth's poetry'. Wordsworth, in turn, 'was not attracted or convinced by the piety of the Evangelicals or by their doctrine of personal salvation through Christ alone' (Moorman, *op. cit.*, p. 106).

Chapter 5: Memory

1. W. Gilpin, *Observations, Relative Chiefly to Picturesque Beauty*, p. xxii.
2. *Ibid.*, pp. 120-1.
3. It was suggested in Toman's *Kilvert: The Homeless Heart* (p. 73) that before the Tintern Abbey visit he had seen *Antiquities of Great Britain*, vol. II, by Hearne and Byrne, but it is likely that he had read Gilpin and Howitt too. There is such close similarity of phrasing between Howitt's description of his visit to Tintern and Kilvert's that it is clear that the latter knew the former's *Ruined Abbeys and Castles of Great Britain*.
4. *Kilvert's Diary*, vol. III, p. 203.
5. Generally, when viewing ruins he commented on the presence or absence of ivy. 'It is very curious that these ruins [Llanthony] are quite free from ivy. . . .' (vol. I, p. 80); 'the old ivy-grown castle. . .' [Hay] (vol. I, p. 89); 'its cold chimney still ivy-clustered' [Whitehall farmhouse] (vol. I, p. 122); Holditch Court's 'ruined ivied tower' (vol I, p. 392).
6. *Ibid.*, vol. III, p. 28.
7. W. Wordsworth, *Guide to the Lakes* (1810), E. de Selincourt (ed.), Oxford, Oxford University Press, 1977, p. 36.
8. W. Wordsworth, *The Prelude*, Book XII, 153-6.
9. *Ibid.*, Book XII, 114-6.
10. *Rural Life of England*, p 287. Howitt's picture of the landscape of Annesley included this meditation: 'There is nothing in all the histories of broken affections and mortal sorrows, more striking and melancholy than the idea of this lady, so bright and joyous-hearted in her youth, sitting in her latter years, . . . alone and secluded . . . in this old house' (p. 288).
11. W. Wordsworth, *The Prelude*, Book XII, 118-121.
12. Houghton, *The Victorian Frame of Mind*, p. 267.
13. S. Prickett, *Romanticism and Religion. The tradition of Coleridge and Wordsworth in the Victorian Church*, Cambridge, Cambridge University Press, 1976, pp. 87-8 and p. 71. His italics.
14. *Kilvert's Diary*, vol. II, pp. 176-7. Cf. Milton describing Adam and Eve leaving Paradise after the Fall near the end of Book I of *Paradise Lost*: 'with wandering steps and slow / Through Eden took their solitary way'.
15. J. Jones, *The Egotistical Sublime*, p. 31.

16. W. Wordsworth, *The Prelude*, Book II, 76-7 and 302-3.
17. *Ibid.*, Book VI, 173-5.
18. *Kilvert's Diary*, vol. III, p. 74.
19. *Ibid.*, vol. III, pp. 36-7. Cf. Cowper, who liked to 'wander . . . in remote / And silent woods, far from . . . the peopled scene' (*The Task*, Book III, 117-9).
20. *Kilvert's Diary*, vol. I, p. 83.
21. W. Wordsworth, *The Prelude*, Book IV, 360-6.
22. *Kilvert's Diary*, vol. I, p. 307.
23. W. Wordsworth, *The Prelude*, Book I, 464-6.
24. J. Jones, *op. cit.*, pp. 31-2.
25. W. Wordsworth, *The Prelude*, Book II, 155-8.
26. Quoted in R. Treble, *Van Gogh and his Art*, London, Hamlyn, 1981, p. 15.
27. *Kilvert's Diary*, vol. I, p. 90.
28. *Ibid.*, vol. I, p. 42.
29. *Ibid.*, vol. I, p. 89.
30. *Ibid.*, vol. I, p. 124.
31. *Ibid.*, vol. I, p. 214.
32. *Ibid.*, vol. I, p. 260.
33. Brooke, *Life and Letters*, vol. I, p. 193. Another well-known *Diary* entry shows Kilvert deciding, after a long search, that the right word for 'the shimmering glancing twinkling movement of the poplar leaves in the sun and the wind' was 'dazzle'. 'The dazzle of the poplars' (*Kilvert's Diary*, vol. III, p. 91).
34. *Ibid.*, vol. I, pp. 308-9.
35. W. Wordsworth, *Peter Bell*, 266-70.
36. Salvesen, *The Landscape of Memory*, p. 69.
37. W. Wordsworth, *Peter Bell*, 286-7 and 248-50.
38. W. Wordsworth, *Tintern Abbey*, 107-11.
39. *The Prelude*, Book II, 302-9 and 384-6.
40. W. Wordsworth, *The Prelude*, Book III, 141-3.
41. *Ibid.*, 185-8.
42. Patricia M. Ball, *The Central Self. A Study in Romantic and Victorian Imagination*, London, Athlone Press, 1968, p. 64.
43. Brooke, *op. cit.*, vol. I, pp. 193-4.
44. W. Wordsworth, *The Prelude*, Book XII, 208 and 214-5.
45. *Kilvert's Diary*, vol. III, pp. 166-7. The passage characteristically highlights feminine features of landscape.
46. *Ibid.*, vol. III, pp. 168-9.
47. *Ibid.*, vol. III, p. 72.
48. Ball, *op. cit.*, p. 8 and p. 11.
49. *Kilvert's Diary*, vol. II, p. 279. The phrase 'lingering longing' is another allusion to Gray's *Elegy* and takes us back to Kilvert's Cornish holiday when he used it (in its right form 'longing lingering') to convey his reluctant departure from Emma Hockin.
50. *Ibid.*, vol. II, pp. 113-4.
51. *Ibid.*, vol. III, pp. 190-1. Again there is an echo of Gray's *Elegy* in 'long lingering glow'.
52. W. Wordsworth, *The Prelude*, Book I, 551-8.
53. The Wanderer in Wordsworth's *The Excursion* told of the pleasure he

derived from standing on the top of a hill to watch the sun rise — God's 'bounteous gift' — or to watch the sun set. 'Then, my spirit was entranced / With joy exalted to beatitude; / The measure of my soul was filled with bliss, / And holiest love' (Book IV, 115-121).

54. *Kilvert's Diary*, vol. III, p. 75.
55. *Ibid.*, vol. III, pp. 214-5.
56. *Ibid.*, vol. III, pp. 22-3.
57. Three weeks later he had a similar experience, though this time vicariously, for the loss of existence was the fate of another. Sir Henry Oglander of Nunwell had died without an heir and 'his place knows him no more and a stranger . . . sits in his seat' (*ibid.*, vol. III, p. 36). Nunwell is on the Isle of Wight.
58. *Ibid.*, vol. II, p. 274.
59. Salvesen, *op. cit.*, p. 2.
60. Legh Richmond, *The Dairyman's Daughter*, in *Annals of the Poor*, pp. 129-30. The orthodox emphasis on life after death, missing from Gray's *Elegy*, that is in Kilvert's elegy, had been derived from the Richmond passage: Kilvert referred to the churchyard's inmates 'waiting for . . . the General Resurrection of the dead' and Richmond said they were 'waiting the resurrection of the dead'.
61. T. Gray, 'Elegy Written in a Country Churchyard', in *Thomas Gray and William Collins. Poetical Works*, R. Lonsdale (ed.), Oxford, Oxford University Press, 1977.
62. *Kilvert's Diary*, vol. III, p. 308. Because Kilvert's stance towards keepsakes matches Robertson's so closely, it seems to be another instance of the influence on him of the brilliant Brighton preacher and writer. Robertson developed his approach to them in remarks he made about pantheism. Whereas High Churchmen localised God only in sacred places (churches) and at special times (services), pantheists found the god-like everywhere. Wordsworth, however, believed that sanctity was a relative, not an intrinsic, phenomenon — existing in the attitude and belief of worshippers i.e. they sanctified a place, any place, by their reverence (Brooke, *op. cit.*, vol. II, p. 170). Robertson recognised a similar process with regard to objects commemorating individuals. Localising a deity in any place that had significance for worshippers corresponded to 'that which an affectionate imagination does in reference to the presence of any loved person; an act which has only reference to his or her own mode of conceiving that presence — as when a relic or keepsake is preserved, or a chair felt to be sacred' (*ibid.*, pp. 193-4). Kilvert's treatment of keepsakes is essentially that of 'an affectionate imagination', the stance of a man for whom 'sympathy' was a guiding principle.
63. *Kilvert's Diary*, vol. I, p. 258.
64. *Ibid.*, vol. III, pp. 268-9.
65. *Ibid.*, vol. III, p. 197.
66. *Ibid.*, vol. I, p. 208.
67. *Ibid.*, vol. III, p. 260.
68. *Ibid.*, vol. III, p. 378.
69. *Ibid.*, vol. III, p. 149.
70. W. Wordsworth, *The Prelude*, Book I, 607-12.
71. *Kilvert's Diary*, vol. III, p. 333.

72. J. Jones, *op. cit.*, pp. 94-5.

73. Salvesen, *op. cit.*, p. 90.

74. W. Wordsworth, *The Excursion*, Book I, 206-10.

75. M. Abrams, *Natural Supernaturalism: Tradition and Revolution in Romantic Literature*, London, Oxford University Press, 1971, p. 281.

76. Hartman, *Wordsworth's Poetry*, p. 170.

77. Jay (*The Religion of the Heart*, p. 202) said that 'Cowper's poetry and hymns did much to recommend to Evangelicals the practice of reading and writing devotional poetry. . . .' She also noted that other good examples of Evangelicals who wrote poetry existed in Legh Richmond, Mrs Hemans and Robert Montgomery.

78. W. Cowper, *The Task*, Book VI, 6, 11-12, 16-18.

79. *Ibid.*, Book V, 748-52.

80. *Kilvert's Diary*, vol. II, p. 445.

81. Tennyson, *In Memoriam*, section 53. Robertson, too, had experienced the total despair of which Tennyson wrote: 'It is an awful moment when the soul begins to find that the props on which it has blindly rested for so long are, many of them, rotten, and begins to suspect them all; when it begins to feel the nothingness of many of the traditionary opinions which have been received with implicit confidence, and in that horrible insecurity begins also to doubt whether there be anything to believe at all. It is an awful hour – let him who has passed through it say how awful – when this life has lost its meaning, and seems shrivelled into a span; when the grave appears to be the end of all, human goodness nothing but a name, and the sky above this universe a dead expanse, black with the void from which God Himself has disappeared' (Brooke, *op. cit.*, vol. I, p. 103).

82. *Kilvert's Diary*, vol. III, p. 241.

83. Lord Tennyson, *In Memoriam*, sections 100 and 101. Kilvert probably also knew Cowper's poem, *On Receipt of My Mother's Picture out of Norfolk*, in which he wrote: 'Where once we dwelt our name is heard no more / Children not thine have trod my nursery floor. . . .' Reed's view that 'For many Victorians, memory meant personal memory of childhood representing an inviolable sanctuary' could be cited as one explanation of this fierce resentment of interlopers in the family home (see Reed, *Victorian Conventions*, p. 403).

84. The experience being described seems akin to that of Wordsworth's Wanderer for whom natural objects 'lay / Upon his mind like substances'.

85. *Kilvert's Diary*, vol. I, p. 374.

86. Salvesen, *op. cit.*, p. 81.

87. Richmond, *The Dairyman's Daughter*, p. 27. Wordsworth, too, noted how recollected childhood scenes in particular could appear perfect:

> Those recollected hours that have the charm
> Of visionary things, those lovely forms
> And sweet sensations that throw back our life,
> And almost make remotest infancy
> A visible scene, on which the sun is shining.
> (*The Prelude*, Book I, 631-5)

88. Landow, *Approaches to Victorian Autobiography*, p. xxxix.

89. *The Rocks of Aberedw* in *Collected Verse by the Reverend Francis Kilvert*.

Chapter 6: The Very Culture of the Feelings

1. The phrase was used by John Stuart Mill to describe what Wordsworth's poetry meant to him in the winter of 1826-7 when he was facing a mental breakdown. 'What made Wordsworth's poems a medicine for my state of mind, was that they expressed, not mere outward beauty, but states of feeling, and of thought coloured by feeling, under the excitement of beauty' (*Autobiography of John Stuart Mill*, [1873], New York, Columbia University Press, 1944, p. 104).

2. The NLW edition of *Kilvert's Diary*, April-June 1870 (Kathleen Hughes and Dafydd Ifans (eds.), Aberystwyth, 1982) gives several references to the poem that are omitted from Plomer's edition. Kilvert began the poem on 30 April, put in a further two hours on it on 2 May, tested it first on Miss Chaloner, his landlady's daughter, on 7 May, and read it to Mrs Chaloner two days later.

3. This is a 'popular theme' currently in the cultural history of landscape (P. Dunham, ' 'An Angel-Satyr Walks these Hills': Landscape and Identity in Kilvert's Diary', in *Landscape History after Hoskins*, P. Barnwell and M. Palmer (eds.), Macclesfield, Windgather Press, 2007 p. 169).

4. Celeste Langan, *Romantic Vagrancy. Wordsworth and the Simulation of Freedom*, Cambridge, Cambridge University Press, 1995, p. 13. The quoted lines are from *The Prelude* (1805 edition), Book XII, 83-7.

5. *Ibid.*, pp. 16-17.

6. Quotations are from pp. 171-178 of Dunham, *op. cit.*

7. W. Wordsworth, Preface to the *Lyrical Ballads*. His italics.

8. W. Wordsworth, *The Excursion*, Book I, 343-7.

9. *Ibid.*, 364-72. Kilvert also had the example of Cowper, who declared that the 'law of love' dictated that we should compare our own troubles with those of others and 'sympathise with others' suffering more' (*The Task*, Book IV, 337-340).

10. Brooke, *Life and Letters*, vol. I, p. 192.

11. *Ibid.*, vol. I, p. 130. His church in Cheltenham was called Christchurch.

12. *Ibid.*, vol. I, p. 115.

13. *Ibid.*, vol. I, p. 111.

14. *Ibid.*, vol. I, p. 348. Undated letter of 1850.

15. *Kilvert's Diary*, vol. I, p. 235. The reference in the passage to French manners derives from the fact that Kilvert was reading at the time Adelaide Sartoris's novel, *A Week in a French Country House*. His critique of English manners was directed largely at the higher gentry families around Clyro and is explored in Toman's *Kilvert: The Homeless Heart* (chapters 5 and 10). He also showed his anger at upper-class arrogance when he wrote of the 'patronising manner' in which labourers and old people, some his own parishioners, were 'preached at by *their betters?*' (his italics and question mark) at the Chippenham Agricultural Meeting (*Diary*, 29 Nov 1872). The *Devizes and Wiltshire Gazette* (5 Dec 1872) account of it shows that Sir George Jenkinson, MP for North Wilts, and the Rev Green (West Kington) used an occasion that should have been a celebration of labourers' worth to read them a lecture on their moral deficiencies. Kilvert's informant about what occurred at the meeting was Miss Mewburn, who was related to the Kearys, one of the local middle-class families, with whom the Kilverts were closely involved (Annie

Keary's novel, *Castle Daly*, celebrated the worth of smallholders). It is also significant that Frederick Robertson was known to the Keary family (Brooke, *op. cit.*, vol. I, p. 30). *Castle Daly* is a fine novel and Kilvert's appreciation of it ('I told Miss Keary how much I liked her story', vol. III, p. 128), is another sign of his literary acumen. A major theme of it is the difference between the Irish (Celtic) and the English (Saxon) character – a subject of considerable interest to Kilvert (see chapter nine).

16. Brooke, *op. cit.*, vol. II, p. 166.
17. *Ibid.*, vol. I, p. 270.
18. *Ibid.*, vol. I, p. 292.
19. *Ibid.*, vol. I, p. 204. 'He reached the most dense in a Sunday-school class'.
20. Howitt, *The Rural Life of England*, p. 403.
21. Quoted in S. Gill, *Wordsworth and the Victorians*, Oxford, Clarendon Press, 1998, p. 15.
22. J.R. Watson, *English Poetry of the Romantic Period*, p. 176.
23. P. Ball, *The Central Self*, pp. 153-4. Perkins noted that the early nineteenth-century ideal of poetry was that it was 'personal utterance; therefore it is or should be veracious; it is passionate and spontaneous. . . . And on the whole the emotions expressed in a poem arise from the writer's personal life and refer back to it' (David Perkins, *Wordsworth and the Poetry of Sincerity*, Cambridge, Harvard University Press, 1964, p. 34).
24. He used 'touching' to register what he admired in, for example, Lamb's *Essay*, in his *Essays of Elia*, on 'The Tombs in the Abbey' (*Kilvert's Diary*, vol. III, p. 76).
25. R. Altick, *The English Common Reader. A Social History of the Mass Reading Public 1800-1900*, Chicago, University of Chicago Press, 1957, p. 122.
26. *Kilvert's Diary*, vol. III, p. 38.
27. From the 'Memoir of the Author' that prefaces Richmond's *Annals of the Poor*. 'How much they lose who are strangers to serious meditation on the wonders and beauties of nature', he wrote in *The Dairyman's Daughter* (p. 29). While curate of Brading and Yaverland, he developed the habit of seeking out beautiful places that could help to form 'pleasing and useful associations'. *The Dairyman's Daughter* has one landscape description that occupies three pages and ends with a meditation contrasting natural beauty with the sinful nature of man.
28. The Evangelical mind would also find 'romance' in the fact that she was vain, irreligious and given to dressing herself in the finest clothes she could afford until, on listening to a sermon on the text 'Be ye clothed with humility', she became convinced of her sinful nature and was converted.
29. J. Uglow, *Elizabeth Gaskell: a Habit of Stories*, London, Faber and Faber, 1993, p. 237. Mrs Gaskell characterised *Ruth*, the one novel of hers we know Kilvert read, in terms of a story she *had* to tell. The same compulsive need drove Kilvert to tell many of the stories he told.
30. Quoted in Dugdale, *William Barnes of Dorset*, p. 113.
31. Richmond, *The Dairyman's Daughter*, p. 22.
32. *Ibid.*, p. 71.
33. W. Wordsworth, *The Excursion*, Book IV, 790-1.
34. In this passage there is an echo of Gray's *Elegy*. At Gaston's farm, 'Daddy! Daddy! cried the children as their father passed the window', returning

from his day's work; the *Elegy* refers to children running to 'lisp their sire's return'. The *Diary* entry (vol. III, pp. 302-7) dealing with Kilvert's visit to the small farm of Chieflands, also near Chippenham, is another complete statement on the morality of rural life. It figures in the last chapter.

35. Ball, *op. cit.*, pp. 81-2.
36. Ball noted that the 'reacting mind' is a structural feature of the poems (*ibid.*, p. 68).
37. Garber, *Wordsworth and the Poetry of Encounter*, p. 14.
38. *Ibid.*, p. 5.
39. *Ibid.*, p. 16.
40. Hartman, *Wordsworth's Poetry*, p. 9.
41. Dunham, *op. cit.*, p 176.
42. Garber, *op. cit.*, p. 19.
43. Introduction to *Kilvert's Diary*, vol. II, p. 11.
44. Garber, *op. cit.*, p. 50.
45. W. Wordsworth, *The Prelude*, Book VII, 619-625.
46. Garber underlined that background or context was important since distinct objects exist in a context (of other discrete things) and are therefore not absolute (pure and unattached) or independent (unattached and alone) or single (without context). If an object is without context, it is deadened because it has no share in the life around it (*op. cit.*, p. 29).
47. To Garber, this statement had 'immense significance' (*ibid.*, p. 45).
48. These passages are in *Kilvert's Diary*, vol. II, pp. 83, 65, 98, 125, 61, 56, 228. They represent only about half of those that could have been cited.
49. *Ibid.*, vol. II, pp. 26-7.
50. Vol. II, pp. 433, 447, 58, 56, 149. Kilvert was sensitive to the effects of singularity in others' depiction of landscapes. Describing Darby's painting of Calypso, he drew attention to light: 'Here and there solitary lamps glitter like glow worms about the darkening cliffs'. He had a letter from his sister Emily, who was in India, and he wrote: 'She gives a beautiful description of a landscape. . . . The lofty rock, the abode of the fakir. One Tree Hill, the little temple crowning the hill. . . .' (vol. II, pp. 107 and 222).
51. Garber, *op. cit.*, p. 51.
52. *Ibid.*, p. 54.
53. Garber noted that all the major Romantic poets made use of the disembodied voice, the most well-known example being Keats's *Ode to a Nightingale*.
54. Cf. the 'small voice singing' and the bee humming, which were used so effectively at the end of the Whitehall passage quoted in chapter one, and the bird singing 'below Tybella', quoted in chapter one.
55. These passages are in *Kilvert's Diary*, vol. II, pp. 334, 358, 375; see also pp. 354 and 128.
56. Garber, *op. cit.*, p. 41.
57. *Ibid.*, p. 14. Compare the excitement and joy of those Hardenhuish passages with Garber's statement: 'The exaltation of the moment of encounter drives the observer to an extreme pitch of consciousness of all that he sees and of himself in that context' (*ibid.*, p. 17). Watson spoke of the *Lyrical Ballads* as exercises in 'consciousness raising' (*op. cit.*, p. 179).
58. *Ibid.*, p. 40.
59. *Ibid.*, p. 42.
60. In the interim, he had escorted them on a round of visits.

61. *Kilvert's Diary*, vol. I, pp. 324-5. He had experienced a parallel situation some time earlier in relation to a Miss Lyne, but his reaction is not marked by the despair of the later one, though his concern with 'chance' meetings and the possibility of 'knowing' another person is there: 'It is so provoking that just as I have become acquainted with her and like her so much, . . . and she had become so friendly and cordial, she goes away and perhaps I shall never see her again' (*ibid.*, vol. I, p. 177).

62. Donald Wesling, *Wordsworth and the Adequacy of Landscape*, London, Routledge, Kegan Paul, 1970, p 44.

63. *Kilvert's Diary*, vol. II, pp. 231, 226, 229.

64. Garber, *op. cit.*, p. 27.

65. *Kilvert's Diary*, vol. II, p. 231, my italics. Kilvert did mention Price again but only to note that 'the poor strange Solitary' had fallen in the fire and burnt himself 'dreadfully' (*ibid.*, vol. III, p. 163).

66. Averill, *Wordsworth and the Poetry of Human Suffering*, p. 149. Wordsworth made a study of Dr Darwin's *Zoonomia*, a large medical treatise containing instances of human behaviour that illustrated 'the laws of organic life'. Wordsworth obtained the story of Goody Blake from this source.

67. *Kilvert's Diary*, vol. I, pp. 282-3.

68. Garber, *op. cit.*, pp. 42-3.

69. *Kilvert's Diary*, vol. I, p. 283.

70. Cf. *Kilvert's Diary*, vol. III, p. 250: 'The apricot blossoms were blowing and under the silver weeping birch the daffodils were dancing and nodding their golden heads in the morning wind and sunshine. . . . The daffodil is one of my favourite flowers. I love the sweet daffodil tide, . . . when the green dawn is breaking on the trees . . . and the air is full of hope'. The moment expressed a religious as well as a sensuous joy in the harmony of the universe (cf. vol. III, p. 380).

71. These poems come later than the *Lyrical Ballads*. They are variations on the theme of loss and loneliness and complement Ferris's story in that they focus on the grief of mothers who have been separated from their sons.

72. *Kilvert's Diary*, vol. III, p. 156. J. Jones (*The Egotistical Sublime*, p. 53) commented: 'Wordsworth was blind to sin, which is the direct way to a Christian understanding of suffering'. Jay noted that Evangelicals saw a close link between sin and suffering: 'Evangelicals did not see the relief of suffering as their main objective'. Where they met with it, they preferred to focus on the evil in men's souls that was its cause (*The Religion of the Heart*, p. 173). The 'good advice' which Kilvert said he gave Ferris as they parted no doubt contained some moral reflections.

73. *Kilvert's Diary*, 13 July 1870. National Library of Wales edition of *Kilvert's Diary, June-July 1870*, edited by Dafydd Ifans, Aberystwyth, 1989, p. 88.

74. 1801 Preface to W. Wordsworth's *Lyrical Ballads*.

75. 7 June 1802 letter to John Wilson in the *Letters of William and Dorothy Wordsworth: The Early Years 1787-1805*, vol. I, A.G. Hill (ed.), Oxford, Clarendon Press, 1967.

76. Jacobus, *Tradition and Experiment in Wordsworth's 'Lyrical Ballads'*, p. 260.

77. J.R. Watson, *op. cit.*, p. 181.

78. David B. Pirie, *William Wordsworth: the Poetry of Grandeur and Tenderness*, London, Methuen, 1982, p. 51.

79. *Kilvert's Diary*, vol. I, p. 59.

80. *Ibid.*, vol. II, p. 116.

81. Bredwardine is on the Wye in Herefordshire. Kilvert became its vicar in November 1877.

82. *Ibid.*, vol. III, pp. 352-3.

83. Her husband worked at the Llwyngwillim Farm run by John Vaughan, son of the Newchurch vicar, David Vaughan, with whom Kilvert was very friendly.

84. *Kilvert's Diary*, vol. II, pp. 163-4.

85. Cf. Garber (*op. cit.*, p. 99): 'The process and effect of sentimental morality found echoes and analogues everywhere in Wordsworth. The stress of this mode is on human response to the human, universal man responding through sympathy and identification to the pained world of other men'. There are elements of Emma Griffith's situation in Wordsworth's *She Dwelt among the Untrodden Ways* and *The Complaint of a Forsaken Indian Woman*.

86. 'Many of the *Lyrical Ballads* suggest that [Wordsworth] is trying to imitate motions of thought observed in others' (Perkins, *op. cit.*, p. 45).

87. *Kilvert's Diary*, vol. II, pp. 46-8. Her death certificate, which describes her as a 45-year-old labourer, makes no mention of suicide but says simply 'found drowned'.

88. 1801 *Preface* to W. Wordsworth's *Lyrical Ballads*.

89. John Beer said that the key to *The Thorn* is the idea of the infinity of suffering. Martha herself expresses this in the image she presents of grief that can find no relief, no adequate expression (*Wordsworth in Time*, London, Faber and Faber, 1979, p. 133).

90. Garber, *op. cit.*, pp. 85 and 89.

91. Wesling, *Wordsworth and the Adequacy of Landscape*, p 9.

92. Schor, *Bearing the Dead*, pp. 185-6.

93. This was demonstrated in chapter four in relation to the ambiguous ending of *Simon Lee*; it was also perceptive of him to pronounce Macdonald's novel, *The Marquis of Lossie*, inferior to his *Malcolm* (*Kilvert's Diary*, vol. III, p. 370). He was completely alert to the defects of *Puck* by the popular novelist, Ouida: 'Finished reading *Puck*, clever, bitter, extravagant, full of repetitions and absurdities and ludicrous ambitious attempts at fine writing, weak and bombastic' (vol. I, p. 303). Nor is it tenable to hold to the view that everything he read in fiction was ephemeral; *Puck* is ephemeral. The same cannot be said of the following prose works read by him: the Macdonald novels referred to above, Kingsley's *Alton Locke*, Keary's *Castle Daly*, Mrs Gaskell's *Ruth*, Trollope's *Is He Popenjoy?*, Mrs Sartoris's *A Week in a French Country House*, Dorothy Wordsworth's *Journal*, Margaret Ossoli's *Summer on the Lakes*, Lockhart's *Life of Sir Walter Scott*, the *Autobiography* of Lamartine, Sterne's *Tristram Shandy*, Newton's *Cardiphonia*. It is enough to point to Kilvert's wide and deep (certainly in relation to Wordsworth) knowledge of poetry as evidence that he was a serious reader.

Chapter 7: Mountain Beauties

1. A. Sedgwick, *A Discourse on the Studies of the University of Cambridge*, Cambridge, John Deighton, 1850, supplement to the appendix, pp. 316-8.

2. Grice, *Francis Kilvert and his World*, p. 218.

3. *Ibid.*, p. 226.

4. *Kilvert's Diary* entry for 27 April 1876, 'I had a grand romp with Polly Sackville', is typical of many. He was quite unashamed about such

behaviour and the romps often occurred in the presence of parents. This
is how he behaved in the home of the St Harmon's church clerk: 'As I was
at luncheon the children came in from school. . . . I drew one pretty girl
to me, put my arm round her waist and kissed her, whereat a small boy
surprised out of his propriety laughed pleasantly'. As he left, having just
shaken hands with the girl's parents, he 'kissed the pretty girl once more
on her blooming cheek and sweet lips. . . .' (vol. III, p. 290). Cf. Charles
Dickens: 'I kiss almost all the children I encounter in remembrance of
their sweet faces, and talk to all the mothers who carry them' (Letters
to his wife in November 1852, quoted in Arthur Adrian, *Dickens and the
Parent-Child Relationship*, Ohio, Ohio University Press, 1984, p. 30).

5. Grice, *op. cit.*, p. 223.

6. O'Brien observed that his 'ever-rushing emotionalism' was accompanied
   by 'a good rough stream of coarseness, of plain sensuality of thought,
   and of shameless enjoyment of the beating of children'. However, she
   believed that 'he got through so decently, as man and as writer, simply
   by the grace of God and the luck of the innocent' (K. O'Brien, *English
   Diaries and Journals*, London, William Collins, 1943, pp. 43 and 41). Blythe
   noted his 'sensuous vision of nature' but was convinced that because
   of his art and his 'erotic heart', the desires which he confesses into the
   Diary do not make the reader uncomfortable as well they might, but
   endear him to the reader (R. Blythe, *From the Headlands*, London, Chatto
   and Windus, 1982, p. 186). The innocence of his erotic fantasies was
   stressed by Le Quesne, who pointed out that our knowledge of Freud
   has destroyed our innocence. Le Quesne also saw sexual repression as
   the main source of the 'intense sensuousness' of the *Diary* (Le Quesne,
   After Kilvert, pp. 133 and 130). Kilvert was 'probably shy and sensitive',
   in Addison's view, and 'No doubt lacked the courage to give effect to his
   desires, and was, it seems, innocent of their implications . . . so that his
   diary has to be read without too much thought of Freudian psychology'
   (W. Addison, *The English Country Parson*, London, Dent, 1948, p. 184).

7. Ivor Lewis, *Kilvert's Divided Personality*, Kilvert Society Newsletter, June
   1983.

8. Brooke, *Life and Letters*, vol. I, pp. 163 and 165-6. Robertson replied
   to criticisms of his lecture on Wordsworth by the *South Church Union
   Chronicle* (a Brighton paper) with the following statements, amongst
   others: 'The tendency of Pantheism is to see the god-like everywhere,
   the personal god nowhere. The tendency of High Churchism is to
   localise the personal Deity in certain consecrated places, called churches;
   certain consecrated times, called Sabbaths . . . ; certain consecrated acts,
   sacramental and quasi-sacramental. I endeavoured to show that there
   are High Churchmen, like Wordsworth, who recognise in such places,
   persons, and acts, a sanctity only relative, and not intrinsic. . . .' (*Ibid.*,
   vol. II, p. 170).

9. *Ibid.*, vol. I, pp. 227-8. His italics. In essence, Robertson was advancing
   the *sacramental* view of physical beauty that Kilvert embraced and which
   informs his *Honest Work* statement of belief.

10. Peter Gay, *The Tender Passion*, vol. II of *The Bourgeois Experience. Victoria
    to Freud*, New York, Norton, 1999, p. 55.

11. *Kilvert's Diary*, vol. III, p. 275. While staying in Oxford with Mayhew,
    his Wadham contemporary, he watched 'the father dressed for dinner

[come] in to see his children and wish them "Good night".' Kilvert was allowed to play the father by escorting Mayhew's daughter Ruthie around Oxford and as he went past the gates of Wadham, the porter remarked '"What a pretty little girl that is". How proud and fond I felt of her' (*ibid.*, vol. III, pp. 321-2).

12. p. 363. The story contrasts the naturalness of family life with the unnaturalness of the cloister. On 10 October 1873, Kilvert attended a section of the Bath Church Congress on 'The Religious wants and claims of children', when he heard Rev Randall (All Saints, Clifton) state: 'the truest education of the child is the home. . . . Holy homes make holy children'.

13. A.S. Kilvert, *Home Discipline*, p. 52.

14. Jay, *The Religion of the Heart*, p. 54. Bradley observed that 'Evangelicals constantly reminded [children] of their own sinfulness and depravity' (*The Call to Seriousness*, p. 186).

15. Hugh Pyper observed: 'Victorian piety cooed over the picture of God as an innocent, loving baby' (*Oxford Companion to Christian Thought*, p. 110).

16. Davidoff, *Worlds Between*, pp. 54-5.

17. Mary Poovey, *Uneven Developments: the Ideological Work of Gender in mid-Victorian England*, Chicago, Chicago University Press, 1988, pp. 49-50.

18. *Ibid.*, p. 157.

19. Brooke, *op. cit.*, vol. I, p. 268.

20. F.K. Brown, *Fathers of the Victorians. The Age of Wilberforce*, Cambridge, Cambridge University Press, 1961, p. 437.

21. Houghton, *The Victorian Frame of Mind*, p. 359.

22. Bradley, *op. cit.*, p. 97.

23. *Kilvert's Diary*, vol. II, p. 418. The previous day he recorded that his father preached 'an admirable sermon to mothers on driving away evil influences from their children'.

24. *Ibid.*, vol. II, p. 380.

25. For example *Kilvert's Diary*, vol. I, p. 144 (housemaid at the Venables' vicarage made pregnant by their coachman); vol. I, p. 262 (a farm servant 'cracked a commandment' and came home 'in the family way'); vol. I, p. 336 (the last housemaid at the home of the Rev Thomas of Llanthomas 'gave birth to a child in the house'). He associated primroses with both young girls and purity. His interest in the symbolism of flowers manifested itself also in the entry in which he dwelt on wild snowdrops, which had the same associations: 'How white and pure and stainless they looked . . . [these] Fair Maids of February' (*ibid.*, vol. II, p. 128).

26. Michael Mason, *The Making of Victorian Sexual Attitudes*, Oxford, Oxford University Press, 1994, pp. 2-3.

27. *Ibid.*, p. 17. Mason thought that the account given by Houghton (*op. cit.*, chapter 13 on Love, Woman and Sex) of the prevailing anti-sensual tone of Victorian society was misleading, largely because he dealt with leading literary figures who represented the 'classic moralism' of the establishment. Evangelicalism, on the other hand, was 'less restrictive in its moral views' than the establishment.

28. Mrs Charles, *Chronicles*, p. 142.

29. *Kilvert's Diary*, vol. I, p. 78. Prentiss's *Stepping Heavenward* adopted the same stance towards monastic communities: 'The best convent for a woman, is the seclusion of her own home. There she may find her vocation and . . .

may learn the reality and earnestness of life' (p. 241).

30. *Kilvert's Diary*, vol. III, p. 31.

31. Jay, *op. cit.*, p. 55.

32. Brooke, *op. cit.*, vol. I, p. 254.

33. Kilvert tried his hand at tracing the loss of infant consciousness upon growing up in a poem of his own in which ideas and phrases of the *Immortality Ode* recur frequently. In *Life's Weather*, he stated that 'life and weather . . . change still together', and he drew a parallel between the span of a day and that of a human life. The day began with a misty morning 'in the heart's childhood prime', when a radiance made up of the shifting light of 'pearl' and 'opal' surrounded the natural forms that in Wordsworth's poem were 'Apparelled in celestial light'. In Kilvert's second stanza the echoes multiply. Where Wordsworth said 'nothing can bring back the hour of splendour in the grass', Kilvert had 'Now the dew hoary / dries from the meadow grass'; the *Ode*'s 'there hath past away a glory from the earth' became in *Life's Weather* 'from life's morn doth pass / The first bright glory'; 'the glory and freshness of a dream' was changed in Kilvert's poem to 'In youth's first freshness' [some children] 'once sainted . . . stand disenchanted / 'Neath manhood's sultry noon'; for Wordsworth's 'The clouds gather round the setting sun' Kilvert wrote 'Thick clouds have blurred the sun'. The day that is life ended for Kilvert with 'Till at sun-setting / . . . Hope spreads her arch on high, — / Love unforgetting; / Lo! the pure even star, / Beacons us homing'. In Wordsworth's account of life, he found hope in the fact that the child came 'Not in entire forgetfulness, / . . . But trailing clouds of glory' and reflected that 'the Soul that rises with us, our life's Star, / Hath elsewhere its setting'.

34. In spring 1872, when Kilvert was entranced by the sight of Clyro with all its trees in blossom, he commented particularly on 'The torch-trees of Paradise'. Paradise Farm could yield less heavenly associations: Eleanor's brother was suffering from 'the itch' in June 1870 and Kilvert recommended to his mother that the child be treated with 'sulphur and hog's lard'.

35. J. Keble, *Lyra Innocentium: Thoughts in Verse on Christian Children, their Ways, and their Privileges*, London, John Henry Parker, 1846. He said his collection of poems was intended for teachers and nurses 'and others who are much employed about Children'.

36. Cf. Wordsworth's sonnet, *By the Sea Shore, Isle of Man*:
    Why stand we gazing on the sparkling Brine,
    With wonder smit by its transparency,
    And all-enraptured with its purity?
    Because the unstained, the clear, the crystalline,
    Have ever in them something of benign;
    Whether in gem, in water, or in sky,
    A sleeping infant's brow, or wakeful eye
    Of a young maiden, only not divine.

37. Harold Bloom, *The Visionary Company. A Reading of English Romantic Poetry*, Ithaca, New York, Cornell University Press, 1971, p. 271.

38. G. Wilson Knight, *The Starlit Dome*, Oxford, Oxford University Press, 1943, p. 45.

39. *Kilvert's Diary*, vol. II, p. 248.

40. Judith Plotz, *Romanticism and the Vocation of Childhood*, New York, Palgrave, 2001, p. 2. U.C. Knoepflmacher noted, however, that Victorians were ambivalent towards the Wordsworthian child of Nature —this 'mythic archetype', who represented the search for 'an elemental harmony'. In the Victorian treatment of it, there was 'a mixture of nostalgia and criticism', more of the latter than of the former. 'Despite their frequently sentimental portraits of divine and innocent children, the Victorians tended to look sceptically at the Wordsworthian child, because they knew that children are far from divine and may only be mini-adults with limited understanding' (*Mutations of the Wordsworthian Child of Nature*, Knoepflmacher and G.B. Tennyson (eds.), Berkeley, University of California Press, 1977, pp. 394 and 400).

41. He wrote in his preface to *Alice's Adventures under Ground*: 'Anyone that has ever loved one true child will have known the awe that falls on one in the presence of a spirit fresh from God's hands, on whom no shadow of sin . . . has yet fallen' (quoted in Morton N. Cohen, *Lewis Carroll. A biography*, London, Macmillan, 1995, p. 105).

42. Plotz, *op. cit.*, p. 4. Cohen traced it back to Traherne, Vaughan and Prior, who focused on the child, while Thomson, Gray and Cowper expressed 'nostalgia for lost children' without addressing 'the phenomenon of childhood itself' (Cohen, *op. cit.*, p. 106). H.J. Massingham (*The Southern Marches*, London, Robert Hale, 1953 p. 217) stated that Traherne, like Vaughan, 'saw in childhood a symbol of the Golden Age but to him the loss of it was the more tragic from the loss of happiness it entailed. He shared with Kilvert that quality of passionate awareness of and sensibility to the world of sense-data which was the means to that happiness'.

43. Cohen, *op. cit.*, p. 107. Carroll was also influenced particularly by Blake: 'His view of children is Blakean; he too revered the mystic combination of the primitive and the pure, the noble and the divine'.

44. K. Leach, *In the Shadow of the Dreamchild. A New Understanding of Lewis Carroll*, London, Peter Owen, 1999, pp. 16 and 62.

45. The only other mention of it occurs almost two months later (23 March 1870) when he stated that he had lent it to his literary farmer friend, Lewis Williams.

46. Part of a review of the book by the *Journal of Education* is quoted on its title page: 'Its object is to bring before the young pupil, in a familiar manner, the different phenomena of nature. It presents a variety of subjects for the child's consideration, the knowledge of which is useful, and besides, admirably calculated to draw out his powers of observation.' The book is divided into parts subdivided into numerous sections. For example, Part Two, 'Of the Earth and its Nature', has sections on the earth in general, the highest mountains, valleys and craters, plains, mountains' relative heights. The very expansive Part Three, 'On Water and Phenomena Pertaining to It', deals with its fluidity, transparency, specific gravity, evaporation, clouds and rain and frost, snow, ice and hail, icebergs, rivers and lakes and so on. Part Six, 'Of Light and Luminous Bodies', concerns sun, moon and stars, meteors, lightning, twilight, and the properties of light. Each section has the format of questions from the schoolmaster, followed by pupil answers, indicating the factual, rote-learning pattern characteristic of nineteenth-century schooling. In spite of the strong overtones of piety in the book's preface, its approach to learning is scientific and inductive

rather than religious and imaginative (Von Türk, *The Phenomena of Nature*, London, Effingham Wilson, 1832).

47. Kilvert would have recognised, as we can recognise, other clear echoes of Wordsworth in the preface to *Phenomena of Nature*. When Von Türk wrote 'Happy is he who understands how to read the Book of Nature', he was paraphrasing Wordsworth's lines in *The Excursion*: 'Happy is he who lives to understand, / Not human nature only, but explores / All natures. . . .' (*Excursion*, Book V, lines 332-4). And in Von Türk's 'for him who studies the Book of Nature in this spirit new pleasures are daily springing up', providing 'a talisman against the errors of vice and the sway of the passions', we can hear Wordsworth's 'For the Man — / Who in this spirit communes with the Forms / Of nature, who with understanding heart, / Both knows and loves such objects as excite / No morbid passions. . . .' (*Excursion*, Book V, lines 1208-12).

48. Wordsworth thought of himself as an educator and saw his poetry as didactic, which is the way Victorians saw it. Ward set out to trace his influence in poetry anthologies, educational journals and biographies in the Victorian period. His conclusion, with some reservations, was that it was 'deep and pervading' (J.P. Ward, ' "Came from Yon Fountain": Wordsworth's Influence on Victorian Educators', *Victorian Studies*, Indiana University, vol. XXIX, Number 3, Spring 1986, p. 406). Wordsworth's teaching was based primarily on the *Immortality Ode* and *The Excursion*, and consisted in a belief in the moral influence of Nature and a reverence for the young child as the first subject and carrier of its beneficent power. Little is known of how, and how much of, his poetry was taught in classrooms. Alice Meynell (1847-1922), the poet, wrote: 'In quite early childhood I lived upon Wordsworth. I don't know that I particularly enjoyed him, but he was put into my hands and, to me, his poetry was the normal poetry, *par excellence*' (quoted in Cruse, *The Victorians and their Books*, p. 177. Meynell's italics). One 300-page anthology of his poetry was published for schools in 1831. This was the only major one before 1866; another appeared in 1874. His poems appeared with those of other poets in the *Classbook of English Literature* (1865), though there were only six by him. Ward underlined this strange imbalance, which is also evident in educational journals of the time: his poetry is often cited but his name is not mentioned. 'Allusions to him are indirect or unacknowledged' (Ward, *op. cit.*, p. 410). It seems that Victorians were uneasy about Wordsworth in the classroom.

49. Wilderspin's *Infant System* (1834, 1840, 1852 editions), quoted in P. McCann and F. Young, *Samuel Wilderspin and the Infant School Movement*, London, Croom Helm, 1982, p. 188 and p. 192.

50. Augustus Hare, *The Story of My Life*, London, George Allen, 1896, vol. I, p. 173. He also recorded the keeping of small animals at the school — another Wilderspin recommendation. Highly critical of the school in general, Hare did not think much of the 'field trips'.

51. In effect, this completely revolutionised the teaching of geography and became the basis of the modern approach to it as a school subject (P. Elliott and S. Daniels, 'Pestalozzi, Fellenberg and British Nineteenth Century Geographical Education', *Journal of Historical Geography*, vol. XXXII, 2006, p. 752).

52. *Kilvert's Diary*, vol. II, p 237.

53. *Kilvert's Diary*, NLW edition, June-July 1870, pp. 57-8. By 'special subject', Kilvert meant what the 1862 Revised Code called 'extra subjects', designed to extend the curriculum and the older pupils. It is significant that he taught for 16 months (April 1865 - July 1866) alongside Miss Henrietta Coleburn, who had trained at the Home and Colonial Infant School Society College, which was founded on Pestalozzian principles.

54. *Kilvert's Diary*, vol. III, p. 228. Kilvert had already been given the motivation and the method of inducting the young into God's book of Nature by Legh Richmond in his story *The Young Cottager*, which appears in *Annals of the Poor*. In the story we are told that a minister had a special concern for the young because they were most open to influence and his work with them is pictured thus: 'What a gratifying occupation it is *to an affectionate mind* to walk through the fields, and lead a little child by the hand . . . striving to improve the time by some kind word of instruction' (*op. cit.*, p. 128, my italics).

55. Pestalozzi's diary entries for 2 and 15 February 1774, quoted in John Russell, *Pestalozzi. Educational Reformer 1746-1827*, (1888) London, George Allen and Unwin, 1926, p. 16.

56. Jones, *The Egotistical Sublime*, p. 70.

57. Kilvert's key poem, *Honest Work*, shows the influence of *Lucy Gray*. He wrote in *Honest Work* that the 'Heaven-sown flower of happiness . . . blooms uncultured and wild' in cottages. He also used in his poem the phrase 'sun and shower' that appears in Wordsworth's title, *Three Years she Grew in Sun and Shower*.

58. Frances Ferguson, *Wordsworth: Language as Counterspirit*, New Haven, Yale University Press, 1977, p. 178. Mason (*Lyrical Ballads*, p. 256) noted that 'Wordsworth is recorded as saying in a conversation in 1816 that "he removed from his poem all that pertained to art . . . it being his object to exhibit poetically entire *solitude.* . . ." '

59. Hartman, *Wordsworth's Poetry*, p. 158. Averill insisted that Wordsworth did not want the reader to believe in a supernatural explanation of the Lucy story. The statement at the end of *Lucy Gray*, that 'some maintain that . . . she is a living child', draws attention, according to Averill, to the 'fictitiousness of the poem's ending' (Averill, *Wordsworth and the Poetry of Human Suffering*, p. 198).

60. Watson, *English Poetry of the Romantic Period*, p. 199.

61. From Kilvert's poem *The Flower of Slaughterford*.

62. *Kilvert's Diary*, vol. I, p. 136. It was 16 May 1870, and Emily had just returned from India.

63. *Ibid.*, vol. I, p. 44. The Geneva brooch was very probably a present from Kilvert that he had bought there, along with his musical box, during his visit while on holiday in summer 1869.

64. *Ibid.*, vol. I, p. 123.

65. S. Parrish, *The Art of the Lyrical Ballads*, Cambridge, Harvard University Press, 1973, p. 14.

66. Ferguson, *op. cit.*, pp. 174-5.

67. *Kilvert's Diary*, vol. II, p. 55. The poem has been lost.

68. Cf. the end of *Three Years she Grew*: 'The memory of what has been, / And never more will be'.

69. The 'storm blown hawthorn on the mountain top' recalls the thorn 'High on a mountain's highest ridge' in Wordsworth's *The Thorn*.

70. Cf. the entry for 5 September 1871 which recorded that 'In the first Newchurch field the turkeys ... were *mourning* in the stubbles and a *black* pony was gazing *pensively* over the hedge'. My italics.

71. Bloom, *op. cit.*, p. 189.

72. Averill, *op. cit.*, p. 198.

73. Ferguson, *op. cit.*, p. 176.

74. *Kilvert's Diary*, vol. I, p. 156. Cf. Howitt: 'what sweet faces and lovely forms issue from these little cabins ... making [them] little temples of rare beauty. . . .' (*Rural Life of England*, p. 405).

75. Lucy Gray inhabits the 'lonesome wild'; she dwelt 'among the untrodden ways'; she is described as 'wild' and like the fawn that 'up the mountain springs' in *Three Years she Grew*.

76. W. Wordsworth, *The Prelude*, Book XIII, 251-3.

77. Keble stated in one of his *Occasional Reviews* (quoted in B.W. Martin, *John Keble*, p. 86) that 'mountainous districts are more favourable to the poetical temper than unvaried plains, the habits of the country than those of the town. . . .'

78. *Kilvert's Diary*, vol. I, p. 87. The *OED* defines 'spirituelle' as 'marked by refinement, grace or delicacy, used chiefly of women'.

79. *Kilvert's Diary*, vol. III, p. 272. Abiasula Price was another member of this group. Once Kilvert was looking for her and described her thus: 'the cottage was silent and deserted, the dark beautiful face, the wild black hair and beautiful wild eyes of the mountain child were nowhere to be seen' (vol. II, pp. 57-8). Later (p. 61), he said she was 'a little gipsy'.

80. *Kilvert's Diary*, NLW edition, June-July 1870, p. 58.

81. *Kilvert's Diary*, vol. I, p. 168.

82. See start of this chapter.

83. Plotz, *op. cit.*, p. 26.

84. James R. Kincaid, *Child Loving. The Erotic Child and Victorian Culture*, New York, Routledge, 1992, p. 241.

85. Leach, *op. cit.*, p. 63.

86. Kincaid, *op. cit.*, p. 198. He added that in Victorian England 'the alliance of purity and sexuality ruled its religion, its poetry, its commerce; it reached its zenith in the home, and in the centre of the domestic sphere, the child'.

87. Kincaid commented on this and similar *Diary* episodes: 'How much awareness Kilvert allowed himself of the nature of interests like these we cannot know, just as we cannot be sure what exactly his consciousness of such matters really could amount to' (*op. cit.*, p. 242).

88. 'Millais's growing popularity in the 1860s was fuelled by simple, charming studies of children' (Laurel Bradley, 'Millais, our Popular Painter', in *John Everett Millais. Beyond the pre-Raphaelite Brotherhood*, New Haven, Yale University Press, 2001, p. 187). His most famous child portrait was *Bubbles*, showing his grandson Willie holding a bowl of soap suds and a pipe; it became an advertisement for Pears's soap. Others were *My First Sermon*, *New Laid Eggs*, *Puss in Boots*, *Pomona*, *Little Miss Muffet* and *Cherry Ripe*.

89. Mary Bennett, *Millais. An Exhibition Organised by the Walker Art Gallery Liverpool and the Royal Academy of Arts London, January-April 1967* (London, Royal Academy of Arts) introduction, p. 10.

90. *Kilvert's Diary*, vol. III, p. 44. Georgie Gale was the daughter of one of Kilvert's Langley Burrell parishioners.

91. Plotz, *op. cit.*, p. 39. The process of 'sequestering' the child was, Plotz

believed, a reflection of the political and social context of the period — the idealised child filled the gap left by the increasing loss of religious faith and by 'the waning of historical utopianism that followed both the French Revolution and the failed revolutions of 1848'. The Child was for Victorians 'a non-threatening means of commitment to social hope'. Adults, by identifying themselves with 'true timeless children', could insulate themselves from despair and the actual exploitation of children. Plotz noted that the idealisation of the Child coincided with the greatest exploitation of the child in factories and mines and with the emergence of children's literature. It is also connected with the emergence of the family, the emphasis on family relations and affections.

92. *Ibid.*, p. 22. Plotz saw the incident in which Kilvert took a young girl under his wing at the concert in Llowes school hall (see chapter four) as a characteristic Wordsworthian 'story' or 'plot' in which an adult 'discovers, intervenes, and rescues' a child, the rescuing having the dual aspect of comforting both the child and himself and assimilating the child's 'power' into himself as a source of moral/spiritual authority (*ibid.*, p. 44). We can see how Plotz's summing up of the event in terms of Kilvert carrying away a 'psychological love-token, an inner assurance of this delicate child's gratitude', fits in with patterns of Kilvert's emotional and moral world that have been examined in earlier chapters. Essentially what is happening is that the Llowes child enters into the circle of sympathies in which she and Kilvert both feel gratitude for what the other can offer. Collecting 'love-tokens', actual and symbolic, was for him a significant activity.

93. Her real name was Elizabeth Jones. Perhaps her mother had married in Pontypool and continued to live there. Mary Williams of Penllan farm was also in moral danger. Her mother's second marriage was to William Phillips, 14 years younger than herself. He was of dubious character. Kilvert found Mary extremely attractive and wrote a highly sensuous entry in which he imagined himself as the sun entering her bedroom in the morning and kissing her 'scarlet lips' and viewing her half-uncovered bosom, praying at the same time that 'the fatherless girl may ever be good, brave, pure and true' (vol. I, p. 173). He emphasised the wordless sympathy that existed between Mary and himself: 'People know instinctively whether they are liked and appreciated' (NLW edition, June-July 1870, p. 47). Another vulnerable child was Marianne Price, who lived in the dangerous, squalid part of Hay and was looked after by her grandmother. Though not a mountain child, she resembled Lucy Gray, with her 'slender delicate figure . . . bright sweet smile . . . and dark eyes. . . . She has a very sensitive affectionate nature and wants to be loved fondled and caressed' (*ibid.*, p. 85). Selina Evans, 'a fine bonny girl', was 9 in 1871 and lived, in danger Kilvert thought, with grandparents who were in their 80s and an unmarried 50-year-old son.

94. His certainty over the date shows the significance of the meeting for him.

95. *Kilvert's Diary*, vol. III, pp. 162-3. It was of considerable significance to Kilvert that, as he noted, Sarah, the child of solitude, was visited 'when she lay a-dying' by the Solitary of Llanbedr.

96. *Kilvert's Diary*, vol. III, pp. 125-6. Her 'wild' career had been 'stopped' by a severe back injury. Kilvert almost invariably used 'wild' in this sense in

relation to women, though occasionally about men.

97. *Ibid.*, vol. II, p. 426. My italics. Kilvert noted that three years before — to the day — he was tearing around her garden with her in a wheelbarrow; she was a child then, nearly a woman now. It seems he was reluctant to admit that she had grown up.

98. Howitt, *The Rural Life of England*, p. 333.

99. *Kilvert's Diary*, vol. I, pp. 100-3.

100. *Ibid.*, vol. I, p. 255.

101. *Ibid.*, vol. II, p. 206. He repeatedly praised naturalness in women: the Duke of Norfolk's two sisters were 'pleasant unaffected girls' (vol. II, p. 328); Mrs Adderley had a 'simple, unaffected . . . manner' (vol. III, p. 243); Amelia de Winton's manner was 'open, simple and natural' (NLW edition, June-July 1870, p. 89).

102. *Ibid.*, vol. III, p. 286. She was also 'perfectly unconscious of her own beauty' (*ibid.*, vol. III, p. 272). The earlier quotation regarding Florence, her sister and mother is from vol. III, p. 278.

103. *Ibid.*, vol. I, pp. 123-4.

104. Chadwick, *The Victorian Church*, Part I, p. 444. Chadwick's source was Mrs Trollope's anti-Evangelical novel *The Vicar of Wrexhill*.

105. *Kilvert's Diary*, vol. III, p. 142. What is more, he gave it religious overtones — her 'glorious hair spread shining like a halo'. Kilvert knew that St Paul had urged (I Corinthians 11.15) that woman's long hair was a 'glory' to her.

106. For Schiller, an important component of Nature was the unselfconscious, spontaneous mode of consciousness characteristic of children (Plotz, *op. cit.*, pp. 6-7). Christian perfection was defined by R.N. Flew (*The Idea of Perfection in Christian Theology*, London, Oxford University Press, 1934) as 'a freedom from anxiety and fettering self-consciousness' (quoted in R.E. Brantley, *'Wordsworth's "Natural Methodism"'*, p. 127).

107. She was also aristocratic in appearance yet was in a third-class carriage. Kilvert subsequently made enquiries about her identity but drew a blank (see *Kilvert's Diary*, vol. II, p. 347).

108. Uncle Francis's poem, 'Renunciation of Human Wisdom in order to live in childlike simplicity' ('Commonplace Book', vol. II), has a quotation from Fénelon as its epigraph. Uncle Francis also memorialised Fénelon in his *Pinacothecae Historicae Specimen*. Aunt Sophia frequently quoted Fénelon in her *Home Discipline* (e.g. p. xiv and p. 57).

109. Flew, *op. cit.*, p. 274.

110. *Kilvert's Diary*, vol. II, p. 431.

111. J.H. Davies, *Fénelon*, Boston, Twayne, 1979, p. 22 and p. 85.

112. Flew, *op. cit.*, p. 268 and p. 292.

113. The Authorised version is quoted here because it would have been familiar to Kilvert. In the Revised version, the passage reads: 'I know a Christian man . . . was caught up into paradise and heard words so secret that human lips may not repeat them'. Victor Furnish said that St Paul was referring to a heavenly journey but unlike other ancient accounts of such journeys had nothing to say about what he saw in Paradise (*II Corinthians*, vol. XXXIIa of the *Anchor Bible*, New York, Doubleday, 1984, pp. 544-5).

114. *Kilvert's Diary*, vol. II, pp. 345-6.

115. Leach, *op. cit.*, p. 63.

116. Alexander, *William Plomer*, p. 217.
117. *The Autobiography of William Plomer*, London, Jonathan Cape, 1975, p. 372.
118. *Ibid.*, p. 366.
119. Cf. 'Enough of Science and Art; / Close up those barren leaves' in Wordsworth's *The Tables Turned*. Plomer probably was also thinking of the disillusioned adult in the *Immortality Ode*, for whom years had brought 'the inevitable yoke' and 'custom . . . Heavy as frost'.
120. Plomer, *op. cit.*, p. 366.
121. Plomer showed an insight into the importance for Kilvert of the Wordsworthian notion of the *power* of singularity by drawing attention in *Angel Satyr* to Kilvert 'glowing' like 'a luminous rose', a reference to the 'glowing' Clyro Vicarage roses (see chapter five).
122. Grice, *Francis Kilvert and his World*, p. 218. It seems virtually certain that Kilvert's kissing and cuddling of girls, much of which went on with their parents' knowledge, was not considered unwholesome at the time, something which Grice underlined: 'the outside world seems to have found very little in his conduct to censure' (*ibid.*, p. 227). Other commentators made the same point. Massingham wrote (*The Southern Marches*, p. 77): 'Nor do the folk [i.e. Kilvert's parishioners] seem at all to have bridled at his caressing and appraising eye for their pretty daughters'. This was the judgement of the editor of the NLW edition of the June–July 1870 edition of the *Diary*: 'The same essential innocence surely pervades those passages about young girls that have been so cruelly misinterpreted' (p. xx).

Chapter 8: Superstition and Dreams

1. *Kilvert's Diary*, vol. I, p. 103.
2. R. Kilvert, *Memoirs*, p. 12. The girl's action vis à vis the 'spirit' of the door handle may have been prompted by her knowledge of his Evangelical upbringing, with its insistence on *watching* oneself and on God seeing all.
3. *Ibid.*, p. 72.
4. *Kilvert's Diary*, vol. II, pp. 398-9. It is possible that for Kilvert and his mother this dream symbolised not only the certainty of immortality but also sympathy with the dead.
5. Rack, *Reasonable Enthusiast*, p. 385. The quotes are from Wesley's letters. Rack went on: 'Wesley shared with his followers a strong propensity to believe in witches and supernatural happenings because he knew that God was capable of disturbing natural laws' (p. 387). 'What is significant is the strangely supernaturalist character of the evangelical mentality even among the educated leadership, including Wesley himself' (p. 172). Similarly, Nuttall asked whether there was a certain mentality, 'a psychologically recognisable type', that is particularly susceptible to religious experiences of an 'enthusiastic' (i.e. evangelical) kind. He believed there is a link between this kind of temperament and the poetic one in that both are highly sensitive to the most minute impressions (Geoffrey F. Nuttall, *Howell Harris, Evangelist, 1714-1773. The Last Enthusiast*, Cardiff, University of Wales Press, 1965, p. 50).
6. The opinion of Lois Lang-Syms, quoted in Grice, *Francis Kilvert and his World*, p. 130.
7. *Kilvert's Diary*, vol. II, pp. 149-150. The *Diary* contains several similar

passages. On 13 May 1874, he had planned an excursion to collect wild flowers with Georgie Gale (the child who resembled the subject of Millais's painting, *A Picture of Health*) and Kilvert had a sudden premonition that she was dead: 'I began to grow anxious . . . a shadow fell upon my mind'.

8. It has already been noted that he included Scott in the list of poets he discussed with his friend Lewis Williams (*Kilvert's Diary*, vol. I, p. 264), that he quoted from Scott's *Marmion* in his description of Bowood (vol. III, p. 106) and that on 21 March 1870 he was reading Lockhart's *Life of Scott*.

9. Wyndowe, 'Rambling Recollections', p. 119. She was given by her father Scott's *Tales of a Grandfather*, a book of Scottish history, for an early birthday but the book was so big and the print so small that she never read it through.

10. One Victorian, to whom the Waverley novels were read at the same period as they were read to the Kilvert children, wrote that 'children were turned loose into the fair domain of the Waverley novels, as into a garden where no poisonous plants were to be feared.' The Victorian was William Archer and his words are quoted in Cruse, *The Victorians and their Books*, p. 294. The novels (called 'Waverley novels' because the series began in 1814 with the first entitled *Waverley*) were read to him in the 1850s.

11. This conflicted with the picturesque view of landscape, which centred on an observer of natural scenery whose awareness of the aesthetic rules governing its appreciation would have been disturbed by inhabitants.

12. It is of some significance that Scott was, like Kilvert (at his best), a border writer. The history and culture of border territories are particularly rich, romantic, full of tensions and violence. As he recorded border stories, Scott was very much in the role of ethnographer, in which Dunham pictured Kilvert (see chapter six).

13. From Lockhart's biography of Scott, quoted in Carlyle, *Critical and Miscellaneous Essays*, vol. IV, London, Chapman and Hall, 1838, p. 46.

14. Quoted in Edgar Johnson, *Sir Walter Scott, the Great Unknown: vol. 1, 1771-1821*, London, Hamish Hamilton, 1970, p. 541.

15. Carlyle, *op. cit.*, p. 74. Lars Hartveit wrote of Scott's 'deep sympathy for the common people and their lot. His sympathy is linked with his awareness of [their] permanence' (*Dream Within A Dream. A Thematic Approach to Scott's Vision of Fictional Reality*, Oslo, Norwegian Research Council, 1974, p. 23).

16. *Works*, vol. V, T.C. Cook and A. Wedderburn (eds.), London, George Allen, 1904, p. 340. Ruskin found that the 'dreaming love of natural beauty' was most intense in 'modern times' (he meant from the seventeenth century onwards) in 'persons not of the first order of intellect, but of brilliant imagination, quick sympathy, and undefined religious principle, suffering also under strong and ill-governed passions'. He placed Scott, Wordsworth and Tennyson in this group. One would feel inclined to include Kilvert in it too. He added that feelings of delight in natural objects, though not indicative of 'the highest mental powers', nevertheless were a mark of mind, 'endowed with sensibilities of great preciousness to humanity'. Love of Nature, 'because it is itself a passion, [is] likely to be characteristic of passionate men' ('The Moral of Landscape', *Works*, vol. V, pp. 359-361 and p. 372).

17. *Ibid.*, p. 354. Kilvert extended his understanding of Scottish landscape

and people by reading the 'autobiography' of Flora Macdonald and the novels of George Macdonald.

18. Introduction to *The Antiquary*, which is set, Scott said, 'in the last ten years of the eighteenth century' (i.e. the period of the *Lyrical Ballads*). Wordsworth was also an admirer of traditional ballads, as has been noted. Daniel Cottom traced the democratic emphasis of Wordsworth's *Preface* to earlier eighteenth-century writing, which 'reflected the values of middle-class sentimentality' and represented the lower classes 'with — to use the all-important word of the new values — sympathy'. 'Nature in its unrestrained wildness becomes the model for beauty of all sorts' and the idea takes root that even uneducated people can appreciate it. 'More emphasis is laid upon the fineness of feeling than upon the fineness of one's birth or rank' (*The Civilised Imagination. A study of Ann Radcliffe, Jane Austen, and Sir Walter Scott*, Cambridge, Cambridge University Press, 1985, pp. 27-8). Kilvert's early immersion in Scott's fiction can therefore be seen as further reinforcement of the morality of 'sympathy' inculcated by his uncle Francis.

19. And presumably the examples of uncle Francis and of William Barnes.

20. Martin Price noted that in the eighteenth century there grew up an interest in and sympathy for the primitive mind and its capacity for imaginative life. In this interest, merged the Gothic novel and the concern with folklore, legends, ballads and antiquarianism ('The Dark and Implacable Genius of Superstition', in *Augustan Worlds*, Hilson, Jones and Watson (eds.), p. 242).

21. 'Druid' is from Greek 'drus' an oak tree and 'wid' the Indo-European word for 'know'. Celts saw trees as a hierarchy with the oak as its head (Alistair Moffat, *The Sea Kingdoms*, pp. 97-8).

22. *Kilvert's Diary*, vol. III, pp. 263-4. Britton (*The Beauties of England and Wales*, vol. XVII, p. 38) noted that the Druids performed their ceremonies in oak groves and regarded the oak as sacred. Cf. Kilvert writing of the 'blasted oak' near Llowes, 'the uncanny oak, the haunted oak which bears such a bad repute. . . .' (*Kilvert's Diary*, vol. II, p. 128). It was suggested in Toman's *Kilvert: The Homeless Heart* (p. 69) that Kilvert saw in the frightening features of the Moccas oaks the emergent working class that he feared; it seems more accurate to see them as representations of the pagan past, of which the militant working class was a reminder.

23. His ambivalent stance towards the remote past has been seen in chapter three in relation to Tintagel Castle —'so ancient, simple and primitive' — yet he knew it had seen battles and brutality. He also identified the indigenous peoples of Britain's colonies with a savagery that belonged to the primitive past, as in his description of the cruelties and mutilations inflicted by Indians on British women and children (*Kilvert's Diary*, vol. II, pp. 310-11).

24. Scott, *The Antiquary*, vol. II, Edinburgh, A. and C. Black, p. 48. What is being defined here is the appeal of the Gothic (horror) novel.

25. *Kilvert's Diary*, vol. I, p. 313.

26. Cottom, *op. cit.*, p 148.

27. *Kilvert's Diary*, vol. III, p. 274.

28. *Ibid.*, vol. I, p. 301. Kilvert was disgusted that the Bible was used in this way, that pain was caused to an animal, and that an innocent person

could be accused as a result of it.

29. Halliday was told of a peasant boy called Saxon, who was a 'Prophet' capable of predicting events, one of which was his own death by 'famine'. Kilvert noted that this 'came to pass' when a gentleman, not wishing the peasant boy to speak to his servants, locked him in a room, taking the key with him. He returned some days later to find the boy had died of hunger (*Kilvert's Diary*, vol. III, pp. 154-5).

30. *Ibid.*, vol. II, pp. 352-3.

31. *Ibid.*, vol. I, p. 247. My italics.

32. *Ibid.*, vol. I, p. 299. He appears to take it for granted that fairies *did* teach men the Welsh country dance, while his 'why?' question implies 'why did the dance have that name if it wasn't for that reason?' Howitt devoted a chapter of his *Rural Life of England* to 'Fairy Superstitions', in which he acknowledged that fairies used to haunt the countryside, though they departed some time ago. His book shows a relish for rural superstition (e.g. pp. 157-8).

33. *Kilvert's Diary*, vol. I, p. 281.

34. *Ibid.*, vol. II, p. 264. Cf. vol. III, p. 52 where Kilvert was involved in the conflict with Squire Ashe over music in Langley Burrell Church and, while reading a passage in Ecclesiastes, 'a word in season came to me like a message in the fourth verse . . . [it] came like a bit of good advice from the Wise Man. . . .'

35. *Ibid.*, vol. II, p. 263. He went to a farmhouse near Bredwardine to see a Holy Thorn in bloom and was given a piece of it, which he brought home 'as a curiosity' (vol. III, p. 355). In another entry, Priscilla Price told him about the Holy Thorn and mentioned the superstition that oxen wept on Christmas Eve (vol. III, p. 354).

36. *Ibid.*, vol. II, p. 432.

37. *Ibid.*, vol. III, p. 226. The description by Britton (*op. cit.*, vol. XV, pp. 74 and 91) has the same tone and some of the same emphases as Kilvert's: 'The origin of this ancient city is unknown. . . . It was once proud, populous and flourishing . . . but now it displays nothing of human art, but ditches and banks . . . partly overgrown with wild brushwood. . . . The present appearance of Old Sarum is wild, dreary, and desolate'.

38. *Kilvert's Diary*, vol. I, p. 55.

39. *Ibid.*, vol. II, pp. 129-30.

40. *Ibid.*, vol. I, pp. 71-2.

41. There is a suggestion that he associated Cross Ffordd stone with superstitious rites which he preferred not to contemplate in the entry in which he noted 'as I passed Cross Ffordd the frogs were croaking snoring and bubbling in the pool under the full moon' (*ibid.*, vol. I, p. 58).

42. *Ibid.*, vol. II, p. 433.

43. 'The essential task of ghosts was to ensure reverence for the dead. . . .' (Keith Thomas, *Religion and the Decline of Magic*, London, Penguin Books, 1971, p. 719). It is interesting that Kilvert pictured himself as a spirit revisiting the Hardenhuish birthplace and the Oxford college he loved.

44. The difference is made clear later in the entry when he met Mr Pinniger, who explained to him that the Roman road from Calne to Marlborough made a detour around Silbury Hill, thus proving that the Hill was older.

45. It was probably influenced by his reading of Britton, who made much

of the fact that all such structures were the ancient Britons' way of commemorating the dead. Standing stones may, he said, 'have been regarded with religious reverence by the ancient Britons'. He added that 'the greater number of barrows in Wiltshire are raised over the remains of the early Celtic inhabitants of the island'. He drew attention particularly to Silbury Hill and connected such huge 'funeral heaps' to the more modest graves of more recent times: 'It is also evident . . . that the custom of raising barrows over the deceased survived the introduction of Christianity'. And, in an emphasis redolent of Gray's *Elegy*, said that 'The small earthly mound still heaped over the remains of those who had had trodden a humble path in life, is evidently a diminutive representation of the ancient barrow' (Britton, *op. cit.*, 'Introduction', pp. 82-3, 86-8).

46. Anthony Aveni, *The Book of the Year. A Brief History of our Seasonal Holidays*, Oxford, Oxford University Press, 2003, p. 71.

47. Cf. Massingham (*The Southern Marches*, pp. 73-4): 'It is clear that Kilvert himself had a strong touch of the pagan in his spiritual constitution, one too that notably encouraged his strong aesthetic consciousness'. This latter quality manifested itself, Massingham said, in Kilvert's 'passionate love . . . of landscapes'. Massingham added: 'But this pagan flavour by no means compromised and may even be said to have enriched his Christian faith and zeal as a parish priest'.

48. Anonymous, *Folklore, Myths and Legends of Britain*, London, Readers Digest Association, 1977, p. 22.

49. Aveni, *op. cit.*, p. 102. Kilvert also marked the Quarter Days — 1 May, 1 August, 1 November, 1 February — of the old Celtic calendar. He was also punctilious about recording important dates in the Church Calendar, as for example 'Advent Sunday' on 3 December 1871 and 'Mid-Lent' on 10 March 1872. The dates such as Michaelmas, Childermas, etc. are of course also in the Church Calendar. He regularly recorded saints' days and Mothering Sunday, Brothering Monday, Sistering Tuesday, Holy Thursday, Lady Day, as well as Maundy Thursday and the Easter festival.

50. Overlaid with the Christian feast of St Michael.

51. The Celtic calendar began on this date. The Christian Church counteracted its supernatural associations by instituting the feast of All Saints on this date.

52. Christ's birth is celebrated on 25 December though the real date is unknown. The licentious Roman festival of Saturnalia ended on 25 December. In the Christian calendar 28 December is Holy Innocents day.

53. It was also a Roman festival. The Church observed the date as the Feast of the Purification of the Virgin Mary.

54. 'Monat' is Anglo-Saxon for month. Kilvert used other Anglo-Saxon words to stress the agricultural significance of dates, e.g. Trimilki (1 May) — the month when, with the availability of spring pasture, cows could be milked three times a day; Sproutkele (1 February), which presumably refers to spring growth (Anglo-Saxon 'sprout' means a green shoot).

55. He linked wild Nature to poetic creativity. On 28 December 1871, he wrote that there was 'the wind, wild, wild, a tempest of wind', and followed it with a passage about poetic inspiration: 'Today my mind

has been full of that divinely gifted marvellous man Robert Burns. There abode the divine spark. . . .' Abrams (*The Correspondent Breeze*, p. 26) noted the reiteration of 'wind' in Wordsworth's poetry and in Romantic poetry in general, as 'a property of landscape' and a source of 'visionary power'.

56. *Kilvert's Diary*, vol. I, pp. 67-9. He appears to have read or heard about the Mill, referring to it as 'famous' and 'old'. He described it as 'the picturesque old mill' and as 'the cosy old picturesque ivy-grown mill'.

57. Part of Kilvert's approval derived from the fact that he was 'having a romp with a little girl'.

58. Kilvert attributes this information to Hannah Whitney, who used to live near there.

59. *Folklore, Myths and Legends of Britain*, p. 30. James Rattie underlined what water meant to the pagan mind: 'Water is "other". Its moods are strange and various. By turns it is quiet, and violent; it can refresh or it can kill. It emerges in a miraculous way from the earth . . . from below, from darkness, from the place where the dead . . . are buried. . . .' (*The Living Stream. Holy wells in historical context*, Woodbridge, Boydell Press, 1995, p. 10). '[Celtic] reverence for springs was widespread' (Barry Cunliffe, *The Ancient Celts*, Oxford, OUP, 1997, p. 199). Kilvert was brought up knowing that the great healing spring of Bath – called by the Romans 'Aquae Sulis' – commemorates Sulis, the Celtic goddess of the spring (Miranda Green, *The Gods of the Celts*, Stroud, Sutton Publishing, 2004, p. 144).

60. *Kilvert's Diary*, vol. I, p. 247.

61. The two quotations are from Violet Alford, *Introduction to English Folklore*, London, G. Bell and Sons, 1952, pp. 36-7. She wrote 'The Christian Easter may have purposely been celebrated in the spring to take the place of a pagan festival' (pp. 36-7). 'Eostre' is an Anglo-Saxon word. Spring and summer were the most popular times for visits to wells when the waters were believed to be most potent. Many well rituals were associated with Easter and are probably of Christian origin (Francis Jones, *The Holy Wells of Wales*, Cardiff, University of Wales Press, 1954, p. 89).

62. *Kilvert's Diary*, vol. III, p. 168. The sun on this pool had importance for him. In his tribute to the beloved 'mountain child', Sarah Bryan (see last chapter), he wrote of meeting her again 'by the shore of the crystal sea which shall shine brighter even than Llanbychllyn Pool' (vol. III, p. 162).

63. *Ibid.*, vol. I, p. 228.

64. Roy Palmer, *The Folklore of Radnorshire*, Almeley, Logaston Press, 2001, p. 2.

65. *Kilvert's Diary*, vol. I, p. 383.

66. *Ibid.*, vol. II, p. 126. Old Mrs Jenkins of Bredwardine, a woman '*full of strange stories of the countryside*' and possessed of second sight, told Kilvert she 'predicted the coming of the great rainstorm and waterspout which fell on the Epynt hills in the summer of 1845. . . .' (vol. III, p. 343, my italics).

67. His poem *Clyro Water* exults in the 'roaring of the brook / . . . as it thundered / [bringing] a message from the hill / Of torrent rain and tempest still'. He also said he loved to hear its voice whatever mood it was in.

68. F. Jones, *op. cit.*, p. 12.

69. *Kilvert's Diary*, vol. I, p. 174. There were also St Mary's Wells in Radnorshire at Rhayader and Pilleth, according to Palmer. The Penllan one was known for 'help with eye problems such as styes' (*op. cit.*, pp. 12 and 14). 97 wells in Wales were exclusively healing wells and 7 of them were in Radnorshire (F. Jones, *op. cit.*, p. 97). Kilvert was drawn to the idea of wells' healing powers. Cf. the entry for 4 June 1870 in which he went into detail about the properties of the Builth waters.

70. *Kilvert's Diary*, vol. III, p. 37.

71. *Ibid.*, vol. II, p. 358. The naturalness of so doing is emphasised in the entry in which he described a pubescent girl naked on the beach: 'She seemed a Venus . . . fresh risen from the waves' (*ibid.*, vol. III, p. 208). His attitude is similar to that of Kingsley, who described himself as 'the most sensuous (not sensual) of men'. In one letter to his wife, he wrote: 'Matter is holy, awful glorious matter. . . . Our animal enjoyments must be religious ceremonies' (Susan Chitto, *The Beast and the Monk. A life of Charles Kingsley*, London, Hodder and Stoughton, 1974, p. 80).

72. W. Stark, *The Sociology of Religion*, vol. II, p. 277.

73. William C. Braithwaite, *The Beginnings of Quakerism*, London, Macmillan, 1912, p. 149.

74. F. Jones (*op. cit.* pp. 124-5) noted that there are early references to fairies and beautiful women appearing at wells, which is a reminder of the nature-sprites Kilvert encountered at Mouse Castle.

75. *Kilvert's Diary*, vol. II, p. 149. 'Mawn' is the Welsh word for peat.

76. *Radnorshire Legends and Superstitions*, Radnorshire Transactions, vol. XXIV (1954). Mrs Essex Hope was Kilvert's niece, daughter of his sister Thersie. Plomer obtained the original Kilvert diaries from Mrs Essex Hope's brother, Perceval Smith.

77. *Ibid.*, p. 4.

78. *Ibid.*, quoted on p. 5. In his manuscript, Kilvert wrote about beliefs in fairies and witches, the power of fire, Holy Thorns, Halloween, the premonition of death, and the terrifying waterfall of Craig Pwll Du.

79. On some occasions, he registered its association with water and baptism, as on 24 June 1874 — 'my little godchild Sybil Francis Awdry was christened'. He also showed awareness of the day's water associations by observing: 'Blessed, blessed rain fell all evening upon the parched and thirsty ground'. Aveni (*op. cit.*, pp. 102-3) noted that midsummer was a festival of water as well as of fire and that the Church overlaid it with the feast of St John the Baptist. Cf. Alford (*op. cit.*, p. 4): 'the Church took advantage of the fertilising water magic of pagan ritual by merging it with the figure of St John the Baptist. . . .'

80. On Sunday 18 April 1875, he wrote 'A beautiful peaceful cloudless Sunday'; on Easter Sunday, 16 April 1876, he stated 'Thank God for a bright beautiful happy Easter Day'. He relished cloudless days in autumn too, for example 20 September 1870: 'The sky a cloudless deep wonderful blue'.

81. The *Diary* is full of such descriptions. He admired too the painting of a sunset in Danby's *Calypso* (vol. II, p. 107) and sought to capture the effect of sunlight on 4 December 1871 (vol. II, p. 92). He noted his own joy at sunshine in May and that Robert Burns 'had a peculiar love for such a day as this — the first fine Sunday in May' (vol. I, p. 329). No doubt Kilvert's love of the sun was influenced especially by Wordsworth who,

referring to his boyhood, wrote: 'already I began / To love the sun. . . .' (see *The Prelude*, Book II, 177-188 and 191-4).

82. Cf. the *Diary* entry on 5 November 1871: 'Thank God for this beautiful bright morning, this brilliant frost *in this dark time of the year*' (my italics).

83. His awareness of what the summer solstice meant is evident in his comment: 'The strong light glow in the North showed that the Midsummer sun was only just travelling along below the horizon, ready to show again in five hours'. He also knew the superstition about the appearance of supernatural beings on Midsummer Night because he and his friend told ghost stories all the way home.

84. Aveni, *op. cit.*, p. 100.

85. Morres had graduated from Kilvert's college, Wadham, the year he went there. He was vicar of Britford, near Salisbury.

86. Howitt, *The Rural Life of England*, p 606.

87. Kilvert regularly used 'Acre of God' in relation to churchyards.

88. Kilvert probably knew Mrs Hemans's poem, *Superstition and Revelation*, which traces the shift from paganism to Christianity. She too showed sympathy with pagans, acknowledging that all human beings 'have need to bid our hopes repose / On some protecting influence'. She also could see that in pagan times 'wild Nature' was 'clothed with a deeper power' because the hold of superstition was stronger, and 'Art had not tamed the mighty scenes which met / Their searching eyes'. Accordingly, they 'shaped unearthly presences, in dreams . . .' (i.e. made natural forms into spirits). Like Kilvert, Mrs Hemans was acutely sensitive to the moods of the seasons (see 'Memoir of Mrs Hemans', in *Works*, p. 66). She was no doubt influenced in her positive view of paganism by Wordsworth, who had stressed in *The Excursion* (which Kilvert knew well) that the early Britons did not worship idols but were aware of 'spiritual presences' that 'filled their hearts / With joy, and gratitude, and fear, and love' (Book IV, 920, 927, 929-32).

89. The stories were told to him by old Hannah Whitney. In one a man and his horse 'fell over the Blue Rocks of Blaen Cwm on a dark night and both were killed'. Hannah had just explained that the Blue Rocks were the place where fairies were last seen. The other story was particularly haunting to Kilvert for it told of a man drowned one night in a mawn pool, the sides of which were marked by the man's fingers as he scrabbled to get out (vol. II, pp. 130-1). The Rhos Goch mawn pools had claimed another victim.

90. *Oxford Companion to Christian Thought*, p. 574.

91. Ford K. Brown, *Fathers of the Victorians*, p. 68.

92. Cecil, *The Stricken Deer*, p. 81.

93. *The Thought of the Evangelical Leaders, Notes of the Discussions of the Eclectic Society*, London, 1798-1814 (1856), J.H. Pratt (ed.), Edinburgh, Banner of Truth Trust, 1978, p. 77.

94. Kilvert's poem *The Pilgrimage*.

95. *Oxford Companion to Christian Thought*, p. 182.

96. Pratt (ed.), *op. cit.*, pp. 80-2. Dreams were treated in the Bible as revelations from God (David P. Melbourne, Dr Keith Hearne, *The Dream Oracle*, London, Quantum, 2000, p. 25). Cf. Howitt, who endorsed the idea that 'there is an immediate and direct revelation of God to the souls of men, more evident . . . than the ordinary operations of nature.' He argued that

'to destroy the faith in the sensible intercourse of spirit with spirit', as the Church of England did, was a crime. Spiritual communication was, he said, a manifestation of the Holy Spirit, of God's power (*The History of the Supernatural*, London, Longman Green, 1863, vol. I, pp. 9-12, 86-7).

97. Jennifer Ford, *Coleridge on Dreaming. Romanticism, Dreams and the Medical Imagination*, Cambridge, Cambridge University Press, 1998, p. 3. She noted that Southey, Shelley, Leigh Hunt, Hazlitt, Crabbe and Keats either kept journals of dreams or wrote about them.

98. See chapter ten.

99. *Kilvert's Diary*, vol. II, p. 385. He was perhaps only half awake as he sat one burning hot summer's day under a tree and experienced a struggle between right and wrong. Immediately after, he saw (or thought he did) 'an angel in an azure robe ... but it was only the blue sky' (*ibid.*, vol. II, p. 356). However, he believed he really did see an angel (or heard it) on 28 April 1870: 'I heard the great sudden flap of an unseen wing. Angels were going about the hill in the evening light'. He added: 'What sights there are to be seen about these hills, especially by those who walk alone!' (NLW edition, April-June 1870). His conscious awareness of poetic images of landscape is evident in the entry dealing with 'the beautiful Cwm of Llandewi', where he saw 'a deep-wooded gorge, romantic and picturesque [seen] from above as fairy land and *leaving room for play of the imagination*' (*Kilvert's Diary*, vol. I, p. 59, my italics). This is very much in the Romantic tradition of writing and has obvious echoes of Coleridge's *Kubla Khan*.

100. An interest manifested in his *The Rime of the Ancient Mariner, Kubla Khan* and *Christabel*.

101. *Kilvert's Diary*, vol. III, p. 227.

102. *Ibid.*, vol. I, p. 283.

103. For example, as when 'half asleep' on the library sofa he 'had a strange and uncomfortable attack in the head and seemed to be struggling for my life with a mysterious and dreadful Power. . . .'(*ibid.*, vol. III, pp. 433-4). The occasion when Kilvert's mother, in a dream, wrestled with death about Langley Burrell churchyard, 'especially by Lessiter's tomb', was a similar case. Superstitious fears centred on Lessiter's tomb (*ibid.*, vol. II, p. 352). Coleridge was concerned about dreams that had evil sources. Keats used a dream-like state to represent evil in *La Belle Dame Sans Merci*.

104. In the introduction to *Ivanhoe*, Scott stated 'The passions . . . are generally the same in all ranks and conditions, all countries and ages' (Edinburgh, printed for A. Constable, 1820).

105. Kilvert blurred them too by his unhistorical attitude towards history, generally shunning evidence in favour of a Scottsian romanticism.

106. It is extremely ironic that he showed an almost hysterical preoccupation with the real-life story of the Tichborne Claimant, the essence of which is the search for the lost heir to the Tichborne property in Hampshire and the establishment of true identity (see Toman's *Kilvert: The Homeless Heart*, pp. 298-311).

107. See the beginning of this chapter.

108. He referred, for example, to Hannah Whitney's past as 'the simple kindly *primitive* times' and to the '*primitive* ancient simple religion' of the British Church at Gwythian (*Kilvert's Diary*, vol. I, p. 246 and p. 204).

Chapter 9: Mountains and Mystery

1. *Kilvert's Diary*, vol. II, p. 246.
2. Moir, *The Discovery of Britain*, p. 129.
3. Schama, *Landscape and Memory*, p. 469.
4. K. Thomas, *Man and the Natural World*, pp. 258-60.
5. J. Brewer, *The Pleasures of the Imagination*, p. 118.
6. Through his friendship with Bishop Warburton of Gloucester, Hurd was invited to Prior Park and became a close friend of Ralph Allen, its owner. Hurd buried Allen at Claverton on 5 July 1764. Kilvert clearly knew all about these friendships which, for their learning and piety, were the adornment of Bath in its heyday, because he wrote of 'the vast parties where Pope, Allen and Warburton used to sit and talk' (*Kilvert's Diary*, vol. II, p. 407). Richard Kilvert's daughter, Maria, never forgave uncle Francis for writing Hurd's life, perhaps because she thought the task belonged to her father (*Kilvert's Diary*, vol. I, p. 266). Biography and its problems were part of the Kilvert family history from an early stage.
7. In his letter of 21 December 1757 to Mason, Hurd noted that Mason was researching the Welsh background to *Caractacus* from books on Druids sent to him by their mutual friend William Warburton (1698-1779), Bishop of Gloucester (*The Early Letters of Bishop Richard Hurd 1739-1762*, edited Sarah Brewer, Woodbridge, Boydell Press, 1995, letter 194). In letter 185 to Gray, 16 August 1757, Hurd complained that Mason neglected him because he had 'gone to pay a visit to his Druids' in Anglesey, where *Caractacus* is set. Warburton's interest in Welsh things is reflected in the fact that he possessed a copy of Arise Evans's *An Echo from Heaven*, a seventeenth-century work containing ancient prophecies (A.W. Evans, *Warburton and the Warburtonians. A Study in some Eighteenth Century Controversies*, Oxford, Oxford University Press, 1932, p. 190).
8. William Powell Jones, *Thomas Gray, Scholar*, Cambridge, Harvard University Press, 1937, p. 99.
9. *Ibid.*, pp. 90-6.
10. *Memoirs of the Life and Writings of the Right Reverend Richard Hurd*, p. vi. Francis stressed Hurd's 'gradual ascent . . . from an inferior to an exalted station' which afforded 'an interesting subject for contemplation'.
11. Hurd had expressed his grief in a letter of 13 September 1771 (*ibid.*, p. 110). Francis's tribute is on p. 184. He also indicated in his book that he had retained in his old age his eighteenth-century literary taste by stressing how Hurd valued 'finished elegance' and 'dexterous use of thoughts already struck out' instead of the current literary criteria of 'energy' and 'originality' (*ibid.*, p. 66). Cf. Roger Lonsdale's statement that the middle of the eighteenth century was 'an age dubious about the value of direct personal utterance' (*Thomas Gray and William Collins*, R. Lonsdale (ed.), Oxford, Oxford University Press, 1977, p. xiv).
12. He meant that he intended as far as possible to let Hurd speak for himself by citing many of his letters. It is the method Brooke used in his life of Frederick Robertson.
13. Though published in 1775, it was written in 1769.
14. W.G. Hoskins, *The Making of the English Landscape* (1955), London, Hodder and Stoughton, 1995, p. 18.
15. Gray, in a letter of 11 June 1755 to Mason, said he had sent a revised

version of the poem to Hurd (McCarthy, *Thomas Gray*, p. 186).

16. Schama, *op. cit.*, pp. 469-70. Kilvert was aware of the Williams-Winn family's importance in Welsh cultural history; he noted (vol. I, 361) that the current Sir Watkin kept no private harper, though his sister did.

17. *The Bard*, Thomas Gray.

18. There were also versions by Paul Sandby, Loutherbourg and Fuseli.

19. *Kilvert's Diary*, vol. I, p. 59. Collins fed the early Victorian taste for idealised rural scenery.

20. He linked another Radnorshire scene to Cuyp in this entry: 'In the meadow below Wern y Pentre the white sheep and lambs were standing and grazing upon the little hillocks in the evening sunshine, reminding me vividly of some of Cuyp's pictures' (*ibid.*, vol. II, p. 172). Visiting Dulwich Picture Gallery in June 1876, he referred to seeing 'Albert Cuyp's cows grouped on a knoll at sunset ... looking placidly over the wide level pastures of Holland' (*ibid.*, vol. III, p. 335). The country life pictures of Collins, Morland, and Cuyp were, according to Hálevy, in the same tradition as Turner and Constable, evoking 'a land of mist and cloudy skies, an atmosphere which possessed a life of its own.' Evangelicals warmed to 'this type of art of a supreme chastity and permeated by a vague mysticism' more than any other. (*A History of the English People in 1815*, London, Fisher Unwin, 1924, p 433).

21. W.G. Constable noted that the line between such paintings and imaginative landscapes is very thin (*Richard Wilson*, London, Routledge Kegan Paul, 1953, p. 43). 'The fashion for the Welsh view stemmed from ... Richard Wilson' (Prys Morgan, 'From a Death to a View: the Hunt for the Welsh Past in the Romantic Period', in *The Invention of Tradition*, Hobsbawm and Ranger (ed.), Cambridge, Cambridge University Press, 1983, p. 88).

22. Schama, *op. cit.*, p. 469.

23. Ann Sumner and Greg Smith, *Thomas Jones. An artist rediscovered*, New Haven, Yale University Press, 2003, p. 90.

24. The quoted phrase is from Jones's *Memoirs* and is cited in Sumner and Smith, *op. cit.*, p. 122.

25. William Stukeley (1687-1765) doctor and antiquary. He was a friend of Sir Isaac Newton and became a Fellow of the Royal Society in 1718. He was a founder member and first secretary of the Society of Antiquaries. 'His principal publishing achievement was two monographs on the ancient stone circles of Stonehenge and Avebury in Wiltshire: *Stonehenge: a temple restored to the British Druids* (1740) and *Avebury: a temple of the British Druids* (1743) ... it was the publications of Stukeley, and his Cornish correspondent William Borlase, which established the popular association of stone temples with druids in the public imagination' (*DNB*). Moffat (*The Sea Kingdoms*, p. 89) noted that Stonehenge was in fact erected 'at least 2,500 years before the first signs of Celtic culture appeared in Britain'.

26. Kilvert's account appears in vol. III, pp. 222-4 of the *Diary*; Gilpin's appears in his *Observations on the Western Parts of England*, London, T. Cadell, 1798, pp. 78-84. Britton, too, asserted that 'The Druids held it unlawful to adore the Gods within walls and under roofs. Their places of worship were invariably in the open air, and covered only by the canopy of the heavens' (*op. cit.*, 'Introduction', p. 28). He gave a sympathetic account of Druidical/Bardic religion, which Kilvert had no doubt absorbed. The foundation

of it, Britton said, was 'the principle of benevolence . . . a second general principle was the investigation of truth; and a third was the perfect equality of its members'. (Previous chapters have noted that these were also principles of Kilvert's ministry.) 'The Bards believed in one creator . . . of the universe, pervading all space' (*op. cit.*, vol. XVII, pp. 34 and 36). Furthermore, they 'taught the doctrine of the immortality of the soul', and that it transmigrated into other bodies. 'Under their influence, the Briton was induced to worship the sun, moon and stars' (*ibid.*, 'Introduction', p. 28). The Druids did go in for human sacrifices and had a belief in magic powers. For Kilvert, the most important notion regarding the Druids that he would find in Britton was William Owen's opinion (in his sketch of Bardism, prefixed to a translation of the work of Llywarc Hen) that 'the reason of the Britons having embraced Christianity with more openness than other nations was, the Bardic being less repugnant than any other pagan systems to the doctrines of the gospel', and that the Bards actually exercised the functions of the Christian priesthood (Britton, *op. cit.*, vol. XVII, p. 39). Britton doubted this because 'the principles of the two institutions are utterly incompatible'. Kilvert's romantic imagination, on the other hand, could well have warmed to this notion. Even Britton concluded that Druidical religion was 'captivating but perverse'. He also praised their knowledge of astronomy, natural philosophy, and mechanics (*op. cit.*, 'Introduction', pp. 29-31).

27. W. Wordsworth, *The Prelude*, Book XIII, 319-20 and 339-349. Cf. also Frederick Robertson: 'who has not . . . in a moment of deep enthusiasm, knelt down amidst the glories of Nature, . . . canopied only by the sky above him, and feeling that none were awake but the Creator and himself. . . .' This was the way, he said, that 'the ancient pagans . . . expressed their feelings of the deep sacredness of that life that there is in Nature' ('Lecture on Wordsworth', in *Lectures and Addresses on Literary and Social Topics*, London, Smith and Elder, 1858, pp. 222-3).

28. As chapter two has shown, uncle Francis was the centre of a network of tourist/antiquarians.

29. Moira Dearnley, *Distant Fields. Eighteenth Century Fictions of Wales*, Cardiff, University of Wales Press, 2001, p. xiv.

30. (London, Dent, 1906). It contains many emphases similar to ones in the *Diary*, but that is true of so many tours of Wales.

31. *Poetry and the Renaissance of Wonder*, New York, 1916, quoted in R.D. Havens, *The Mind of a Poet. A study of Wordsworth's thought*, Baltimore, the Johns Hopkins University Press, 1941, p. 487.

32. Moir, *op. cit.*, p. 131.

33. *Ibid.*, p. 132.

34. *A Walk through Wales in 1798*, Bath, T. Cruttwell, 1799, pp. 173-4 — his italics. Warner was of the strong opinion that the only way to see Wales was on foot; it was not accidental that he called his book *A Walk through Wales* and advised his reader in the 'Advertisement' to it that maps were provided for the 'Pedestrian'. Byng (*Tour of North Wales 1793*, vol. III of *The Torrington Diaries*, p. 248) ridiculed an English baronet he met in a Welsh inn who had come in his carriage 'in great pomp and parade' with valets in 'green and red and gold!' Borrow declared firmly: 'it is impossible to see much of Wales unless you walk' (*op. cit.*, p. 236). Kilvert also had this general advice from Wordsworth (*The Excursion*, Book IV,

508-518):

> Oh! What a joy it were, in vigorous health,
> To have a body . . .
> And to the elements surrender it.
> As if it were a spirit! — How divine . . .
> To roam at large among unpeopled glens
> And mountainous retirements, only trod
> By devious footsteps; regions consecrate
> To oldest time!

35. Byng, *A Tour of North Wales 1784*, vol. I of the *Torrington Diaries*, p. 141. Warner was impressed by the cleanliness of the Welsh, especially because of the link he saw between 'personal decency and ethical excellence' (*op. cit.*, p. 28).

36. *Kilvert's Diary*, vol. I, p. 109. The occasion was the opening of a new chapel.

37. Byng, *op. cit.*, p. 142.

38. Warner, *A Walk through Wales in August 1797*, Bath, T. Crutwell, 1798, p. 206.

39. Borrow, *op. cit.*, p. 151. The face of a young cottager 'looked the picture of kindness, I was now indeed in Wales among the real Welsh' (*op. cit.*, p. 417).

40. Warner, *A Walk through Wales in August 1797*, p. 28. Watts-Dunton wrote of his novel *Aylwin*: 'And as to the charm of the Welsh girls, no one who knows them as you and I do, can fail to be struck by it continually. Winifred Wynne I meant to be the typical Welsh girl as I have found her — affectionate, warm-hearted, self-sacrificing and brave' (quoted in introduction to Borrow's *Wild Wales*, p. xv).

41. *Kilvert's Diary*, vol. I, p. 99.

42. Warner, *op. cit.*, pp. 40-1.

43. *Ibid.*, p. 20.

44. See chapter four.

45. The first was on 3 November 1860, the others on 8 December and 26 January 1861. Kilvert had studied Homer and in January 1878 was reading *The Iliad* with Henry Bates, son of the Bredwardine schoolmaster.

46. In addition to the *Cornhill*, he read *Macmillan's Magazine* and the *Saturday Review*. That he read regularly this last-named periodical ('In the *Saturday Review* for last week . . .' he wrote on 16 November 1870) is proof that he was a serious reader. Keeping up with it alone was no small undertaking since its closely argued, highly intellectual articles amounted each week to 36,000 words! Bevington called it 'the most brilliantly written critical journal of the time' (Merle Mowbray Bevington, *The Saturday Review 1855-1868. Representative educated opinion in Victorian England*, New York, Columbia University Press, 1941, p. 25). Its tone was characterised by its critics as 'cynical, sceptical, hypercritical, malicious and destructive' (*ibid.*, p. 43). It was commonly known as the 'Saturday Reviler' and the 'Saturday Snarler'. Bearing this in mind, it is remarkable that Kilvert read it at all; that he did so is further confirmation that he valued intellectual debate. He sought out George Venables, one of its main contributors, for the same reason. The journal's basic quarrel with Victorian manners and morals is contained in a sentence from 'Nineteenth Century Sentiment', an article in its 2 November 1867 number: 'It may reasonably be doubted whether there

has ever been a more thoroughly sentimental time than the present'. (It
regularly attacked Dickens's novels for their sentimentality.) In contrast,
the *Saturday Review* was frankly utilitarian, empirical and relativistic
in its morality. There are signs that Kilvert could adopt the *Saturday
Review*'s opinion of some things, as for example his quite unsentimental
view of Father Lyne's experiment in monasticism at Capel y Ffin (12
miles from Clyro). Kilvert's accounts of it (vol. I, pp. 76-9 and 220-4)
show the influence of the article 'Ignatius in Extremis' (*Saturday Review*,
vol. XXI, 19 May 1866).

47. Nicholas Murray (*A Life of Matthew Arnold*, London, Sceptre, 1996,
pp. 233-5) noted that the central premise of his *New Poems* (1865) was
that Christianity, though 'vitally necessary, must adapt its message to
a changing world', and that Evangelical journals disliked the poems
because of their religious doubts and pantheism.

48. R. Samuel, *Theatres of Memory*, vol. II, London, Verso, 1998, p. 59. In
archaeology, it meant anything pre-Roman. In post-Darwinian science,
it stood for mankind in an aboriginal state. Antiquarians used it to mean
a style of decoration. It was much used to indicate the romantic poets of
Cornwall.

49. M. Arnold, *On the Study of Celtic Literature*, London, Smith and Elder,
1867, p. 343.

50. *Ibid.*, p. 296.

51. Kilvert was in the habit of reading both these papers and probably
followed the exchange.

52. Arnold, *op. cit.*, p. 291. Arnold was recalling a summer he spent at
Llandudno when he looked across the river Dee to Liverpool.

53. His meeting with her is described thus: '. . .there was an attractive power
about this poor Irish girl that fascinated me strangely. I felt irresistibly
drawn to her. The singular beauty of her eyes, a beauty of deep sadness,
a wistful sorrowful imploring look, her swift rich humour, her sudden
gravity and sadnesses, her brilliant laughter, a certain intensity and
power and richness of life and the extraordinary sweetness, softness
and beauty of her voice in singing and talking gave her a power over me
which I could not understand nor describe, but the power of a stronger
over a weaker will and nature.' Such are the similarities between Kilvert's
response to the girl and *The Solitary Reaper* that it is hard to believe that
he didn't have some memory of Wordsworth's poem in his head when
he wrote up the entry concerning Irish Mary (*Diary*, vol. II, 208-11). She
has obvious affinities with both Lucy Gray and the Mouse Castle sprites.
Ursula Hamilton, the heroine much admired by Kilvert (he called her
'Dear Ursula') of Mrs Sartoris's novel, *A Week in a French Country House*,
is presented throughout the story as spontaneous, impulsive and highly
changeable.

54. He wrote, for example, of the Clyro hills: 'Oh these kindly hospitable
houses about these hospitable hills' (*Kilvert's Diary*, vol. I, p. 257). He
was alluding to the nexus of qualities covered by 'demonstrative' in the
following entries: 'Mrs Meredith . . . with [her] hearty cordial manner
and plenty to say for herself' (*ibid.*, vol. II, pp. 80-1); 'benevolent-looking'
older women going to Rhayader market (*ibid.*, vol. I, p. 104); the 'good-
humoured . . . courteous . . . lively animated' Builth market folk (*ibid.*,
vol. III, p. 167). The earlier quotations from Arnold's *Celtic Literature* are

from pp. 343-7 and p. 374.

55. The illustrations are from the Three Romances of *The Mabinogion*, the stories of which are 'among the finest flowerings of the Celtic genius', which create a 'fantastic and primitive world where birds and beasts are as important as men, a world of hunting, fighting, shape-shifting and magic' (introduction to *The Mabinogion*, Gwyn Jones and Thomas Jones (eds.), London, Dent, 1975, pp. ix and xxi).

56. Arnold, *op. cit.*, pp. 374-5. The 'mysterious life' of Nature that he had in mind is found in the semi-supernatural worlds of Coleridge's *The Rime of the Ancient Mariner, Christabel* and *Kubla Khan*, of Keats's 'faery lands forlorn', and the 'huge and mighty forms that do not live like living men' and 'souls of lonely places' of Wordsworth's *Prelude*.

57. Samuel, *op. cit.*, p. 58.

58. Cf. Britton (*op. cit.*, vol. XVIII, p. 908): '[Aberedw] is one of the most enchanting spots in the principality. Nothing can exceed in grandeur and picturesque beauty the scenery by which it is surrounded in every direction.'

59. Arnold, *op. cit.*, p. 370. He also referred to Celticism's 'love of emotion, sentiment, the inexpressible' (p. 355).

60. Blythe, *Divine Landscapes*, p. 41.

61. W. Wordsworth, *Guide to the Lakes*, pp. 78-81. The basis of his objection to white was that it is 'scarcely ever found in Nature'. Gilpin 'notices this', he added. Wordsworth's book was first published in 1810 as the introduction to a large folio volume entitled *Select Views of Cumberland, Westmoreland and Lancashire*, a book of drawings by Rev Joseph Wilkinson. The fifth and final edition of Wordsworth's essay (1835) was called *A Guide through the District of the Lakes in the North of England, with a Description of the Scenery, for the use of Tourists and Residents*. A re-issue of it in 1842 included three letters on the geology of the district by the Professor Sedgwick who was known to Kilvert's uncle Francis.

62. *Kilvert's Diary*, vol. II, p. 64.

63. *Ibid.*, vol. II, p. 65.

64. J. Brewer, *op. cit.*, p. 652. Even picturesque theorists like Gilpin saw this translation as a loss because authentic Nature was supposed to be about wildness, whereas to collect it in books of prints represented a taming of it. There was a loss too because 'the picturesque tourist was a spectator rather than a part of the natural world he observed. . . . When [he] looked at peasants on the Welsh hillside or at Highlanders . . . he did not expect or want them to look back' (*ibid.*, p. 654).

65. J. Brewer supported this last statement by citing instances from travel literature of the second half of the eighteenth century which showed this preference for a blend of pastoral and wild.

66. *Kilvert's Diary*, vol. II, p. 64.

67. *Ibid.*, vol. II, p. 71.

68. *Ibid.*, vol. III, p. 288.

69. *Ibid.*, vol. III, p. 292.

70. *Ibid.*, vol. II, p. 58. His emphasis on the 'solitary' tree is notable.

71. *Ibid.*, vol. I, p. 80. In the remainder of this entry, he can be seen picture-making in the picturesque manner, aware of the 'rule' that said that particular landscapes should be viewed in appropriate weathers. On this occasion, he viewed the scene around Llanthony in sunshine. 'How

different from the first day that I pilgrimaged [it was another place, like St David's, that he approached with reverence] down the Vale of Ewyas under a gloomy sky, the heavy mist wreathing along the hillsides cowling the mountain tops, till as dusk came on the dreary melancholy deserted track looked dark and savage as the Valley of Desolation and the Abbey seemed in mourning. But it is well to have seen it all under different circumstances'. Another passage where he revelled in the blue appearance of hills is vol. I, p. 231: 'The sky a cloudless deep wonderful blue, and the mountains so light blue as to be almost white. The slight mist of an early autumn afternoon hanging over the gorgeous landscape.'

72. Robertson, *Lecture on Wordsworth*, p. 215.

73. Prys Morgan, 'From Long Knives to Blue Books', in *Welsh Society and Nationhood. Historical essays Presented to Glanmor Williams*, various eds., Cardiff, University of Wales Press, 1984, p. 202.

74. P. Morgan, *From a Death to a View*, p. 45.

75. Warner, *A Walk through Wales in August 1797*, p. 2. Cf. the quote from Borrow's *Wild Wales* that prefaces this chapter.

76. Matless, *Landscape and Englishness*, p. 14. His book contrasts an 'organic' sense of rural life with one that looks only to its commercial exploitation. The former typically includes the celebration of traditional crafts, folklore and regional dialects. In his discussion of 'organic' views of landscape, he noted the prevalence of an east-west split. This was the thesis of David Dimbleby's programme, *Mystical West* in his series *A Picture of Britain* (BBC1, 10 July 2005). The programme made much of Richard Wilson's paintings of Welsh landscapes and also included the observation that 'Hardy's novels are a lament for a landscape that was disappearing'. It is the thesis of this book (and of Toman's *Kilvert: The Homeless Heart*) that *Kilvert's Diary* is an elegy for *his* threatened landscapes.

77. It is also virtually certain that Kilvert's wide knowledge of Wordsworth included the poet's *Ecclesiastical Sonnets*, Part I, entitled *From the Introduction of Christianity into Britain to the Consummation of the Papal Dominion*. Sonnet II refers to the ability of prophets to foretell the means by which the 'sacred well / Of Christian Faith' provided 'this savage Island . . . / With its first bounty'; it also refers to the wanderings of St Paul 'through the *west*' of Britain (my italics). *Trepidation of the Druids* is the title of Sonnet III and it concerns the Archdruid's fear as he looks towards the 'mystic ring' of standing stones and contemplates the destruction of pagan belief by Christianity. Sonnet V links together such sacred places as 'Snowdon's wilds', 'the plain of Sarum' and 'bleak Iona', where men await confirmation that the tiny stream of early Christianity will grow to a flood. King Arthur is pictured in Sonnet X defending Christian faith against pagans, urged on by the harp music of bards. In Sonnet XXVI, Arthur is 'Lord of the harp and liberating spear'.

78. M. Richter, *Giraldus Cambrensis. The growth of the Welsh Nation*, Aberystwyth, National Library of Wales, 1976, p. 75. This tradition was reinforced in Geoffrey of Monmouth's *History of the Kings of Britain* (c. 1139).

79. J. Morris, *The Age of Arthur*, London, Weidenfeld and Nicholson, 1973, p. 119. As usual, Britton was keen to play down fanciful claims about Arthur, whose achievements were 'renowned in the works of minstrels and fabulous historians' (*op. cit.*, 'Introduction', p. 212). Kilvert took some trouble on 9 February 1878 to locate Arthur's Stone ('the great *mysterious*

stone', he called it, my italics), between his parish of Bredwardine and Dorstone. On another visit to it (26 June 1878), a local man told him that the marks of a man's knees and fingers imprinted on a rock lying near Arthur's Stone 'were believed to have been made by King Arthur when he heaved this stone up on his back and set it upon the pillars'. These were the kind of details Kilvert loved. Given the level of his interest in landscape relics of Arthur, it seems likely that he would have asked his Gower hosts to take him to see the Arthur's Stone on Cefn Bryn, 'the most impressive of the communal tombs built 4000 years ago by early agriculturalists in the Gower' (Morris, *op. cit.*, p. 99).

80. From the end of the Roman empire up to the Norman Conquest, the Welsh were defined as 'Brython' (Britons), a name which meant in Roman times the indigenous people of south and western Britain (Prys Morgan, 'Keeping the Legends Alive', in *Wales: the Imagined Nation. Studies in Cultural and National Identity*, Tony Curtis (ed.), Bridgend, Poetry of Wales Press, 1986, p. xx).

81. *Kilvert's Diary*, vol. III, p. 95.

82. Paul Hill, *The Age of Athelstan: Britain's Forgotten History*, Stroud, Tempus Publishing, 2004, p. 71. (Castle Combe is seven miles from Langley Burrell.) For 500 years the Scrope family owned Castle Combe. William Scrope erected the tower Kilvert called Scrope's Folly (it was variously known as Castle Tower and Alfred's Tower) in the early nineteenth century. It was demolished before the Second World War. A much larger tower, also a folly, dedicated to King Alfred is located on the Wilts-Somerset border near the landscape garden of Stourhead created by Henry Hoare II. He intended it to form part of picturesque views on his estate and to show off his learning and wealth. Erected in 1722, it is over 150 feet high and bears a statue of Alfred, who was alleged to have raised his standard before the battle of Ethandune on the hill where the folly stands. Below the statue is the inscription: 'The light of a Benighted Age, a Philosopher and a Christian, the Father of his People'. Kilvert would have read about Ethandune in Britton (*op. cit.*, vol. XXV, pp. 18-19).

83. Beram Saklatvala, *The Christian Island*, London, Dent, 1969, p. 113. William of Malmesbury repeated the story of the Battle of Badon. A.H. Williams (*An Introduction to the History of Wales*, vol. I, Cardiff, University of Wales Press, 1962, p. 148) underlined that the Danes were very prone to raid Wales in order to plunder its fertile country and monasteries and churches such as St David's.

84. Saklatvala, *op. cit.*, p. 118.

85. Richter, *op. cit.*, p. 34.

86. William Greswell, *Chapters on the Early History of Glastonbury Abbey*, Taunton, The Wessex Press, 1909, p. 97.

87. *Kilvert Society Journal*, Number 10, March 2003, pp. 13-14.

88. H.R. Loyn, 'The Conversion of the English to Christianity: some comments on the Celtic contribution', in *Welsh Society and Nationhood*, various eds., Cardiff, University of Wales Press, 1984, p. 5.

89. Britton, *op. cit.*, vol. XVII, p. 48.

90. Kilvert's *veneration* for the Bishops was entirely his own.

91. Henry Mayr-Harting, *The Coming of Christianity to Anglo-Saxon England*, London, Batsford, 1972, p. 34. Cf. A.H. Williams, *op. cit.*, p. 2: 'The

outstanding fact in Welsh history is that Wales is a mountainous country to the west of the English plain. . . . For this reason it has been exposed to wave after wave of invaders . . . and each movement [of invaders] spent itself in the mountains of Wales'.

92. During the Welsh revival, the Druids were rediscovered and this sparked a new interest in monuments such as Stonehenge, which they were supposed to have built. In the early eighteenth century the Druids came to represent 'the sage or intellectual defending his people's faith and honour' (Prys Morgan, *From a Death to a View*, pp. 62-3).

93. Blythe, *Divine Landscapes*, p. 47.

94. Athelstan became King of Wessex in *c*. AD 924 and was 'determined to exact a real submission from his vassals the princes of Wales', in the form of gold, silver and cattle. He also fixed the Wye as the boundary between them and his territory. The great Welsh prince, Hywel the Good, acquiesced to these demands, not out of servility but as an admirer of English civilisation (A.H. Williams, *op. cit.*, p. 162).

95. Mayr-Harting, *op. cit.*, p. 192. The main source of information on Aldhelm is the *Gesta Pontificium* of William of Malmesbury. Kilvert may have learned about Aldhelm from his uncle Francis, who would have respected William of Malmesbury because he was an antiquarian like himself.

96. A clergyman he knew 'opened his eyes wide' when Kilvert told him of his round trip and Mary Knight, one of Kilvert's parishioners, said: 'you must have had a good nerve to walk to Malmesbury and back. I always heard you were a noted walker in Wales. . . .' (vol. III, p. 95). Kilvert's pride in his walking prowess may have been a response to the challenge Warner issued in his *Literary Recollections* (vol. II, p. 135) where he noted that during his 1797 Welsh tour he averaged 26 miles a day over 18 days. Kilvert boasted of walking 25 in one day (vol. I, p. 81; see also vol. 2, p. 157).

97. Britton, *op. cit.*, vol. XV, p. 601.

98. Hill, *op. cit.*, caption to photo facing p. 160.

99. R.F. Treharne, *The Glastonbury Legends. Joseph of Arimathea, the Holy Grail and King Arthur*, London, Cresset Press, 1966, p. 24.

100. Actually in a mid thirteenth-century interpolation in his *De antiquitae Glastonensis ecclesiae*.

101. He had no doubt read in Wordsworth's Ecclesiastical Sonnet XXI, *Dissolution of the Monasteries*, how Glastonbury Abbey 'displaced, as story tells, / Arimathean Joseph's wattled cells'.

102. *Kilvert's Diary*, vol. II, p. 263. The portress showed him a piece of 'black holly staff' found in a stone coffin by one of the Glastonbury abbots.

103. According to Treharne (*op. cit.*, p. 120), this well was an eighteenth-century invention. Kilvert most probably knew Warner's *History of the Abbey of Glastonbury and the Town of Glastonbury* (Bath, Cruttwell, 1826), which records Warner's excavation of the well. 'Not surprisingly the well was at once dubbed "holy", and attracted much public attention at the time' (Philip Rhatz, *English Heritage Book of Glastonbury*, London, Batsford, 1993, p. 84).

104. The Isle was known as 'Insula Avalonia', either from Avalloc, a Celtic chief, or from 'aval', an apple. Cadbury Castle is 12 miles south-east of Glastonbury.

105. Giraldus Cambrensis wrote an account of the episode.

106. Felicity Riddy, 'Glastonbury, Joseph of Arimathea and the Grail in John Hardyng's Chronicle', in *The Archaeology and History of Glastonbury Abbey*, L. Abram and James P. Carley (eds.), Woodbridge, Boydell Press, 1991, p. 320.

107. Treharne, *op. cit.*, p. 35. Cf. Greswell (*op. cit.*, p. 59): 'Glastonbury . . . was from the earliest times the spiritual centre of Christian "Celtica".'

108. Rhatz, *op. cit.*, p. 42. The myths grew up mainly because of the efforts of the monks of Glastonbury to attract visitors to their Abbey. Cf. Treharne (*op. cit.*, p. 114): The Grail 'was pure myth and fantasy grafted on to the Arthurian legend before 1240'. William of Malmesbury differentiated the real Arthur from the legendary Celtic one. He rejected the Celtic legends about Arthur. 'The non-Celtic world ignored the [Celtic Arthurian stories] as uncouth, barbaric fantasies. . . .' (Treharne, *op. cit.*, p. 42). It is these stories that form part of *The Mabinogion*.

109. The connections between these locations depended on geographical and historical factors as well as on mythical ones. There was a well-established sea route in Celtic times from the Mediterranean, via Spain and Brittany, into the Bristol Channel, to the Somerset coast and on to Wales, Ireland and Strathclyde (Rhatz, *op. cit.*, p. 55). Artefacts found at Glastonbury confirm that cargoes (and missionaries) came this way. Greswell (*op. cit.*, p. 56) pointed out that Glastonbury was on the main shipping route linking Tintagel to Tewkesbury, south to Brittany, north to Strathclyde. This is the 'western route' identified by A.H. Williams (*op. cit.*, p. 4).

110. They also discussed Wordsworth and the local family connection between him and Mrs Henry Dew of Whitney. Since 'Holy Grail' is not italicised (as it is in the 1 June entry), it must mean that the *subject* of the Grail was discussed, although since Tennyson is mentioned, his poem no doubt figured in the talk too. *The Holy Grail* was one of four long poems published with the title *The Holy Grail and Other Poems*.

111. Quoted in *The Poems of Tennyson*, vol. III, edited by Christopher Ricks, London, Longman, 1969, pp. 463-4.

112. J. Philip Eggers, *King Arthur's Laureate. A study of Tennyson's Idylls of the King*. New York, New York University Press, 1971, p. 53.

113. The poem contains four visions of the Second Coming: Arthur's, Lancelot's, Sir Percivale's, and Sir Galahad's.

114. Perhaps it had special significance for Kilvert because of its associations with Bishop Gower, whose family owned land there.

115. It is also known as the Parc-le-Breos Tomb.

116. The first quotation has not been traced. B. Lile ('Kilvert in Gower: some footnotes', *Kilvert Society Newsletter*, spring 1992, p. 1) found the latter phrase 'odd' but made no attempt to explain it or trace the quotation.

117. The tombs date from 3500 BC. Other tombs in Gower are even older. The Swayne's Howes on Rhossili Down, which have several chambers like the Giant's Grave, are 6000 years old according to Robert Lucas (*Rhossili: a Village Background*, Tonypandy, Hackman Printers, 1998, p. 16). Lawrence Rich wrote of Swayne's Howes: 'These are Neolithic burial chambers built by the earliest families in Gower between 4000 and 5500 years ago. . . .' (*The Gower Peninsula*, National Trust, 1991, no page ref.). There is a King Arthur association in Gower in the form of Arthur's Stone on Cefn Bryn (moorland running the length of the peninsula), described by Morris as 'the most impressive of the communal tombs built 4000

years ago by early agriculturalists in the Gower' ('Gower Prehistory and History', in *A Guide to Gower*, Don Strawbridge and Peter J. Thomas (eds.), Swansea, Gower Society publication, 1991, p. 99). Britton (*op. cit.*, vol. XVIII, p. 731) mentioned Arthur's Stone on Cefn Bryn.

118. Madoc/Madog is based on the form Mo-aid-og (E.G. Bowen, *The Settlements of the Celtic Church in Wales*, Cardiff, University of Wales Press, 1956, p. 97). 'Mo' is a contraction of the Welsh 'dim o' — '[There is] none like'. The close cultural relations between Ireland and Wales at this time led to the dedication of Welsh churches to Irish saints. David Walker pointed out that St David's was 'a natural point of departure for Ireland and the large Irish population of Dyfed, where St David's is located, witnessed to the contact between south Wales and Ireland' (*A History of the Church in Wales*, Penarth, Church in Wales Publications, 1976, p. 13).

119. A. Butler, *The Lives of the Saints*, vol. I, London, Burns and Oates, 1956, p. 214.

120. *Ibid.*, p. 214. Giraldus Cambrensis (quoted in Butler) wrote: 'as long as the holy youth Aidan dwelt in the districts of the Britons with St David, the Saxons dared not come thither'. In one of his miracles, a stag took refuge with him from pursuing hounds and the saint made it invisible so the hounds went away frustrated.

121. Flemish people were among several foreign peoples who settled in Gower. Kilvert wrote '*We* suggested . . .' to include Westhorp in his notion about the housekeeper's Flemish blood. Cf. Wesley's response to Gower: 'all the people talk English, and are in general the most plain, loving people in Wales and ready to receive the Gospel' (*Journal*, vol. IV, July 1764).

122. She wore a Puritanical 'severe and full cap border'.

123. *Kilvert's Diary*, vol. II, p. 186.

124. Anyone who has visited Gower will confirm that a strong wind always seems to be blowing.

125. The path that Kilvert took brought him very close to another burial chamber, some mention of which may have appeared in the *Diary's* original manuscript. It is extremely difficult to find now as fern and brambles have grown to a height of over six feet around it; it was perhaps more visible then. One of the stone supports has collapsed and the capstone is at an angle. A mound of earth and stones used to cover it, as at the Giant's Grave. The National Trust leaflet, *Penmaen Burrows*, gives its age as 4000-5500 BC.

126. Brown, 'Walk Softly, Mr Kilvert', p. 5.

127. 'The Vicar said that when he came to the place [Llan Madoc] the Church was meaner than the meanest hovel in the village' (*Kilvert's Diary*, vol. II, p. 184).

128. Lile, *op. cit.*, p. 6.

129. The fact that he was accompanied again by his father, as he was on his St David's visit, suggests that both trips had special character: they had been prepared for with some care and much was expected of them. Kilvert was experiencing daily the Wales of the borderland; he also spent a few days in the Gower peninsula; the trips to St David's and Snowdonia meant penetrating to the most remote, imaginatively stimulating parts of Wales.

130. Moir, *op. cit.*, pp. 129 and 133.

131. Rev Warner, *A Walk through Wales in August 1797*, p. 182. The quoted

phrase, from Pope's *An Essay on Man*, refers to the man who, 'Slave to no sect, . . . takes no private road, / But looks through Nature, up to Nature's God'.

132. Warner's list overlaps a good deal too with Arnold's Celtic qualities. Warner found these qualities among 'the lower orders', who 'continue to think and act as nature dictated'.

133. This is another indication of the way in which his major excursions into Welsh culture were prepared for beforehand. There must have been a long tradition of harpers at the Hand Hotel because John Byng heard one play there in July 1793. During his 1784 tour of Wales, Byng sought harpers out wherever he could. At Dolgelly, he requested one to play while he had supper. A boatman at Bala told him that 'harping and dancing were decreasing in Wales, by the interdiction of the Methodists'. At Caernarvon '[We] listened to the best harper we had yet met with. . . .' So pleased was Byng with the harper's performance that he requested him to repeat 'the tunes of the greatest antiquity; such as might formerly have gladdened the breast of Llewellyn, and urged Glendower to face the field of Shrewsbury' (*A Tour to North Wales*, 1784, pp. 142, 145-6, 161).

134. Wyndowe, 'Rambling Recollections', p. 105. Kilvert had probably read as a schoolboy the tribute in Britton (*op. cit.*, vol. XVII, pp. 129 and 133) to Welsh poetry and song: 'The ancient Britons were exceedingly partial to poetry. Wales . . . was early the seat of the poetic muse. . . . Their music is as varied and expressive as their language'. (The volumes on Welsh counties in Britton were written by Rev J. Evans, who highlighted the role of the harp in Welsh music.)

135. For example, in *The Prelude* (Book VII, 564-5) Wordsworth referred to 'the Bard / Whose genius spangled o'er a gloomy theme'. *Glen Almain* celebrates Ossian, 'last of his race' (i.e. of bards).

136. Quoted in Abrams, *The Correspondent Breeze*, p. 56.

137. *The Harp of Wales* expresses the hope that its song would never be stilled: 'Wake with the spirit and power of yore', says the first verse. Other verses recall the harp's rallying power during the time of Roman and Edward I's invasions. See also *Chant of the Bards before their Massacre by Edward I, The Dying Bard's Prophecy, To Mr Edwards, the Harper of Conway, The Meeting of the Bards*.

138. *Kilvert's Diary*, vol. I, p. 361. Kilvert's idealisation of Florence Hill included the idea that 'She seemed to me to be the daughter of the Bards' (*Diary*, vol. III, p. 286).

139. Brewer, *op. cit.*, p. 636.

140. In 'a good deal of talk' they had after he had played, the harper told Kilvert that young people in Wales learnt the double stringed English harp, which was easier to play than the treble stringed Welsh one. Cf. Rev Warner (1798 *Walk through Wales*, p. 318): 'The Welsh harp is very superior to the one common in England, having three sets of strings. . . .'

141. My italics. It has been noted that the idea of trance, spell or enchantment in relation to imaginative experience had particular significance for Kilvert.

142. 1797 tour, pp. 148-9. Conway was the most appropriate place to hear a harper because Gray's *The Bard* located his harper there (Warner quoted from the poem at this point in his narrative). Cf. Kilvert's description of

Hugo's *Les Misérables* as 'that extraordinary *pathetic*' (*Kilvert's Diary*, vol.
I, p. 30).

143. The three stringed harp itself was a legend, as Prys Morgan explained.
It had, he said, replaced the 'old simple Welsh harp' in the seventeenth
century and by 1800 'patriots were certain that the triple harp . . . was the
ancient national instrument', though it was originally an Italian baroque
instrument (Prys Morgan, *From a Death to a View*, p. 77). Dearnley (*op.
cit.*, p. xiv) wrote that the harp was 'the bardic instrument — cherished
vehicle of Welsh nationalism and emblem of the organic relationship
between a people, their land and their culture. . . .'

144. *Kilvert's Diary*, vol. I, p. 362.

145. Moir, *op. cit.*, p. 136.

146. *Kilvert's Diary*, vol. I, p. 352. Cader Idris would have been the most
prominent mountain he saw when he wrote during his Snowdonia trip:
'From Barmouth Junction . . . we travelled up the beautiful valley of
Dolgelly beside the noble estuary of the Mawddach, mountains standing
close on either side'. Richard Wilson's painting, *Valley of the Mawddach,
with Cader Idris*, shows this view.

147. Kilvert referred to discussing Tyndall's 'discoveries in science and
sound, Swiss mountaineering' with a clergyman (*Diary*, vol. III, p. 183).

148. He found it appropriate in his poem, *Honest Work*, to picture the
Christian life in terms of toiling up 'duty's steep', on whose summit the
'blossoms / Which love 'mid crags and storms to blow' are to be found.
These rewards of the spirit are not found 'warm below'.

149. *Kilvert's Diary*, vol. I, p. 359. He gave its title as *A Night upon Cader Idris*.

150. This note prefaced Mrs Hemans's poem.

151. Kilvert followed Warner in hiring a guide for the ascent of Cader
Idris. Byng (*Tour of North Wales 1784*, p. 147) noted that a guide, Robin
Edwards, who had been guiding tourists over Cader Idris for forty
years was available, but Byng declined to climb the mountain because 'I
hate distant views; am giddy on heights; and very hot and nervous. . . .'
Pennant (*Journey to Snowdon*, 1781, quoted in Moir, *op. cit.*, p. 136) said
that the ascent of that mountain was only for those with 'a degree of
bodily activity' and 'strength of head'.

152. *Kilvert's Diary*, vol. I, p. 354.

153. Cf. his pleasure at the way Florence Hill was '*entranced* . . . according
to the progress and the passion of the tale' which he told her (*Kilvert's
Diary*, vol. III, p. 285).

154. 'Old Pugh says the fairies used to dance near the top of the mountain and
he knows people who have seen them', Kilvert noted. BBC Wales featured a
programme on 26 February 2003 in which the Rev Geraint ap Iorworth told
of his belief that the spirit of the ancient Earth Goddess is on Cader Idris.

155. There are close similarities of phrasing between Mrs Hemans's account
of her experiences on the mountain top and Kilvert's. Where she wrote
'I viewed the dread beings around us that hover, / Though veiled by the
mists of mortality's breath', he had 'the mists and clouds began to sweep
by us in white thin ghostly sheets as if some great dread Presences and
Powers were going past. . . .' She wrote of how 'the powers of the wind
and the ocean, / The rush of whose pinions bears onward the storms; /
Like the sweep of the white-rolling wave', while in his description the
mountain's peak is seen 'looming large and dark through the cloud and

rain and white wild driving mist, . . . It is an awful place in a storm'. Both writers experienced relief to leave the dark turmoil of the summit. Mrs Hemans saw 'Day burst on that rock with the purple cloud crested, / And high Cader Idris rejoiced in the sun'. Kilvert went 'Down, down and out of the cloud into sunshine, all the hills below and the valleys were bathed in glorious sunshine. . . .'

156. Hartman, *Wordsworth's Poetry*, p. 64.
157. *Kilvert's Diary*, vol. III, p. 167.
158. *Ibid.*, vol. II, p. 86. Field sports were offensive to both Quakers and Evangelicals. Kilvert was also likely to have been influenced by Cowper particularly, for whom they were a travesty of country life. Hunting with hounds he called 'Detested sport, / That owes its pleasures to another's pain' (*The Task*, Book III, 326-8).
159. *Kilvert's Diary*, vol. I, p. 235.

Chapter 10 The Spirit of the Dream

1. Borrow, *op. cit.*, p. 173. Kilvert could have come across the word 'awen' in (i) Scott's *The Antiquary* (vol. I, p. 216) where Oldbuck refers to Lovel as possessor of the 'awen' of the Welsh bards, and (ii) in Barnes's 'Thoughts on Beauty and Art' (*Macmillan's Magazine*, June 1861).
2. It is not clear which the poem is that Kilvert referred to. It could be *Twilight*, which states that 'The choristers are mute, / Save for the mellow flute / Of some late ouzel at his evensong'. *Evensong*, too, refers to birds singing 'in the fading light'. In both poems is the idea of night *mourning* the death of the day that is reminiscent of the beginning of Gray's *Elegy*: 'The curfew tolls the knell of parting day'. Neither of the Kilvert poems refers to a valley.
3. Dunham's essay, 'An Angel-Satyr Walks these Hills', p 175.
4. Wordsworth referred also to 'the still sad music of humanity', which, in the intervening period, had had 'ample power / To chasten and subdue'.
5. Jacobus, *Tradition and Experiment in Wordsworth's Lyrical Ballads*, p. 107.
6. Kilvert's sense of Oxford as a dream landscape may have contained a memory of what Wordsworth had written of his time at Cambridge: 'I was the Dreamer, they the Dream' (*The Prelude*, Book III, 29). 'They' referred to students, tutors, shopkeepers. After the loss of the Kilvert family fortunes, the importance of the family's success in obtaining an Oxford education for several of its sons can scarcely be over-estimated.
7. *Kilvert's Diary*, vol. II, p. 277.
8. *Ibid.*, vol. II, p. 265.
9. Frederick Garber, *Self, Text, and Romantic Irony. The Example of Byron*, Princeton, New Jersey, Princeton University Press, 1988, p. 118. Kilvert may have been introduced to *The Dream* by his uncle Francis, who acknowledged that Byron fascinated him: 'During confinement with lumbago, read in extenso an admirable life of Lord Byron — one of the most striking psychological specimens ever exhibited to the student of . . . human nature' (F. Kilvert, 'Commonplace Book', vol. II, BCL).
10. Mary was two years older than Byron and infatuated with Jack Musters, who was 'a handsome, womanising, musical fox-hunter' (Ian Gilmour, *The Making of the Poets. Byron and Shelley in their time*, London, Chatto and Windus, 2002, p. 84). Kilvert had experienced a similar situation

and a similar landscape on 11 August 1874, when he too was on the verge of a new love affair, this time with Katharine Heanley, whom he had just met at the Findon (Sussex) wedding of Adelaide Cholmeley. The 'woods and cornfields' of Byron's landscape were matched by the 'bright plain and green pastures, blue hill and golden corn' of the Sussex one Kilvert contemplated. The two landscapes had a particular feature in common — a circle of trees on the hills' summits. Byron's hill was 'crowned with a peculiar diadem of trees, in circular array'; in Kilvert's case it was Chanctonbury Ring, which is a ring of trees on top of one of the Downs, and his entire situation there must have recalled Byron's poem. Both landscapes betokened, like Kilvert's 'dream' landscapes of Cwm Dingle and Oxford, visions of promise, of perfect happiness.

11. In Armstrong's essay, ' 'Tintern Abbey': from Augustan to Romantic', in *Augustan Worlds*, Hilson, Jones and Watson (ed.). I am indebted to her perceptive analysis.

12. Cf. Legh Richmond describing the clean, homely cottage interior of the dairyman in *The Dairyman's Daughter* (p. 71): 'Just now the setting sun shone brightly . . . into the room. It was reflected from three or four rows of bright pewter plates and white earthenware'.

13. The strongest suggestion that Wordsworth's poem was in his mind lies in his reference to the 'high and *tufted* woods' on the sides of the Cwm, which recalls the 'orchard-tufts' of *Tintern Abbey*. In an earlier entry (3 February 1872), he had written of the valley's 'tufted copse', putting the phrase in inverted commas as though quoting; he was misremembering Wordsworth's 'orchard-tufts' that lost themselves in 'copses'. (The idea of trees as 'tufts' appealed to Kilvert: he used it in his description of the river Glasnant, quoted in the last chapter.)

14. Dunham, *op. cit.*, p 174.

15. W. Wordsworth, *The Prelude*, Book II, 325-6 and 348-352.

16. Hartman (*Wordsworth's Poetry*, p. 183) pointed out that Wordsworth wanted the eye quieted because the sense of sight was likely to dominate the other senses. 'He does not want to blind a faculty but to cleanse a gate of perception'. He wanted all the senses to work together, hence the stress on *harmony*.

17. Cf. *The Prelude* I, 340-1: 'the immortal spirit grows / Like harmony in music'; Book II, 415: 'One song they sang' (speaking of the unity of all natural forms and creatures).

18. *The Prelude*, Book XII, 200.

19. Cf. Warner (*A Walk through Wales in August 1797*, p. 71), who referred to the way the imagination 'pourtrays with her magic pencil to the mind, wonders that exceed reality. . . .' We are reminded too of the 'magicalised Romance touch' that Arnold saw as characteristic of Celtic imagination.

20. Barth, *The Symbolic Imagination*, p. 43.

21. *Ibid.*, pp. 47 and 55.

22. Houghton, *The Victorian Frame of Mind*, p. 152. Wordsworth saw the imagination both as the creative power of the artist and the actual physical data of sense impressions. The imagination unified the data into a coherent 'reality' in which they became spiritualised in the sense that their beauty and order demonstrated the basic physical laws that revealed God's hand in the universe.

23. Maber and Tregoning, *Kilvert's Cornish Diary*, p. 122.

24. Abrams, *Natural Supernaturalism*, p. 123. Cf. Jacobus (*Tradition and Experiment*, p. 105): 'The link between landscape and the poetic imagination ... is central to Wordsworth's exploration of changing identity'.
25. 1847 letter by George Macdonald to his father, quoted in Greville Macdonald, *George Macdonald and his Wife*, London, George Allen and Unwin, 1924, p. 108.
26. *Kilvert's Diary*, vol. II, p. 426.
27. Houghton, *op. cit.*, p. 77.
28. James, 'Landscape in Nineteenth-Century Literature', p. 62.
29. R. Williams, *op. cit.*, p. 49.
30. In the entry for 5 September 1871, he referred to trees '*embosoming* the little church' of Newchurch overlooked by the 'little lonely tree' that mourned Emmeline Vaughan (my italics). On 12 June 1875 he wrote of the way 'the wind swept back the tresses of the birch from her bared white limbs. . . .'
31. Cf. Kilvert's description of the landscape around Silbury Hill (see chapter eight).
32. *Kilvert's Diary*, vol. III, pp. 302-6. The use of 'plaintive' (i.e. mournful) is interesting. Was Kilvert acknowledging that the kind of rural society Chieflands represented was really dead and gone? In his Chieflands there are echoes of Howitt's picture of life in a secluded region: 'a spot where the inhabitants are passing through life ... in a dream-like pilgrimage, half unconscious of its trials and evils' (*Rural Life of England* p. 200).
33. *Kilvert's Diary*, vol. I, p. 392.
34. Brooke, *Life and Letters*, vol. II, p. 12. His italics.
35. Davidoff observed that Victorians looked on the village community as a haven from the troubles of the industrial world (*Worlds Between*, p. 49).
36. Keith, *The Rural Tradition*, p. 12.
37. Keith (*op. cit.*, p. 12) spoke of a 'challenging radicalism' in such writing, while R. Williams (*The Country and the City*, p. 49) distinguished in it 'a persistent rural-intellectual radicalism; genuinely and actively hostile to industrialism and capitalism; opposed to commercialism and to the exploitation of environment'. Cobbett, Barnes and George Sturt were exponents of it.
38. Toman's *Kilvert: The Homeless Heart* deals with these issues fully in chapters seven and nine.
39. Brooke, *op. cit.*, vol. I, pp. 183-4. Letter of 22 February 1849.
40. One could argue that if he belonged anywhere (and a very strong impression given by the *Diary* is that his personality, his Evangelicalism, and his writing meant that he would always be something of a solitary) it was with the Clyro people whom he called 'the usual set that one ... knows so well. Dews, Thomases, Webbs, Wyatts, Bridges, Oswalds, Trumpers etc' (vol. I, p. 175). These were the area's upper-middle class/professional people, who were the equivalent of the Kearys and the clergy families of Langley Burrell.
41. *Kilvert's Diary*, vol. II, p. 162. His satisfaction at his ready response to the man's pathetic condition is evident in his statement 'My heart melted within me'.
42. Eggers, *King Arthur's Laureate*, p. 93.
43. *Ibid.*, p. 93.

Bibliography

Unpublished Material

Cennick, John. (undated) 'John Cennick's Diary'. East Tytherton Archive Moravian Church Centre, Muswell Hill, London.

Grigg, A. 'Some Account Of The Life Of The Single Sister Ann Grigg Who Departed At Tytherton, Dec. 11th 1814, Written by Herself'. East Tytherton Archive Moravian Church Centre, Muswell Hill, London.

Gubi, Rev P.M. (1998) 'Whither John Cennick?' Unpublished M.A. thesis, Cheltenham and Gloucester College of Higher Education.

Kilvert, F. (undated) 'Commonplace Books'. Bath Central Library (vol. I – D803598, vol. II – D803599).

'Tytherton Congregation Diary' (September 1st 1813-December 31st 1824) East Tytherton Archive Moravian Church Centre, Muswell Hill, London.

Published Material

Abrams, M.H. (1971) *Natural Supernaturalism. Tradition and Revolution in Romantic Literature*. London: Oxford University Press.

Abrams, M.H. (1984) *The Correspondent Breeze. Essays on English Romanticism*. New York: Norton.

Ackroyd, P. (1990) *Dickens*. London: Minerva.

Adams, A. (1996) *The Creation Was Open To Me: an Anthology of Friends' Writings on that of God in all Creation*. London: Library of the Society of Friends.

Addison, W. (1948) *The English Country Parson*. London: Dent.

Adrian, A. (1984) *Dickens and the Parent-Child Relationship*. Ohio: Ohio University Press.

Aguilar, G. (1852) *Home Influence*, (1853) *A Mother's Recompense*. London: Evans.

Alexander, P. (1990) *William Plomer: a Biography*. Oxford: Oxford University Press.

Alford, V. (1952) *Introduction to English Folklore*. London: G. Bell and Sons.

Altick, R.D. (1957) *The English Common Reader. A Social History of the*

Mass Reading Public 1800-1900. Chicago: University of Chicago Press.

Altick, R.D. (1973) *Victorian People and Ideas*. London: Dent.

Andrews, M. (1999) *Landscape and Western Art*. Oxford: Oxford University Press.

Anonymous. (1977) *Folklore, Myths and Legends of Britain*. London: Readers Digest Association.

Armstrong, I. (1978) ''Tintern Abbey': from Augustan to Romantic'. In: Hilson, Jones and Watson (eds.), *Augustan Worlds: Essays in Honour of A.R. Humphreys*. Leicester: Leicester University Press.

Arnold, F. (1886) *Robertson of Brighton*. London: Ward and Downey.

Arnold, M. (1867) *On the Study of Celtic Literature*. London: Smith and Elder.

Ashby, M.K. (1974) *The Changing English Village*. Kineton: Roundwood Press.

Aveni, A. (2003) *The Book of the Year. A Brief History of our Seasonal Holidays*. Oxford: Oxford University Press.

Averill, J. (1980) *Wordsworth and the Poetry of Human Suffering*. Ithaca: Cornell University Press.

Baker, F. (1970) *John Wesley and the Church of England*. London: Epworth Press.

Ball, P.M. (1968) *The Central Self. A Study in Romantic and Victorian Imagination*. London: Athlone Press.

Banks, R. (1980) *Paul's Idea of Community*. Exeter: Paternoster Press.

Barker, J. (2003) *Wordsworth: a Life in Letters*. London: Penguin.

Barnes, W. (1861) 'Thoughts on Beauty and Art'. In: *Macmillan's Magazine*, June.

Barnes, W. (1996) *Humilis Domus: Some Thoughts on the Abodes, Life and Social Conditions of the Poor*. London: Routledge/Thoemmes Press.

Barnes, W. (1996) *Views of Labour and Gold*. London: Routledge/Thoemmes Press.

Baron, M. (1995) *Language and Relationship in Wordsworth's Writing*. London: Longman.

Barth, J.R. (1977) *The Symbolic Imagination. Coleridge and the Romantic Tradition*. New Jersey: Princeton University Press.

Bath Chronicle, 2 December 1858.

Battiscombe, G. (1963) *John Keble. A Study in Limitations*. London: Constable.

Bauer, J.B. (ed.) (1970) *Encyclopedia of Biblical Theology*. London: Sheed and Ward.

Beer, J. (1977) *Coleridge's Poetic Intelligence*. London: Macmillan.

Beer, J. (1979) *Wordsworth in Time*. London: Faber and Faber.

Bennett, M. (1967) *Millais. An exhibition organised by the Walker Art Gallery Liverpool and the Royal Academy of Arts, January-April 1967*. London: Royal Academy of Arts.

Berry, R. (1999) *Working with Dreams*. Oxford: How To Books.

Bevington, M.M. (1941) *The Saturday Review 1855-1868. Representative*

Educated Opinion in Victorian England. New York: Columbia University Press.

Bickersteth, E. (1832) *The Christian Student*. London: Seeley and Burnside.

Bloom, H. (1971) *The Visionary Company. A Reading of English Romantic Poetry*. Ithaca, New York: Cornell University Press.

Blunt, J.J. (1857) *The Acquirements and Principal Obligations and Duties of the Parish Priest*. London: John Murray.

Blythe, R. (1982) *From the Headlands*. London: Chatto and Windus.

Blythe, R. (1998) *Divine Landscapes. A Pilgrimage through Britain's Sacred Places*. Norwich: Canterbury Press.

Borrow, G. (1906) *Wild Wales*. London: Dent.

Bottrell, W. (1980) *Traditions and Hearthside Stories of West Cornwall*. Newcastle-on-Tyne: Frank Graham.

Bowen, E.G. (1956) *The Settlements of the Celtic Church in Wales*. Cardiff: University of Wales Press.

Bradley, I. (1976) *The Call to Seriousness. The Evangelical Impact on the Victorians*. London: Jonathan Cape.

Bradley, L. (2001) *John Everett Millais. Beyond the pre-Raphaelite Brotherhood*. New Haven: Yale University Press.

Braithwaite, W.C. (1912) *The Beginnings of Quakerism*. London: Macmillan.

Brantley, R.E. (1975) *Wordsworth's 'Natural Methodism'*. New Haven: Yale University Press.

Brantley, R.E. (1989) *Locke, Wesley and the Method of English Romanticism*. University of Florida Press.

Bready, J.W. (1938) *England Before and After Wesley. The Evangelical Revival and Social Reform*. London: Hodder and Stoughton.

Brewer, J. (1997) *The Pleasures of the Imagination. English Culture in the Eighteenth Century*. London: Harper Collins.

Brighton and Hove Herald, 20 August 1853.

Britton, J. and Brayley, E. (1801-1818) *The Beauties of England and Wales: Or, Delineations Topographical, Historical and Descriptive of Each County*. London: various publishers.

Brooke, S.A. (1891) *Life and Letters of the Rev F.W. Robertson*, 2 vols. London: Kegan Paul, Trench and Trübner.

Broughton, T.L. (1999) *Men of Letters, Writing Lives, Masculinity and Literary Arts / Biography in the Late Victorian Period*. London: Routledge.

Brown, F.K. (1961) *Fathers of the Victorians. The Age of Wilberforce*. Cambridge: Cambridge University Press.

Brown, Rev R.L. (1974) 'Walk softly, Mr Kilvert'. In: *Kilvert Society Newsletter*, autumn.

Burns, R. (1985) *Poems, Chiefly in the Scottish Dialect*. D. Low (ed.). London: Dent.

Butler, A. (1956) *The Lives of the Saints*, vol. I. London: Burnes and Oates.

Butts, D. and Garrett, P. (2006) *From the Dairyman's Daughter to Worrals of the WAAF*. Cambridge: Lutterworth Press

Byng, J. (1934) *The Torrington Diaries. A Selection from the Tours of the Hon.*

Byng between the years 1781 and 1794, vol. I. C.B. Andrews (ed.). London: Eyre and Spottiswoode.

Carlyle. (1838) *Critical and Miscellaneous Essays*, vol. IV. London: Chapman and Hall.

Cecil, Lord D. (1929) *The Stricken Deer*. London: Constable.

Chadwick, O. (1966) *The Victorian Church*, 2 vols. London: Adam and Charles Black.

Chandler, A. (1971) *A Dream of Order. The Medieval Ideal in Nineteenth Century English Literature*. London: Routledge and Kegan Paul.

Chapman, R. (1961) *Father Faber*. London: Burns and Oates.

Charles, Mrs. (1864) *The Diary of Mrs Kitty Trevylyan. A Story of the Times of Whitefield and the Wesleys*. New York: M.W. Dodd.

Charles, Mrs. (1895) *Chronicles of the Schönberg-Cotta Family (1862)*. London: Nelson.

Chitto, S. (1974) *The Beast and the Monk. A Life of Charles Kingsley*. London: Hodder and Stoughton.

Claridge, L. (1992) *Romantic Potency: the Paradox of Desire*. Ithaca, New York: Cornell University Press.

Clark, A.M. (1969) *Sir Walter Scott: the Formative Years*. Edinburgh: Blackwood.

Clark, G.K. (1973) *Churchmen and the Condition of England 1832-1885*. London: Methuen.

Clark, J.W. and Hughes, T. (1890) *The Life and Letters of the Reverend Adam Sedgwick*, 2 vols. Cambridge: Cambridge University Press.

Cockshut, A.O.J. (1969) *The Achievement of Walter Scott*. London: Collins.

Cohen, M.N. (1995) *Lewis Carroll. A Biography*. London: Macmillan.

Coleridge, S.T. (1825) *Aids to Reflection in the Formation of a Manly Character on the Serveral Grounds of Prudence, Morality, and Religion*. London: Taylor and Hersey.

Coleridge, S.T. (1969) *Biographia Literaria*, vol. III. J. Shawcross (ed.). Oxford: Oxford University Press.

Colloms, B. (1977) *Victorian Country Parsons*. London: Book Club Associates.

Constable, W.G. (1953) *Richard Wilson*. London: Routledge Kegan Paul.

Cottom, D. (1985) *The Civilised Imagination. A study of Ann Radcliffe, Jane Austen, and Sir Walter Scott*. Cambridge: Cambridge University Press.

Cowper, W. (1981) *Letters and Prose Writings of William Cowper*, vol II. J. King and C. Ryskamp (eds.). Oxford: Oxford University Press.

Cowper, W. (1994) *The Task and Selected Other Poems*. J. Sambrook (ed.). London: Longman.

Crittall, E. and Crowley, D.A. (eds.) (1953) *A History of Wiltshire*. London: Oxford University Press.

Cross, F.L. (ed.) (2001) *Oxford Dictionary of the Christian Church*. Oxford: Oxford University Press.

Cruse, A. (1936) *The Victorians and their Books*. London: Allen and Unwin.

Cunliffe, B. (1997) *The Ancient Celts*. Oxford: Oxford University Press.

Curtis, T. (ed.) (1986) *Wales: the Imagined Nation. Essays in Cultural and National Identity*. Bridgend: Poetry of Wales Press.

Dale, A. (1989) *Brighton Churches*. London: Routledge.

Danby, J.F. (1972) 'Simon Lee and the Idiot Boy'. In: A.R. Jones and W. Tydeman (eds.), *Wordsworth's Lyrical Ballads*. London: Macmillan.

Davidoff, L. (1995) *Worlds Between: Historical Perspectives on Gender and Class*. Cambridge: Polity Press.

Davidoff, L. and Hall, C. (1987) *Family Fortunes: Men and Women of the English Middle Class, 1780-1850*. Chicago: University of Chicago Press.

Davies, J.H. (1979) *Fénelon*. Boston: Twayne.

Dearnley, M. (2001) *Distant Fields. Eighteenth Century Fictions of Wales*. Cardiff: University of Wales Press.

De Laura, D. (1979) 'The Allegory of Life: the Autobiographical Impulse in Victorian Prose'. In: G.P. Landow (ed.), *Approaches to Victorian Autobiography*. Athens: Ohio University Press.

Devizes and Wiltshire Gazette, 5 December 1872.

De Vries, A. (1991) *Dictionary of Symbols and Imagery*. Amsterdam: North Holland Publishing Company.

Dimbleby, D. (2005) *A Picture of Britain*. London: Tate Publishing.

Dugdale, G. (1953) *William Barnes of Dorset*. London: Cassell.

Dunham, P. (2007) 'An Angel-Satyr Walks these Hills: Landscape and Identity in Kilvert's Diary'. In: P. Barnwell and M. Palmer (eds.), *Landscape History after Hoskins*, vol. III. Macclesfield: Wingather Press.

Edwards, A.G. (1912) *Landmarks in the History of the Welsh Church*. London: John Murray.

Edwards, D.L. (1981) *Christian England from the Reformation to the 18th Century*, vol. II. London: Collins.

Eggers, J.P. (1971) *King Arthur's Laureate. A study of Tennyson's Idylls of the King*. New York: New York University Press.

Elliott, P. and Daniels, S. (2006) 'Pestalozzi, Fellenberg and British Nineteenth Century Geographical Education', *Journal of Historical Geography*, vol. XXXII.

Elwell, W.A. (ed.) (1984) *Evangelical Dictionary of Theology*. Basingstoke: Marshall Pickering.

Espriella, don M.A. (1967) 'Letters from England'. In: R.P. Chope (ed.), *Early Tours in Devon and Cornwall*. Newton Abbot: David and Charles.

Essex Hope, Mrs. (1954) 'Radnorshire Legends and Superstitions'. *Radnorshire Transactions*, vol. XXIV.

Evans, A.W. (1932) *Warburton and the Warburtonians. A Study in Some Eighteenth Century Controversies*. Oxford: Oxford University Press.

Extracts from unpublished parts of Kilvert's Diary relating to the Dew and Bevan Families. (undated) Hereford: Kilvert Society publication.

Ferguson, F. (1977) *Wordsworth: Language as Counterspirit*. New Haven: Yale University Press.

Ferguson, S. and Wright, D. (eds.) (1988) *A New Dictionary of Theology*. Leicester: Inter-Varsity Press.

Figes, C. (1993) *250 Years of the Moravian Settlement at East Tytherton, 1743-1993*. Privately printed.

Fisher, E. (1839) *Sketches and Souvenirs*. Bath: privately printed.

Flanagan, O. (2000) *Dreaming Souls. Sleep, Dreams and the Evolution of the Conscious Mind*. Oxford: Oxford University Press.

Flew, R.N. (1934) *The Idea of Perfection in Christian Theology*. London: Oxford University Press.

Ford, J. (1998) *Coleridge on Dreaming. Romanticism, Dreams and the Medical Imagination*. Cambridge: Cambridge University Press.

Forsyth, R.A. (1967) 'The Conserving Myth of William Barnes'. In: I. Fletcher (ed.), *Romantic Mythologies*. London: Routledge and Kegan Paul.

Fothergill, R.A. (1974) *Private Chronicles. A Study of English Diaries*. London: Oxford University Press.

Fox, G. (1962) *The Journal of George Fox*. Cambridge: Cambridge University Press.

Frank, G. (2000) *The Memory of the Eyes. Pilgrims to Living Saints in Christian Late Antiquity*. Berkeley: University of California Press.

Freud, S. (1976) *The Interpretation of Dreams*. Harmondsworth: Penguin.

Furnish, V. (1984) *Anchor Bible*. New York: Doubleday.

Garber, F. (1971) *Wordsworth and the Poetry of Encounter*. Urbana, Chicago: University of Illinois Press.

Garber, F. (1988) *Self, Text and Romantic Irony. The Example of Byron*. New Jersey: Princeton University Press.

Gay, P. (1995) *The Cultivation of Hatred*, vol. III of *The Bourgeois Experience: Victoria to Freud*. London: Fontana.

Gay, P. (1999) *The Tender Passion*, vol. II of *The Bourgeois Experience: Victoria to Freud*. New York: Norton.

Gidding, R. (1967) *The Tradition of Smollett*. London: Methuen.

Gill, F.C. (1937) *The Romantic Movement and Methodism: A Study of English Romanticism and the Evangelical Revival*. London: Epworth Press.

Gill, S. (1998) *Wordsworth and the Victorians*. Oxford: Clarendon Press.

Gilley, S. (1994) 'The Church of England in the Sixteenth Century'. In: S. Gilley and W.J. Shiels (eds.), *A History of Religion in Britain*. Oxford: Blackwell.

Gilmour, I. (2002) *The Making of the Poets. Byron and Shelley in their Time*. London: Chatto and Windus.

Gilpin, W. (1786) *Observations, Relative Chiefly to Picturesque Beauty, made in the year 1772 of Several parts of England, Particularly the Mountains and Lakes of Cumberland and Westmorland*. London: printed for R. Blamires.

Gilpin, W. (1798) *Observations on the Western Parts of England*. London: T. Cadell.

Girouard, M. (1981) *Return to Camelot. Chivalry and the English Gentleman*. New Haven and London: Yale University Press.

Gray, T. and Collins, W. (1977) *Thomas Gray and William Collins. Poetical Works*. R. Lonsdale (ed.). Oxford: Oxford University Press.

Green, F. (ed.) (1927) *Menevia Sacra*. London.

Green, M. (2004) *The Gods of the Celts*. Stroud: Sutton Publishing.

Greswell, W. (1909) *Chapters on the Early History of Glastonbury Abbey*. Taunton: The Wessex Press.

Grice, F. (undated) *Francis Kilvert and his World*. Horsham: Caliban Books.

Grice, F. (1975) *Francis Kilvert Priest and Diarist 1840-1879*. Leamington Spa: Kilvert Society.

Hagstrum, J.H. (1989) 'Description and Reflection in Gray's *Elegy*'. In: J.R. Watson (ed.), *Pre-Romanticism in English Poetry of the Eighteenth Century*. Basingstoke: Macmillan Education.

Halévy, E. (1924) *A History of the English People in 1815*. London: Fisher Unwin.

Hamilton Jenkin, A.K. (1990) *Cornwall and its People*. Newton Abbot: David and Charles.

Handley, C.G.M. (1948) *Charles Simeon*. London: Inter-Varsity Fellowship.

Hare, A.J.C. (1896) *The Story of my Life*, vol. I. London: George Allen.

Hartman, G. (1971) *Wordsworth's Poetry 1787-1814*. London: Yale University Press.

Hartveit, L. (1974) *Dream Within a Dream. A Thematic Approach to Scott's Vision of Fictional Reality*. Oslo: Norwegian Research Council.

Harvey, A.E. (1970) *Companion to the New Testament*. Cambridge: Cambridge University Press.

Hastings, A., Mason, A. and Pyper, H. (eds.) (2000) *The Oxford Companion to Christian Thought*. Oxford: Oxford University Press.

Havens, R.D. (1941) *The Mind of a Poet. A Study of Wordsworth's Thought*. Baltimore: the Johns Hopkins University Press.

Helsinger, E.K. (1979) 'Ulysses to Penelope: Victorian Experiments in Autobiography'. In: G.P. Landow (ed.), *Approaches to Victorian Autobiography*. Athens, Ohio: Ohio University Press.

Hemans, Mrs. (1839) *Works*. Edinburgh: Blackwood.

Hennell, M. (1979) *Sons of the Prophets. Evangelical Leaders of the Victorian Church*. London: SPCK.

Hepworth, D. (1994) 'Kilvert and the Classics'. In: *Kilvert Society Newsletter*.

Herbert, G. (1981) *The Country Parson, The Temple*. J. Wall (ed.). London: SPCK.

Hervey, J. (1843) *Reflections on a Flower Garden, the Works of the Rev J. Hervey*. Edinburgh: Thomas Nelson.

Hill, P. (2004) *The Age of Athelstan: Britain's Forgotten History*. Stroud: Tempus Publishing.

Hillhouse, J.T. (1970) *The Waverley Novels and their Critics*. New York: Octagon Books.

Hilson, J.C., Jones, M.M.B. and Watson J.R. (eds.) (1978) *Augustan Worlds: Essays in Honour of A.R. Humphreys*. Leicester: Leicester University Press.

Hilton, B. (1988) *The Age of Atonement. The Influence of Evangelicalism on Social and Economic Thought, 1795-1865.* Oxford: Clarendon Press.

Horne, R.H. (1848) *A New Spirit of the Age*, vol I. London: Smith and Elder.

Hoskins, W.G. (1995) *The Making of the English Landscape.* London: Hodder and Stoughton.

Houghton, W.E. (1957) *The Victorian Frame of Mind, 1830-1870.* New Haven: Yale University Press.

House, H. (1942) *The Dickens World.* London: Oxford University Press.

Howitt, M. (1847) *The Children's Year or The Story of a Happy Home.* London: Nelson.

Howitt, M. (1854) *A Pictorial Calendar of the Seasons.* London: Bohn's Illustrated Library.

Howitt, M. (1857) *My Own Story.* London: William Tegg.

Howitt, M. (1889) *An Autobiography* (edited by her daughter, Margaret Howitt), two vols. London: William Isbister.

Howitt, W. (1838) *The Rural Life of England* (third edition, 1844). London: Longman, Brown, Green.

Howitt, W. (1839) *The Boy's Country Book.* London: Hodder and Stoughton, no date.

Howitt, W. (1842) *Visits to Remarkable Places: Scenes Illustrative of Striking Passages in History and Poetry*, second series. Philadelphia: Carey and Hart.

Howitt, W. (1849) *The Homes and Haunts of the Most Eminent British Poets*, two vols.: The Early Poets and The Modern Poets. London: Richard Bentley.

Howitt, W. (1862) *Ruined Abbeys and Castles in Great Britain.* London: Bennett.

Howitt, W. (1863) *The History of the Supernatural in all Ages and Nations, and in all Churches, Christian and Pagan*, two vols. London: Longman Green.

Hulme, T.E. (1936) *Speculations. Essays on Humanism and the Philosophy of Art.* London: Kegan Paul.

Humphreys, A.R. (1937) *William Shenstone. An Eighteenth Century Portrait.* Cambridge: Cambridge University Press.

Hurd, R. (1995) *The Early Letters of Bishop Richard Hurd 1739-1762.* S. Brewer (ed.)Woodbridge: Boydell Press.

Hylson-Smith, K. (1988) *Evangelicals in the Church of England 1734-1984.* Edinburgh: Clark.

Ifans, D. (ed.) *The Diary of Francis Kilvert, June-July 1870.* Aberystwyth: NLW.

'Ignatius in Extremis'. (1866) *Saturday Review*, vol. XXI, 19 May.

Inglis-Jones, E. (1955) *The Story of Wales.* London: Faber.

Jacobus, M. (1976) *Tradition and Experiment in Wordsworth's Lyrical Ballads.* Oxford: Oxford University Press.

Jacobus, M. (1989) 'Nature, God and the Imagination – from Thompson to

Wordsworth'. In: J.R. Watson (ed.), *Pre-Romanticism in English Poetry of the Eighteenth Century*. Basingstoke: Macmillan Education.

James, L. (1989) 'Landscape in Nineteenth-Century Literature'. In: G.E. Mingay (ed.), *The Rural Idyll*. London: Routledge.

Jarvis, R. (1997) *Romantic Writing and Pedestrian Travel*. London: Macmillan Press.

Jay, E. (1969) *The Religion of the Heart. Anglican Evangelicalism and the Nineteenth Century Novel*. Oxford: Clarendon Press.

Johnson, E. (1970) *Sir Walter Scott, the Great Unknown: vol. 1, 1771-1821*. London: Hamish Hamilton.

Johnson, E.D.H. (1974) *The Poetry of Earth: a Collection of English Nature Writing*. New York.

Jones, B. (2004) *Francis Kilvert's Poetry. A study*. Kilvert Society publication.

Jones, F. (1954) *The Holy Wells of Wales*. Cardiff: University of Wales Press.

Jones, G. and Jones, T. (eds.) (1975) *The Mabinogion*. London: Dent.

Jones I.G. (1981) *Explorations and Explanations. Essays in the Social History of Wales*. Aberystwyth: Gwasg Gomer.

Jones, J. (1970) *The Egotistical Sublime: a History of Wordsworth's Imagination*. London: Chatto and Windus.

Jones, W.P. (1937) *Thomas Gray, Scholar*. Cambridge: Harvard University Press.

Jordan, J.E. (1976) *Why the 'Lyrical Ballads'?* Berkeley: University of California Press.

Kaplan, F. (1975) *Dickens and Mesmerism. The Hidden Springs of Fiction*. Princeton: Princeton University Press.

Kaplan, F. (1987) *Sacred Tears. Sentimentality in Victorian Literature*. Princeton, New Jersey: Princeton University Press.

Keary, A. (1875) *Castle Daly*. London: Smith and Elder.

Keary. (1883) *Memoir of Annie Keary, by her Sister*. London: Macmillan.

Keats, J. (1958) *Letters of John Keats*. Cambridge: Cambridge University Press.

Keble, J. (1846) *Lyra Innocentium: Thoughts in Verse on Christian Children, their Ways and their Privileges*. London: Parker.

Keble, J. (1863) *The Christian Year: Thoughts in Verse for the Sundays and Holydays Throughout the Year*. Oxford: Henry and Parker.

Keble, J. (1912) *Lectures on Poetry*, 1832-1866. E.K. Francis (trans.). Oxford: Clarendon Press.

Keith, W.J. (1975) *The Rural Tradition*. Hassocks: Harvester Press.

Keith, W.J. (1989) 'The Land in Victorian Literature'. In: G.E. Mingay (ed.), *The Rural Idyll*. London: Routledge.

Keynes, R. (2002) *Annie's Box. Charles Darwin, his Daughter, and Human Evolution*. London: Fourth Estate.

Kilvert, A.S. (1847) *Home Discipline, or Thoughts on the Origin and Exercise of Domestic Authority*. London: Joseph Masters.

Kilvert, F. [uncle] (1827) *Sermons Preached at Christ Church, Bath, before the National Schools*. London: John Taylor.

Kilvert, F. [uncle] (1860) *Memoirs of the Life and Writings of the Right Rev Richard Hurd.* London: Richard Bentley.

Kilvert, F. (1882) *Musings in Verse.* Edward C. Alden.

Kilvert, F. (1938-40) *Kilvert's Diary.* W. Plomer (ed.). London: Jonathan Cape.

Kilvert. F. (1968) *Collected Verse by the Rev Francis Kilvert.* Hereford: Kilvert Society publication.

Kilvert, F. (1982) *The Diary of Francis Kilvert, April-June 1870.* K. Hughes and D. Ifans (eds.). Aberystwyth: NLW.

Kilvert, F. (1989) *Kilvert's Cornish Diary.* R. Maber and A. Tregoning (eds.). Penzance: Alison Hodge.

Kilvert, F. (1989) *Kilvert's Diary, June-July 1870.* Dafydd Ifans (ed.). Aberystwyth: NLW.

Kilvert Society Journal, number 10, March 2003.

Kilvert Society Newsletter, spring 1974.

Kincaid, J.R. (1992) *Child Loving. The Erotic child and Victorian Culture.* New York: Routledge.

Kingsley, C. (1850) *Alton Locke, Tailor and Poet. An Autobiography.* Oxford: Oxford University Press.

Kingsley, Mrs. (1878) *Charles Kingsley. His Letters and Memories of his Life.* London: C. Kegan Paul.

Knight, G.W. (1943) *The Starlit Dome.* Oxford: Oxford University Press.

Knoepflmacher, U.C. and Tennyson, G.B. (eds.) (1977) *Mutations of the Wordsworthian Child of Nature.* Berkeley: University of California Press.

Knox, E.A. (1933) *The Tractarian Movement 1833-1845. A Study of the Oxford Movement.* London: Putnam.

Knox, R.A. (1950) *Enthusiasm. A Chapter in the History of Religion.* Oxford: Clarendon Press.

Kunze, B.Y. (1994) *Margaret Fell and the Rise of Quakerism.* London: Macmillan.

Lamb, C. (1814) 'Review of Wordsworth's 'The Excursion''. In: *Quarterly Review,* vol. XII. October.

Landow, G.P. (ed.) (1979) *Approaches to Victorian Autobiography.* Athens: Ohio University Press.

Langan, C. (1995) *Romantic Vagrancy. Wordsworth and the Simulation of Freedom.* Cambridge: Cambridge University Press.

Langton, E. (1956) *History of the Moravian Church.* London: Allen and Unwin.

Lawton, F.H. (1968) *The Oxford Law School, 1850-1965.* Oxford: Oxford University Press.

Leach, K. (1999) *In the Shadow of the Dreamchild. A New Understanding of Lewis Carroll.* London: Peter Owen.

Lee, A. (1955) *Laurels and Rosemary. The Life of William and Mary Howitt.* London: Oxford University Press.

Le Quesne, L. (1975) 'Suggestions for Further Research'. In: *A Kilvert Symposium.* Hereford: Kilvert Society.

Le Quesne, L. (1978) *After Kilvert*. Oxford: Oxford University Press.

Le Quesne, L. (2003) 'Kilvert and Woodforde – the Diarists Compared'. In: *Kilvert Society Journal*, 12, September.

Lesage, A.R. (1715-35) *The Adventures of Gil Blas of Santillane*. T. Smollett (trans.). London: George Routledge.

Lewis, I. (1983) 'Kilvert's Divided Personality'. In: *Kilvert Society Newsletter*, June.

Lile, B. (1992) 'Kilvert in Gower: Some Footnotes'. In: *Kilvert Society Newsletter*, spring.

Lockwood, D. (1975) 'Sidelight on the Character of Francis Kilvert'. In: *A Kilvert Symposium*. Hereford: Kilvert Society.

Lockwood, D. (1990) *Francis Kilvert*. Bridgend: Seren Books.

Loyn, H.R. (1984) 'The conversion of the English to Christianity: some Comments on the Celtic Contribution'. In: Davies, Griffiths, Jones and Morgan (eds.), *Welsh Society and Nationhood. Historical Essays Presented to Glanmor Williams*. Cardiff: University of Wales Press.

Lucas, R. (1998) *Rhossili: a Village Background*. Tonypandy: Hackman Printers.

Lytton, B. (1971) *England and the English*, vol. I. Shannon: Irish University Press.

McCann, P. and Young, F. (1982) *Samuel Wilderspin and the Infant School Movement*. London: Croom Helm.

McCarthy, E. (1997) *Thomas Gray: the Progress of a Poet*. Madison: Farleigh Dickinson University Press.

Macdonald, G. (1924) *George Macdonald and his Wife*. London: George Allen and Unwin.

McFarland, T. (1981) *Romanticism and the Forms of Ruin. Wordsworth, Coleridge and Modalities of Fragmentation*. New Jersey: Princeton University Press.

Malcomson, C. (2004) *George Herbert. A Literary Life*. Basingstoke: Palgrave Macmillan.

Martin, B.W. (1976) *John Keble: Priest, Professor and Poet*. London: Croom Helm.

Martin, R.H. (1983) *Evangelicals United: Ecumenical Stirrings in pre-Victorian Britain, 1795-1830*. Metuchen, New Jersey: Scarecrow Press.

Mason, M. (1992) *Lyrical Ballads*. London: Longman.

Mason, M. (1994) *The Making of Victorian Sexual Attitudes*. Oxford: Oxford University Press.

Massingham, H.J. (1953) *The Southern Marches*. London: Robert Hale.

Matless, D. (1998) *Landscape and Englishness*. London: Reaktion Books.

Mayr-Harting, H. (1972) *The Coming of Christianity to Anglo-Saxon England*. London: Batsford.

Melbourne, D.P. and Hearne, Dr K. (2000) *The Dream Oracle*. London: Quantum.

Mill, J.S. (1944) *Autobiography of John Stuart Mill*. New York: Columbia University Press.

Millais, G. (1979) *Sir John Everett Millais*. London: Academy Editions.

Millais, J.G. (1899) *The Life and Letters of John Everett Millais*. London: Methuen.

Moffat, A. (2001) *The Sea Kingdoms. The Story of Celtic Britain and Ireland*. London: Harper Collins.

Moir, E. (1964) *The Discovery of Britain. The English Tourists 1540-1840*. London: Routledge Kegan Paul.

Molesworth, M. (1869) *Stray Leaves from the Tree of Life*. London: William Macintosh.

Montgomery, R. (1828) *The Omnipresence of the Deity*. London: Samuel Maunder.

Moore, A. (1993) 'Moravian Women'. In: C. Figes (ed.), *250 Years of the Moravian Settlement at East Tytherton, 1743-1993*. Privately printed.

Moorman, M. (1965) *William Wordsworth: a Biography. The Later Years 1803-1850*. Oxford: Clarendon Press.

Moorman, M. (1969) *William Wordsworth: a Biography. The Early Years 1770-1803*. Oxford: Clarendon Press.

Morgan, P. (1983) 'From a Death to a View: The Hunt for the Welsh Past in the Romantic Period'. In: E. Hobsbawm and Ranger (eds.), *The Invention of Tradition*. Cambridge: Cambridge University Press.

Morgan, P. (1984) 'From Long Knives to Blue Books'. In: Davies, Griffiths, Jones and Morgan (eds.), *Welsh Society and Nationhood. Historical Essays Presented to Glanmor Williams*. Cardiff: University of Wales Press.

Morgan, P. (1986) 'Keeping the Legends Alive'. In: T. Curtis (ed.), *Wales: the Imagined Nation. Studies in Cultural and National Identity*. Bridgend: Poetry of Wales Press.

Morris, J. (1973) *The Age of Arthur*. London: Weidenfeld and Nicholson.

Mullan, J. (1988) *Sentiment and Sociability. The Language of Feeling in the Eighteenth Century*. Oxford: Clarendon Press.

Murray, N. (1996) *A Life of Matthew Arnold*. London: Sceptre.

Mylne, V. (1965) *The Eighteenth Century French Novel*. Manchester: Manchester University Press.

Nadel, I.B. (1984) *Biography. Fiction, Fact and Form*. London: Macmillan.

Newman, J.H. (1849) *Lyra Apostolica*. London: Mozley.

Newton, J. (1781) *Cardiphonia or the Utterance of the Heart in the Course of a Real Correspondence*. London: Buckland and Johnson.

Nicholson, N. (1951) *William Cowper*. London: John Lehmann.

Nuttall, G.F. (1965) *Howell Harris, Evangelist, 1714-1773. The Last Enthusiast*. Cardiff: University of Wales Press.

O'Brien, K. (1943) *English Diaries and Journals*. London: William Collins.

Oliphant, Mrs. (1882) *The Literary History of England in the End of the Eighteenth and Beginning of the Nineteenth Century*, vol. III. London: Macmillan.

Overton, J. (1894) *The English Church in the Nineteenth Century (1800-1833)*. London: Longmans Green.

Oxenden, A. (1859) *The Pathway of Safety*. London: Macintosh.

Palmer, R. (2001) *The Folklore of Radnorshire*. Almeley: Logaston Press.

Parrish, S. (1973) *The Art of the Lyrical Ballads*. Cambridge: Harvard University Press.

Payne, J. and Lewsey, R. (1999) *The Romance of the Stones*. Fowey: Alexander Associates.

Pearce, J. (1964) *The Wesleys in Cornwall*. Truro: Bradford Barton.

Pearse, R. (1983) *The Land Beside the Celtic Sea. Some Aspects of Ancient, Medieval and Victorian Cornwall*. Redruth: Truro.

Perkins, D. (1964) *Wordsworth and the Poetry of Sincerity*. Cambridge: Harvard University Press.

Phelps, E.S. (1868) *The Gates Ajar*. London: Milner.

Piette, M. (1937) *John Wesley and the Evolution of Protestantism*. London: Sheed and Ward.

Pirie, D.B. (1982) *William Wordsworth: the Poetry of Grandeur and Tenderness*. London: Methuen.

Plomer, W. (1973) *Collected Poems*. London: Jonathan Cape.

Plomer, W. (1975) *The Autobiography of William Plomer*. London: Jonathan Cape.

Plotz, J. (2001) *Romanticism and the Vocation of Childhood*. New York: Palgrave.

Poovey, M. (1988) *Uneven Developments: the Ideological Work of Gender in mid-Victorian England*. Chicago: Chicago University Press.

Pope, A. (1987) *Selected Prose*. Paul Hammond (ed.). Cambridge: Cambridge University Press.

Pratt, J.H. (ed.) (1978) *The Thought of the Evangelical Leaders, Notes of the Discussions of the Eclectic Society*. Edinburgh: Banner of Truth Trust.

Prentiss, E. (undated) *Stepping Heavenward*. London: Sunday School Union.

Price, Rev D.T.W. (1975) 'Francis Kilvert as a Clergyman'. In: *A Kilvert Symposium*. Hereford: Kilvert Society.

Prickett, S. (1976) *Romanticism and Religion. The tradition of Coleridge and Wordsworth in the Victorian Church*. Cambridge: Cambridge University Press.

Pritchett, V.S. (1942) *In My Good Books*. London: Chatto and Windus.

Purkis, E.M. (1931) *William Shenstone. Poet and Landscape Gardener*. Wolverhampton: Whitehead Brothers.

Rack, H.D. (1989) *Reasonable Enthusiast. John Wesley and the Rise of Methodism*. London: Epworth Press.

Rattie, J. (1995) *The Living Stream. Holy Wells in Historical Context*. Woodbridge: Boydell Press.

Reed, R. (1975) *Victorian Conventions*. Athens: Ohio University Press.

Rhatz, P. (1993) *English Heritage Book of Glastonbury*. London: Batsford.

Rich, Lawrence. (1991) *The Gower Peninsula*. The National Trust.

Richardson, A. and Bowden, J. (eds.) (1983) *A New Dictionary of Christian Theology*. London: SCM Press.

Richmond, L. (1859) *Annals of the Poor*. London: Nelson.

Richter, M. (1971) 'Giraldus Cambrensis'. In: *National Library of Wales Journal*, Aberystwyth, xvii.

Richter, M. (1976) *Giraldus Cambrensis. The Growth of the Welsh Nation*. Aberystwyth: National Library of Wales.

Riddy F. (1991) 'Glastonbury, Joseph of Arimathea and the Grail in John Hardyng's Chronicle'. In: L. Abram and J.P. Carley (eds.), *The Archaeology and History of Glastonbury Abbey*. Woodbridge: Boydell Press.

Rivers, I. (1978) ' 'Strangers and pilgrims': Sources and Patterns of Methodist Narrative'. In: Hilson, Jones and Watson (eds.), *Augustan Worlds: Essays in Honour of A.R. Humphreys*. Leicester: Leicester University Press.

Robertson, F. (1854) *Sermons, Preached at Trinity Chapel, Brighton*. London: Smith and Elder.

Robertson, F. (1858) *Lectures and Addresses on Literary and Social Topics*. London: Smith and Elder.

Robertson, F. (1859) *Expository Lectures on St Paul's Epistle to the Corinthians*. London: Smith and Elder.

Rowse, A.L. (1945) *The English Spirit. Essays in History and Literature*. London: Macmillan.

Ruskin, J. (1904) *The Moral of Landscape, the Works of John Ruskin*, vol. V. T.C. Cook and A. Wedderburn (eds.). London: George Allen.

Russell, G.W.E. (1903) *The Household of Faith. Portraits and Essays*. London: Hodder and Stoughton.

Russell, J. (1926) *Pestalozzi. Educational Reformer 1746-1827*. London: George Allen and Unwin.

Sadie, S. (ed.) (2001) *The New Grove Dictionary of Music and Musicians*, vol. XVII. London: Macmillan.

Saklatvala, B. (1969) *The Christian Island*. London: Dent.

Salvesen, C. (1965) *The Landscape of Memory. A study of Wordsworth's Poetry*. London: Edward Arnold.

Samuel, R. (1998) *Theatres of Memory*, vol. II. London: Verso.

Schama, S. (1995) *Landscape and Memory*. London: Harper Collins.

Schor, E. (1994) *Bearing the Dead. The British Culture of Mourning from the Enlightenment to Victoria*. Princeton: Princeton University Press.

Scott, Sir W. (1815) *The Antiquary*. Edinburgh: A. and C. Black.

Scott, Sir W. (1816) *Guy Mannering*. Edinburgh: A. and C. Black.

Scott, Sir W. (1820) *Ivanhoe*. Edinburgh: printed for A. Constable.

Scott, Sir W. (1833) *The Poetical Works of Sir Walter Scott, Bart*. (vol. VIII). Edinburgh: Printed for R. Cadell.

Sedgwick, A. (1850) *A Discourse on the Studies of the University of Cambridge*. Cambridge: John Deighton.

Shaw, M. (1973) 'Tennyson and his Public 1827-1859'. In: D.J. Palmer (ed.), *Tennyson, Writers and their Background*. London: Bell.

Showalter, E. (1972) *The Evolution of the French Novel 1641-1782*. Princeton: Princeton University Press.

Shumaker, W. (1954) *English Autobiography: its Emergence, Materials and Form*. Berkeley and Los Angeles: University of California Press.

Skinner, R.F. (1964) *Nonconformity in Shropshire (1662-1816)*. Shrewsbury: Wilding.

Smith, B. (1989) 'The Hockins and the British Church'. In: *Kilvert Society Newsletter*, February.

Smith, M. (ed.) (2003) *Victorian Wessex. The Diaries of Emily Smith, 1836, 1841, 1852*. Norwich: Solen Press.

Smyth, C. (1940) *The Art of Preaching*. London: SPCK.

Solkin, D.H. (1982) *Richard Wilson. The Landscape of Reaction*. London: The Tate Gallery.

Somervell, D.C. (1936) *English Thought in the Nineteenth Century*. London: Methuen.

Spangenburg, A.G. (1959) *Idea Fidei Fratrum*, third English edition. Moravian Church USA.

Stark, W. (1967) *The Sociology of Religion. A Study of Christendom*, vol. II. London: Routledge, Kegan Paul.

Stephens. (ed.) (1986) *Companion to Welsh Literature*. Cambridge: Cambridge University Press.

Sterne, L. (1983) *A Sentimental Journey through France and Italy*. Oxford: Clarendon Press.

Sterne, L. (1983) *Tristram Shandy*. Ian Campbell Ross (ed.). Oxford: Clarendon Press.

Strawbridge, D. and Thomas, P.J. (eds.) (1991) *A Guide to Gower*. Swansea: Gower Society.

Sumner, A. and Smith, G. (2003) *Thomas Jones. An Artist Rediscovered*. New Haven: Yale University Press.

Temperley, N. (1979) *The Music of the English Parish Church*, vol. I. Cambridge: Cambridge University Press.

Tennyson, A. (1969) *The Poems of Tennyson*, vol. III. C. Ricks (ed.). London: Longman.

Tennyson, G.B. (1977) 'The Sacramental Imagination'. In: U.C. Knoepflmacher (ed.), *Nature and the Victorian Imagination*. Berkeley: University of California Press.

Thomas, E. (1993) *The South Country*. London: Everyman.

Thomas, K. (1971) *Religion and the Decline of Magic*. London: Penguin Books.

Thomas, K. (1983) *Man and the Natural World. Changing attitudes in England 1500-1800*. London: Allen Lane.

Tillotson, K. (1965) 'Tennyson's Serial Poem'. In: G. Tillotson and K. Tillotson (eds.), *Mid-Victorian Studies*. London: Athlone Press.

Toliver, H. (1993) *George Herbert's Christian Narrative*. Pennsylvania: Pennsylvania University Press.

Toman, J. (2001) *Kilvert: The Homeless Heart*. Almeley: Logaston Press.

Toman, J. (2002) *The Books that Kilvert Read*. Kilvert Society.

Towlson, C. (1957) *Moravian and Methodist*. London: Epworth Press.

Tracy, C. (1987) *A Portrait of Richard Graves*. Toronto: Toronto University Press.

Treble, R. (1981) *Van Gogh and his Art*. London: Hamlyn.

Treble, R. (1989) 'The Victorian Picture of the Country'. In: G.E. Mingay (ed.), *The Rural Idyll*. London: Routledge.

Treharne, R.F. (1966) *The Glastonbury Legends. Joseph of Arimathea, the Holy Grail and King Arthur*. London: Cresset Press.

Trollope, A. (1987) *An Autobiography*. Oxford: Oxford University Press.

Turner, F.M. (1990) 'The Victorian Crisis of Faith and the Faith that was Lost'. In: R.J. Helmstadter and B. Lightman (eds.), *Victorian Faith in Crisis. Essays in Continuity and Change in Nineteenth Century Religious Belief*. London: Macmillan.

Turner, P. (1989) *Victorian Poetry, Drama and Miscellaneous Prose 1832-1890*. Oxford: Clarendon Press.

Tuveson, E.L. (1960) *The Imagination as a Means of Grace. Locke and the Aesthetics of Romanticism*. Berkeley: University of California Press.

Twistleton-Davies, Sir L. and Edwards, A. (1939) *Welsh Life in the Eighteenth Century*. Feltham: Country Life.

Tyte, W. (1898) *A History of Lyncombe and Widcombe*. Bath: William Tyte.

Uglow, J. (1993) *Elizabeth Gaskell: a Habit of Stories*. London: Faber and Faber.

Virgin, P. (1989) *The Church in an Age of Negligence*. Cambridge: James Clarke.

Von Türk. (1832) *The Phenomena of Nature*. London: Effingham Wilson.

Walker, D. (1976) *A History of the Church in Wales*. Penarth: Church in Wales Publications.

Walker, L. (1979) 'The Invention of Childhood in Victorian Autobiography'. In: G.P. Landow (ed.), *Approaches to Victorian Autobiography*. Athens: Ohio University Press.

Ward, J.P. (1986) '"Came from yon fountain": Wordsworth's Influence on Victorian Educators'. In: *Victorian Studies*, Indiana University, vol. XXIX, no.3, spring.

Warner, Rev R. (1798) *A Walk through Wales in August 1797*. Bath: T. Cruttwell.

Warner, Rev R. (1799) *A Walk through Wales in August 1798*. Bath: T. Cruttwell.

Warner, Rev R. (1809) *A Tour through Cornwall in the Autumn of 1808*. Bath: R. Cruttwell.

Warner, Rev R. (1826) *History of the Abbey of Glastonbury and the Town of Glastonbury*. Bath: Cruttwell.

Warner, Rev R. (1830) *Literary Recollections*. London: Longman.

Watson, J.R. (1985) *English Poetry of the Romantic Period*. London: Longmans.

Wesley, J. (1909) *John Wesley's Journal*. N. Curnock (ed.). London: Robert Culley.

Wesley, J. (1909-16) *Journal*. J. Curnock (ed.). London: Culley.

Wesling, D. (1970) *Wordsworth and the Adequacy of Landscape*. London: Routledge, Kegan Paul.

Wilberforce, W. (1797) *A Practical View of the Prevailing Religious System of Professed Christians, in the Higher and Middle Classes in this Country, Contrasted with Real Christianity*. London: printed for T. Cadell.

Williams, A.H. (1962) *An Introduction to the History of Wales*, vol. I. Cardiff: University of Wales Press.

Williams, G. (1985) *When was Wales? A History of the Welsh*. Harmondsworth: Penguin.

Williams, I. (1893) *The Autobiography of Isaac Williams*. Sir G. Prevost (ed.). London: Longmans Green.

Williams, J. (1996) *William Wordsworth. A Literary Life*. Basingstoke: Macmillan.

Williams, R. (1975) *The Country and the City*. St Albans: Paladin.

Williams, T. and Grice, F. (1982) *The Other Francis Kilvert: Francis Kilvert of Claverton 1793-1863*. Hay-on-Wye: Kilvert Society.

Woodbridge, K. (1970) *Landscape and Antiquity. Aspects of English Culture at Stourhead 1718-1838*. Oxford: Clarendon Press.

Woof, R. (2001) *Wordsworth: The Critical Heritage*, vol. I, 1793-1820. London: Routledge.

Wordsworth, W. (1905) *The Poetical Works of William Wordsworth*. T. Hutchinson (ed.). London: Oxford University Press.

Wordsworth, W. (1920) *The Poetical Works of William Wordsworth*. Oxford: Oxford University Press.

Wordsworth, W. and Wordsworth, D. (1939) *The Letters of William and Dorothy Wordsworth, The Later Years*, vol. I, 1821-1830. E. De Selincourt (ed.). Oxford: Clarendon Press.

Wordsworth, W. (1944) *Wordsworth's Poetical Works*, vol. III. E. De Selincourt and H. Darbishire (eds.). Oxford: Oxford University Press.

Wordsworth, W. and Wordsworth, D. (1967) *The Letters of William and Dorothy Wordsworth: The Early Years, 1787-1805*. A.G. Hill (ed.). Oxford: Clarendon Press.

Wordsworth, W. and Wordsworth, D. (1969) *The Letters of William and Dorothy Wordsworth, The Middle Years*, part I, 1806-1811, and part II, 1812-1820. A.G. Hill (ed.). Oxford: Clarendon Press.

Wordsworth, W. (1974) *Essay Upon Epitaphs, Prose Works of W. Wordsworth*, vol. II. W.J.B. Owen and J. Smyser (eds.). Oxford: Clarendon Press.

Wordsworth, W. (1974) *Guide to the Lakes*. E. De Selincourt (ed.). Oxford: Oxford University Press.

Wordsworth, W. (1974) *Wordsworth's Literary Criticism*. W.J.B. Owen (ed.). London: Routledge, Kegan Paul.

Wyndowe, E. (undated) 'Rambling Recollections'. In: *More Chapters from the Kilvert Saga*. Leamington Spa: Kilvert Society publication.

Young, C.R. (1995) *Music of the Heart. John and Charles Wesley on Music and Musicians*. Illinois: Hope Publishing.

Young, E. (1989) *Edward Young. Night Thoughts*. S. Cornford (ed.). Cambridge: Cambridge University Press.

Index

Printed in the United Kingdom
by Lightning Source UK Ltd.
135204UK00002B/40-249/P